VA

James. Madison.

FIVE PARTNERSHIPS THAT BUILT AMERICA

MADISON'S GIFT

DAVID O. STEWART

SIMON & SCHUSTER

NEW YORK   LONDON   TORONTO   SYDNEY   NEW DELHI

Simon & Schuster
1230 Avenue of the Americas
New York, NY 10020

First Simon & Schuster hardcover edition February 2015

SIMON & SCHUSTER and colophon are registered trademarks of Simon & Schuster, Inc.

For information about special discounts for bulk purchases, please contact Simon & Schuster Special Sales at 1-866-506-1949 or business@simonandschuster.com.

The Simon & Schuster Speakers Bureau can bring authors to your live event. For more information or to book an event contact the Simon & Schuster Speakers Bureau at 1-866-248-3049 or visit our website at www.simonspeakers.com.

Interior design by Akasha Archer

Manufactured in the United States of America

10   9   8   7   6   5   4   3   2   1

Library of Congress Cataloging-in-Publication Data

Stewart, David O.
Madison's gift : five partnerships that built America / David O. Stewart.
pages cm
Includes bibliographical references and index.
1. Madison, James, 1751–1836. 2. Madison, James, 1751–1836—Friends and associates. 3. Madison, James, 1751–1836—Marriage. 4. Madison, James, 1751–1836—Influence. 5. Presidents—United States—Biography. 6. Statesmen—United States—Biography. 7. Friendship—Political aspects—United States—History. 8. United States—Politics and government—1775–1783. 9. United States—Politics and government—1783–1865. I. Title.
E342.S74 2015
973.5'1092—dc23
[B]
2014021393

ISBN 978-1-4516-8858-0
ISBN 978-1-4516-8860-3 (ebook)

CONTENTS

To Nancy

1

---❖---

The End of the Beginning

The great news reached Philadelphia in November of 1783, when James Madison was packing for home. Britain had signed a peace treaty that recognized American independence, redeeming eight years of bitter sacrifices by the American rebels. They had defeated the most powerful nation on earth and won the right to govern themselves.

Madison and his three million countrymen faced fundamental questions. Could the thirteen states remain united across fifteen hundred miles of Atlantic coast and almost as far into the western forests? Could they maintain a republic in a world of monarchies? Could they avoid anarchy at one extreme and autocratic rule at the other?

The thirty-two-year-old Madison, who was finishing four years as a Virginia delegate to Congress, faced questions of his own. After a spell of ill health and aimlessness as a wealthy graduate of the College of New Jersey (now Princeton), he had found purpose in the Revolution. A month with his county militia in 1775 established that the bookish Virginian was a poor candidate for soldiering. He not only was short and slight—no taller than five feet six inches and a bit over one hundred pounds—but also suffered from chronic intestinal woes and fits that resembled epilepsy. He put down his musket and applied his revolutionary ardor to politics. After serving in Virginia's provisional government, Madison went to Congress in 1779, still only twenty-eight. Through hard work and talent, he became a central figure in a legislative body crowded with the second-raters.

The past year had been a turbulent one. Madison had lost his heart to Kitty Floyd, the fifteen-year-old daughter of a New York delegate who lived in the same Philadelphia boardinghouse as Madison. He had hoped to marry Kitty and had courted her assiduously. In late April, when the Floyd family journeyed to New Jersey, the infatuated Madison rode sixty miles with them, then returned to Philadelphia.[1]

But by early August the affair was off; within a year, Kitty would be engaged to a medical student much nearer her own age. The blow fell hard on Madison. Fifty years later, the hurt was still so sharp that he blacked out portions of an old letter that mentioned the failed romance.[2]

Madison's public life had also brought disappointments. The new nation could not pay its bills, starting with huge debts to France and to its own citizens. The government created by the Articles of Confederation could impose taxes only with the consent of all thirteen states. Because no tax ever commanded such unanimous support, Congress had to ask the states, politely, to send money to pay for the war, and now for the peace. Voluntary state payments always fell below what was needed, so Congress gasped along on whatever came to hand.

The lack of money ignited a crisis in the winter of 1783. Unpaid soldiers, camped on the Hudson River above New York City, grumbled about mutiny. A delegation of officers carried a petition to Congress in Philadelphia, demanding their back pay. In late February, Madison joined five congressional delegates in a dramatic evening session with the disgruntled soldiers. By the flickering firelight, delegate Alexander Hamilton of New York made dark pronouncements. A former army officer himself, Hamilton warned that some officers aimed to oust George Washington as commander and to remain in arms until they were paid.[3]

Congress made more promises to the soldiers, as did state officials, but they were empty ones. There was no money. It was a recipe for insurrection: an army with no enemy to fight and real grievances against its own government.[4] Inflammatory letters circulated among the officers, urging an end to the waiting. Lest they "grow old in poverty, wretchedness and contempt," one railed, the soldiers must "change the milk and water style" of their demands.[5]

In Congress, Madison urged the fractious states to agree on a national tax that would pay the nation's soldiers and its debts. Without such action, he predicted, "a dissolution of the Union would be inevitable"; the southern states would go one way, New England another, the middle states a third, each seeking alliances with European powers.[6] Congress appointed Madison to a committee charged with developing a fiscal solution.

While Congress dithered, one man prevented mutiny. General Washington called an assembly of officers for March 15, the ides of March. For those who knew their Shakespeare, it must have seemed a portentous date.

Standing before his brother officers, Washington recalled sacrifices shared through battle and privation, misery and loss. This was not the time, he said, to "open the floodgates of civil discord and deluge our rising empire in blood." It was not his prepared statement, but a theatrical aside, that carried the day. When he began to read a letter aloud, Washington stumbled over the words, then donned a pair of spectacles. "Gentlemen," he said. "You must pardon me. I have grown gray in your service and now find myself growing blind." Some wept. Most were ashamed. All were moved. The mutiny dissolved with a unanimous resolution supporting Washington.

In the breathing space won by the general, Madison concocted a plan. It was a political hodgepodge. He proposed a twenty-five-year import tax that was set too low to pay off the debt, so he wishfully assumed that states would continue to contribute money to the national government, plus additional revenues from the sale of western lands. In a closing exhortation, Madison argued that through this plan "the cause of liberty will acquire a dignity and luster which it has never yet enjoyed." Continued drift, he warned, would mean the failure of "the last and fairest experiment in favor of the rights of human nature."[7]

Six weeks later, Washington echoed Madison's appeal in his own "Circular Letter of Farewell to the Army." The states' actions on the national tax would determine, he wrote, "whether the Revolution must ultimately be considered . . . a blessing or a curse, not to the present age alone, for with our fate will the destiny of unborn millions be involved."[8]

Neither appeal worked. Virginia, home to both Madison and Washington, refused to adopt the plan, killing it outright. Worse was coming.

Within days of Washington's circular, disgruntled Pennsylvania soldiers surrounded Philadelphia's State House, where Congress was sitting, and demanded their back pay. When Pennsylvania's governor refused to call out his state's militia to oppose the mutineers, the congressional delegates fled, resolving to reconvene in tiny Princeton, New Jersey.

Although Madison had spent three happy years in Princeton as a student, he despised it as the nation's temporary capital. He was depressed by the spectacle of Congress cowering in a remote village to escape its own soldiers. The room he shared with another Virginian measured "not more than 10 square feet." For one roommate to dress, the other had to remain in the single bed. The only position available for writing "scarcely admits the use of any of my limbs."[9] On top of the rejection by Kitty Floyd, his world was turning bleak.

For the first time in his career, Madison began to play hooky. He missed more than half of the congressional sessions between June 30 and early November, when his term expired. Unless he was needed in Princeton to achieve a quorum, he stayed in Philadelphia. Even when he was in Princeton, Madison was listless. Usually a compulsive note taker, he wrote down nothing about the debates. He offered no excuse for his inattention to duty. One letter recorded, almost defiantly, that he was composing it "in bed in my Chamber in the Hotel" at six-thirty in the evening. When Virginia again missed its voluntary payment to Congress, Madison's disenchantment grew stronger.[10]

Madison was changing his focus. With the end of the war and the end of his congressional term, he was lifting his gaze from the daily struggles in Congress to the largest challenge facing Americans: whether they could create a government that preserved the Revolution's exhilarating ideals yet functioned effectively. *This* would be the work of his life.[11]

For the next three decades, Madison's contributions to his country would be incomparable. Without Madison, the Constitutional Convention of 1787 might never have happened. But for him, that gathering could have ended in failure. He led the difficult fight to ratify the Constitution, then a lonely crusade for the Bill of Rights. In the first months of the new government in 1789, it was Madison who advised President Washington on the critical decisions and legislation that established the new republic on a solid footing. When political conflict began to tear the infant nation apart in the 1790s, Madison joined with Thomas Jefferson to form the first true political party and steer it to a position of dominance. And when the republic faced its first foreign war, the profoundly unmilitary Madison, as America's first war president, unsteadily coaxed an unprepared nation to a surprisingly satisfactory peace and a flowering prosperity.

In Philadelphia in 1783, at the threshold of this extraordinary future, Madison's mind did not hold dreams of power or of political office. Instead, he turned inward, resolving to improve himself through a course of study in law, government, and history. To meet the mighty challenges before it, America would need wisdom and judgment. Madison aimed to deepen his knowledge and powers of reason so he could serve the nation better.[12]

Earlier in 1783, Madison had intended to pursue his course of study as a newlywed in cosmopolitan Philadelphia. When Miss Floyd's inconstancy sent that plan up in smoke, he resolved to return to Montpelier, his father's sprawling plantation in the western hills of Virginia, setting another pattern for the rest of his life. Past thirty and unmarried, Madison's ties remained strong to his parents and five surviving siblings (he was the eldest). Though the young Madison had chafed against Virginia's aristocratic slave culture, Montpelier was his home and a comfortable one at that. He would never really leave it. Until he was fifty, he honored and was financially dependent upon his father; he shared Montpelier with his mother until he was seventy-eight. Mother and son also shared a steady disposition that carried both through troubled times. An old friend recalled Mrs. Madison possessing "a certain mildness and equanimity for which I ever considered her remarkable."[13]

As he prepared to leave Philadelphia in late 1783, Madison bought gifts for his sisters and a new carriage for his father, plus medicine for his mother, whose recent illness alarmed him.[14] At home in Virginia, he shed the political and personal failures of the last year. By the new year, he was deep into his reading. He celebrated the harsh winter in a letter to Thomas Jefferson, claiming it kept visitors from Montpelier and left him more time for study.[15]

Despite its disappointments, 1783 proved to be a pivotal year in James Madison's life, not for what he did but for what he prepared himself to do, beginning with his self-prescribed course of study and thinking. A man of the mind in so many ways—surely among the most intellectual of American leaders—he aspired to serve America's Revolution directly. Small, reserved in company, never a soldier, he was not an obvious candidate to leave a large imprint on the founding of the new republic. Lacking the narcissism of most political leaders, Madison did not elbow his way into the limelight or preen on public stages. Avuncular with friends, he could be ill at ease at public events. Rather than thrust himself forward, Madison preferred to blend his talents with those of others.

Madison's indelible imprint on the new nation sprang in large part from his ability to form rich partnerships with five talented contemporaries, an ability that blossomed in 1783. Those five partnerships underlay his greatest achievements. Late in life, when a correspondent tried to christen him the Father of the Constitution, Madison would have none of it. The Constitution was not, he insisted, "like the fabled Goddess of Wisdom, the offspring of a single brain. It ought to be regarded as the work of many hands and many heads." And so, he plainly thought, was the launching of the American republic.[16]

His steady disposition was central to his many partnerships. "Nothing could excite or ruffle him," wrote a longtime friend. "Under all circumstances he was collected, and ever mindful of what was due from him to others, and cautious not to wound the feelings of any one." That description captures an unusual leadership style, one focused on what "was due from him to others" and careful to impose no injury. Collegiality can be undervalued in public life. The solitary hero, the man on horseback, readily commands emotional attention. Madison's heroic moments tended, like him, to be quiet ones.

Madison brought many gifts to his public career. He combined a sharp understanding of political and economic forces with an inspiring vision of a government that could achieve public goals while respecting personal liberty. But ultimately it was his gift for working with others that allowed him to play an outsize role in building the nation.[17]

Students of America's early years often neglect Madison, a mistake his contemporaries did not make. They named fifty-nine counties and towns after him, more than any other president. He is the only president to have a major avenue in Manhattan named after him; indeed, that street named an entire industry—advertising—which carries his name: Madison Avenue.[18]

Yet he has become easy to miss in accounts of the early republic. His soft voice has carried little better in the halls of history than it did in public chambers. His manner was unobtrusive. Some misjudged his talents. "Madison," claimed the acid-tongued John Randolph of Roanoke, "was always some great man's mistress—first Hamilton's, then Jefferson's." Even Jefferson, on his deathbed, betrayed a core misunderstanding of the man who was his closest friend. After fondly reciting Madison's virtues, the dying man added, "But, ah! He could never in his life stand up against strenuous opposition." It would have been more accurate to say that Madison wasted little time in frontal assaults on entrenched opponents but, rather, searched for ways to persuade or work around those who disagreed with him, including Jefferson.[19]

Madison forged the five defining partnerships of his life with strikingly different characters. The small man from Virginia could assume different roles, adapting himself to the situations and personalities around him. Three of his partners were revolutionary leaders— Alexander Hamilton, George Washington, and Jefferson—each of whom radiated the personal magnetism that Madison lacked. The fourth, fellow Virginian James Monroe, was sometimes a sharp rival, sometimes a key ally, usually a warm friend. Through alliances with these four men, all of whom had talents he lacked, Madison was able to extend his own reach and amplify his own influence over events. With each, he assumed a different role, one that suited the situation and the partnership.

With Hamilton, a contemporary and intellectual peer, he joined in brotherly combat on behalf of the new Constitution. Washington was a generation older and the nation's great leader, so Madison was a confidential adviser and consummate aide to the first president. With Jefferson he formed the deepest and most complex connection: political partnership, intellectual camaraderie, and personal friendship. With Monroe, who was younger and more impulsive, he played the role of elder brother, guide, and friend. In turn, each relied heavily on Madison at critical moments of their careers.

Those four partnerships all can be traced to 1783, but not the fifth. Though Madison and his fifth partner both lived in Philadelphia that year, not for ten more years would Madison meet Dolley Payne Todd and win her as his wife. To her, like the others, Madison conceded the spotlight, helping her become a public figure in her own right, sometimes called the "Lady Presidentess." He happily yielded public acclaim to his gracious and outgoing partner. In return, she brought cheer and warmth into his life and became an integral part of his political success.

Two centuries later, James Madison's America can exist only in our imaginations, framed by the words he and his contemporaries wrote, the land on which they lived, the objects they used, and the buildings they walked through. It was a world lit by the sun or the glow of candle, oil lamp, or fireplace. Travel was grueling, sometimes nightmarish. Foul weather delayed ships for weeks or months. Roads were cloying bogs on wet days, then rutted corduroy on dry ones. Wooden-wheeled vehicles punished the body even when not overset by drunken hostlers. In summer, river crossings were slow and ferry schedules unpredictable; winter gallops across frozen streams carried the constant risk of crashing through into frigid waters.

Home, even for the wealthy, was drafty and dark, heated by smoky fires. Personal hygiene was a challenge, hot water a luxury. Human waste was deposited in containers and sometimes thrown into the street, sometimes carried to disposal sites. Washing clothes was hard physical labor. Food preparation consumed hours. Unreliable drinking water drove most to prefer distilled or fermented beverages. Medical care featured the bleeding of ill patients. Death was a constant companion. Of James Madison's ten siblings, five died by the age of seven and three others in middle age. (Some Madisons, though, reached great age:

James lived to eighty-five; his father, a brother, and a sister all came close to that number; his mother died at ninety-seven.)[20]

Though many elements of Madison's world are unfamiliar, the human beings in it are not. We recognize immediately their feelings and thoughts, their conflicts and affections. Through his correspondence, essays, and speeches, Madison primarily addressed the public issues of his time, often similar to those of our time. In letters with Dolley and close friends, the private Madison spoke directly, with genuine feeling. His sentences could be wooden, but his sentiments and ideas are as winning today as they were to his friends.

Madison lived in a network of intimate connections, from his large family to the most fertile political partnerships in our history, to a loving marriage that spanned four decades. With James Madison, often depicted in history as a dry creature of intellect, the core of his life was a genuine heart.

I

ALEXANDER HAMILTON

2

IMPATIENT YOUNG MEN

Alexander Hamilton's hardscrabble youth was unique among America's Founders, and not at all like Madison's upbringing. Born on the island of Nevis, a flyspeck in the Caribbean, Hamilton knew turbulence and squalor. His parents, who lived together but never married, struggled financially. His father was the wastrel son of a landed Scottish family. He left when Hamilton was ten. Hamilton's mother died of fever not long after, leaving two sons in the care of a cousin who soon committed suicide.

At fourteen, Hamilton began to clerk in a trading house on the island of St. Croix. With an intuitive grasp of business (and most other subjects), the energetic Hamilton began the steep climb to success. Local businessmen sent him to mainland America for formal education, first at a New Jersey academy and then at Kings College, now Columbia University.[1] Hamilton leapt into the Continental Army, serving as an artillery captain before he was twenty. Washington, who had a keen eye for talent, installed him as a close aide. By war's end, Hamilton was the hero of Yorktown as protégé of the great Washington and had married an heiress. In an eighteenth-century world that did not celebrate upward mobility, Hamilton crashed the highest reaches of American society.

Madison trod an easier path, his way smoothed by a prosperous father, the wealthiest planter in Orange County. His grandfather Ambrose began to assemble the family's holding in the 1720s, when Virginia's Piedmont was raw frontier. The future president, born in March 1751 to James Sr. and the nineteen-year-old Nelly Conway Madison, grew up on Montpelier's roughly five thousand acres. Several dozen slaves managed livestock, cut timber, and raised tobacco; they worked in the master's contracting business, ironworks, and brandy still. They cooked and cleaned and washed clothes.[2]

Violence shadowed Madison's youth. Periodic Indian unrest sparked waves of terror on the Virginia frontier, particularly during the war between Britain and France in the late 1750s. Slave insurrection, always a danger, haunted Montpelier after Ambrose Madison died at thirty-six, a victim of poison. A slave was hanged for murdering him; two others were whipped. Though Madison never commented on his grandfather's murder, such a lurid crime sticks in the mind and passes as a whispered story down the generations. In late 1783, when Madison returned to Montpelier, the plantation held eighty-eight slaves. Madison's younger brother, also named Ambrose, owned another thirty.[3]

Though sickly, Madison at age eleven began attending a boarding school seventy miles away. When he reached sixteen, his parents took a fateful step. The Madisons feared the climate at the College of William and Mary in Williamsburg, where fevers periodically swept through town. So they sent their eldest son to the College of New Jersey, far removed from Virginia's plantation culture.

Attending Princeton dramatically expanded the horizons of the bright young Virginian. Madison rode past the small, neat farms of Pennsylvania and New Jersey, where owners and hired workers, not slaves, tilled the fields. He lived with young men from Philadelphia and New Jersey and New York, whose merchant and professional families had ties in many colonies and in other lands. His instructors were scholars from Great Britain, many of them Scots. This early experience sowed the seeds of Madison's appreciation for the factors that divided Americans north and south, as well as his hankering to leave Virginia for a community that felt more free. It would be many years before he abandoned that longing and reconciled to his birthright as a Virginia squire.

His college teachers, inspired by a dissenting political tradition and a muscular form of Presbyterianism, encouraged the application of an individual's reason to the physical and spiritual world; they educated a disproportionate share of America's future Revolutionaries. Madison worked prodigiously, as he would through life. He completed the college curriculum in two years but stayed for a third year of studies directed by the college president. The effort exhausted him. After suffering a physical and emotional breakdown, Madison returned to Montpelier in 1772.

At home, while tutoring his younger siblings, Madison slid into gloom. Writing to William Bradford, a college friend from Philadelphia, he confided, "My sensations for many months past have intimated to me not to expect a long or healthy life." He plotted a trip to

Bradford's city "if I should be alive and have health sufficient." Orange County, Virginia, felt small. Madison scorned its narrowness. "I want again to breathe your free air," he wrote to Bradford in 1774. Madison deplored intolerance in the Anglican Church, of which he was a nominal member, denouncing "pride, ignorance and knavery among the priesthood and vice and wickedness among the laity."[4]

Madison's dissatisfaction with Virginia spurred his enthusiasm for northern society's "inspiration of liberty," both civil and religious.[5] For a young man so devoted to liberty, Montpelier's slave society—where slaves outnumbered the Madisons by at least ten to one—would be oppressive. Through his life, Madison chafed over the contradiction between his dependence on slavery and his devotion to liberty, while also fearing the dangers of slave insurrection. Indeed, as the colonies slid toward rebellion in 1774, he worried that the British would promote an uprising by slaves. Yet Madison never left the slave-dependent society that reared him.[6]

The Revolution stirred Madison from his slough of despond. Boosted by his father's position, Madison plunged into the political world. He served at Virginia's constitutional convention in 1775, then in the state's new legislature, and then on its executive council. He was representing Virginia in Congress, already an established politician, when Alexander Hamilton arrived in December 1782 as a delegate from New York.

Both were rising young men. Hamilton was sponsored by Washington and by his rich father-in-law, General Philip Schuyler of upstate New York. Hamilton and Madison became political allies, though never soulmates. For an evening's entertainment, Hamilton might lead the singing in a tavern as the punch bowl drained, or play the gallant to charming ladies in a drawing room. For company, Hamilton preferred the raconteur and rake Gouverneur Morris.[7] Madison's close friends were Virginians like Edmund Randolph or Thomas Jefferson. He enjoyed an evening in earnest conversation, with good wine, perhaps some cards and chess, or a moonlight ramble in the countryside.

Hamilton's flamboyance contrasted with Madison's sobriety. Below medium height and slender, Hamilton's military carriage and athletic grace made him seem larger. With reddish-brown hair and sparkling blue eyes, the ebullient New Yorker favored bright fashions. Always conspicuous, he combined battlefield élan with a sexually charged vitality. The last quality drove John Adams to grouse that Hamilton had "a superabundance of secretions which he could not find whores enough to draw off."[8] Hamilton's passions alternated with a haughtiness that could repel. A French diplomat described him as "one of those rare men who has distinguished himself equally on the field of battle as at the [legal] bar," adding that he "owed everything to his talents." Yet the Frenchman also found the young American "has a bit too much affectation and too little prudence." A later observer emphasized Hamilton's combative nature, calling him a "political porcupine, armed at all points, [who] brandishes a shaft to every opposer."[9]

Little about Madison made a strong first impression. Small and quiet, with a receding hairline and pale blue eyes, he usually dressed in black. He generated no sexual tension, tending to disappear at social gatherings, his reserve sometimes mistaken for hostility or rudeness. The wife of a political foe dismissed him as "a gloomy, stiff creature," who had "nothing engaging or even bearable in his manners—the most unsociable creature in existence."[10]

Those who worked with him knew a different man entirely. "He is easy and unreserved among his acquaintances," one wrote, "and has a most agreeable style of conversation." Outside the drawing room, he showed "a remarkable sweet temper" and "a soul replete with gentleness, humanity, and every social virtue."[11] All agreed on his intelligence and industry. A Frenchman thought Madison "can be more profound than Mr. Hamilton, but less brilliant."[12]

Through life, contemporaries would find in Madison a personal timidity that may have grown from his small stature, his dodgy health, and his social reserve. Though he had women friends, marriage long eluded him. Alone among the Founders, Madison never traveled by sea, repeatedly declining public offices that would subject him to the risks of the briny deep. He may have feared the impact of open waters on his epileptic-like symptoms. Yet timidity in some matters could mislead political adversaries. In political contests, Madison could be tenacious.

Princeton expanded Madison's horizons, but Hamilton exploded them. Making no effort to cloak his brilliance or defer to his elders, Hamilton demonstrated that raw talent could make its way in the American world. With his cosmopolitan flair and driving urgency, Hamilton fascinated many, including the quiet Virginian. Two principal factors brought them together despite their contrasting temperaments.

Both wished for a stronger national government and feared that the states would never form a workable union under the loose amalgamation achieved by the Articles of Confederation, which had been in effect only since 1781. In addition, they shared a precocious genius for government. Hamilton was more impetuous, Madison more deliberate, but each recognized the other's talents. For the next five years, they formed a potent force for making permanent the American experiment in self-government.

Hamilton was first to conclude that a new government was needed. In September 1780, as a twenty-five-year-old army officer, he declared the Articles inadequate before they even took effect. "The fundamental defect is a want of power in Congress," he wrote; the government needed "more decision, more dispatch, more secrecy, more responsibility." The solution, he predicted, was to summon a convention of state representatives to revise the Articles.[13]

Hamilton was not a man to abandon a penetrating insight. In July 1782, he and his father-in-law, General Schuyler, persuaded the New York legislature to call for "a general convention" to rewrite the Articles. Their resolution stated that "the radical source of most of our embarrassments is the want of sufficient power in Congress."[14]

Hamilton's dismay with the Articles grew sharper a few months later when he entered Congress at the Pennsylvania State House (later renamed Independence Hall), where each state had one vote. Attendance was spotty. For weeks at a time, Congress lacked the required quorum of seven state delegations. Major actions required the votes of nine states; it took the unanimous vote of thirteen state legislatures to amend the Articles or levy a national tax. The new delegate from New York, though often the youngest man in the chamber, freely voiced his dissatisfaction. On Hamilton's very first day, according to Madison's notes, he "warmly and cogently espoused" that Congress should accept a prisoner exchange involving British commander Lord Cornwallis.[15]

The quiet Virginian and the aggressive New Yorker served together on many committees, including one on disposing property seized from the British, another on a Dutch commercial treaty, a third addressing the peace negotiations with Britain, and a "grand committee" that struggled with the nation's vexing financial problems.[16] They agreed on the most pressing issue before Congress: the need for a revenue source other than begging from the states. Having served as "Continental Receiver General" in New York, Hamilton knew that state tax systems were often unfair and favored the influential. He thought a national tax would be more reliable, more just, and simpler to enforce.[17]

The political barriers to solving the problem were immense, beginning with what one delegate called Americans' "peculiar repugnance . . .

to taxes." People who had fought for eight years against British taxes were in no hurry to tax themselves. Nevertheless, Americans in the 1780s were not greed-ridden pinchpennies with only a crabbed vision of a national future. Money was short and times were hard. To sustain the war effort, states had imposed heavy taxes on people who were already suffering. The British pillaged farms, destroyed homes, and burned crops. Americans also paid through involuntary exactions, including paper currency that quickly inflated away personal wealth. American soldiers and government agents often seized food and supplies, leaving behind only scribbled promises of future payment.[18] With the end of the war and its urgent needs, many Americans hoped to reduce their financial contributions to the common good.

Madison understood the difficulty of solving the nation's financial woes. He wrote to a friend that when the delegates considered taxation they sank into "despondence and timidity." The Articles required that each state support the national government according to the proportionate value of its land, but the grand committee had neither statistics nor methodology for allocating that burden. Congress debated the question without finding a solution, with Hamilton and Madison sometimes venting their frustrations with the inconclusive deliberations.[19]

In April, Hamilton revived his idea that a national convention should rewrite the Articles. He drafted a resolution to that effect but did not press it. Even Madison, who shared Hamilton's despair over congressional paralysis, was not ready for that drastic step.[20] Instead, Congress approved Madison's rickety plan to repay the debt through an import tax for twenty-five years, voluntary payments by the states, and the sale of western lands. Hamilton, thinking the scheme impractical, voted against it. An exasperated Madison attributed the New Yorker's nay vote to his "rigid adherence . . . to a plan which he supposed more perfect."[21]

Despite voting against Madison's plan, Hamilton served on the committee that recommended it to the thirteen state legislatures. The committee's "Address to the States by Congress," written by Madison, framed the crisis in powerful terms. Rejecting the plan would open the way to "tyranny and usurpation." Despite Madison's passionate language and a separate appeal from Hamilton, the Rhode Island and Virginia legislatures scuttled the plan by voting against it.[22]

Through these defeats, Madison and Hamilton grew closer. The New Yorker sought the Virginian's support when he was blamed for Congress's ignominious flight from irate Pennsylvania soldiers in June.

Hamilton, a former soldier, had managed the congressional response to the troops; gossip flew that he had been inept or even cowardly. At Hamilton's request, Madison wrote that the New Yorker had resisted abandoning Philadelphia "except in the last necessity." For someone as sensitive about his honor as Hamilton was, Madison's statement was gratifying.[23]

But by that point in the summer of 1783, both men were looking beyond Congress. Madison's term would expire soon. Hamilton longed to be back with his family and to begin amassing the sort of fortune that his friend from Virginia would inherit. In a passage that Madison could have written, Hamilton complained that the victory over Britain had eliminated any sense of urgency over the nation's business: "Every day proves the inefficacy of the present confederation, yet the common danger [Britain] being removed, we are receding instead of advancing."[24]

By late November, each man was headed home. In New York City, where a joyous celebration marked the British departure from their American headquarters, Hamilton settled his young family on Wall Street. The city was in a transition, virtually hollowed out by the war. Parts of it had burned down during the British occupation. Thousands of loyalist New Yorkers had fled on Royal Navy ships. But New York's harbor and location were too fine for the city not to rebound quickly, and Hamilton aimed to share in its prosperity. A year later, he helped found the city's first bank and enjoyed a thriving law practice.[25]

Madison traveled to Montpelier through heavy rains and a countryside also wounded by war.[26] As he settled in at home, he retired to the library to study. His father still managed the estate, assisted by third son Ambrose. By May, Madison was back in public office, representing Orange County in the Virginia House of Delegates. Within two years, he would win enactment of the Virginia statute for protecting religious freedom, the first guarantee of freedom of worship in human history. He did not yet, however, agree with Hamilton that a national convention was the only way to address America's crisis.

No one planned the process that produced America's Constitution. The road was a twisting one, marked with improvisation and luck. Many Americans, including Madison, felt that a divine will watched over them through those pivotal years; little else could explain how they avoided perils by a hairsbreadth, how small-mindedness unexpectedly yielded to vision.

The weakness of the national government afflicted daily life. There was no uniform currency. Any transaction might be conducted in federal dollars, British pounds sterling, Spanish doubloons, Prussian carolines, or the inflated paper money issued by individual states. When Madison served as delegate to Congress in 1782, his pay came in Portuguese "johannes." The humblest purchase could become a currency negotiation. Even with the many forms of currency, there was not enough of it, which gave rise to widespread barter. Virginia accepted bales of tobacco as tax payments. The absence of uniform weights and measures further stymied economic activity. "Next to the inconvenience of speaking different languages," Madison wrote, "is that of using different and arbitrary weights and measures."[27]

The states' contempt for the national government went beyond refusing to pay its soldiers or its creditors. A Virginia delegate to Congress described the national government as "always an object of derision . . . it's like a man's attempting to walk with both legs cut off." Under the treaty with Great Britain, the United States promised that British merchants could sue in American courts to collect debts incurred before the war. This debt overhang was acute in Virginia, where many planters had survived on credit from British traders. Virginia thumbed its nose at the treaty by blocking collections of those debts through Virginia courts. In retaliation, the British retained military posts in the western frontier lands.[28]

With the central government weak, the states quarreled. New Hampshire and New York competed to control the future state of Vermont. Connecticut laid claim to part of Pennsylvania, while Virginia claimed the region around the current city of Pittsburgh. Seven states pressed conflicting claims to western lands beyond the Appalachian Mountains. States with good harbors taxed goods destined for neighboring states. In Madison's words, "New Jersey, placed between Philadelphia and New York, was likened to a cask tapped at both ends: and North Carolina between Virginia and South Carolina to a patient bleeding at both arms." Commercial rivalries festered. Massachusetts placed higher taxes on imports from Connecticut than on those from Britain.[29]

While Hamilton practiced law in New York, Madison traveled to Richmond in May 1784 to serve in the Virginia legislature. He was soon appointed one of four commissioners to negotiate with Maryland over fishing and navigation rights to the Potomac River, the boundary between the two states. The negotiations lay dormant for six months until General Washington traveled to Annapolis. The general, a longtime advocate of the Potomac's commercial potential, prodded both states to start the process.[30]

The talks began inauspiciously in March 1785. The Maryland commissioners sent a letter to George Mason of Alexandria, announcing that they would soon arrive to parley with him and his Virginia colleagues. Mason, who had received no notice of his appointment as commissioner, was puzzled. His neighbor, General Washington, urged that he proceed nonetheless. Mason lassoed a nearby Virginia commissioner for the talks, but the other two Virginians, including Madison, were too distant to summon.[31]

To propel the business, Washington housed the conferees at his comfortable Mount Vernon mansion. Sheltered from the raw weather of late winter, enjoying the general's larder and wine cellar, the negotiators agreed on tolls, navigation rights, port duties, fishing practices, and lighthouses.[32] More important, the Mount Vernon conference became a model for greater economic cooperation among the states and the first step on the road to a constitutional convention.

For a year, Madison and others had been chewing over Hamilton's notion of a national convention to rewrite the Articles. When Jefferson traveled in Massachusetts, he found that New Englanders supported a stronger federal government. "I have no hopes," another Virginian wrote to Madison, "but in a convocation of the states." Another found lively interest in a national convention to "enable Congress to execute with more energy, effect, & vigor, the powers assigned to it."[33]

Madison agreed that the Articles should be replaced by a strong union, but he was uncertain how to make that happen. Charting that course, he wrote in late 1784, required "a knowledge greater than I possess of the temper and views of the different states."[34] After the Mount Vernon conference and a trip to New York and Philadelphia, Madison warmed to the idea of a national convention. From Richmond in late 1785, he reported that the Virginia legislature was considering calling for a meeting of all thirteen states "for the purpose of digesting and reporting the requisite augmentation of the power of Congress over trade." Such a session, he explained, naturally grew out of the Mount Vernon conference.[35]

After the Virginia legislature again refused to expand congressional powers, Madison and his allies slipped through a proposal for a national conference. Madison had given up on asking state legislatures to increase congressional authority; the states would never embrace a reduction in their own powers. In a national convention, Madison calculated, a stronger national government would have "fewer enemies."

The final legislation named eight commissioners from Virginia, including Madison.[36]

Madison still feared that the convention "will probably miscarry." The convention process seemed protracted and strewn with obstacles: "[T]he states must first agree to the proposition for sending deputies—that these must agree in a plan to be sent back to the states, and that these again must agree unanimously in a ratification of it. I almost despair of success." With a shrug, he concluded it was all that the Virginia legislature would approve.[37]

Virginia called on every state to send commissioners to Annapolis on the first Monday in September, 1786. Maryland's sleepy capital was selected for its central location and its distance from the commercial power of New York and Philadelphia. Madison's doubts about the event seemed prophetic when Maryland, the host, refused to appoint delegates. In August, as Madison was leaving for the convention, his expectations remained low. Even mere commercial reform, he wrote to Jefferson, seemed unlikely.[38]

Hamilton, however, embraced the Annapolis session. According to a friend, the New Yorker saw it as "a stepping stone to a general convention." While traveling to Maryland for the meeting, Hamilton confided that he preferred "a convention to revise the whole of our mode or system of general government."[39]

Madison prepared for the conference by reading, studying, and thinking. Two years before, when Jefferson was dispatched to Paris as United States Minister, Madison had asked his friend to undertake for him "the occasional purchase of rare and valuable books." Jefferson agreed. By January 1786, two trunks filled with precious volumes had arrived at Montpelier.[40] Madison found that Jefferson's "literary cargo" was "perfectly to my mind."[41]

Armed with Diderot's massive *Encyclopédie*, several multivolume histories of Europe, and studies of ancient Greece and Rome, Madison went to work. He examined previous confederacies, starting with the classical era, then moving on to more recent ones (the United Provinces of the Netherlands, the Swiss cantons, and the German empire). For each, he analyzed their governments, their laws, and why they failed. Except for Germany, dominated by the royal Hapsburg family, Madison concluded that the great flaw was the weakness of the ties binding together the parts of each confederacy. Jealousy among those parts, or alliances with foreign powers, undermined each. That was what Madison feared for the United States: that quarreling American states would fall into the arms of European monarchies. The risk, he wrote to Jefferson, was "the danger of having the same game played on our confederacy by which Philip [of Macedon] managed that of the Grecian state." Only a stronger government could sustain the American union against petty rivalries and foreign princes.[42]

Madison arrived in Annapolis on the first day of September 1786, exactly on time. Two other delegates, both from New Jersey, were in town. Rugged travel conditions often confounded punctuality in 1786, yet Madison was rarely late. Knowing that at least eight other states had appointed delegates to the meeting, he settled in at George Mann's tavern, an upscale establishment that featured more than a hundred beds and stables for fifty horses. He waited.[43]

After a few days, Madison wrote to his brother Ambrose. A few commissioners were arriving, he reported, but he doubted there would be enough for the meeting to be "respectable," even though the nation's situation was critical:

> Nothing can bear a worse aspect than our federal affairs. . . . No money comes into the public treasury, trade is on a wretched footing, and the states are all running mad after paper money, which among other evils disables them from . . . paying the public debts.

As Madison posted the letter to his brother, Hamilton arrived in Annapolis. He too wrote home, though his missive was a love note to his wife: "In the bosom of my family alone must my happiness be sought, and in that of my Betsey is everything that is charming to me." The prospect of spending two weeks away, he moaned, "fills me with an anxiety."[44]

Through more idle days in Annapolis, the few delegates grew fretful. Hamilton's impatience with America's political malaise began to infect them all. They were impatient with those not yet present, impatient with the states that appointed no delegates, impatient with the feeble national government, and impatient with the tortuous process of amending the Articles. As they shared their frustrations, according to Madison, they talked "of the expediency of a more radical reform." He wrote to Ambrose that unless many delegates arrived soon, "it is proposed to break up the meeting with a recommendation of another time and place, and . . . extending the plan to the other defects of the Confederation."[45]

The next day, twelve delegates gathered in Maryland's Senate chamber, which sat on the highest point in Annapolis, overlooking its small harbor. Congress had met in the small, elegant chamber for almost a year, and in December 1783 it received Washington's resignation from the army there. Now, nearly three years later, two other Virginians sat with Madison, along with three delegates each from Delaware and New Jersey, a lone Pennsylvanian, plus Hamilton and another New Yorker. A few more delegates were on the way. Three from Massachusetts had just left New York, with Rhode Islanders close behind. Another New Yorker and a North Carolinian were nearing Annapolis. But the delegates in the Maryland Senate chamber were finished with waiting.[46]

The Pennsylvanian rose to question the unfair fees that states levied on goods from other states, but he was quickly squelched. Madison and Hamilton had no intention of working within the narrow mandate of the Annapolis meeting. Rather, they insisted, the delegates should disband and call for a new convention to review every part of the Articles—the plan Madison had described to his brother. The slender justification for this bold move came from four words in New Jersey's charge to its delegates: that they should address commercial issues "*and other important matters.*" On that slight linguistic thread, the Annapolis delegates hung the nation's future.

The boldness of their action is easy to miss. Twelve public men met in a coastal town. Their business failed, so they called for another session with a wider agenda. The currents of history swirled on, or so it might seem.

But for those in the Maryland Senate chamber, the occasion was both immense and immensely risky. Four years later, in a letter to Madison, the Pennsylvanian remembered that moment with a note of wonder. It was the time, he wrote, when "I hazarded a vote unsupported, and unauthorized by my powers."[47] None of the delegates—except possibly the three from New Jersey—was authorized to cross that political Rubicon, to go beyond writing impatient letters to friends or newspapers, beyond complaining in local taverns. Nevertheless, they rose and proclaimed that the nation was on the wrong road, in the wrong political vehicle, pointed at the wrong destination. Only three years after the peace with Britain, the Annapolis delegates pronounced that Americans were making a hash of their independence and needed to rethink the whole business.

Madison and Hamilton led them. Their impatience, the impatience of young men, fueled an impetuous gamble on a second convention, double or nothing. When it came to being impatient and impetuous, Hamilton had few peers. Recognizing the power of his passion and his vision, his fellows asked him to draft a resolution calling for a second convention to consider changes to every part of the Articles.[48]

Hamilton, not for the last time in his life, overdid it. The other delegates balked at his violent denunciation of the Articles. Madison drew the New Yorker aside. Hamilton should revise the resolution, he said, so every delegate could join it. Hamilton toned down the draft, and the delegates adopted it three days after convening.

The final resolution expressed the "earnest and unanimous wish . . . [for] a general meeting of the states" that would consider *all* of the "embarrassments which characterize the present state of our national affairs." That next convention, meeting in Philadelphia "on the second Monday in May next," should "devise such further provisions as shall appear to them necessary to render the constitution of the Federal Government adequate to the exigencies of the Union."[49]

Over those few days in September 1786, Hamilton and Madison formed a real alliance. For the next two years, they prodded America to embrace a new idea of itself through a structure of self-government that could stand for centuries.

For the Philadelphia Convention to attract broad participation, the Virginia legislature's endorsement was essential. Madison traveled to Richmond to make that happen.

Richmond had been Virginia's state capital for only a few years. Hot, humid, and feverish through the summer, it sheltered some two thousand residents. Trading ships, blocked by the falls of the James River from passing farther upstream, nestled at piers near tobacco warehouses. Residents shared the unpaved streets with goats and hogs. A visitor in 1785 admired the views from Richmond's hills but dismissed the town as "one of the dirtiest holes of a place I was ever in." Early autumn brought the horse-racing season as well as the state's legislators; the latter did not much impress another visitor. Their conversation, he reported, was of "insignificant or irrelevant matters," including "horse-races, runaway negroes, yesterday's play, politics."[50]

Madison worried that the proposal for the Philadelphia Convention would be undermined by a dispute with Spain over access to the Mississippi River. By barring American goods from shipment through New Orleans, the Spaniards were blocking western settlers from sending their produce to world markets. A tentative deal proposed that the United States relinquish Mississippi access for twenty-five years in return for the right to trade directly with ports in Spain, a great benefit for Northern merchants. Angry Virginians and westerners thought the deal would sacrifice their interests to favor northerners. By sharpening sectional mistrust, Madison feared, the episode might weaken support for the Philadelphia Convention.[51]

Two developments, however, allowed Madison to overcome any opposition to a convention. First came strife in western Massachusetts. In what became known as Shays' Rebellion, New England farmers and mechanics protested taxes they could not pay, which caused courts to seize their land and property. They barricaded courthouses, thwarting debt collection. No one knew how far the movement would go, but the unrest reinforced Madison's message that something must be done.[52]

In addition, Madison was able to invoke Washington's prestige. Though the general had not authorized it, Madison placed Washington atop the list of proposed delegates for the Philadelphia meeting. Few Virginians would vote against a resolution with Washington's name on it.[53]

In November, the Virginia legislature unanimously called for the Philadelphia Convention and appointed seven delegates, beginning with Washington. Madison was an equally obvious choice. In quick succession, five more states approved similar resolutions (New Jersey, Pennsylvania, Delaware, North Carolina, and Georgia).[54]

But there the momentum stalled, becalmed by the failure of Congress to act on the Annapolis report. New Englanders were leery of the report's broad mandate, while New York was reluctant to risk losing its ability to tax goods shipped through its harbor to its neighbors. The Philadelphia initiative needed another push. Hamilton and Madison provided it.[55]

In mid-February 1787, Madison arrived in New York to start a new term in Congress. There he found Hamilton, newly elected to the New York Assembly. With the New York legislature and Congress meeting mere steps apart, the two men executed a deft political minuet. On February 15, Hamilton urged the state assembly to adopt the import tax proposed by Congress years before. When his motion failed, Hamilton presented a fallback motion, imploring the assembly to instruct its congressional delegates to support the Philadelphia Convention. When the New York delegates to Congress adopted that position a few days later, Madison pounced. On his motion, Congress finally endorsed the Philadelphia Convention.[56]

The congressional resolution was narrower than either Madison or Hamilton wished, as it called for a convention "for the sole and express purpose of revising the Articles of Confederation." But it was enough to propel the convention proposal. Twelve states—all but Rhode Island—appointed delegates for Philadelphia.[57]

For the next three months, Madison remained in New York, close to Hamilton. Though both still had legislative duties, they also could focus on the extraordinary opportunity now before them: the chance to reinvent the United States government.

3

A POWERFUL EFFECT ON OUR DESTINY

Madison, full of anticipation, arrived in Philadelphia at the beginning of May, eleven days early for the convention. With forty thousand residents, the city was America's largest and most sophisticated. Madison settled among old friends and familiar surroundings at Mrs. House's establishment, where he always stayed in Philadelphia. Hamilton, a busy lawyer and family man, would not arrive for many days.

Both men craved firm action to confront America's crisis. The national government was too weak to develop its own revenue and currency. Shays' Rebellion had ended in a bloody confrontation at the Springfield Arsenal. Westerners feared that a deal with Spain would sacrifice their access to the Mississippi.[1]

Madison saw little prospect for improvement under the Articles of Confederation. "No respect is paid to the federal authority," he wrote in late February. "Not a single state complies with the requisition[s], several pass them over in silence, and some positively reject them." He did not flinch from his conclusion: "It is not possible that a government can last long under these circumstances." If the Philadelphia Convention did not act decisively, most Americans "will probably prefer the lesser evil of a partition of the Union into three or more practicable and energetic governments." Congressional delegates spoke of dividing into a New England confederacy, one of the middle states, and a southern union.[2]

Madison had composed for himself a twelve-count indictment of the Articles, titled "Vices of the Political System of the United States." Not only, he stressed, did the states fail to support the national government; they actively assumed federal authority. Georgia made its own peace treaties with Indian tribes. Massachusetts used state troops to stop the Shays rebels. Maryland and Virginia entered independently into their own agreement over the Potomac River. Virginia flouted trade treaties between the United States and France and the Netherlands. Some states imposed taxes that discriminated against citizens of other states. Some printed their own currency. There were too many state laws, Madison worried, and they changed too often.

The union was fragile. Because state legislatures had adopted the Articles, any state could dissolve the government by revoking its ratification. Madison dreamt of a nation bound by ties among its people, not among its states. To achieve that goal, its founding document had to be ratified by the people through special conventions.

Madison inserted a jarring observation in his "Vices" memorandum: "Where slavery exists the republican theory becomes still more fallacious." This flat statement neither followed from the previous sentence nor connected to the ones after it. Rather, it was an almost involuntary burst from Madison's innermost mind. No intelligent person in 1787 could miss the contradiction between American slavery and the principles of human liberty. The British lexicographer Samuel Johnson had seized upon it during the Revolution, asking why "we hear the loudest yelps for liberty among the drivers of negroes." Despite Madison's usual reticence about that contradiction, this unguarded moment suggests his dismay over the hypocrisy that tainted the American experiment.[3]

Madison's preparation covered more than the sins of the confederacy. In letters to Washington and others, Madison urged a "radical" revision of the government; halfway measures, he insisted, "will dishonor the councils which propose them." He wanted national taxes and trade laws, a national judiciary, a federal veto over unwise state legislation, and a change from per-state voting in Congress to representation based on population. The federal legislature should have two branches, as most state legislatures did, though Madison had not yet worked out his ideas for an executive branch. He was not alone in identifying most of these priorities, but Madison had thought about them longer and harder than most others had.[4]

He did not devote all his time to matters of state but also performed family errands. In Richmond, he had somewhat limply pressed his father's claim to a disputed land title.[5] On another journey to Richmond, Madison bought an advertisement in the *Virginia Gazette* that offered twenty dollars for the return to Montpelier of "a mulatto slave, named Anthony, about 17 years old." While in Philadelphia on this current trip, he sold tobacco for his father and sought a foundry that could fashion tools needed back home.[6]

Ten days passed before a second delegate, George Washington, arrived in Philadelphia. Despite blustery weather, a company of cavalry escorted the general over the Schuylkill River bridge. Thirteen cannons boomed, church bells rang, and crowds cheered. Washington's arrival established, as no other event could, that this convention was a serious matter that might change the nation.[7]

The other delegates did not match the punctuality of the Virginians. On the scheduled opening day, May 14, Virginians numbered five of the eight delegates at the Pennsylvania State House. The other three were Pennsylvanians who lived in Philadelphia, including the eminent Benjamin Franklin.[8] Three days later, all seven Virginia delegates were present, including Governor Edmund Randolph and George Mason, the elder statesman who drafted Virginia's Declaration of Rights of 1776. Because they represented the largest state, which also had issued the first call to Philadelphia, the Virginians decided to lead the Convention's deliberations with an outline of a new government charter.[9]

For the next week, the Virginians conferred in morning sessions at Mrs. House's. In the afternoon, they walked to the State House to greet arriving delegates.[10] They soon learned that one of the Convention's dividing lines would run between small states and more populous ones (Massachusetts, Pennsylvania, and Virginia). The battleground would be representation in Congress: Should each state continue to have an equal vote, or should congressional seats be assigned on the basis of population?

The Pennsylvanians wanted to eliminate per-state voting in the Convention itself, but the Virginians disagreed. That step, Madison feared, might panic the small-state delegates, making it more difficult to secure population-based representation in the final charter. The small-state delegates recognized their peril. A Delaware delegate urged a colleague "to keep a strict watch upon the movements and propositions from the larger states."[11]

In contrast to the Virginians' unity, the New York delegation was sharply split between Hamilton, who sought radical change, and two upstate followers of Governor George Clinton, who saw no reason to strengthen the national government.

Robert Yates, almost fifty, was a leading judge; the younger John

Lansing was mayor of Albany. By temperament and politics, they were natural adversaries to Hamilton, who radiated the energy of the embryo metropolis on Manhattan Island. Five years before, Hamilton had sneered that Lansing's "friends mistook his talents when they made him a statesman." A Georgia delegate to the Constitutional Convention agreed: "[Lansing] has a hesitation in his speech, that will prevent his being an orator of any eminence—his legal knowledge I am told is not extensive, nor his education a good one." Judge Yates attracted fewer adverse comments, yet he was equally conservative politically. In Hamilton, they had a trying colleague. The same Georgian found that Hamilton's "manners are tinctured with stiffness, and sometimes with a degree of vanity that is highly disagreeable." Madison warned Washington that Yates and Lansing were "likely to be a clog on" Hamilton.[12]

In fact, the rules established by the New York legislature neutered Hamilton throughout the Convention. Two New York delegates had to be present to cast the state's one vote, and a majority of the delegation determined that vote. Hamilton's two colleagues could overrule him on every question; one of them alone could stymie him; both could render him powerless simply by jointly boycotting a session. Though Hamilton traveled to Philadelphia with Yates and they stayed at the same inn, any façade of cordiality crumbled quickly. In a slight overstatement, a delegate observed later that "Yates and Lansing never voted in one single instance with Hamilton."[13]

On Friday, May 25, however, those conflicts lay in the future. After almost two weeks of restless waiting, a quorum of seven state delegations was finally present. With mingled feelings of eagerness and dread, they began the convention that could determine whether the United States would remain a nation.[14]

Americans in 1787 had more experience writing constitutions than virtually any other society in history. Over the previous eleven years, they had written thirteen state constitutions and the Articles of Confederation. Madison had first entered public service as a twenty-five-year-old delegate to the convention that drafted Virginia's state constitution. For more than a decade, Americans had debated how frequently legislative elections should be held, how much discretion executive officials should have, what the role of courts should be, and how judges should be selected. Each state charter and the Articles struck a different balance among these and dozens of other difficult questions, and the Philadelphia delegates had opinions about the consequences of those different balances. America had become a laboratory of constitution writing, an experience that prepared well the men who met in Philadelphia.

As the Convention began, Hamilton and Madison immediately stepped forward, propelled by their identification with General Washington, who was the unanimous choice as the Convention's presiding officer. Madison took the desk next to the general at the front of the chamber, intending to take notes on the summer's debates. In his study of earlier republics, Madison had searched in vain for accounts of why certain government structures were created. To ensure that the Philadelphia Convention would leave no such void, Madison resolved "to preserve as far as I could an exact account of what might pass in the Convention." At a desk that faced the delegates, Madison could record every speech in his own shorthand, which he transcribed and corrected at night. The effort proved grueling. He later said it almost killed him, and it may have limited his role at the Convention. His notes, though, remain the essential starting point for any study of that body.[15]

On the first day, Hamilton was named to the rules committee chaired by legendary Virginia judge George Wythe. The final rules included features that proved essential through the summer: votes were recorded by state and not by individual delegate, all proceedings were secret, and no vote was conclusive until a final document was approved. Secrecy allowed the delegates to inquire widely about the issues before them, to explore creative yet ill-formed ideas without fear of public embarrassment. The third rule allowed them to reconsider their views as the work proceeded. For example, a decision about the structure of the legislative process might seem unwise after later debates over the executive branch.

The stage was set. "The whole community is big with expectation," Madison wrote, "and there can be no doubt but that the result will . . . have a powerful effect on our destiny."[16]

On May 29, Edmund Randolph rose to present the "Virginia Plan," which had been hammered out in Mrs. House's parlor. It had been a cool May, with little hint of the infernal temperatures that would torment the delegates in the coming weeks. Young and attractive, Randolph had a large speaking voice and was comfortable at center stage. Though Madison was the moving force behind the Virginia Plan, he registered no frustration when Randolph took the star turn. Madison concentrated on taking the notes.

Randolph detailed the Articles' defects, then unveiled fifteen resolutions that would scrap the Articles and build a new government. Under the Virginia Plan, the people would elect a lower house of the legislature, which would elect an upper house; both houses together would adopt laws on matters where "the separate states are incompetent" and would be able to void state laws; they also would choose an executive branch and national judiciary. A number of delegates were stunned. They had come to Philadelphia to revise the Articles, but the Virginians—including both Washington and Madison—wanted to reinvent the government.[17]

Dissension among the New Yorkers surfaced immediately. When Randolph sat down, Hamilton insisted that the delegates must resolve whether the states were committed to "one government" or wished to continue their "separate existence connected only by leagues offensive and defensive and treaties of commerce." His colleague Yates, in his notes, complained that Randolph proposed "a strong consolidated union, in which the idea of states should be nearly annihilated." The following day, Yates questioned whether he should be at the Convention at all. "My forebodings," he wrote to a friend, "are too much realized," adding, "How long I shall remain future events must determine." Lansing raised the same question in a letter to his brother.[18]

The contrast between the prudent Madison and the headstrong Hamilton also emerged early. Hamilton did not speak frequently, but his views were often bold, full of emotion as well as reason; one observer called his presentation "flowing and rapturous."[19]

Madison's manner was prosaic. Although always "the best informed man of any point in a debate," one delegate recalled, "he cannot be called an orator." His speeches were "cool," based on reason; a colleague would later call him "too much of a book politician." His small size and soft voice did not command attention: "[T]he warmest excitement of debate was visible in him only by a more or less rapid and forward seesaw motion of his body." Yet Madison's reasoning and insight could win adherents, and he was not shy about presenting his views. At the Convention he spoke often and at length.[20]

With an acute sense of timing, Madison sometimes strained to shunt an issue aside, hoping for a better resolution on another day.[21] Several times, he presented historical analysis from his "Vices" memorandum. An early Madison speech, an observer wrote, "pointed out all the beauties and defects of ancient republics; [then] compared their situation with ours wherever it appeared to bear any analogy." The Virginian stressed the principle that has come down to us as a central tenet of American government: to control government power, there must be "checks and balances" among its branches.[22] Though Madison's theoretical forays elicited little response from the other delegates, Hamilton listened closely to him. During debates, the New Yorker jotted occasional notes. He especially noted Madison's remarks, sometimes with comments on them, almost a silent dialogue with the Virginian.[23]

Through most of the summer, delegates from ten or eleven states met from ten o'clock in the morning to three in the afternoon, Monday through Saturday. Rhode Island never sent delegates, while the New Yorkers left in early July; New Hampshire's delegates did not arrive until late in that month. The men from Delaware considered going home in the early weeks, when they realized they might lose per-state voting, but they stayed.

The Convention's early days were uneven. "[W]e [are] wandering from one thing to another," Madison complained, "without seeming to be settled in any one principle."[24] As the delegates worked through the Virginia Plan, three interconnected questions kept confounding them: per-state voting versus population-based representation; how the states would survive with a stronger central government; and just how democratic the government should be. Lurking underneath was an issue none cared to address: slavery.

For many delegates, Shays' Rebellion had tarnished the idea of democracy. "The people," announced a Connecticut delegate, "should have as little to do as may be about the government. They want information and are constantly liable to be misled." A Massachusetts delegate agreed: "The evils we experience flow from the excess of democracy. The people do not want virtue; but are the dupes of pretended patriots." Mason of Virginia rejoined that no matter the problems with democracy, "the genius of the people is in favor of it."[25]

When it came to democracy's virtues, both Madison and Hamilton held contradictory views. Madison insisted that the people must directly elect one branch of the legislature or else they "would be lost sight of altogether." Both men strongly supported proportional representation rather than per-state voting because it treated individual citizens equally. Yet Madison also argued for "successive filtrations" of the popular will through institutions insulated from the people. Stability, he insisted, was as important as democracy. Hamilton shared this ambivalent view that democratic processes were important, but should be constrained.[26]

The debate over representation forced the delegates to think about

America's slaves. To allocate congressional representatives on the basis of population, the question arose whether the enslaved also should be counted. Delegates from northern states objected. Slaves were property and did not vote, they proclaimed, just like horses and oxen. Perversely, southerners insisted on the human qualities of their slaves, eager to have them count for representation purposes. Women and white men without property also could not vote, they argued, yet they would be counted when allocating representatives. At issue, of course, was power. Of the more than three million Americans recorded by the 1790 census, roughly six hundred thousand were slaves and most lived in the South. If the slaves counted in the allocation of congressional seats, southerners would gain votes in Congress.

A political deal narrowly carried the day. The three large states (Massachusetts, Pennsylvania, and Virginia) and the three states of the Deep South (the Carolinas and Georgia) cobbled together a grimy compromise. Popular representation would prevail in both houses of Congress, with each slave counting as three-fifths of a person. On June 11, the Convention adopted the deal.[27]

Alarmed by this outcome, the small-state delegates demanded a recess to develop an alternative. For two days, delegates from Delaware, New Jersey, New York, and Connecticut thrashed out their own proposal, the "New Jersey Plan." It looked a lot like the Articles, retaining a one-house Congress with per-state voting and denying Congress the power to levy taxes.[28] Lansing of New York praised it, warning that the "states will never sacrifice their rights," but it was anathema to Madison, Hamilton, and others who despaired of government under the Articles.

Hamilton was in a hopeless position, his own delegation sponsoring a plan he despised. He was not, he told the Convention, "in sentiment with either plan." Then he offered his own audacious ideas.[29]

For nearly five hours on June 18, Hamilton told the delegates that they should not give power to the people because they "seldom judge or determine right." Power should go to "the rich and well born." The states, he urged, should be "reduced to corporations, and with very limited powers." To speed that process, Congress should have the power to appoint state governors and veto state laws. Because no effective executive could be based on republican principles, Hamilton urged an executive modeled on the British system, which he called "the best in the world." That meant that the chief executive—Hamilton called him a "monarch"—should serve for life, as should senators.[30] Hamilton wanted to take self-government out of American government.

It was a courageous speech in some respects, but also a foolhardy one, very nearly amounting to political self-immolation. Hamilton's suggestions had no chance of success. A convention of former American rebels was never going to embrace an American copy of the British government. Americans demanded something different.

Hamilton became a whipping boy for other delegates. James Wilson of Pennsylvania archly assured the Convention that, unlike Hamilton, he wished to preserve the states. Lansing pronounced that the greatest objection to Hamilton's ideas was "the repugnance of the people to them." A Connecticut delegate observed that Hamilton's speech "has been praised by everybody, [but] he has been supported by none."[31]

Offering no comment on Hamilton's rash pronouncements, Madison showed extraordinary solicitude for his colleague. After transcribing his notes of Hamilton's incendiary speech, Madison appreciated how controversial it was and how it would look to history. So he read his version to Hamilton and allowed the New Yorker to make corrections. Through the summer, Madison accorded that courtesy to only one other delegate.[32]

Though Hamilton's statements threatened to reduce him to pariah status, he did not recant or modify them. Two days later, after insisting he had been misunderstood, he repeated that the national government must have "indefinite authority" and that the states "*as states . . .* ought to be abolished." A day later, he expressed the hope that state governments "might gradually dwindle into nothing."[33] Despite the thundering lack of support for Hamilton's ideas, he would not trim them.

Like Hamilton, Madison recognized that the convention was at a pivotal moment in that third week of June. He too wished to guide it toward a stronger national government, but his strategy was more conventional. Rather than champion a junior version of the British government, on June 19 he went on the attack, dissecting the New Jersey Plan in excruciating detail.

Madison's theme was that the New Jersey proposal would not solve America's problems. It would not prevent states from violating foreign treaties, or encroaching on federal authority, or "execut[ing] their unrighteous projects against each other." Nor would it enable the country to quell rebellions such as the Shays affair. Oddly, he added the observation from his "Vices" memo that "where slavery exists, the Republican theory becomes still more fallacious," again not bothering to explain that point.

Madison concluded that the "great difficulty" before the convention was "the affair of representation," per-state voting versus proportional representation: "If this could be adjusted, all others would be surmountable." Yet Madison offered no counterproposal. Rather, he insisted that the small states swallow proportional representation.[34] Though his critique of the New Jersey Plan was incisive, Madison had not helped resolve the convention's impasse.

The delegates approved the Virginia Plan over the New Jersey Plan, but that only made the small states more intransigent. The conflict boiled over on June 29, again over representation in Congress. Madison and Hamilton passionately opposed a renewed motion for per-state voting in Congress. Hamilton described the small states as engaging in "a contest for power, not for liberty." The people of Delaware, he added, would not be less free if they cast votes equal in weight to people in Pennsylvania. He appealed for them to reconsider their views: "It is a miracle that we were now here exercising our tranquil and free deliberations on the subject. It would be madness to trust to future miracles."[35]

The day before, Madison had pointed out that the large states had never banded together in Congress against the smaller states; the large states, he explained, differed from each other in customs, religion, and economic interests. There was, Madison now observed, an elemental divide in American politics, but it was a different one:

> The great danger to our general government is the great southern and northern interests of the continent being opposed to each other. Look to the votes in Congress and most of them stand divided by the geography of the country, not according to the size of the states.[36]

Madison's insight—that geography, North against South, defined the conflicts in American politics—made little impression on his colleagues or on the final Constitution. Yet it established Madison as a political seer, the man at the Philadelphia Convention who most worried about the forces that would dictate America's political life for the next century. Yet when Madison attempted to translate that insight into a meaningful proposal, the results were decidedly odd. He proposed that one house of Congress be structured to defend the interests of the southern slave states, while the other represented the interests of the other states. To that end, representatives to one house should be allocated based on the number of free inhabitants plus the *whole* number of slaves; the allocation of seats in the other house should exclude slaves altogether.[37]

The convention did not dwell on either Madison's insight or his odd proposal. Instead, the speech of an overwrought Delaware delegate underscored that the delegates stood at the edge of a precipice. He insisted that without per-state voting, the small states would have no choice but to form alliances with European powers. This was exactly what Madison most feared. Sobered by that threat, the delegates appointed a "grand committee" consisting of one delegate from each state. Its charge was to find a way back from the edge. Neither Madison nor Hamilton, partisans of proportional representation, was on the committee. Compromise was the order of the day.

The committee adopted an idea that John Dickinson of Delaware had offered on the eighth day of the Convention: that one house of Congress have proportional representation; in the other house, the states would enjoy equal voting power. As a sop to the large states, the branch with proportional representation (now the House of Representatives) would originate legislation about revenue matters. Madison disliked the compromise. He ached to call the small states' bluff and insist on proportional representation in both houses.[38]

By the time the committee reported, all three New York delegates had left Philadelphia. Lansing and Yates were certain their views would never prevail; Hamilton knew that the makeup of his delegation, combined with his ill-considered speech, left him with little influence. Yet even when not in Philadelphia, Hamilton's mind remained on the Convention. "I am seriously and deeply distressed," he wrote to General Washington, "that we shall let slip the golden opportunity of rescuing the American empire from disunion, anarchy, and misery. No motley or feeble measure can . . . finally receive the public support."[39]

Washington agreed. Matters at the Convention, he wrote back, "are now, if possible, in a worse train than ever." The general also was losing hope: "I *almost* despair of seeing a favorable issue to the proceedings." He joined Hamilton in dismissing the "men who oppose a strong and energetic government" as "narrow minded politicians," and he added words that must have lifted Hamilton's sore spirits: "I am sorry you went away—I wish you were back."[40]

Madison would never leave while the Convention sat. His mild demeanor masked steely determination. During ten more days of wrangling, Madison's opposition to the grand committee's compromise grew more strident and his proposals more far-fetched. He again argued that one house of Congress should represent slave interests with the other house representing nonslave interests. He suggested doubling the number of representatives so the smaller states could have more of them, though only in proportion to their populations. He even proposed that voting in Congress could vary according to subject: votes could be cast on a per-state basis when "the government is to act on the states as such," but on a proportional basis when the government "is to act on the people." On July 14, he once more explained that the "real difference of interests lay, not between the large and small but between the Northern and Southern states. The institution of slavery and its consequences formed the line of discrimination."[41]

The delegates ignored him.[42] By undermining the alliance between the large and the slave states, the grand committee's compromise prevailed. On the morning of July 16, many large-state delegates met to discuss their options. According to a dejected Madison, "The time was wasted in vague conversation." The small states had won.[43]

After ten more days of quarreling in the late-July heat, the delegates appointed a five-man Committee of Detail to translate their work into a draft constitution. The convention would stand in recess for ten days while the committee worked.

4

A System to Last for Ages

During the break, some delegates rushed home to see family and attend to business. Others escaped to cooler locales outside of Philadelphia. General Washington went fishing with Gouverneur Morris, then toured the site of the Continental Army's winter camp at Valley Forge a decade before. Madison remained in town even though Randolph was the Virginian on the pivotal committee, again having won an assignment that Madison might have coveted. Perhaps Madison still seemed too much the partisan to serve on such a key committee. Or perhaps the delegates were weary of the man who kept yammering about conflict between North and South.[1]

Madison used the break to attend to personal matters. He sent his ailing father his "fervent wish that this may find your health thoroughly re-established" and confessed to difficulties managing the personal slaves he had brought with him to Philadelphia. One, Anthony, was neglecting his duties. Billey, who had served Madison in Philadelphia before, "either knows or will tell nothing of the matter." John, in contrast, was "very attentive and faithful," which Madison attributed to threats he had made to John that "have never lost their effect."[2] This intimate view of the thirty-six-year-old Madison managing his human property suggests he was more comfortable with the affairs of the nation than with his role as slavemaster.

When the delegates reconvened on August 6, the Committee of Detail presented a comprehensive draft. It clarified some of the agreements reached before the break, altered others, and dropped some altogether. After a day to study the draft, the debates resumed. Hamilton, unable to stay away, returned to Philadelphia. He took an active part in the following week's debates even though New York could cast no vote so long as Lansing and Yates stayed home. At least Hamilton did not have to watch the other two cast New York's vote contrary to his views.[3]

Madison's talents suited the Convention's work over its last six weeks. Sentence by sentence, the delegates worked through the draft, shuffling the most contentious issues off to committees to be compromised, then scouring the compromises. They had to weigh the meaning and implications of each word while gauging how a provision would interact with other provisions. The task required intellect, discipline, and stamina. Madison had all three.

Repeatedly, Madison targeted ambiguities and offered thoughtful improvements. An example was the provision giving Congress the power to "make war." What if, Madison asked, the nation was invaded and Congress was not in session? Because the president would have to respond immediately to the invasion, Congress should have the power only to "declare" war, leaving the president the power "to repel sudden attacks." The delegates agreed. Other Madison amendments ensured that Congress could establish federal trial courts and that the right to hold national office would not be confined to landowners.[4]

Madison offered amendments to every part of the draft. He sponsored language ensuring that the congressional power to punish piracy included the power to define it. In the clause requiring states to honor judgments handed down in other states, Madison won a change of "ought to" to "shall" in one passage and of "shall" to "may" in another. He rewrote the oath of office for federal officials. Madison did not prevail on every issue, but his attention to detail was unflagging.[5]

The Virginian repeatedly urged provisions that would accommodate a growing nation. "In framing a system which we wish to last for ages," he explained, "we should not lose sight of the changes which ages will produce." He worried that an expanding population would demand so many representatives that Congress would become unwieldy, and that landholding requirements for voting would become divisive if population growth made it impossible for most people to own land.[6]

During Hamilton's August week in Philadelphia, he and Madison joined forces in trying to shorten the residency qualification for federal legislators. Hamilton, an immigrant, opposed any minimum residency, urging that any citizen should be eligible to serve in Congress. Madison supported him. America, he argued, "was indebted to emigration for her settlement and prosperity." The motion failed. The Convention required seven years of citizenship to serve in the House of Representatives and nine for the Senate. All who were citizens when the Constitution took effect, like Hamilton, also would be eligible.[7]

Madison was at the center of two late controversies that could have derailed the Constitution. The first involved slavery. In the first week after the break, Gouverneur Morris of Pennsylvania challenged the protections for slavery in the committee draft. Though few delegates cared to address slavery directly, momentum built to cut off the importation of slaves. The bestial conditions aboard slave ships from Africa, which inflicted a punishing mortality rate, led some delegates to denounce the slave trade. Though roughly a third of the delegates were slaveholders like Madison, others like Hamilton belonged to abolition societies; at least two had emancipated their slaves. On August 22 a committee was appointed to address the question. Madison, the delegate most concerned about conflict between North and South, was on it.[8]

The committee offered a compromise: slave imports could be taxed and would continue until 1800, at which point Congress could end it. In a concession to New England merchants, a simple majority in Congress—not a two-thirds vote—could enact laws regulating commerce.

In the ensuing debate, Madison's complicated feelings about slavery spilled out. He objected to a South Carolina proposal to lengthen the guarantee of slave imports until 1808, calling the provision "more dishonorable to the national character than to say nothing about it in the Constitution." Indeed, when the delegates adopted the longer term, the slaveowning Madison grew fastidious over the language used. He moved to eliminate the word "slave" from the Constitution, insisting that it would be "wrong to admit in the Constitution that there could be property in men."[9] By these steps, Madison looked beyond the narrow interests of his region and urged a turn away from slavery.[10]

The second major issue of the closing days was how to choose the president. Few questions so puzzled the delegates. The world of 1787, dominated by hereditary monarchies, provided no models of public executives who were both effective and accountable to the governed. Most state governors, chosen by and subservient to their legislatures, were weak. The delegates sought a method of choosing the president that would make him independent, yet not a despot. The Virginia Plan and the draft produced by the Committee of Detail allowed Congress to choose the president. But such a president, many feared, would be the "creature" of Congress.

The committee appointed to address the presidency leaned toward having Congress choose the president. Then it reconsidered. As one delegate recalled it, "James Madison took a pen and paper, and sketched out a mode for election" with each state choosing individual electors whose votes would elect the president. The elector system, first proposed by James Wilson of Pennsylvania, remains in the Constitution today.[11]

As the pace of work accelerated during the convention's final weeks, tempers frayed, speeches became shorter, and Madison took fewer notes. Complaints swelled over the duration of the convention. General Washington, not known for drollery, wrote: "If something good does not proceed from the [Convention] the defects cannot with propriety be charged to the hurry with which the business has been conducted."[12]

Through ill-tempered days, Madison's focus did not waver. He pressed new suggestions and opposed others. He spoke thirty times in the final eleven days, addressing the selection of the president, the privileges of congressmen, filling presidential vacancies, treaty making, impeachment, corporate charters, state militias, and the presidential pardon power.

By September 6, Hamilton was back on the Convention floor. He had invited Lansing and Yates to return to Philadelphia with him, but they declined. When Hamilton first addressed the delegates in September, he admitted he had "been restrained from entering into the discussions by his dislike of the scheme of government in general." But, he added, he "meant to support the plan to be recommended, as better than nothing."[13]

No longer part of an official state delegation, Hamilton pitched into the final debates. When Madison moved to expand the number of representatives in the lower house of Congress, Hamilton supported him "with great earnestness and anxiety." He and Madison won a change to make it easier to amend the Constitution; they lost a joint effort to require a three-fourths vote of Congress (rather than two-thirds) to override presidential vetoes of legislation.[14]

When the moment arrived to produce the final draft, the delegates named a five-man Committee of Style to do so. That Madison was appointed was little surprise. But the inclusion of Hamilton, who had been absent for at least half of the Convention, was almost shocking. Evidently the New Yorker's brilliance outweighed both his long absences and his disagreement with many of the Constitution's principles. Though virtually nothing in the final document can be traced to his efforts, he was selected for this final committee ahead of two dozen delegates who had attended all summer. In the end, it made little difference that Madison and Hamilton were on this final committee. Working alone, Gouverneur Morris produced the final Constitution in a marvelously productive forty-eight-hour effort.

In the Convention's last days, Mason and Randolph of Virginia became disenchanted. Mason, joined by a Massachusetts delegate, moved on September 12 to insert a bill of rights, which would "give great quiet to the people." In the worst blunder of the summer, the weary delegates resoundingly defeated Mason's proposal; ten states voted against it. When Mason and Randolph resolved not to sign the Constitution, the mighty Virginia delegation, which had dwindled from seven to five, barely supported the final document by a 3–2 margin.[15]

On the last day, September 17, Gouverneur Morris and Dr. Franklin urged unanimous support for the Constitution, but Mason, Randolph, and Elbridge Gerry of Massachusetts would not sign. Hamilton could not sit silent. "No man's ideas were more remote" from the Constitution than his, he admitted, but he rejected "anarchy and convulsion on one side," in favor of "the chance of good to be expected from the plan on the other."[16] Madison, in contrast, did sit silent, completing his summer-long mission of making the record of the convention for later generations.

For the signing ceremony, the delegates lined up by state delegation, from north to south. As convention president, General Washington signed first, affixing the name that Americans most wanted to see. Hamilton, the only New Yorker, was the seventh signature. Madison was the twenty-ninth to sign, as "James Madison, Jr.," below his nowforgotten Virginia colleague John Blair.

Madison had many doubts about the Constitution. He thought Congress should have a veto over state laws and that a joint executive-judicial body should be able to veto federal legislation. He detested per-state voting in the Senate and feared that the Constitution had no mechanism to mediate conflicts between North and South. "Should it be adopted," he wrote to Jefferson, he feared the Constitution "will neither effectually answer its national object nor prevent the local mischiefs which everywhere excite disgusts." Yet, like Hamilton, Madison would support a document he thought gravely flawed. "If the present moment be lost," he explained to Jefferson, "it is hard to say what may be our fate."[17]

Through the deliberations at the Pennsylvania State House that summer, Madison had been far more prominent than Hamilton, whose participation was hamstrung by his balky New York colleagues and his own outlier views. As the battle for America's future moved to the states, however, the partnership between the two young men would become much more equal. Each state would elect its own convention to decide whether to ratify the Constitution. If nine states ratified, the Constitution would take effect. In that battle, Madison and Hamilton helped remake the nation.

5

---◆---

CREATING *THE FEDERALIST*

Afew weeks after the Philadelphia Convention adjourned, Hamilton was worried about the Constitution. A burst of praise greeted the proposed charter in mid-September, but then critics began to carp. Essays in New York newspapers denounced the powers of the proposed Senate. Some argued that the United States was too large to be a single republic. On a Hudson River sloop, traveling home from court business in Albany, Hamilton came up with the idea for a series of newspaper essays that would make a powerful case for ratification. Hamilton's idea became *The Federalist*.[1]

Madison, in New York City as a Virginia delegate to Congress, shared Hamilton's worries, even after Congress voted unanimously to refer the Constitution to the states for ratification. "The newspapers here," he wrote to General Washington, "begin to teem with vehement and virulent calumniations of the new government." More opposition was coming. George Mason and Elbridge Gerry of Massachusetts would repeat complaints they raised during the convention, as would Yates and Lansing of New York.[2] Hamilton and Madison might lose the gamble they made in Annapolis more than a year before. Unless nine states ratified, their work would go for naught while the nation drifted into regional confederacies.

A decade earlier, Tom Paine's electrifying pamphlet *Common Sense* demonstrated that the written word could shape American opinion. For a people who lived in rural settings or small towns, large gatherings were impractical. A pamphlet or newspaper essay could circulate from hand to hand and be read aloud to dozens more ears. No other method spread ideas so well. Ratification, Washington wrote in early October 1787, would depend "upon literary abilities, and the recommendation of [the Constitution] by good pens should be openly, I mean publicly afforded in the Gazettes."[3]

Hamilton, skeptical of both republican governments and the Constitution, was an unlikely candidate for the task, but he resolved to justify the Constitution in an ambitious series of newspaper essays. He sketched out six broad topics: the importance of the union; the inadequacy of the present confederation; the need for an "energetic" government; how the Constitution conformed to "the true principles of republican government"; how the Constitution copied the thirteen state constitutions; and the need for ratification.

Hamilton projected the project would require twenty articles, "or at the utmost twenty-five."[4] Once he started writing and recruited essential support from Madison, with minor aid from John Jay of New York, the effort turned into a Vesuvius of advocacy and political theory. For more than six months, New York newspapers carried seventy-seven essays now preserved as *The Federalist*. Combined with eight more essays Hamilton wrote solely for a bound volume, which some newspapers published later, the collection totaled 190,000 words. And the authors never reached the last two topics on Hamilton's outline.

The Federalist began as propaganda to support ratification, but its immediate impact on the ratification campaign was far from clear. Even the serious readers of the eighteenth century struggled with 190,000 words of close analysis. "This book is of no utility to educated people," a French diplomat sniffed in early 1788, "and it is too learned and too long for the ignorant." Distribution of the essays beyond New York was spotty, and some dismissed it entirely. One scholar has found *The Federalist*'s effect on New York's ratification was "negligible" compared to a much shorter pamphlet by Jay.[5]

Once Hamilton and Madison started writing, though, they could not stop. Each had been thinking for more than a decade about the largest question of political life: how to maintain a stable society that balances the rights of the individual with the needs of the group. They had analyzed the nation's crisis in countless conversations, speeches, and letters. They had argued at the Philadelphia Convention with America's most talented politicians. They were bursting with ideas they had honed for years. As they wrote, they had to know they were producing something extraordinary, so they kept writing until time ran out on them.

They were too young to be so wise: Madison was thirty-six, Hamilton thirty-two. Between them, they had served barely a dozen years in public office. They combined that experience with insights gleaned from voracious reading of history, law, and political theory, and with their mutual inclination to dash off breathtaking generalizations. A contemporary observation about Hamilton applied to both men: "[T]here is no skimming over the surface of a subject with him, he must sink to the bottom to see what foundation it rests on."[6]

The Federalist can be viewed as propaganda, as political philosophy, as literature, or as historical artifact. In all of these guises, it still looms large in twenty-first-century America. Chief Justice John Marshall insisted that it "will be read and admired when the controversy in which that valuable treatise on government originated, shall be no longer remembered." Jefferson proclaimed it "the best commentary on the principles of government." Political theorists and constitutional law professors relentlessly sift it, insisting either that Hamilton and Madison got it exactly right, or completely wrong, or pathetically contradicted themselves, or each other. Lawyers and judges search *The Federalist* for support for opposing positions, seeking refuge in its status as *the* authoritative explication of the Constitution.[7]

How did it happen?

The sloop from Albany delivered Hamilton to New York City around October 10. The first two men he invited to join in the project did not work out. One declined and the other quickly demonstrated that he was not equal to the task.[8] John Jay accepted Hamilton's invitation and wrote four early essays, but then he fell ill and could not work for many weeks.[9]

That left Madison. The Virginian was not part of the effort when Hamilton's first essay appeared in the *New York Independent Journal*, under the pen name "Publius." In 1787, political writers commonly used pseudonyms to conceal their identities. The classically educated would appreciate Hamilton's choice of "Publius," a leader who vanquished Rome's enemies in the fifth century B.C. but then was suspected of kingly ambitions. To show his humility, Publius razed his hilltop house and rebuilt it on low ground, then restored the Roman republic. Hamilton too was recanting any monarchical inclinations, or he wished to appear to do so.

In early November, Madison left New York for Philadelphia without deciding whether to join Hamilton's project. By November 18, with Jay's first four essays in print along with three by Hamilton, Madison was back in New York. He enlisted in the Publius effort.[10]

With Hamilton's initial outline as a guide, the project became a months-long improvisation by two men with demanding day jobs.

Hamilton practiced law while Madison served as a Virginia delegate to the weak Congress that the Constitution would replace. In late January, Hamilton also joined Congress, further adding to his workload.[11]

They published sixty-nine essays between November 20 and June 14 (Jay contributed one in early March). Madison eased into the rotation. He wrote two in the second half of November and collaborated with Hamilton on three more in December. Beginning on January 11, the Virginian took over, writing twenty-two essays that ran consecutively for almost six weeks. After contributing two more in late February, Madison left New York to stand for election to Virginia's ratifying convention. Hamilton finished the effort with his own solo turn, scratching out twenty-two essays from March until May.

The two principal writers divided the topics roughly according to their interests. Hamilton addressed the need for energy in government and defended the new executive and judicial branches, subjects that drew on his military experience, his economic expertise, and his legal training. Madison, a veteran legislator, defended the proposed Congress and explained how the new government and the states would coexist harmoniously.

The pace was punishing. As many as four essays appeared in a week, requiring that the principal authors produce an average of a thousand words per day. Because New York had no daily newspaper, Publius ran in four different papers: the *Independent Journal,* the *Packet,* the *Daily Advertiser,* and the *Journal.* Essays were reprinted in multiple newspapers, prompting the Constitution's critics to protest that New York's printers were "cramming us with the voluminous PUBLIUS."[12] Madison recalled the work as frenetic: "It frequently happened that whilst the printer was putting into type the parts of a number, the following parts were under the pen, and to be furnished in time for the press." Sometimes the printer hovered at the author's elbow, needing to set the piece in type immediately.[13]

Fortunately for the authors, the state ratifications unfolded at an eighteenth-century rhythm. Each state legislature had to call for a convention and schedule elections for delegates. Local political and legislative schedules often dictated when. As of November, when Madison enlisted in *The Federalist* effort, six states had issued calls for conventions and only Pennsylvania had chosen delegates. Delaware ratified first, on December 7. Pennsylvania, New Jersey, and Georgia did so by the end of that month.

As ratification news trickled in, many became obsessed with the process. One woman complained in late December 1787 that New York's social life had shriveled because "the minds of all ranks of people appear effected with the situation of this country, [and] a general anxiety for the event suspends the love of pleasure." She added that "[a]ll the men are immersed in politics; and the women say, 'Life is not life without them.'" In Virginia, talk about the Constitution sometimes flagged, Edmund Randolph wrote, "from downright weariness." Yet in March 1788, a delegate to Congress reported that "[t]he prospect of a new Constitution seems to deaden the activity of the human mind as to all other matters."[14]

Madison was a hub for pro-Constitution activities. His correspondents eagerly reported news from other states and begged for the same from him. They feared mounting opposition in Massachusetts, New York, and Virginia.[15] Some asked Madison to relay their messages to Hamilton, understanding that both were leading the ratification effort.[16]

Hamilton and Madison, both in New York, frequently conferred, shared correspondence, and laid their plans. Madison was boarding with Mrs. Elsworth on Maiden Lane. Hamilton's home, a quarter-mile away at Wall Street and Broadway, was on Madison's route as he walked to Congress through New York's bustle and unpenned pigs. With no surviving record of their conversations, the imagination can project the two men—Madison jotting notes while Hamilton paces before the fireplace—listing the topics to address, the arguments to answer and those to press. A Hamilton infant might wander by to be petted absentmindedly as his father emphasizes a new idea.

Through shared battles and mutual respect, the two very different men from very different worlds developed a genuine personal warmth, their differences put aside or even enhancing their mutual attraction. For most who encountered him, Hamilton was a fascinating exotic, with his Caribbean childhood, military swagger, and flashing intellect. To Madison, who found Virginia's culture narrow, stunted by slavery, and morally undeveloped, Hamilton offered a window into other worlds. To Hamilton, Madison embodied the gentry lifestyle to which he aspired, sharpened with a powerful mind and passionate political commitment. Over the next two years, the two friends could be seen walking around New York in animated conversation. A neighbor remembered them engrossed in an exchange in Hamilton's yard, then stopping to laugh and play with a pet monkey next door. Always the two men talked, conversations that were among the most productive in American history.[17]

Before pitching into the ratification battle, Madison allowed himself a moment of detachment. "Companies of intelligent people," he wrote in late October 1787, would be "equally divided, and equally earnest" in contending that the new government would be too strong or too weak. "Unanimity," he concluded, "is not to be expected in any great political question: that the danger is probably exaggerated on each side, when an opposite danger is conceived on the opposite side."[18]

The *Federalist* authors were not publicly revealed until four years later, when a bound volume in France listed all three.[19] The title of the essays reflected a canny move to claim the appellation "Federalists," though it was a misnomer. The confederacy under the Articles was a "federal" system. The Constitution would replace it with one that was more "consolidated," leaving less power in the states. By calling themselves Federalists, ratification advocates appropriated the term and cast their opponents as Anti-Federalists—grasping the public relations orthodoxy that an "anti" label is less appealing.[20]

To produce *The Federalist*, the partners had to trust one another. Events called each of them away during the ratification campaign: Hamilton turned to his law practice in January and February 1788, then Madison left for Virginia. Each left his reputation in the other's hands, trusting that future essays would provide effective advocacy yet say nothing that would haunt either in the future. Even before those bravura solo efforts, there rarely was time to review each other's writings before publication. They knew each other from their joint service in Congress, in Annapolis, and at the Philadelphia Convention. They trusted one another.

Publius undertook an impossible task: to justify a structure for self-government by human beings who cannot be trusted to rule themselves, to judge right, or to rule others. An invincible distrust of human nature is the bedrock of *The Federalist*. In No. 6, Hamilton warned that "men are ambitious, vindictive, and rapacious," adding in No. 28 that they do not behave well in groups: "[S]editions and insurrections are, unhappily, maladies as inseparable from the body politic as tumors and eruptions from the natural body." Few can read Hamilton's passage in No. 70 without nodding in agreement:

> Men often oppose a thing merely because they have had no agency in planning it, or because it may have been planned by those whom they dislike. . . . [O]pposition then becomes, in their estimation,

an indispensable duty. . . . They seem to think themselves bound in honor, and by all the motives of personal infallibility, to defeat the success of what has been resolved upon contrary to their sentiments.

Thus, Hamilton concluded, "how often the great interests of society are sacrificed to the vanity, to the conceit, and to the obstinacy of individuals."[21]

Madison's view of his fellow humans was equally skeptical, though slightly less dark. In No. 55, he noted "a degree of depravity in mankind which requires a certain degree of circumspection and distrust," but he also described "other qualities in human nature which justify a certain portion of esteem and confidence." Madison particularly mistrusted people in groups. He wrote in No. 49 that groups are easily misled and often violent, as people acquire "firmness and confidence" when they act in groups.

The Federalist carries many hallmarks of advocacy, with Hamilton more likely to reach for rhetorical high notes, especially when bemoaning the parlous state of the nation. He began the series in a mild tone. In No. 1, he wrote soothingly that there were "wise and good men on the wrong as well as on the right side of the question." His pen, however, was more often sharp than soothing.

In No. 15, he lamented that the existing confederation's "frail and tottering edifice seems ready to fall upon our heads and to crush us beneath its ruins." The current structure, he added in No. 21, "afford[s] the extraordinary spectacle of a government destitute even of the shadow of constitutional power to enforce the execution of its own laws." In No. 25, he answered with contempt the Anti-Federalists' claim that the nation should have no standing army, calling it:

the most extraordinary spectacle which the world has yet seen. . . . [T]he presence of an enemy within our territories must be waited for [before the government may] begin its levies of men for the protection of the State. We must receive the blow before we could even prepare to return it.

Under the Articles of Confederation, Hamilton wrote in No. 22, the unanimity requirement for approving taxes was "poison." He fulminated in No. 27 that the states resembled "feudal baronies." He found "a striking incoherence" in Anti-Federalist arguments in favor of state militias, which did not "inspire a very favorable opinion of the sincerity or fair dealing of their authors" (No. 29). In No. 67, he accused his adversaries of wandering into "regions of fiction" in their portrait of the president under the Constitution. Writing with a sensuality that was alien to the straitlaced Madison, Hamilton scorned portrayals of all-powerful future presidents with "terrific visages of murdering janizaries" and "unveiled mysteries of a future seraglio." He questioned whether "language can furnish epithets of too much asperity for so shameless and so prostitute an attempt to impose on the citizens of America."

In contrast, Madison's essays called often for "prudence" and "stability." In No. 37, he strove for a sober tone, observing: "It is a misfortune, inseparable from human affairs, that public measures are rarely investigated with that spirit of moderation which is essential to a just estimate of [them]." He also described the frustrations of searching for the correct words to convey his meaning. Though Madison's career depended heavily on his pen, he was never a graceful writer. Vibrant passages are occasional oases in arid expanses of Madisonian prose.

Ideas, he observed in No. 37, "should be expressed by words distinctly and exclusively appropriate to them." The task, however, is more easily described than performed. "[N]o language is so copious as to supply words and phrases for every complex idea," he wrote, which meant that an idea could be betrayed "by the inaccuracy of the terms in which it is delivered." Yet he managed to complete this thought with a near-perfect sentence.

> When the Almighty himself condescends to address mankind in their own language, his meaning, luminous as it must be, is rendered dim and doubtful by the cloudy medium through which it is communicated.

Both *Federalist* authors stressed America's unique opportunity to build a new manner of government. "It belongs to us," Hamilton wrote in No. 11, "to vindicate the honor of the human race." He added an edge of anti-European feeling, calling for the thirteen states to "[erect] one great American system . . . able to dictate the terms of the connection between the old and the new world!" In No. 14, Madison stressed the novelty of the American experience, insisting it was "the glory of the people of America that, whilst they have paid a decent regard to the opinions of former times and other nations, they have not suffered a blind veneration for antiquity, for custom, or for names, to overrule the suggestions of their own good sense, the knowledge of their situation, and the lessons of their own experience."

The Federalist addressed controversial issues head-on. Hamilton wrote seven essays that justified empowering the new government to impose taxes (Nos. 30–36). These essays reflected Hamilton's commercial sensibility, first honed as a clerk for a St. Croix trading house. In the eighteenth century, merchants sat at the center of an international web of information about wars, politics, crops, weather, and innovation. Every ship brought news. The brilliant young Hamilton used that information to understand the forces that moved men and goods, navies and armies. In No. 35, he addressed how taxes work in the real world. A merchant might attempt to pass a tax on to consumers, he wrote, but "a division of the duty, between the seller and the buyer, more often happens" because the seller must keep his prices low.

In eleven essays on the executive branch, Hamilton denied that the president would be a kingly figure. To the contrary, a strong president would preserve liberty against the tyranny of the mob. "Energy in the executive is a leading character in the definition of good government," he wrote in No. 70. That energy was essential to the protection of property, the regular conduct of courts, and "to the security of liberty against the enterprises and assaults of ambition, of faction, and of anarchy."

The New Yorker's brilliant explanation of the judicial branch in No. 78 prefigured the development of judicial review by Chief Justice John Marshall. Hamilton disarmingly wrote that the judiciary will be the "least dangerous" branch of government because it controls neither sword nor purse. Though the courts could strike down laws as unconstitutional, that power did not make the courts superior to Congress, but made "the power of the people," expressed in the Constitution, "superior to both."

Not every effort was a masterpiece. In May, Hamilton's No. 84 took on the difficult task of answering the "loud clamors" for a bill of rights. His response was anemic. The Constitution need not guarantee freedom of the press, Hamilton wrote, because it created no power to restrict the press. He insisted that the people's rights would be protected by "public opinion, and . . . the general spirit of the people and of the government," bulwarks that can only be described as vaporous.

Both Hamilton and Madison defended the apparently broad language in Article I, Section 8, empowering Congress to enact laws "which shall be necessary and proper for carrying into Execution the foregoing Powers." Critics, as Hamilton put it in No. 33, saw the provision as "the hideous monster whose devouring jaws would spare neither sex nor age, nor high nor low, nor sacred nor profane." Hamilton called the clause "perfectly harmless" though "it may be chargeable with tautology or redundancy." In a few short years, Hamilton would use that perfectly harmless clause to justify a wide range of economic legislation that Madison thought beyond federal power.

Yet Madison struck a similar note in No. 44, in a passage that Hamilton would later use against him. "No axiom is more clearly established in law, or in reason," Madison wrote, "than that wherever the end is required the means are authorized." Even if the Constitution did not include the "necessary and proper" language, he added, Congress would have the same powers "by unavoidable implication." Madison would later express a different view.

Madison stumbled worst when he defended the slavery provisions in the Constitution. He could not escape the assignment. Hamilton opposed slavery; he could hardly be expected to defend the charter's slavery clauses. In No. 44, Madison expressed regret over the twenty-year guarantee of slave imports, but he called it "a great point gained in favor of humanity" that such imports might end thereafter. As a slaveholder, Madison struck a jarring note when he pointed an accusing finger at other nations: "Happy would it be for the unfortunate Africans, if an equal prospect lay before them of being redeemed from the oppressions of their European brethren!"

More embarrassing still was Madison's defense of the clause that treated slaves as three-fifths of a person when apportioning representatives to Congress. In No. 54, the Virginian declined to defend the provision in the voice of Publius. Instead, he conjured up an imaginary surrogate, "one of our southern brethren," and used that voice to defend it in bracingly frank terms. Slaves are regarded, says his imaginary southerner, "in some respects, as persons, and in other respects as property." He admits that the slave is "at all times to be restrained in his liberty and chastised in his body, by the capricious will of another" and thus he may appear properly "classed with those irrational animals which fall under the legal denomination of property." But the law protects the slave against some forms of violence and punishes him for his own violence, treating him "as a moral person, not as a mere article of property." Accordingly, the Constitution treated slaves "in the mixed character of persons and of property. This is in fact their true character."

The imaginary southerner also responds to the objection that slaves who cannot vote should not count toward legislative representation. Many other Americans could not vote—including women and those without property—but they would be counted for the purposes of representation. In a shamefaced conclusion, Madison reverted to his own voice:

> Such is the reasoning which an advocate for the Southern interests might employ . . . and although it may appear to be a little strained in some points, on the whole, I must confess that it fully reconciles me.

Despite these missteps, two of Madison's contributions to *The Federalist* have become classics of political analysis, required reading on American government. No. 10 and No. 51 rank only slightly behind the Declaration of Independence, the Constitution itself, and the Gettysburg Address as distillations of the American spirit. Though less celebrated, No. 37 rivals them in power.

Madison captured the challenge of governing in No. 51:

> If men were angels, no government would be necessary. If angels were to govern men, neither external nor internal controls on government would be necessary. In framing a government which is to be administered by men over men, the great difficulty lies in this: you must first enable the government to control the governed; and in the next place, oblige it to control itself.

In this rendering, people are too flawed to sustain a society that grants them perfect liberty, though that is the ideal. After all, Madison insists, "Justice is the end of government [and] civil society. It . . . ever will be pursued until it be obtained, or until liberty be lost in its pursuit." Because people cannot be trusted with perfect liberty, government must preserve peace and just dealings. But government will be designed and conducted by people who can no more be trusted with power than they can be trusted with perfect liberty. Worse still, self-government will permit majorities to oppress minorities. Madison dreaded the tyrannical majority as much as the single tyrant.[22]

In No. 10, Madison explored an equal risk to a just government: factions "united and actuated by some common impulse of passion, or of interest, adverse to the rights of other citizens." The spirit of faction might pit debtors against creditors, farmers against merchants, or set members of different religious groups against each other. For Madison, factions were a byproduct of a free society. "Liberty is to faction," he wrote, "what air is to fire." Humans form factions even when there is little reason to do so: "[T]he most frivolous and fanciful distinctions have been sufficient to kindle their unfriendly passions and excite their most violent conflicts."

Madison had wrestled with these problems in his memoranda to himself and in his speeches at the Philadelphia Convention. No system of government, he insisted, can assume the presence of "enlightened statesmen"; such individuals are not always present. Neither can a system assume a virtuous populace. "We well know," he wrote in No. 10, "that neither moral nor religious motives can be relied on." They govern neither individual conduct nor the actions of groups, where anonymity erodes moral constraints.

The solution for Madison, as expressed in the Constitution, was mechanistic, suitable to an age in which clockworks were a powerful metaphor. He wished to design "the interior structure of the government" so "its several constituent parts may, by their mutual relations, be the means of keeping each other in their proper places." He praised an interconnected system of checks and balances between legislative, executive, and judicial branches; between federal and state governments. Congress may legislate, but the Senate (representing the states) and the House of Representatives (representing the people) will often disagree. The president may veto legislation, though two-thirds of Congress may override that veto. The courts may strike down laws as unconstitutional, but only in individual cases. And the president and Senate may influence the courts by appointing new judges or changing their jurisdiction. Congress polices the executive and judicial departments with impeachments. No branch is independent. These complex interworkings bring stability by making government action difficult except on matters of broad consensus.

Madison also reasoned that factions could serve as a self-correcting mechanism in a plural society. On this point, he answered many writers who insisted that a republic was feasible only in a small area, preferably a single city. In No. 51, Madison turned that contention on its head, insisting that "the extended republic of the United States" was ideal. With a "great variety of interests, parties, and sects" in that extended republic, "a coalition of a majority of the whole society could seldom take place on any other principles than those of justice and the general good." Here was a moment of optimism: The larger the society and the more diverse its interest groups, Madison argued, "the more duly capable it will be of self-government."

In No. 37, Madison framed the constitution-writing process as one of balancing "the requisite stability and energy in government with the inviolable attention due to liberty and to the republican form." He noted the perverse truth that stability comes only from a government with enough energy to govern effectively; a weak government, like the one under the Articles, becomes unstable and cannot protect liberty. A clockmaker would find familiar Madison's effort to balance stability and liberty. Power must be entrusted to individuals, but the people must retain control through elections. Every power has its counterweight.

Above all, Madison urged that the Constitution could not be perfect. "A faultless plan," he wrote in No. 37, could never be produced because "the convention, as a body of men," was fallible. In his final plea, Madison struck an ingenuous tone that remains persuasive more than two centuries later: "The real wonder is that so many difficulties should have been surmounted, and surmounted with a unanimity almost as unprecedented as . . . unexpected."[23]

The choice, he emphasized, was between the Constitution and the Articles. The Constitution need not be perfect if the Articles are "more imperfect" (No. 38).

By December, newspapers in other cities were reprinting many of the *Federalist* essays. Hamilton and Madison decided to publish a bound volume of them for a national audience. The first volume, released in late March of 1788, included thirty-six essays. Shortly afterward, Hamilton wrote to Madison that he had to stop work on the project.[24] Nevertheless, when the second volume of *The Federalist* was published in late May, it included seven new Hamilton essays, which also ran in several newspapers in June.[25]

Hamilton, centrally located in New York, distributed the volumes. He sent fifty-two to Edmund Randolph in Virginia, while a friend of Madison's asked for another thirty to forty; Washington requested three or four. Sixty copies went to Stephen Van Rensselaer in New York, and Hamilton spread them around his home state. The focus on New York and Virginia matched the ratification process, which was reaching a critical point in those states.[26]

By late April, seven states had ratified. If two more agreed, the new government would be approved. South Carolina was expected to ratify soon, but New Hampshire's convention took no vote before adjourning in late February. The Virginia and New York conventions, scheduled for June, loomed large. Anti-Federalist forces in those states were formidable; even if both South Carolina and New Hampshire ratified and thus created the new government, the nation could hardly begin its existence without Virginia and New York; they were, respectively, the largest state and a centrally located state with the finest seaport. As a French diplomat wrote, "without Virginia and New York the new government will exist more in name than in fact." There also was a very specific problem if Virginia did not ratify: George Washington could not be the first president.[27]

Madison and Hamilton had written *The Federalist* most often in parallel, not in close collaboration. Each author wrote many essays without comment by the other. Nevertheless, the shared effort brought them closer. They certainly understood that they had produced something remarkable that neither could have done alone. In old age, Madison looked back on the essays with pride, calling them "the most authentic exposition of the text of the federal constitution."[28]

A mundane indicator showed the increasing closeness between Hamilton and Madison. In their era, the signature of a letter carried meaning, though those farewell phrases strike the modern ear as ritualistic. Signature as "your humble and obedient servant" reflected formal respect. More intimacy came with the terms "friend" and "affectionate." A signature as "affectionate friend" meant real closeness.

By April, Hamilton was signing his letters to Madison "your affectionate and obedient servant"; in May, he signed "Believe me with great attachment, Yours" and "with great sincerity and attachment." By June, Madison had escalated to the simple "Yours affectionately," which Hamilton reciprocated in July.[29]

The fortunate son from a Virginia plantation and the striving immigrant had become brothers in the constitutional struggle. Their joint fight for ratification would take the monochromatic Madison to the Virginia Convention in Richmond. The multihued Hamilton traveled to the New York Convention in Poughkeepsie. Each would press the arguments they had honed in the voice of Publius. Through tense and exhausting days in the summer of 1788, their partnership would flourish.

6

◆

RATIFICATION BATTLES

Before the Constitution was drafted, Hamilton had already started the campaign to win ratification by the states. In July 1787, back home from the Philadelphia Convention, his article in a New York newspaper accused Governor George Clinton of a "dangerous predetermination" to oppose any new charter of government.[1]

In fact, Clinton had made no public statement about the Articles, the Philadelphia Convention, or a new constitution. A bluff, military sort, Clinton avoided disputation about political theory. But Hamilton correctly anticipated that the popular governor would be New York's most powerful opponent to the Constitution. Hamilton's attack was the political equivalent of yanking the whiskers of the largest man in a peaceful tavern while insulting his parentage. Hamilton evidently reasoned that he would have to fight Clinton sooner or later, so he might as well start. The governor's surrogates speedily replied in print; one referred to Hamilton with the scatological epithet "Tom S**t."[2] But pro-Constitution observers applauded Hamilton's pugnacity. He has "boldly taken his ground in the public papers," a Virginian wrote to Madison, and "it is to be hoped he will stem the torrent of folly and iniquity."[3]

The ratification campaign began in earnest in autumn, and five states had ratified by mid-January 1788 (Delaware, Pennsylvania, New Jersey, Georgia, and Connecticut). No pattern was emerging: One was a "large" state and four were "small"; one was in the deep south, one in New England, and three were middle states.

By late January, all eyes watched the Massachusetts Convention, where the pro and anti forces were roughly equal. "Our prospects are gloomy," wrote a Boston Federalist to Madison, "but hope is not entirely extinguished." In the state that spawned Shays' Rebellion twelve months earlier, class resentment still ran high. The antis, according to the same Federalist, thought the Constitution "the production of the rich and ambitious" aimed at "the establishment of two orders in the society, one comprehending the opulent and great, the other the poor and illiterate."[4]

To break the deadlock, Massachusetts Federalists worked a compromise. They agreed that the state convention could propose amendments for the new Congress to consider. Two of the proposed amendments related to individual rights. Seven more aimed to restrict the powers of Congress and federal courts.[5]

Massachusetts's ratification, though by a margin of only 187–168, brought sighs of relief from Federalists. In a letter to Jefferson, Madison unconsciously confirmed the accusations of class bias, insisting that the Massachusetts Federalists numbered "all the men of abilities, of property, and of influence." He dismissed the proposed amendments as a sop to assuage the doubts of "the people."[6]

Madison had not planned to attend Virginia's ratifying convention, thinking that ratification should not be decided by the same men who had produced the Constitution. When other veterans of the Philadelphia Convention participated in their state conventions, friends urged Madison to do the same. He could, he admitted, "contribute some explanations and information" to the other delegates.[7] Moreover, the Constitution's prospects in Virginia were uncertain. If Virginia failed to ratify, he worried, "it would be truly mortifying."[8]

Madison asked his brother and father to pass the word in Orange County that he would accept a seat as a delegate. Still serving in Congress and busy writing *The Federalist*, Madison made no plans to campaign for the late-March election. Then warnings came from Orange County: The antis were strong; Madison had to campaign. Some voters, his father wrote, "suspend their opinion till they see you," while others "will endeavor to shut you out."[9] On March 4, Madison departed New York, leaving Hamilton to finish *The Federalist* alone.[10]

On election day in Orange, Madison found what he called "absurd and groundless prejudices against the federal Constitution." By his account, he delivered a "harangue" of almost two hours in windy, raw weather. When he finished, the voters elected him and another Federalist by a four-to-one majority. Had he not returned home, he conceded, "a very different event would have taken place."[11]

For the next two months, Madison stayed at Montpelier to do what he always did: prepare. Waiting for him in Richmond was his greatest adversary, Patrick Henry.

• • •

Madison and Henry had clashed before. Four years earlier, Madison thwarted Henry's move to enact a tax to benefit Virginia's churches, which Madison saw as an intrusion on freedom of conscience. More often, though, Henry prevailed. When Madison and Jefferson prepared reforms of Virginia's constitution and criminal code, Henry blocked them. When Madison pushed for the federal import tax, Henry defeated it. When the peace treaty with Britain required that Americans pay their pre-Revolution debts to British merchants, Henry wrote legislation excluding the British from Virginia's courts. While governor in 1785, Henry failed to inform Madison and three other commissioners that they were to negotiate Potomac River issues with Maryland, an oversight that George Mason overcame by responding promptly when Maryland commissioners arrived on his doorstep for what became the Mount Vernon Conference.[12]

The conflicts were so chronic, and Henry's influence so great, that Jefferson in Paris saw only one solution. "What we have to do," he wrote to Madison, "is devoutly to pray for his death."[13]

Henry, fifty-two, rose to prominence during the struggle against the British. He mixed contradictory elements. His first biographer, who knew him, called Henry's "aversion to study invincible, and his faculties almost benumbed by indolence." From his first job as bartender in his father-in-law's tavern, Henry always enjoyed the taproom. Jefferson disparaged Henry's "fondness for 'fiddling, dancing, and pleasantry.'" That Henry had sixteen children with two wives confirms his sociability. Legend holds that he took his bar examination after reading law for only six weeks, and barely passed.[14]

Yet Henry had a powerful gift for debate. Slender, long-faced, above medium height, he was solemn and impressive on public occasions. "You would swear he had never uttered or laughed at a joke," remembered one observer, who thought Henry displayed "a severity sometimes bordering upon the appearance of anger or contempt." Henry dressed formally in scarlet cloak, black suit, and a dressed wig. He made complicated issues simple, cutting through doubts and qualifications; the contrast with Madison, who perceived complexities everywhere, was stark.[15]

Henry's opposition to the Constitution was no surprise. When he refused to attend the Philadelphia Convention, Madison interpreted Henry's absence as evidence that he wished to divide the nation.[16] After the Constitution was released, Edmund Randolph put the matter succinctly: "Mr. Henry is implacable." Madison echoed that view in December 1787, telling Jefferson, "Mr. Henry is the great adversary who will render the event precarious . . . [and is] working up every possible interest into a spirit of opposition." Federalists dreaded Henry's influence. "The powers of Henry in a large assembly," one wrote, "are incalculable." Madison predicted that "desperate measures will be his game," that this nemesis would propose amendments to gut the Constitution.[17]

Henry was not the only leading Virginian in opposition. After returning from Philadelphia, George Mason circulated his complaints about the Constitution. When the Constitution came before Congress in September 1787, Virginia delegate Richard Henry Lee moved to attach a bill of rights, then insisted that Virginia should propose amendments and withdraw from the union if they were not adopted within two years.[18] After the voters chose Virginia's convention delegates, Madison was worried. "The torch of discord has been thrown in," he told Washington, "and has found materials but too flammable."[19]

In addition to resuming his study of previous republics and confederations, Madison also worked to bring Edmund Randolph back to the Federalist camp. The position taken by Randolph, a popular and influential figure, could be pivotal. Though impressive in public, Randolph was prone to crippling indecision. A cousin compared him to "the chameleon on the aspen, ever changing, ever trembling."[20] On the question of the Constitution, he had both trembled and changed.

He had presented the Virginia Plan at the opening of the Philadelphia Convention, demanding that the Articles be replaced. But after helping draft the new charter, he would not sign it. Explaining his refusal, Randolph stressed that the people had not seen the Constitution. He proposed that a second national convention rework the document based on recommendations from state conventions. Now Madison needed him to change his position again.[21]

Madison exchanged congenial letters with Randolph through the fall of 1787. When Randolph asked why Madison did not respond to his ideas for amending the Constitution, Madison replied carefully: "I wished not unnecessarily to repeat or dwell on points on which our ideas do not accord."[22]

Madison employed flattery as well as tact. Noting that the decision of most citizens on ratification "will be governed by those with whom they happen to have acquaintance," Madison stressed the importance of people like Randolph who commanded "a general confidence of the people." While Madison courted his waffling friend, Henry perversely pursued a contrary course, arguing with Randolph on several occasions.[23]

Madison cemented his arrangements with Hamilton in New York. That state's convention would meet after Virginia's, and the Federalists would be a distinct minority in Poughkeepsie. Though Hamilton won a seat from New York City, the antis held a 46–19 advantage overall. Governor Clinton would control the convention. He now made no secret of his opposition, describing Federalists as "advocates for despotism" and his allies as "friends to the rights of mankind."[24]

From early April through July, Hamilton and Madison exchanged at least twenty letters, by far the most intense period of their correspondence. Facing a hostile majority in Poughkeepsie, Hamilton knew that reason would not carry the day. The only chance, he wrote, "will be the previous ratification by nine states, which may shake the firmness of [Clinton's] followers." He asked Madison to hire an express rider to speed word of Virginia's vote to Poughkeepsie. Hamilton made the same arrangement with delegates at the New Hampshire Convention, which would resume in June.[25]

Anti-Federalists in New York and Virginia attempted to cooperate with each other as well, exchanging supportive letters and using a Philadelphia editor as go-between. Their cooperation did not begin in earnest, however, until May 1788. By then, Hamilton, Madison, and their allies had produced a deluge of pro-Constitution articles and pamphlets and had coordinated Federalist advocacy within state conventions.[26]

Maryland ratified in late April and South Carolina in late May. That made eight states, one short. Rhode Island had refused to ratify, and North Carolina was dragging its feet. Many expected New Hampshire to ratify in June, which would destroy the leverage of antis arguing for "previous amendments"—that is, amendments that must be added to the Constitution before the state would ratify. Once the nine-state threshold was satisfied, the ratifying states would have little incentive to amend the Constitution to gratify a single state.

For New Yorkers, refusal to ratify in those circumstances could have immediate and unnerving consequences. All four of its neighboring states would be part of a foreign country, the United States. For Virginia, a refusal to ratify would leave two foreign states, Pennsylvania and Maryland, on its northern border. No one thought that Virginia, North Carolina, New York, and Rhode Island could form a separate, noncontiguous confederacy. Early in the ratification season, Madison thought that after nine states ratified, the "tardy remainder" would be "either left as outcasts . . . or be compelled to come in, or must come in . . . when they will be allowed no credit for it."[27]

Most antis believed that the Constitution gave Congress too much power, left the states with too little, and was unacceptable without a bill of rights. But they fell out among themselves, as Madison wrote to Jefferson, over what course to follow. Should they try to blow up the Constitution and invite the union to dissolve? Or demand amendments before ratifying? Or follow the Massachusetts example: ratify and propose amendments for future consideration?[28]

The Anti-Federalists never agreed on this strategic choice. Mason in Virginia harshly criticized the Constitution, but he would not have Virginia leave the union. Others insisted that Virginia and New York were so important that the ratifying states would revise the Constitution to satisfy them. The choice for the antis became whether to require previous amendments or to approve mere "recommendatory" amendments. Previous amendments had more visceral appeal, but far more risk; a state holding out for previous amendments might simply be left out of the union.

Most Federalists were willing to accept ratification with recommendatory amendments, but they would not accept anything less. "That the Constitution will admit of amendments is acknowledged by its warmest advocates," Washington wrote from Mount Vernon, but requiring previous amendments "would, in my opinion amount to a complete rejection of it."[29]

For once, Madison was not early. When he arrived for the Richmond Convention on the evening of June 2, the first day's session had just ended.

For the next four weeks, the convention debates electrified Richmond. To accommodate spectators and more than a hundred and fifty delegates, the convention moved to the city's New Theatre on Shockoe Hill, which usually featured performances and instruction in drawing, fencing, dancing, languages, and music. Despite the June heat, hundreds packed the galleries, standing in doorways and passageways. Stagecoach companies beefed up their schedules to deliver spectators from Fredericksburg and Williamsburg.

The cavernous hall was a challenging venue for Madison. The Confederation Congress and the Constitutional Convention excluded the public, creating an atmosphere more congenial to Madison's quiet advo-

cacy. At the capacious New Theatre, Madison's soft voice did not carry.
The shorthand specialist transcribing the debates often could not hear
him. In a setting that did not suit him, Madison entered a desperate
battle.[30]

At the outset, the delegates resolved to take no vote until they
had debated, "clause by clause," every constitutional provision. Patrick
Henry quickly demonstrated that no rule applied to him.[31]

When Henry rose on June 4, there fell "a perfect stillness throughout the House, and in the galleries." He commanded the hall. "He
was emphatic," an observer recalled, "without vehemence or declama-
tion; animated, but never boisterous." Henry urged the delegates "to
be extremely cautious, watchful, jealous of your liberty; for instead of
securing your rights, you may lose them forever." Henry did not object
to anything so small as the structure of the executive, or the powers
of Congress, or the scope of judicial review. Rather, he challenged the
entire constitutional enterprise, the creation of a national government
rather than a confederacy of sovereign states. He demanded:

> [W]hat right had they to say, *We, the People* . . . who authorized
> them to speak the language of, *We, the People,* instead of *We, the
> States*? States are . . . the soul of a confederation. If the states be
> not the agents of this compact, it must be one great consolidated
> national government.[32]

The initial Federalist response came from Randolph, enticed back to
the pro-Constitution side by Madison. The Articles, Randolph insisted,
were a catastrophe, which would allow the union to disintegrate. Flour-
ishing an arm, he claimed to prefer "the lopping of this limb" to the
union's demise. He flung back Henry's challenge to the phrase "We, the
People": "I ask why not? The government is for the people."[33]

Writing letters that evening, Madison exulted that Randolph "has
thrown himself fully into our scale." Also, George Mason's objections
to the Constitution had not resembled Henry's blanket denunciation.
The two leading antis, Madison wrote to Washington, "appeared to take
different and awkward ground."[34]

Within a few days, the convention's pattern was clear. Delegates like
Federalist John Marshall and Anti-Federalist James Monroe might
speak well, but the main contest was between Henry and Mason for
the antis and Randolph and Madison for the Federalists. Henry, rarely
addressing the provision under discussion, cast rhetorical thunderbolts.

"Guard with jealous attention the public liberty," he declaimed one day. "Suspect everyone who approaches that jewel. Unfortunately, nothing will preserve it but downright force: Whenever you give up that force, you are inevitably ruined." He warned against swarms of tax gatherers feasting upon the flesh of citizens. "The federal sheriff," he intoned, "will ruin you with impunity . . . sucking your blood." State sheriffs, "those unfeeling bloodsuckers, have . . . committed the most horrid and barbarous ravages on our people." Henry accused the Constitution of "an awful squinting . . . toward monarchy."[35]

Randolph was almost as dramatic. "I am a child of the revolution," he pronounced. "My country very early indeed took me under its protection, at a moment when I most wanted it." He would not, he insisted, watch that country destroyed.[36]

When Madison spoke, the atmosphere changed. He brought no piercing orator's glare, no premonition of galloping doom. Spectators strained to hear him. The question, he said, was whether the Constitution would "promote the public happiness." He would not appeal to "feelings and passions" but would present "a calm and rational investigation." With the relentlessness he showed at the Philadelphia Convention, Madison demolished the inconsistencies in Henry's fevered speeches.

Henry had applauded the nation's prosperity under the Articles; Madison cataloged its distresses. Henry warned against relying on future constitutional amendments; Madison pointed out that it would be far easier to amend the Constitution than it was to amend the Articles. Henry fulminated against incipient monarchy; Madison replied that the current "factions and divisions" were an open invitation to tyrants.[37]

On the convention's sixth day, Madison again asked the delegates to consult reason, experience, and the history of nations. Continuing the states as independent sovereigns, he argued, "is a solecism in theory, and a mere nullity in practice." The confederation was feeble, and history taught that confederacies lapse into anarchy, "prey to their own dissensions and foreign invasions."[38]

Madison missed a day of the convention with stomach ills. He complained to Hamilton that the sessions were "wearisome beyond expression."[39] Yet he returned to deflect Henry's attacks, finally emerging as the Constitution's leading defender. Madison explained the president's power to make treaties and why Congress should have control over its members' elections. He addressed congressional pay, the origination of money bills in the House of Representatives, and the structure of the militia. He defended the vice presidency and the Senate's power to confirm treaties. He spent days explicating the federal court system. He explored the need for the national government to control its home district, evident since Congress had fled Philadelphia in 1783, as well as the congressional power to enact laws "necessary and proper" to its duties. It was an advanced tutorial by Professor Madison, who always reverted to "rational premises" or "syllogistic reasoning."[40]

The contrast with Henry was acute, a match between a slugger and a boxer. Henry issued slashing appeals to emotion, to first principles, to liberty. When he spoke, a contemporary recalled, "I experienced an instantaneous sympathy with him in the emotions which he expressed."[41] Yet Madison was his equal. The small man, a friend wrote from Richmond, "came boldly forward and supported the constitution with the soundest reason and most manly eloquence I ever heard." Another found that a Madison speech bristled with "such force of reasoning, and display of such irresistible truths, that opposition seemed to have quitted the field." Madison's passion throbbed quietly: "[H]is whole soul is engaged in its success and it appeared to me he would have flashed conviction into every mind."[42]

In correspondence with Hamilton, Madison worried about the plotting between Virginia and New York antis. They might, he wrote, play for time, wearying the convention into an adjournment. To avoid that, the Federalists would propose unconditional ratification plus recommended amendments. There was, he confessed, "a very disagreeable uncertainty" about the outcome.[43]

Madison feared two issues especially. The first was the Spanish bottleneck on the Mississippi River trade. About a dozen delegates came from the future state of Kentucky, then part of Virginia. Based on Congress's earlier flirtation with abandoning Mississippi navigation rights, westerners worried that a government under the Constitution would be similarly inclined. A strong central government, Madison rejoined, would better defend western interests.[44]

The Anti-Federalists also trumpeted statements by Jefferson from Paris that nine states should ratify the Constitution but that four should hold out for a bill of rights. This was uncomfortable for Madison. Jefferson's reputation was high and their friendship was already well formed. This, however, was no moment for sentiment. Describing Jefferson as "an ornament to this state," Madison nevertheless disparaged his friend's opinion, asking whether "we are to submit to the opinion of a citizen beyond the Atlantic." Insisting that Jefferson would vote to ratify, Madison stressed the support for ratification from "a character equally great"—invoking the redoubtable Washington, whose signature appeared first on the Constitution.[45]

After three weeks, the delegates finished debating each section of the Constitution. The ratification vote remained uncertain. "If we have a majority at all," Madison wrote to Hamilton, "it does not exceed three or four."[46]

On June 24, the Federalists presented a motion to ratify the Constitution and recommend that the first Congress consider amendments. The final debate began with high drama as Henry reached into the tool kit of the southern demagogue. He warned that the North would use the Constitution to free Virginia's slaves. Claiming that he personally deplored slavery—"it would rejoice my very soul," Henry cried out, "that every one of my fellow beings was emancipated"—he deplored even more the prospect of freeing them. Emancipation would produce "the most dreadful and ruinous consequences," he said, adding: "We ought to possess them in the manner we have inherited from our ancestors, as their manumission is incompatible with the felicity of the country." Then Henry offered his own resolution calling for a declaration of rights to be adopted *before* ratification.[47]

Randolph scourged Henry's resolution, insisting it would end the union: "The dogs of war will break loose and anarchy and discord will complete the ruin of this country." Then Madison rose to celebrate American self-government, "the first instance from the creation of the world . . . that free inhabitants have been seen deliberating on a form of government, and selecting [it]." Just as mutual concession produced the Constitution, he added, Virginia should trust that amendments would be adopted when experience showed them necessary. Demanding previous amendments, Madison warned, was "pregnant with dreadful dangers."[48]

In reply, Henry pulled out all the stops. He saw before the nation the "awful immensity of the dangers . . . I see it. I feel it." Looking "beyond the horizon that binds human eyes," Henry felt the disapproval of "beings of a higher order," those "intelligent beings which inhabit the ethereal mansion." The choice, he shouted, was between securing "the happiness of one half of the human race," or embracing "the misery of the other hemispheres."

With the hall in Henry's grip, suddenly thunder boomed, torrents of rain cascaded down, and the wind blew open the theater's doors and windows. The storm, an observer wrote, shook the building, making it seem that Henry had "the faculty of calling up spirits from the vasty deep." Another recalled that the fleeing crowd felt that Henry could "seize upon the artillery of Heaven, and direct its fiercest thunders against the heads of his adversaries."[49]

The final vote, cast three days later on June 25, disproved Henry's divine powers. By a margin of 89–79, the delegates ratified without previous amendments. Ecstatic, Madison immediately sent the news to Hamilton. The Virginians thought they were the ninth state aboard and had thus brought the new government into being, but New Hampshire had beaten them by four days.[50]

Two days later, a committee proposed forty amendments to recommend to Congress. Twenty related to rights of individuals and the states, including guarantees of due process of law, jury trials in civil cases, and freedom of religion, speech, assembly, and the press. The other twenty addressed the government structure. The most controversial would allow the national government to tax the citizens of a state only if that state failed to pay a requisition from Congress. Other amendments sought state control over militias, a two-thirds majority requirement for Congress to adopt commercial laws, and a limit on presidential service to eight years out of any sixteen. They were, Madison wrote Hamilton, "highly objectionable," but only recommendatory. He could not stop them. The convention approved all forty.[51]

The express rider carrying Madison's letter arrived in Poughkeepsie on July 2. Governor Clinton was speaking in the two-story stone court-house where the convention met. The news of Virginia's ratification, according to one account, "occasioned such a buzz . . . that little of his Excellency's speech was heard." Only that morning, Hamilton had written to Madison that "there is more and more reason to believe that our conduct will be influenced by yours."[52]

The news from Virginia was the break Hamilton was waiting for. Outnumbered more than two-to-one, the New York Federalists had fiercely debated each constitutional clause, but to no particular effect. Neither side, according to John Jay, made "much impression on the other." Hamilton sent the same message to Madison: "Our arguments confound, but they do not convince." He called the Constitution's prospects in New York "infinitely slender"; they would shrink to "none at all if you [Virginia] go wrong."[53]

Class divisions marked the Poughkeepsie convention as they had in Massachusetts. One anti exulted that not since the Revolution had the "high born . . . felt and appeared so uninfluential." Many Federalists saw themselves as superior. Jay reported that the New York antis were "numerous and indefatigable," but the "balance of abilities and property is against them." Another Federalist referred to the antis as "a set of ignorant Dutchmen." In his first speech, the Anti-Federalist leader Melancton Smith embraced the class distinction, claiming to speak for "[t]hose in middling circumstances."[54]

Before Madison's letter arrived, the Poughkeepsie delegates had learned of New Hampshire's ratification. The news, crowed one New York anti, "made no impression on the convention at all." John Lansing of Albany insisted that "[n]o such event ought to influence our deliberations."[55] With the additional news from Virginia, the Federalists expected their opponents would *finally* see reason. Inexplicably, the antis still acted as though nothing had changed. Governor Clinton's nephew DeWitt Clinton wrote that Virginia's ratification "has made, in my opinion, no impressions upon the republican members."[56]

The Federalists reversed their strategy. They fell silent. They resolved not to answer any argument by an anti, wrote one, "until after the whole of their objections shall be stated." Hamilton's father-in-law, Philip Schuyler, expressed the Federalists' hope that the antis "will not sacrifice their country to the obstinacy of certain desperadoes."[57]

Over the next several days, some antis grew anxious. They feared a report then circulating that the state's southern portion, led by New York City, was prepared to secede and join the new national government on its own. Congress, meeting in New York City, was already beginning the transition to a new government. On July 8, a congressional committee recommended that the states select presidential electors on the first Wednesday in December, and that the electors vote on the first Wednesday of the next month. The new government would begin on the first Wednesday in February, 1789. Many New Yorkers wanted that government to remain in their city, generating business for merchants and landlords. But if New York did not ratify, the national government would move to Philadelphia or Baltimore or a site on the Potomac River.[58]

In Poughkeepsie, the antis brandished proposals for amendments while the Federalists maintained their grim silence.[59] Behind the scenes, the antis met in nervous caucuses. Governor Clinton wanted previous amendments, no matter the political cost. Like Patrick Henry, he flatly opposed a stronger national government. Melancton Smith, who took a less strident view, became the pivot of the convention.[60]

Smith's speeches and letters reveal a thoughtful man of patriotic feelings and solid intellect. When the convention opened, he agreed on "the necessity of union" but wanted to amend the Constitution before ratification.[61] His speeches made a positive impression on his adversaries. One Federalist found him "a man of remarkable simplicity, and one of the most gentle, liberal, and amiable disposition." He spoke, a newspaper wrote, without any "tincture of malevolence."[62]

With ten states having ratified and the new government already forming, Smith was troubled by how intractable his allies were.[63] Demanding previous amendments, Smith decided, no longer made sense, though he resolved to give ground slowly.

Thursday, July 17, began with Hamilton's most ardent address yet. Two days before, he had extended a slight olive branch, offering to support "recommendatory" amendments. Now he asked why, with the new government approved, other states would care if New York demanded previous amendments? He listed the prominent leaders who supported the new government, including Washington and Franklin, "the old grey headed patriot looking into the grave," and invoked the memory of "departed heroes" who died fighting the British. "Let us take care," he begged, "not to oppose the whole country." According to one report, much of the audience wept. Not, however, the antis.[64]

Smith then took a decisive step. He had a proposal, he announced, that "will not please either side," because "neither side can be entirely suited." His motion was convoluted. The convention would ratify the Constitution but also bar federal control of New York's militia or allow federal taxes in New York until amendments were adopted. It would recommend a second constitutional convention, reserving the right to rescind ratification if one did not meet.[65] But it would not demand previous amendments.

Every delegate understood the significance of Smith's motion, the first actual movement of the convention. The antis adjourned to argue among themselves. "Some are much enraged at [Smith's motion] and its author," wrote one, and "detest Smith as much as Hamilton."[66]

Maneuvering consumed the next ten days. Federalists in New York City, who had postponed a celebration of the new government, lost patience. On July 23 they mounted their festival before the Poughkeepsie Convention acted. Five thousand joined a procession through the city. A ten-horse team pulled a fully-rigged, thirty-two-gun ship named the *Hamilton*. Marching trade groups ranged from wig makers to butchers to bakers, from lawyers to brewers to silversmiths to cordwainers. They passed out poems celebrating the Constitution. A giant flag bore the image of Washington on one side and Hamilton on the other. Six thousand celebrants enjoyed a feast at an alderman's farm.[67]

Fittingly, that was the day that Smith and his band of apostate antis found a verbal formulation for ratification that commanded a majority: New York would ratify "in full confidence" that the new government would adopt amendments. The measure passed, 31–29, with twelve antis joining nineteen Federalists in the majority.[68]

Next day, John Lansing moved that New York reserve the right to rescind ratification if a second convention was not summoned within two years. Hamilton rose with a paper in his hand, a letter from Madison. In a rushed exchange, Madison and Hamilton had anticipated Lansing's move. Because Lansing's proposal would be only a "conditional ratification," Hamilton read out, it would bar New York from the new union. According to Madison, New York's ratification had to be without condition, "in toto and forever." Due at least in part to Madison's authority—a New York newspaper account referred to him as "a gentleman of high distinction"—the convention rejected Lansing's maneuver.[69]

The final vote came on Saturday, July 26. A committee including leading Federalists produced thirty-three constitutional amendments, plus a circular to other states calling for a second constitutional convention. The final vote to ratify was 30–27.[70]

Hamilton has long been credited with overcoming the Anti-Federalists in Poughkeepsie. A proposal circulated to change the name of New York City to "Hamiltonia." As the only New Yorker to sign the Constitution, Hamilton was its most visible champion, a visibility reinforced by his natural flamboyance. In Poughkeepsie, as one delegate wrote, "his oratorical abilities ha[ve] pleased his friends and surprised his enemies."[71]

Often, however, Hamilton annoyed his opponents. In the midst of one Hamilton speech, Clinton wrote sarcastically that "the little Great Man [is] employed in repeating over parts of Publius to us." Hamilton recognized the problem, even apologizing to the convention for employing "too vehement" language, excusing it as "the habit of using strong phrases to express my ideas."[72] His contribution in Poughkeepsie was great, though it would have gone for naught without Melancton Smith.[73]

•   •   •

Ratification proved the high-water mark of the partnership between Madison and Hamilton. They would veer away from each other politically over the next three years, ultimately becoming adversaries. In May 1792, Hamilton wrote of this with regret, describing Madison's character as "one of a peculiarly artificial and complicated kind."[74]

But they never fell into rancor and bitterness. Their partnership had been too close for that. Recalling Hamilton years later, Madison stressed his former partner's "intellectual powers of the first order" and his "moral qualities of integrity and honor in a captivating degree." He paid tribute to Hamilton's candor in stating his preference for a strong centralized government and his "greater merit of co-operating faithfully in maturing and supporting a system which was not his choice." But their political differences could not be reconciled. Asked why he had deserted Hamilton politically, Madison fired back that he thought Hamilton had deserted him.[75]

Throughout the ratification struggle, Hamilton and Madison enjoyed the irreplaceable support of General Washington, the most influential man in America. That Washington wanted the Constitution, James Monroe wrote to Jefferson, "carried this government."[76] Madison appreciated the general's unrivaled moral authority. Indeed, he had diligently worked for years to nurture his connection with the man who would be America's first president and Madison's second great partner.

II

GEORGE
WASHINGTON

COURTING THE GENERAL

Madison's partnership with George Washington was no accident. In the late summer of 1783, Madison began an assiduous courtship of America's first citizen. The general had moved his headquarters to be near Congress's temporary home in Princeton. With the war against the British winding down, Washington wanted to influence the nation's postwar defenses. As a member of the congressional committee on that subject, Madison met with the general professionally. As a Virginian who shared a room with one of Washington's old friends, Madison saw him socially. It was a start.[1]

Many factors separated them. Washington was almost twenty years older, a natural athlete with heart-stopping courage on the battlefield. Though high-spirited as a youth, Washington trained himself to maintain a stern self-command in public settings. A powerful six-footer, he commanded attention in every room he entered. Even Abigail Adams, a demanding judge of character, fell under Washington's spell. "He has a dignity which forbids familiarity," she wrote, "mixed with an easy affability which creates love and reverence." She also noted that he "has so happy a faculty of appearing to accommodate and yet carrying his point, that if he was not really one of the best intentioned men in the world he might be a very dangerous one." Washington was an efficient executive whether managing his Mount Vernon estates or mounting an underfunded rebellion against the British Empire. Often overlooked was his political acumen, which allowed him to command the support of both his soldiers and the Congress through eight years of war.[2]

Yet Washington had an area of self-doubt. With an acute sense of his limited formal education, which might be revealed by an unwise or rash remark, he avoided public debate. To compensate for this deficit in intellectual polish, during the war he surrounded himself with bright young men like Hamilton who managed his correspondence and implemented his decisions. As a talent spotter, Washington had few peers. After a few conversations with James Madison, reinforced by the young legislator's reputation, the general understood that the small Virginian was a man of judgment and high intelligence. The powerful have always loaned their stature and sponsorship to the talented young in return for loyalty and services. The Washington-Madison partnership began on that model.

The two men had a good deal in common. They were both products of the Virginia plantation culture and its slave society. Each was reserved in public and had a strong sense of propriety yet liked to unwind with small groups. Both were fervently committed to the ideals of the Revolution and American independence. But the common interest that first bound them together was a shared enthusiasm for the lands between the Appalachian Mountains and the Mississippi River.

Washington's fascination with the West began early. As a teenager, he surveyed western lands, allowing him to identify those with the best soil and water and access to transportation. In 1754, the twenty-two-year-old Lieutenant Colonel Washington led the Virginia militia on a bloody frontier expedition that launched Britain and France into the global Seven Years' War. Armed with his special knowledge of western lands, he amassed sixty thousand acres, mostly in the valleys of the Potomac and Ohio Rivers.[3]

For Washington, the West was not only an investment. Looking beyond the Indian tribes living there, Washington expected the region to lead America's growth when effective transportation links were built. The Potomac, which rose in the Appalachians to flow past Mount Vernon, could be the nation's highway to the West. Before the Revolutionary War, he pressed for river improvements and roads to connect the eastward-flowing Potomac with tributaries of the westward-flowing Ohio.[4]

Madison, raised in the Blue Ridge country almost two hundred miles from the Atlantic Coast, was as close to a westerner as sat in Congress in 1783. He led the effort to persuade the states to abandon their overlapping claims to western land. For the peace negotiations with Britain, Madison pushed for the Mississippi River to be the nation's western boundary. Westerners had to have access to the Mississippi or they might secede from the nation.[5]

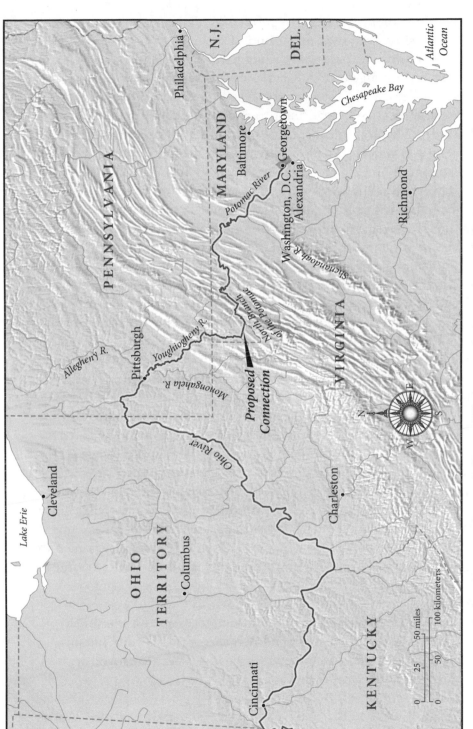

Madison's partnership with George Washington began with joint efforts to connect the Potomac River with the Ohio River, to create a waterway to America's western lands.

In 1784, Thomas Jefferson—another Virginian infatuated with the West—pushed both men to act on improving the Potomac. The river could accommodate oceangoing ships as far as Alexandria, near Mount Vernon, and Georgetown in Maryland. Only small boats could pass beyond the Great Falls. The river's obstructions must be removed in some places and locks and canals built to circumvent them in others. Jefferson urged Madison to enlist Washington to lead the project. It would be, Jefferson wrote, "a noble amusement in his retirement and leave a monument of him as long as the water would flow."[6]

In the early fall, Washington and a companion spent five weeks traveling by horseback through the West. His immediate goals were to collect overdue rents from settlers on his land and to eject squatters. He returned to Mount Vernon with a renewed fire to improve the Potomac. The first step was for Maryland and Virginia to resolve their disagreements over tolls and navigation rights. Washington set out to make it happen.[7]

In late 1784, few would obstruct a proposal from George Washington. The general traveled to Richmond to pursue the business with Madison and other Virginia legislators, then moved on to Annapolis for six days of lobbying over the Christmas holiday. In a late-night letter to Madison, Washington reported both success and "an aching head, having been constantly employed in this business."

When Maryland enacted the necessary law, Madison ensured that the Virginia General Assembly approved an identical bill and also created the Potomac Navigation Company, granting fifty shares to Washington. The state renewed an earlier Madison proposal to negotiate with Maryland and Pennsylvania for links between the Potomac and the Ohio Rivers.[8]

This episode demonstrated for Madison what an irresistible force Washington was. With the general as a partner, a deft politician might move mountains—or at least rivers. Madison, who was accustomed to being the hardest worker in any group, was impressed with Washington's determination:

> The earnestness with which he [Washington] espouses the undertaking is hardly to be described, and shows that a mind like his, capable of grand views and which has long been occupied with them, cannot bear a vacancy.

When it came to the West, Madison's enthusiasm matched Washington's. The river improvements, he wrote, "will double the value of half the lands within [Virginia], will extend its commerces, link with its interests those of the Western states, and lessen the emigration of its citizens." Though Madison missed the Mount Vernon conference in March 1785 because Governor Henry never told him about it, he engineered legislative approval of the deal with Maryland. Within a year, Washington had fifty men working at Harpers Ferry to remove boulders and dredge channels, and another hundred and fifty at the Great Falls. A visitor to Mount Vernon reported that Washington "completely infected me with the canal mania."[9]

The evolving Potomac project drew Madison and Washington together. The general worried about accepting the fifty shares in the Potomac Navigation Company. To smooth over ethical worries, Madison suggested the general donate the shares to "some patriotic establishment." The growing warmth between them led to Madison's first visit to Mount Vernon, in September 1785. Washington, fresh from a trip upriver, was "more and more sanguine" about the Potomac's future.[10]

The Washingtons often had guests at Mount Vernon. Curious travelers freely imposed on the general's hospitality; on most evenings, at least one or two of the extra bedrooms were occupied, and conversation often turned to the Potomac.

A young British merchant recorded a Mount Vernon visit in 1785. He found that Washington kept "a genteel table for strangers that almost daily visit him." The general devoted his mornings to writing letters and managing the farm, often working "with his men himself: strips off his coat and labors like a common man." He greeted his company at midafternoon dinner, dressed in a plain blue coat, white cashmere waistcoat, and black breeches. After the meal and two more hours at his writing desk, Washington returned for supper with powdered hair, a clean shirt, and white silk stockings. He "sent the bottle about pretty freely after dinner," toasting "success to the navigation of the Potomac, . . . which he has very much [at] heart." Because the company that evening included close friends, Washington "got quite merry," laughing and chatting until midnight. When another visitor to Mount Vernon coughed into the night, the general brought a soothing bowl of hot tea to his bedroom. That guest found that Washington's conversation mostly concerned "the interior country, and the opening of the navigation of the Potomac, by canals and locks."[11]

By November, Washington felt comfortable enough with Madison to write a letter that was candid, even chatty. He discussed not only the Potomac but also the larger questions facing the nation. The general confided that the need for Congress to regulate commerce seemed "so self-evident . . . I am at a loss to discover wherein lies the weight of the objection to the measure." Americans, he added, "are either a united people, or we are not." If not, "let us no longer act a farce by pretending to it." Madison responded with news from the state legislature and shared cautious hopes for what would become the Annapolis Convention.[12]

Madison had forged a solid connection with America's most influential man, principally by making himself useful. When Washington wanted the Potomac legislation adopted, Madison was there. When the general worried over whether to accept shares in the navigation company, Madison offered thoughtful advice. When Virginia needed to ratify the results of the Mount Vernon conference, Madison made that happen. Washington learned that this quiet young man could get things done, allowing the general to remain above the daily push and pull of politics. Of course, the squire of Mount Vernon would be the senior partner of any combination. Madison was not troubled that Washington would rank above him in any hierarchy. Madison's ego would not get in the way of using Washington's leadership and stature to achieve their common goals.[13]

For the first two-thirds of 1786, Madison mostly remained at Montpelier, remote from public affairs and from General Washington. He spent the early months exploring Jefferson's "literary cargo" from Paris. After days of study and correspondence, he passed quiet evenings in card-playing, chess, and conversation. Livelier times came when neighbors visited for two or three days of drinking, eating, even dancing. By the summer, Madison was restless, eager to travel north.[14]

After months of indecision, Madison had purchased nine hundred acres in the Mohawk Valley of New York in a joint venture with his friend Monroe. He had admired the area during a journey two years before with the Marquis de Lafayette, and Washington encouraged the land purchase. Still with no independent income, Madison strained to come up with his share of the price. He set off to look at additional parcels in the same area but only got as far as New York City, as Monroe could not join him on the trip to the frontier.[15]

The lure of New York lands was not entirely financial. Madison considered moving there. He confided his goals to his friend Edmund Randolph: "to provide a decent and independent subsistence" and "to depend as little as possible on the labor of slaves." The idea of leaving Virginia tantalized Madison, but moving to the New York frontier would entail many costs. Virginia was not only Madison's home but also was an extraordinary political platform—the most important state in the union and home to its most important citizen, who was now Madison's partner.[16]

After the Annapolis Convention in September 1786, Madison stopped for three days at Mount Vernon. He was on his way to Richmond for Virginia's legislative session. Acting in many respects as Washington's political agent, Madison would secure Virginia's unanimous approval of the call for a national convention in Philadelphia.

Washington balked, however, at serving as a delegate in Philadelphia and offered several reasons: his rheumatism, his "wish for retirement and relaxation from public cares," and his desire to avoid the simultaneous conference in Philadelphia of the Society of the Cincinnati, a controversial organization of former Continental Army officers. Madison brushed off the objections, insisting that Washington's name "could not be spared . . . as a mark of the earnestness of Virginia, and an invitation to the most select characters from every part of the confederacy."[17]

After taking his seat in Congress in New York in early 1787, Madison sent political reports to Mount Vernon, confident that the general would shoulder whatever burden his country needed him to bear. Madison knew his man. By late March, Washington was eagerly explaining to Madison his wish that the upcoming convention in Philadelphia "provide radical cures" for the nation's ills. Madison agreed that only radical steps would defeat the "malignity of the disease" infecting the government. He also provided a preview of the new charter of government he would propose in Philadelphia.[18]

They were the first two out-of-state delegates to arrive in Philadelphia. For a week, they and the other Virginia delegates met in Mrs. House's parlor to draft the Virginia Plan. Through the summer, they sat side by side at the front of the meeting room, facing the other delegates. As presiding officer, Washington had to manage the motions and amendments that flew up at him. Madison, the unofficial secretary of proceedings, was the most reliable resource for determining what precise question was before the presiding officer. For his part, Madison could observe at close quarters the effect of Washington's immense stature, which survived the bitterest contention among delegates. Though the Virginia delegation slowly fragmented, Madison and Washington usually agreed on disputed issues. Madison recorded six contentious votes within their delegation; he and Washington parted company only once on those votes.[19]

By the convention's end, the two men shared a powerful conviction that the Constitution, whatever its flaws, promised the best future for the United States. Once again acting as Washington's agent, Madison rushed to New York to guide the document through Congress, then kept the general fully informed about the state ratification battles. They swapped catty remarks about adversaries like George Mason of Virginia and Charles Pinckney of South Carolina.[20] Madison shipped copies of *The Federalist* to Mount Vernon, and Washington passed them on to friends for publication in Virginia newspapers. Madison also suggested the general urge his Maryland friends to push for ratification.[21]

As the date neared for the Virginia ratifying convention, the partners found their previous roles reversed. Now Washington was urging Madison to mount the public stage. Many Virginians, he wrote, viewed Madison's leadership "of indispensable necessity." Grudgingly, the younger man agreed to serve in Richmond, muttering in terms that blended Washingtonian reluctance with Madisonian syntax:

> I foresee that the undertaking will involve me in very laborious and irksome discussions; that public opposition to several very respectable characters whose esteem and friendship I greatly prize may unintentionally endanger the subsisting connection; and that disagreeable misconstructions . . . may be the fruit of those exertions which fidelity will impose.

Washington assured him that "the consciousness of having discharged that duty which we owe to our country is superior to all other considerations."[22]

Madison sent reports to the general from Richmond, also mentioning his recurring "bilious indisposition." Washington insisted that Madison plan to recuperate at Mount Vernon on his way to Congress in New York. "[M]oderate exercise, and books occasionally," he wrote, "will be your best restoratives." He added a personal remark—an effusive one for Washington—that "no one will be happier in your company than your sincere and affectionate servant."[23]

After Virginia's ratification, Madison lingered at Mount Vernon for three days. Washington doubtless passed the wine around freely to celebrate the new nation. Yet there was time for serious talk about the new government. On one day, Washington's diary states only, "I remained at home all day with Mr. Madison."[24] Knowing he would be America's first president, it was time to review the job with the man who now was his closest ally and adviser.

The new government would not launch itself. Someone had to translate the written Constitution into a national union. Critical decisions lay before Washington, and he wanted Madison's ideas about most of them. "I conceive it to be of unspeakable importance," Washington wrote that summer, "that whatever there be of wisdom and prudence and patriotism on the continent, should be concentred in the public councils at the first outset." Washington understood that the nation's first steps would mark its course for years. He wrote to an old army colleague that "the first transactions of a nation, like those of an individual upon his entrance into life, make the deepest impression and are to form the leading traits in its character." Madison agreed, insisting that "the first year or two will produce all the great arrangements under the new system, and . . . may fix its tone for a long time to come."[25]

The challenges were great. The United States was far from sturdy. It was beginning life with only eleven states; neither North Carolina nor Rhode Island had yet ratified. The new government had to function effectively, unlike the government of shadows under the Articles of Confederation. True executive and judicial branches had to be created while setting a myriad of precedents.

In addition, the new government would have to consider the constitutional amendments demanded by the Anti-Federalists. Madison preferred not to address amendments right away but to wait for the Constitution's flaws to emerge with time and experience. Then amendments could repair the real problems. But there was no time to wait. New York was circulating its call for a second constitutional convention, a proposal that Madison thought had "a most pestilent tendency"; if a new convention met, "the system, which has resisted so many direct attacks, may be at last undermined by its enemies." Anti-Federalist fears of the new government had to be eased.[26]

The partners also had to find a permanent home for the itinerant national government, which had resided in four different cities since 1783. Congress had tried several times to resolve the question, each time stumbling into a thicket of sectional rivalries.

Then there was the problem that drove the drafting of the Constitution in the first place. The American government needed a financial structure, including a tax system, that would pay the debts from the Revolution and allow it to operate.

A final problem was personal to Madison. His clash with Patrick Henry at the Richmond Convention had left the older man filled with anger. Henry was plotting vengeance. Not even General Washington could stop him from striking at Madison.

8

STARTING FROM SCRATCH

By the second half of 1788, Madison was a national political figure. He had been a leader in Congress for much of the previous decade, a prominent sponsor of the Constitution, and the victor in the Virginia ratification fight. His reputation exceeded that of regional figures like Patrick Henry or George Clinton. Within a year, a South Carolina congressman would foresee Madison as president.[1] But a national reputation was not enough to bring him a seat in the new Congress. For that, Madison would have to thread his way through a political obstacle course.

Madison's friends wanted the Virginia legislature to make him that state's first United States senator. Patrick Henry had declined the office, insisting he would swear no oath of loyalty to the Constitution, but neither did he want Madison to have it. In Richmond, Edmund Randolph found the fabled orator "involved in gloomy mystery," perhaps planning something "animated, forcible and violent."[2]

Madison, serving in the expiring Congress, thought the deck was stacked against him on the vote for Virginia's senators. A majority of the state's legislature were "enemies to the government," he wrote, who would find him "obnoxious." Henry charged that Madison could not be trusted to press amendments to the Constitution and was "unworthy of the people." Madison's election to the Senate, Henry predicted, would "produc[e] rivulets of blood throughout the land." General Washington viewed Henry's machinations with disgust, comparing him to an absolute monarch: "He has only to say let this be law—and it is law." And so it was. Madison finished third in balloting for the Senate, behind Henry's candidates.[3]

Madison said he preferred to serve in the less elitist House of Representatives, but Henry moved to block him there too. First, Henry jammed Anti-Federalist counties into the congressional district that included Orange County. Then Henry recruited a handsome war hero to oppose Madison: James Monroe.[4]

A chorus of voices reached Madison in New York. He must campaign against Monroe or face defeat. His presence in the district was "indispensably necessary," one friend wrote. He must meet the voters to confront the accusation that he opposed constitutional amendments. Madison, enduring an attack of the piles, was reluctant. He found office-seeking "not a little grating." Nevertheless, by mid-December he was on his way back home.[5]

The road home led through Mount Vernon, where Madison stayed for a week, leaving on Christmas Day. Madison found the general alarmed about his personal finances. Disappointing crops and high living expenses—which he called "contrary to my wishes, but really unavoidable"—had left the general feeling "more sensibly the want of money, than I have ever done at any period of my whole life." He tried to collect on outstanding loans but with little success. Times were still hard.[6]

For much of a cold and stormy week, Washington abandoned his usual farm routine. Instead, he recorded in his diary, he "remained at home with Mr. Madison." Their partnership had ripened into as close a connection as Washington ever permitted. Indeed, since the Articles of Confederation took effect, they had exchanged at least 175 letters—almost three times as many as passed between Washington and Jefferson, and more than four times the number between the general and Hamilton. He and Madison shared personal concerns as well as public ones.[7]

Raised on a working plantation, Madison could talk with the general about farming as well as politics. Before Mount Vernon's hearths, they reviewed the progress on the effort to clear the Potomac. The younger man was looking at a land investment at the Great Falls, just upriver from Georgetown. Washington, enthusiastic about anything connected to the river, wrote a letter attesting to the promise of the location. Madison forwarded the letter to Jefferson in Paris, asking him to recruit French investors for the project. The general admired a French watch of Madison's and later asked a friend in Paris to acquire one just like it for him.

Facing the contest against Monroe, Madison's tie with Washington provided some political security. Even if Madison lost the race for Congress, Washington could certainly find him a place in the new government. Hamilton hoped to see Madison in "one of the executive departments." Years later, a visitor heard from Madison that "there was nothing that General Washington would not have given [Madison] if he chose it, as they were very well together."[8]

Washington even sought Madison's view on whether he should accept the presidency, a question entertained by few serious candidates for that office. Washington was troubled that when he retired from the army, he had announced "a final leave of public life." Would it seem hypocritical, he worried, now to become president? Madison dismissed the concern. Washington was "indispensable," and he could amply prove his integrity by returning to private life after his presidential term. Then Madison left to fight for his seat in Congress.[9]

He spent January seeking votes in the district's eight counties. He met with voters in several of them, appearing with his opponent, Monroe, in Culpeper, Orange, and Hebron Church. Returning home in icy weather after a meeting with "a nest of Dutchmen," he wrote years later, his nose was frostbitten, "of which I bear the mark now."[10]

As his friends predicted, the principal election issue was whether Madison would support constitutional amendments. He addressed the question in letters to leading figures, letters that were intended for a public audience. In response to Baptist complaints that the Constitution did not protect freedom of worship, Madison announced his "sincere opinion that the Constitution ought to be revised" and pledged to do so during the first congress. He endorsed guarantees of "the rights of conscience in the fullest latitude, the freedom of the press, trials by jury, security against general warrants." He emphasized that he preferred to have Congress propose amendments rather than summon a second national convention, which "containing perhaps insidious characters . . . would . . . spread a general alarm, and be but too likely to turn everything into confusion and uncertainty."[11]

Madison's efforts were sufficient. Despite bitter cold and ten inches of snow on election day, he defeated Monroe, 1,308–972.[12]

Before Madison left for the new Congress, Washington sent him a seventy-three-page draft of his inaugural address, written by one of the general's aides. When Madison stopped at Mount Vernon in late February—his fourth visit in eleven months—he and Washington agreed to start over on the speech. When Washington delivered it two months later, it covered but four pages and took twelve minutes to read.[13]

New York City welcomed the new government in grand style. Managing two hundred workers, French architect Pierre L'Enfant converted

City Hall into Federal Hall, replete with a three-story entrance lobby and a marble floor. The Senate chamber and the octagonal chamber for the House of Representatives both reached two stories high. A New Jersey senator thought nothing equaled it in the country.[14]

The city, which then covered only the lower tip of Manhattan, still bore scars from the British occupation. Streets were paved poorly or not at all. Garbage cluttered the streets until wandering pigs and other animals converted it into something more noxious. The few urban amenities included a theater on John Street, a racetrack, and two pleasure gardens. Society in New York, already the country's financial center, was marked by luxury and ostentation.[15]

The harsh winter delayed the arrival of many congressmen and senators. Veterans of the Philadelphia Convention were thick on the ground: eleven congressmen, eight senators, the new president, and three members of his first cabinet. Most were euphoric to be translating the new government from the written page to reality, and they felt a special burden to make the translation successful. Madison, though, was not impressed with his fellow legislators. "I see on the lists," he wrote to a friend, "a very scanty proportion who will share in the drudgery of business."[16] Because of his prominence and his well-known partnership with Washington, Madison was deluged with requests for plum appointments as diplomats, tax collectors, postmasters, or military officers.[17]

Though Federalists had overwhelming majorities in both houses of Congress, Madison had a plan for reaching out to Anti-Federalists. Through "some conciliatory sacrifices," he hoped to "extinguish opposition to the [Constitution], or at least break the force of it, by detaching the deluded opponents from their designing leaders."[18]

By early April of 1789, Congress had a quorum and could unseal the electoral votes for president. With each elector casting two votes, Washington received a vote from each one and thus won unanimously. John Adams of Massachusetts had the highest total of the electors' second votes and so would be vice president, providing regional balance. Congress was the lone visible symbol of the new government; neither Washington nor Adams had yet arrived in New York. Because the Senate met in secret until 1794, the House of Representatives commanded the greatest public notice. Madison became its preeminent voice, very much like Washington's prime minister.

Madison immediately presented legislation, developed with Washington, to set taxes on imported goods and tonnage duties on merchant ships. By generating revenue, he explained, the bill would deliver the government from its "state of imbecility." He stressed that the structure of taxes was exactly the same that the Confederation Congress had proposed in 1783. He was again the best prepared man in the chamber, reeling off statistics about American trade in molasses, rum, iron products, beer, and anything else under discussion. He had hoped that swift action would allow import taxes to apply during the spring shipping season, but his colleagues preferred protracted debate.[19]

By modern standards, the government was tiny. The House of Representatives numbered sixty-eight, while the Senate had twenty-two members. In a country of four million (including slaves), the army mustered fewer than seven hundred soldiers. Thirty people staffed the Treasury. Seventy-five post offices served the nation.[20] (In 2011, the state of Oregon employed eighty thousand people to serve a population of similar size.)

Washington's inauguration came on April 30. After the violence and privation of the war, then the drift of the Confederation years, the Federal Hall ceremony was profoundly moving. Washington wore a sword and a suit of brown cloth spun in a Connecticut mill. He took his oath on a balcony overlooking a street filled with cheering countrymen. The new president delivered his inaugural address to the senators and representatives assembled in the Senate chamber. A senator thought that Washington "was agitated and embarrassed more than ever he was by the leveled cannon or pointed musket."

Six years had passed since Washington had commanded the Continental Army. "Time has made havoc upon his face," a Massachusetts congressman wrote of the new president, who seemed in the grip of powerful emotions: "His aspect grave, almost to sadness; his modesty, actually shaking; his voice deep, a little tremulous, and so low as to call for attention." The congressman found it "an allegory in which virtue was personified."[21]

Washington's somber demeanor was no act. He was leery of a job that promised to be difficult. Contemplating the presidency, he wrote to Hamilton, brought "a kind of gloom upon my mind." In his inaugural address, he described himself as "inheriting inferior endowments from nature and unpracticed in the duties of civil administration." He feared, he said a week later, "my countrymen expect too much of me."[22]

New Yorkers had no such anxieties. They marked the occasion with two hours of fireworks on the night of the inauguration. Giant backlit illuminations loomed over crowded streets, portraying celestial graces descending upon the new president. Candles blazed from houses and ships in the harbor, while strolling bands serenaded the town. Washington viewed the festivities, then had to walk home. No carriage could pass through the crowd.[23]

Madison composed the response of the House of Representatives to Washington's address, giving him the singular experience of drafting the answer to his own speech. When Washington then asked him to write the presidential reply, he underscored the universal respect Madison commanded.[24]

Washington faced sensitive issues of etiquette and protocol. He had to establish "the dignity of the office" without straying into pomposity or the rituals of monarchies. Few people have had a finer sense for public conduct than George Washington, but on crucial points he asked for advice from those closest to him: Adams, Hamilton, John Jay, and Madison. Before arriving in New York, he had asked Madison to hire lodgings for him so he would not live with a private family, which might imply a preference for that family. As he explained in a letter:

> Many things which appear of little importance in themselves . . . may have great and durable consequences from their having been established at the commencement of a new general government. It will be much easier to commence . . . upon a well adjusted system . . . than to correct errors or alter inconveniences after they shall have been confirmed by habit.[25]

Washington resolved to accept no social invitations and return no visits. He set dates and times when he would receive guests, notably a Tuesday-afternoon levee that some found stuffy. A weekly reception held by his wife, Martha, was somewhat less formal. His dinners included only "official characters": congressmen, senators, executive officials and their spouses. A diner described one event as "the most solemn dinner . . . scarcely a word said." The limited conversation may have been a byproduct of the president's deafness; he could not respond to remarks he did not hear, while his taciturnity tended to silence his guests. Washington struggled to avoid "a seclusion [that] would stop the avenues to useful information from the many, and make me dependent on the few," but he also had to preserve time to do his work.[26]

Congress also strained to strike the correct tone, wrangling at length over the form for addressing the president. Vice President Adams, having spent years in European courts, proposed "His Highness the

President of the United States of America and Protector of Their Liberties." Adams's enthusiasm for titles prompted one senator to refer to the portly vice president as "His Rotundity."

Madison told the House of Representatives that he did not fear titles because they were meaningless but added that they were inconsistent with "the nature of our government or the genius of the people." Representing the House in a conference with senators, Madison rejected any title other than "President of the United States." In a private letter, Washington expressed relief that the simple title was chosen, complaining that Adams's proposal would have created hostility.[27]

Congress had more important work before it, beginning with establishing the executive branch, the courts, and a revenue system.

After less than three months in Congress, Madison vented his frustrations in a letter to Jefferson in Paris. His colleagues in Congress showed "a mortifying tardiness" while indulging "prolixity of discussion." The greatest challenge, though, was conjuring a government from close to nothing. "We are in a wilderness," he wrote, "without a single footstep to guide us." To another friend he admitted that working out the meaning of the Constitution would delay Congress "until its meaning on all great points shall have been settled by precedents."[28]

A constitutional difficulty arose when Madison moved to create the executive departments—Treasury, State, and War—but stumbled upon a disturbing omission from the Constitution. The document clearly directed that the president appoint high executive officers subject to Senate confirmation. But it said nothing about how to remove those officials. Some congressmen argued that they could be removed only by impeachment; others insisted that the removal mechanism should be the mirror image of the appointment process, requiring Senate agreement for each removal from office.[29]

Madison recoiled from such limitations on executive powers—Washington's powers—but made an embarrassing admission. After attentive study, he had determined that the constitutional provision "does not perfectly correspond with the ideas I entertained of it from the first glance." He stressed the question's importance: If Congress got it wrong, the government might "take a direction towards aristocracy or anarchy." He concluded, however, that since the Constitution gave the president the entire "executive power" and instructed him to "take care" that the laws be executed, he must be able to remove executive officials.

Allowing the Senate to share that power would make it a "two-headed monster," part legislative and part executive. Madison's argument carried in the House, but the Senate deadlocked on the question; Vice President Adams cast the tie-breaking vote to give the president unfettered removal power.[30]

Madison did not fear, he wrote, giving the president too much power: "I see, and politically feel that that will be the weak branch of the government." His expectation proved true through the nineteenth century; the massive growth of executive power in the twentieth century was beyond his imagining.[31]

Through the summer of 1789, as Congress created the executive departments and a court system, Washington and Madison collaborated closely. Madison frequented the president's house, consulting on a range of public business. Washington had few people to confer with. Some carryover officials from the prior regime occupied offices. Hamilton, still practicing law in New York, would not become Treasury Secretary until mid-September. Jefferson would not leave France for several more months and would not become Secretary of State until February of 1790. Through those early months, Washington and Madison were the heart of the government.

Because they were in such close quarters, their correspondence consisted mostly of short cover notes or proposals for meetings. Washington's confidence in Madison suffuses his tone of easy familiarity in those quick exchanges. In early May, he shared with Madison confidential records concerning relations with Britain, "as you are upon business which requires every information of the state of the union." A few days later, he asked Madison to draft a reply to a message from the Senate.

In June, the president sent papers relating to developments in the West "which will require to be acted upon in some way or other." The next month he asked Madison's advice on negotiations with Spain over Mississippi River access. Enclosing a draft address to Congress in August, he asked for Madison's help "if you have leisure, by adding to, or striking out such parts as you may think had better be expunged." In September he sent Madison a draft of ideas and suggested he "suffer them to run through your mind between this [evening] and tomorrow afternoon when I shall expect to see you at the appointed time." On another occasion, he modestly apologized for bothering Madison: "I am very troublesome, I know, but you must excuse me. Ascribe it to friendship and confidence, and you will do justice to my motives." Madison stood as close to Washington as anyone ever could.[32]

Perilous days came in mid-June, when the fifty-seven-year-old president developed a dangerous abscess on his thigh. After a day of high fever, a physician drained the infection. Washington recovered but very gradually. Six weeks later he still could lie on only one side. Almost three months later the wound was still open. Madison had no illusion about the risk to the nation. "His death at the present moment," he wrote to a friend, "would have brought on another crisis in our affairs."[33]

Though still largely an invalid, Washington signed the nation's new tariff act into law on the anniversary of independence, July 4, 1789, even though Madison disliked the legislation. The Virginian had fought to impose a graduated scale for tonnage fees on merchant ships, with American ships paying the lowest rate, an intermediate rate for ships of countries with trade treaties with the United States (notably, France), and other nations paying the highest rate. This "discrimination" was targeted at Britain, whose ships dominated American trade. In several speeches, Madison called for retaliation against unfair British trade policies. Britain, he insisted, needed American agricultural goods far more than Americans needed British cloth and manufactured items. "I have, therefore, no fears of entering into a commercial warfare with that nation," he proclaimed. "[I]f fears are to be entertained, they lie on the other side."

Privately, Washington agreed with Madison on the discrimination question, but the Senate removed Madison's provision because it would work against the goal of the law—to raise revenue. A trade war with Britain would reduce imports and revenue from the import tax. The economically sophisticated Hamilton later apologized to a British envoy for Madison's financial naiveté:

> The truth is, that although this gentleman is a clever man, he is very little acquainted with the world. That he is uncorrupted and incorruptible I have not a doubt; he has the same end in view that I have, . . . but [his] mode of attaining it is very different.[34]

The episode was a preview of the political and trade conflicts of the next twenty-five years, which would grow out of the renewed global struggle between Britain and France. Madison served notice early that he would not be a friend to Britain.

Private concerns were on the minds of both Washington and Madison through the summer of 1789. In late August, the president's mother died, at the age of eighty. Though she had been a difficult figure in his life, sometimes complaining about her eminent son, Washington wrote to his sister that her death was "awful, and affecting." Almost as difficult was the dispute over how to distribute Mary Washington's slaves among her heirs.[35]

Madison spent much of the summer troubled about the illness of his own mother. He was an established public figure entering his middle years, yet he was still torn between the great national stage and his Virginia home, where his family dwelt in a slave society that he could not reconcile with his principles. His father, now in his late sixties, was increasing the pressure for his eldest son to pay greater attention to Montpelier. On September 16, 1787—the day the Constitution was unveiled to the nation—his father's new will left Montpelier and the bulk of its lands to James Jr. Madison would have to choose between Virginia, which was his home and his political base, and his longing to escape its slave culture.

Madison also formed a romantic relationship. Years after his unsuccessful engagement to the teenage Kitty Floyd, Madison was seeing Henrietta Colden, the widow of a prominent New York Tory and the mother of two small boys. According to a contemporary, Mrs. Colden was "noted for her masculine understanding and activity, as well as for feminine graces and accomplishment." In a move unusual for women of her time, she invested in western lands in her own name. Madison referred to her only as "an amiable lady . . . within the circle of my acquaintance." Though Madison was discreet in matters of the heart, his habits were not monastic. Only the year before, a French diplomat recorded that Madison was expected to marry a Philadelphia woman, a report that was echoed in another source. Noting that Madison was moving to New York, the sister of a Philadelphia friend wrote of her sympathy for "poor Mrs. T . . . for having known, and after having known, for losing such a lover."[36]

Madison's summer of 1789, however, would be best remembered for his lonely sponsorship of the constitutional amendments that became the Bill of Rights. His partnership with Washington was essential to that effort as well.

9

◆

NOT ALTOGETHER USELESS

M adison thought bills of rights did little good. "Wherever there is an interest and power to do wrong," he wrote to Jefferson in 1788, "wrong will generally be done" even if a bill of rights is in place. "[R]epeated violations of these parchment barriers," he continued, "have been committed by overbearing majorities in every state." Madison believed that the best way to protect liberty was to separate powers among the branches of government and divide powers between state and federal governments. Though not foolproof, those structural protections more effectively restrained government overreaching. He opposed a bill of rights in the Philadelphia Convention, in *The Federalist*, and again at the Richmond Convention.

Madison was not alone in his lack of enthusiasm for bills of rights. Washington also doubted their utility. "Paper declarations of rights," proclaimed future lexicographer Noah Webster, "are trifling things and no real security to liberty." Six of the thirteen state constitutions included no guarantees of individual rights; nor did the Articles of Confederation.[1]

The ratification struggle converted the question from one of theory to one of practical politics. Three key state conventions had narrowly ratified the Constitution largely because they were able to propose amendments: Massachusetts proposed nine amendments, New York thirty-two, and Virginia forty. In all, state conventions proposed 210 amendments, many involving protections of individual rights.[2] Patrick Henry distilled the argument for a bill of rights with characteristic bite: "A Bill of Rights may be summed up in a few words. What do they tell us?—that our rights are reserved.—Why not say so? Is it because it will consume too much paper?" Jefferson also consistently supported a declaration of rights.[3]

Madison thought it rash to consider constitutional amendments before the new government was well established. Only after experience, he insisted, would Americans know the Constitution's flaws. "The public mind," he wrote, "is neither sufficiently cool nor sufficiently informed for so delicate an operation." Washington adopted a softer tone, observing that "there are scarcely any of the amendments which have been suggested, to which I have *much* objection," except the proposal to strip Congress of its power to levy taxes.[4]

Though Madison feared the adoption of ill-considered amendments, he had no doubt that one course would be worse: a second constitutional convention, which both New York and Virginia had endorsed. A second convention, Madison said, would feature "men who will essentially mutilate the system." Mangling metaphors, he predicted that it would be a "dangerous opportunity of sapping the very foundations of the fabric" of the Constitution.[5]

To forestall a second convention, he preferred a less reckless method of adopting a few amendments: by a two-thirds vote of each house of Congress, plus three-fourths of the state legislatures. That was the course he urged in the congressional campaign against Monroe in early 1789.

Madison distinguished between amendments to preserve the rights of individuals and states and those to alter the government structure. He vehemently opposed the latter, even though many of the proposals from the state ratifying conventions fell into that category. Those included provisions to restrain the federal judiciary, to limit congressional powers, or reallocate power between the Senate and the executive. He saw no reason to change those structures before experience showed that they worked or did not work.

Rights guarantees were different. Madison thought them ineffective but also inoffensive. As he explained to a friend, they would "quiet the fears of many by supplying those further guards for private rights which can do no harm to the system." Madison's view was pragmatic. A bill of rights, he wrote, "will either make [the Constitution] better in itself; or without making it worse, will make it appear better to those who now dislike it." Because a bill of rights would reconcile people to the Constitution, he resolved to support one.[6]

Through the campaign against Monroe, Madison professed a "sincere opinion" that the first Congress should revise the Constitution "with a proper moderation and in a proper mode." Madison's qualified enthusiasm for a bill of rights made sense to the voters who elected him.[7]

As the new Congress began, Madison confronted a political puzzle. To mollify Anti-Federalists, he would seek amendments to protect personal rights. But the Federalist majority in Congress held Madison's earlier view that amendments should wait for experience under the Constitution. To secure the amendments he had promised, he would have to persuade his new colleagues to adopt provisions they thought premature and unnecessary. Madison would start with the most influential Federalist of all, Washington.

In his inaugural address, written with Madison after abandoning a draft by another aide, the new president specifically asked Congress to take but a single action. Pointing to Article V of the Constitution, which prescribes the procedure for amendments, he noted that the "occasional exercise" of that power might be warranted by the "objections which have been urged against the system, or by the degree of inquietude which has given birth to them." Professing his "entire confidence" in the ability of Congress to address the question, Washington delivered a firm shove for a bill of rights. He urged Congress to demonstrate "a reverence for the characteristic rights of freemen, and a regard for the public harmony" by considering how those rights "can be more impregnably fortified" in order for that harmony to be "safely and advantageously promoted."

It was not a stirring call to arms. The two Virginians who crafted it were wary of executive intrusion into legislative business. Despite its delicate phrasing, the message was one that Madison could employ as proof of presidential support for amendments protecting personal rights. As draftsman of the House answer to Washington's address, Madison committed that body to act on the president's muted call to arms. The president's endorsement of amendments, Madison's reply stated, "will receive all the attention demanded by its importance; and will, we trust, be decided under the influence of all the considerations to which you allude."

When Madison prepared amendments, Washington gave him a final weapon: a private letter to be shown to other congressmen, placing the president on the side of Madison's proposals. The president's letter spoke with characteristic moderation:

As far as a momentary consideration has enabled me to judge, I see nothing exceptionable in the proposed amendments. Some of them, in my opinion, are importantly necessary, others, though in themselves . . . not very essential, are necessary to quiet the fears of some respectable characters and well meaning men. Upon the whole, therefore, not foreseeing any evil consequences that can result from their adoption, they have my wishes for a favorable reception in both houses.[8]

Madison did not present his amendments until Congress had been meeting for three months, deferring them while his colleagues debated legislation to establish a revenue system and the executive and judicial branches. When deliberations on those subjects stretched on and on, Madison decided to wait no longer. On June 8, he rose in the octagonal House chamber to propose them.

Because the House conducted its business in public, New York's leisured class embraced its sessions as a form of civic theater. Those in the gallery leaned forward to hear Madison's soft voice as he presented the question of amendments. A half-dozen congressmen responded that Congress should resolve more important matters before considering constitutional amendments. Roger Sherman of Connecticut predicted that the amendments "would alarm the fears of twenty of our constituents where it will please one."[9]

Madison pressed on. Speaking to a chamber filled with skeptical Federalists, he did not oversell. His presentation was low-key, even lukewarm. Using terms that might apply to a pair of old shoes, he called a bill of rights "neither improper nor altogether useless."[10]

Despite the tepid rhetoric, the length of Madison's address reflected the importance of the subject. He began with the political benefits. Amendments would, he said, "give satisfaction to the doubting part of our fellow-citizens." Many Americans would support the government "if they were satisfied on this one point." North Carolina and Rhode Island still had not joined the union. Amendments, Madison said, would bring them aboard.[11]

Then Madison emphasized the amendments that should *not* be adopted: "I should be unwilling to see a door opened for a reconsideration of the whole structure of the government." To achieve a "moderate" revision of the government's charter, he proposed nineteen amendments sifted from the scores proposed by the state conventions. He also proposed a new constitutional preamble.[12]

Madison's amendments began by declaring that all power derives from the people, and that the government exists solely for their benefit (the antecedent of the current Ninth Amendment). He proposed to increase the size of the House of Representatives so each state would elect at least two members of that body. If Congress changed its own pay, he suggested, the change should take effect only in the *next* Congress (the current Twenty-seventh Amendment).

Having fought for religious liberty in Virginia, he offered a thorough provision on the subject. It stated that no rights could be abridged due to a person's religious beliefs, that no national religion could be established, and that rights of conscience could not "be in any manner, or on any pretext, infringed." Madison's free speech provision covered the "right to speak, to write, or to publish," along with freedom of the press. All should be "inviolable." (These, modified, make up the First Amendment.)

Madison proposed to preserve the right "to keep and bear arms," adding, "a well armed and well regulated militia being the best security of a free country." (The source of the current Second Amendment.) He also proposed language exempting from military service those "religiously scrupulous of bearing arms." Madison recommended barring the quartering of soldiers in private houses (the Third Amendment).

A single paragraph included the elements of the current Fifth Amendment: protection against being tried a second time for the same crime, against self-incrimination, against losing property to the state without just compensation, and against loss of "life, liberty, or property, without due process of law." Other paragraphs included a ban on cruel and unusual punishment (the Eighth Amendment) and protection against unreasonable searches and seizures (the Fourth Amendment). Another provision granted the right to a speedy and public trial, to be notified of criminal charges, to confront witnesses, and to have a lawyer (the Sixth Amendment). Other proposed amendments, prescribing court procedures, did not pass.

One of Madison's proposals had never been mentioned in a state ratifying convention but, rather, was an idea he had urged unsuccessfully at the Philadelphia Convention: that Congress should be able to veto state legislation. Madison still thought state legislatures were particularly dangerous and needed to be restrained. Because most Anti-Federalists would despise such a veto, Madison proposed it in a limited form. "No state," his provision read, "shall violate the equal rights of conscience, or the freedom of the press, or the trial by jury in criminal cases." During later debates, he would call this provision the most valuable of all.[13] Finally, he presented a provision reserving to the states those powers not delegated to the federal government (the Tenth Amendment).

Somewhat apologetically, Madison admitted that a headstrong legislature or executive could violate these "paper barriers." Yet, he insisted, "as they have a tendency to impress some degree of respect for them, to establish the public opinion in their favor, and to rouse the attention of the whole community, it may be one means to control the majority." In addition, courts could enforce the guarantees in some cases, forming "an impenetrable bulwark against every assumption of power in the legislative or the executive." Madison even suggested that state legislatures—more often the bogeymen of his constitutional vision—might enforce the guarantees. His goal was "tranquility of the public mind, and the stability of the government."[14]

Some of the responses to Madison's speech were gratifying. A former North Carolina delegate to the Constitutional Convention reported that it "dispersed almost universal pleasure" and urged adoption of the amendments before his state's ratifying convention met in November. Anti-Federalists were pleased that Madison was reaching out to them.[15]

Northern Federalists, though, were unhappy. They saw Madison's effort as craven truckling to Virginia voters who disliked a strong national government. Fisher Ames of Massachusetts called Madison the "first man" in the House but thought him too much a Virginian: "[He] thinks that state the land of promise, but is afraid of their state politics and of his popularity there." Another Massachusetts Federalist offered a similar portrait. After giving Madison credit for "fair and honorable intentions," he described him as "haunted with the ghost of Patrick Henry" and subject to paralyzing timidity. A Pennsylvanian portrayed him as "frightened with the anti federalists of his own state." Another dismissed Madison's amendments as empty posturing, "bread pills, powder of paste, and neutral mixtures."[16]

Debate on the amendments resumed in late July, six weeks later. A special committee examined them for a week, rewriting some, then returning them for consideration by the House. For twelve consecutive days in August, the House argued about them.

In that first Congress, floor debate featured men who prepared their own remarks, attended House sessions, and listened to each other. Few other activities competed for their attention while each chamber was in session. Committee work was performed at other times, while fundraising events and media opportunities were not yet invented.[17]

Working through Madison's amendments in sweltering August weather, no one representative dominated the debate. Madison spoke only occasionally. Some questioned the entire enterprise. The amendments, a South Carolinian complained, were "frothy and full of wind, formed only to please the palate; or they are like a tub thrown out to the whale, to secure the freight of the ship and its peaceable voyage." (Mariners supposedly threw wooden tubs from their ships to distract whales from wreaking havoc on the ship itself.)[18]

In private letters, Madison called the congressional debate "nauseous," "extremely wearisome," and "extremely difficult and fatiguing," but he stressed its importance: He hoped the amendments would "kill the opposition everywhere, and [put] an end to the disaffection to the government itself."[19] When the House finished its work, Madison's preamble was gone, more provisions had been rewritten, and only seventeen amendments remained, but their substance tracked Madison's original version. By the required two-thirds margin, the House passed them.

The amendments' progress through the Senate is largely mysterious because that body worked in secret.[20] The Senate considered some twenty amendments of the type that Madison feared: changes to government structure that would limit congressional power to establish an army, would impose term limits on presidents, and would require that the branches of government be "separate and distinct." All failed.

Nevertheless, the senators reduced Madison's amendments from seventeen to twelve and rewrote several. Most disturbing to Madison, they killed the amendment to bar states from denying free speech, freedom of conscience, and jury trials. Madison still feared irresponsible state governments above all else. He complained to a friend that the Senate struck "the most salutary articles." A New Hampshire congressman reported that "Madison says he had rather have none than those [amendments] agreed to by the Senate." Madison was not alone in that view. An Anti-Federalist from Virginia thought the Senate had "mutilated and gutted" the amendments, though it retained protections against federal intrusions on individual rights.[21]

But Madison came around. The amendments were critical to the national reconciliation he fervently sought and also to bringing the last two states into the union. He led the House negotiators in meetings with senators that produced twelve amendments that passed the House, 37–14. The Senate concurred by the required margin and President Washington sent the amendments to the states for ratification.

The amendments achieved one of Madison's primary goals. North

Carolina joined the union in November 1789; Rhode Island followed, grudgingly, in May 1790. Both states ratified most of the amendments. "These amendments," Rhode Island's legislature announced in late September 1789, "have already afforded some relief and satisfaction to the minds of the people of this state."[22]

By the end of January 1790, six states had ratified most of the twelve proposals. New York and Pennsylvania soon followed suit, as did the new state of Vermont in 1791.

Final ratification of the ten amendments in the Bill of Rights had to wait for Virginia. In late 1789, Madison's home state refused to ratify, a final exercise of Patrick Henry's waning powers. Madison took Virginia's rejection in stride, predicting to Washington that the action would harm the state legislature's reputation without injuring the national government. By December 1791, the Virginia legislature finally shrugged off Henry's influence and ratified. The Bill of Rights was law.[23]

The story of the Bill of Rights has little drama. Madison's speeches were measured, not heroic. The congressmen who approved it were impatient to address other matters. No crisis attended the effort. Rather, the Bill of Rights was designed to avoid future crises by reconciling the Constitution's critics to the new government. The supporting statements by President Washington were moderate, though his support was vital.

Madison championed the Bill of Rights out of a sense of obligation, not one of mission. He had won Virginia's ratification, and his own election to the House, by promising amendments. Consequently, he explained in 1789, "As an honest man I feel myself bound." And although he did not prize such declarations of rights, he thought them "not without some influence." The amendments accomplished his immediate political goals, blocking the second constitutional convention and removing many Anti-Federalist objections to the new Constitution.[24]

Yet the intervening centuries have demonstrated that the Bill of Rights achieved far more. In his June 8 speech presenting it, Madison foresaw the educational effect that rights guarantees can have over a long period of time. Though they are weak constraints in an emergency, he said, they can shape public opinion over time to support the enumerated rights. The Bill of Rights might thereby embolden state legislatures to oppose oppressive federal measures and could arm the courts to do the same.[25]

And so it has. It was more than a century before the Supreme Court enforced the First Amendment's guarantees of free expression and freedom of conscience—not until the federal government had expanded well beyond the size and scope that Madison's generation imagined. By then, as Madison predicted, the principles of the Bill of Rights were entrenched in American culture. Even Madison's cherished goal of restricting state governments finally came to pass. In the twentieth century, the Supreme Court used the Fourteenth Amendment, adopted after the Civil War, to apply most of the Bill of Rights against oppressive state actions.

The partnership between Madison and Washington reached its peak when Congress approved the constitutional amendments in September 1789. Madison had displayed a sure feel for Washington's personality, how the general preferred to influence events without engaging in day-to-day politics. He had used Washington's vast prestige and support—sometimes explicit, sometimes implicit—to propel the calling of the Philadelphia Convention, to win ratification of the Constitution, to push the legislation establishing the new government, and to secure the Bill of Rights. Both men could look back with satisfaction over the road they had traveled together. They had breathed life into a new type of self-government, festooned with checks and balances and constrained by concern for the people's liberty, ratified and supported by the people.

In the same month that Congress approved the Bill of Rights, the Senate confirmed Madison's friend Hamilton as Secretary of the Treasury. In a few more months, Jefferson would return from Europe to become Secretary of State. With a close partner as president and another atop the Treasury, with his best friend about to take charge of America's foreign policy, Madison seemed poised to wield ever-greater influence within the nation's executive. Shifting politics, however, would bring about a fundamental shift in his partnerships.

10

THE DEAL

When Congress recessed for the last months of 1789, Madison dawdled in New York for a time, suffering again from piles. The recess was a trying time. His mother remained seriously ill while he stayed at Montpelier, then he contracted dysentery upon his return to New York. Though sometimes dismissed as a hypochondriac, Madison endured more than his share of maladies.[1]

The president used the recess to take a month-long tour of New England. Besieged by crowds, Washington revealed his interests through his itinerary. Though he called agriculture "my favorite amusement," Washington wanted America to have a solid commercial base and was fascinated by emerging industries. He toured four New England factories: a woolen mill in Connecticut and a sailcloth factory and two cotton mills in Massachusetts.[2]

When Madison reached New York in early 1790, he recoiled from a frenzy of financial speculation in government securities, which had been triggered by Hamilton's announcement of a plan to pay America's debts. Suddenly, riches might flow from government bonds previously dismissed as worthless. "I call not at a single house or go into any company," one senator wrote, "but traces of speculation in certificates appear." Agents for investors combed the nation for any government debt paper they could snap up at 15 to 20 percent of face value. Abigail Adams, wife of the vice president, had speculated profitably in those securities for some time, but now the market was supercharged.[3]

The first session of Congress had addressed only those actions needed to start the new government: establishing its procedures, creating its departments, giving it a revenue, and approving constitutional amendments. The next session would address substantive policies. Would it gratify the financial elites of the northeast, who wished for an energetic government on the British model, or would it operate with a smaller revenue and bureaucracy, closer to the pre-Constitution government? Action on the debt question would provide the first answer to this pivotal question.

In 1790, government debt held a towering place in American finance. Its size was prodigious: roughly $77 million, or about 40 percent of the nation's annual economic output. The United States at that time was a largely agricultural nation, with few banks and no uniform currency. Its businesses had rudimentary capital structures, and government had very limited ability to collect revenue. Repaying that much debt seemed unthinkable.[4]

The debt came from the eight years of war against Britain, but different types of debt securities reflected the different circumstances in which they arose. "Certificates" were paper IOUs, often scribbled out by quartermasters for goods they seized to feed or supply soldiers. Soldiers had received a range of IOUs instead of pay, which might also be called certificates. "Stock" or "securities" described IOUs issued by the government when it redeemed paper currency it previously issued, substituting a new promise to pay for an earlier promise to pay. Congress and many state governments had issued stock. "Indents" were IOUs issued when a government could not make scheduled interest payments. By whatever name, the government securities all promised to pay a certain rate of interest, often 6 percent, and to be redeemable at face value in the future.[5]

But no one knew what those promises were worth. By 1786, no government in America was paying any interest, and redemption of any security was literally a matter of speculation. The Confederation Congress, begging for funds from the states, could make no payments unless the Articles were overhauled or replaced. Because of the nation's financial distress, most states chose not to enact the taxes needed to pay their debts. Shays' Rebellion, a protest against Massachusetts taxes, demonstrated the perils of trying to pay down a state's debts. Massachusetts quickly repealed most of the taxes that triggered the unrest.

In addition to its size, other qualities of the public debt made it the principal challenge facing Congress. First, debt speculation promised the sort of profits ordinarily associated with finding buried gold. Through the 1780s, most debt could be purchased at no more than 20 percent of its face value. Imagine an investor purchasing a hundred dollars' worth of certificates at 20 percent of face value, with a promise of 6 percent interest. If those certificates were honored, the investor would receive six dollars per year in interest, or a 30 percent annual return on her investment of twenty dollars. If the certificates were later redeemed at face value, the investor would receive an additional 500 percent return on her initial payment. Small wonder that Mrs. Adams bought them.

Moreover, the validity of America's debt securities depended on whether its governments had the will to honor them. While still in his twenties, Madison had concluded that political factors defined economic realities. Challenging the views of savants like David Hume and Montesquieu, he denied that the value of a nation's currency depended on the quantity in circulation. The key factor, he concluded, was the public trust in the government that issued it.[6]

Madison's insight applied directly to the situation confronting Congress in 1789. Public confidence in all of America's governments was low, which was reflected in the low prices commanded by the debt paper. The new government's policy on the debt would either establish it as worthy of public confidence, or would squander the opportunity to stop the drift under the Articles of Confederation.

Congress faced several key choices. It might pay debts with paper currency, which would lose its value shortly after issuance, or it might pay with specie or "hard money" that would hold its value. It could assume the debts incurred by state governments or it could leave the states to flounder in their own predicaments. It might reduce the interest rates on securities, or redeem them at face value or at some lower value, or repudiate them altogether. At bottom, the questions all boiled down to whether Americans could be inspired to pay the taxes needed to redeem the debt.

Moral considerations influenced the financial choices. Much of the debt was initially held by soldiers and farmers and others who contributed directly to the fight against the British. Because those individuals made great sacrifices during America's darkest hours, they posed a powerful claim for full repayment. Yet most of those original debt holders had long since sold their securities, often for pennies on the dollar, and the securities may have changed hands multiple times. The secondary purchasers were ordinarily people of means who presented a far less compelling moral claim. They were, some argued, mere gamblers, heartless profiteers. In addition, a geographic bias was at work. Secondary holders were clustered in the northeastern and middle states, so those regions were predictably enthusiastic about full repayment. Southerners and westerners, who held much less of the debt by 1789, were much less supportive.[7]

Facing this challenge, Treasury Secretary Hamilton knew that import taxes and excise taxes on products like whiskey would produce some revenues to apply to the looming tower of debt. The government's credit, and its long-term survival, hinged on his ability to deploy those revenues to create a comprehensive and fair package for the debt holders.

Within a few weeks of taking office, Hamilton asked Madison for his views on several questions relating to the debt, including what additional taxes would be least unpopular. In reply, Madison listed several possible taxes and argued for extinguishing the debt entirely. Some debt holders were then arguing that debt should be maintained indefinitely as "a national blessing," with debt paper serving as a financial asset that provided liquidity and investment capital for a growing economy. Madison disagreed. The debt, he warned, would end up in foreign hands, siphoning off America's wealth. He called the debt "a public curse."[8]

Hamilton's "Report on Public Credit," a fifty-one-page pamphlet issued on January 9, 1790, jolted New York. The Treasury Secretary proposed to repay all federal debt with specie over a long period of time, paying nothing to the original holders who sold out to speculators. Current holders would receive different interest rates on different types of securities, but the blended value would be over 4 percent. They also could accept partial payment in the form of western land. Most striking, Hamilton called for the federal government to assume state debts incurred in the shared effort against the British. By taking over the states' debts, Hamilton's policy would make the federal government of central importance to the monied class, which would look to the national government to pay off their investments. Contrary to Madison's recommendation, only a small part of the debt would be extinguished every year, so it would linger for decades.

In the weeks before Hamilton released his proposal, new speculation erupted. Agents carried satchels of cash to southern and western communities, sweeping up any remaining state debt shares and military certificates, sometimes misleading the sellers about the political situation and always having far greater knowledge of Hamilton's likely policy. A North Carolina congressman traveling to New York passed two express riders headed south with money for speculation; a financier sent two ships to South Carolina with goods and cash for buying military certificates. The atmosphere in New York, center of government and of speculation, grew feverish. Madison referred disdainfully to the prevailing "avidity for stock."[9]

As Congress prepared to debate Hamilton's proposals, Madison knew that a major change had occurred. In the 1789 congressional session, working closely with Washington behind the scenes, Madison had sponsored, drafted, or shaped most of the major legislation. Just a few months later, he was playing no role in developing the executive's principal policy initiative. Hamilton was steering the ship of state on financial policy. Though Washington would say little publicly during the legislative battles over the public credit plan, Hamilton plainly had his support. When the plan came before the House, Madison would not be its chief sponsor; indeed, he would oppose two of its central elements. Through six months of debate on the plan, Madison would work closely with Hamilton and Washington, but as a contending political figure, not as a partner. No longer would anyone think Madison was President Washington's prime minister.

Madison held his tongue through the first days of House debate on Hamilton's plan. On February 11, he announced his support for full debt repayment: "No logic, no magic, in my opinion, can diminish the force of the obligation." He questioned, however, "to whom the payment is really due." Madison was disturbed that Hamilton proposed no payments to the original debt holders: the farmers, storekeepers, and soldiers who had extended credit (willingly or unwillingly) to the Revolution. He could see no justice in using taxes paid by those original holders to bestow windfall gains on the speculators who bought securities at a fraction of their face value. He countered with a proposal to pay original holders the highest market price ever commanded by their securities (up to 50 percent of face value), with later purchasers receiving the balance, plus interest.[10]

Madison's amendment met a cascade of opposition. His course, according to northern Federalists, would undermine public credit. The government had promised to pay the face amount to whoever held the security. "Instead of doing what it promised," one scoffed, Madison proposed that the government "do as it pleases." Madison's proposal also was impractical, others complained, due to the patchy records available of who the original debt holders actually were.[11]

Madison answered caustically. Hamilton's plan, he said, would "erect the monuments of [America's] gratitude, not to those who saved her liberties, but to those who had enriched themselves in her funds." Though portrayed in other situations as a dry creature of intellect, Madison pleaded guilty to the accusation that he was following his heart rather than his head: "In great and unusual questions of morality, the heart is the best judge."[12]

Madison's amendment lost thumpingly, 39–13. If Washington had been a congressman, he also would have voted no. The president wrote to a friend that Madison was acting on "the purest motives and the most heartfelt convictions," but he added that "the matter was delicate, and perhaps better not have been stirred." Madison was unfazed by the setback, assuring his father that his proposal was "much better relished I find in the country at large, than it was in this city." After his political tangles with Patrick Henry and James Monroe, Madison was keeping a sharp eye on public opinion, especially Virginia opinion. By June, a Virginian wrote to Washington that "Mr. Madison's conduct on this business has gained him great popularity."[13]

Congressional deliberations in 1790 were interrupted by a burst of the violent passions that erupted whenever events prodded America's rawest nerve: slavery. A group of Quakers submitted petitions to Congress denouncing the importation of African slaves and calling for a ban on those imports. Because the Constitution preserved the right to import slaves until 1808, Congress could not satisfy the Quakers. Nevertheless, the petitions riled many congressmen.

Madison tried to shunt the Quaker petitions off to a quiet demise in committee, but southern congressmen preferred to rise in high dudgeon to defend their property rights. A Georgian called upon the Quakers to buy the Negroes or otherwise "keep themselves quiet." A South Carolinian predicted that the South would never consent to emancipation without a civil war. Madison did not support his fellow southerners. Indeed, he suggested that Congress consider barring the introduction of slaves into the nation's western lands.[14]

A month later, the Quaker petitions were back on the House floor. A committee recommended a resolution that would vaguely commit Congress to act "for the humane objects" of the Quaker petitioners. Though the resolution would have triggered no action, southerners once more mounted the ramparts, offering many of the arguments that would split the union seventy years later. Some insisted that slaves were humanely treated and that emancipation would come gradually, in due course. Others denounced the Quakers as ignorant meddlers. One asked rhetorically if any of them had ever married a Negro or would "suffer their children to mix their blood with that of a black." He quoted from Jefferson's writings about the inherent inferiority of Negroes and predicted that mixing races would result in the massacre of one race or the other. Though some northern congressmen defended the committee report, the House jettisoned any negative references to slavery.[15]

In private correspondence, Madison deplored the performance of his fellow southerners. They had overreacted, he thought, to "the most distant approach of danger." They should have "let the affair proceed with as little noise as possible." Washington agreed, calling the Quaker petitions "an ill-judged bit of business."[16]

Shortly before the Quakers presented their petitions, Madison was approached by an advocate of relocating freed slaves to Africa. In a memorandum prompted by that overture, Madison examined "colonization" as a solution to the problem of holding "600,000 unhappy negroes" in bondage. Free blacks, he observed, could never live as equals in America because of "the prejudices of the whites." He concluded that colonization might encourage masters to emancipate their slaves by providing a "proper external receptacle" for free blacks.[17]

With the slavery question stuffed back out of sight, Madison strained to modify Hamilton's funding plan. The greatest controversy surrounded the assumption of state debts by the federal government, a proposal that most congressmen viewed in terms of their own state's self-interest. Massachusetts, Connecticut, and South Carolina, drowning in unpaid debts, demanded assumption. States like Virginia had repaid some of their debts, so they were reluctant to assume the burdens of their sister states. Madison found a way for the plan to treat states in Virginia's position more fairly (that is, more generously). The key was "settlements."

The settlements issue grew from a pledge in the Articles of Confederation that each state would be reimbursed for its spending "for the common defense or general welfare." The principle was straightforward: If a state was the scene of many battles (say, South Carolina or New Jersey), it had likely spent more to prosecute the war than did a state that saw relatively little conflict (say, New Hampshire). Those states that had paid more than their share would be reimbursed by the others. Like many straightforward principles, it proved tricky to apply. For starters, no state conceded that it did less or spent less than any other state during the war; each trumpeted its extraordinary sacrifices.[18]

States also disagreed over whether specific expenditures were authorized by Congress or even assisted the war effort. Some saw Virginia's western expedition, led by George Rogers Clark, as advancing Virginia's western claims, not the nation's welfare. Virginia had a larger problem with the settlement process: Its accounting records were incomplete, sometimes nonexistent. Other southern states had similar problems. In contrast, the mercantile northerners had maintained precise accounts. As the settlement process proceeded, southerners realized that many of their claims would fail unless they could loosen the documentation standards.[19]

In late February, Madison told his colleagues that it was "preposterous" to adopt assumption before settlements were completed, and he offered an amendment requiring that settlements be part of any assumption of state debts. Over the next few days, he changed the motion several times in an effort to cobble together a majority. His proposal would pile up additional federal debt, but Madison insisted that fairness required it. He was complicating matters for the Treasury Secretary, and for the president.[20]

On April 12, the House defeated assumption by a narrow vote. Massachusetts representatives grew frantic; one denounced the "violent and unjust" action of the House and warned of "dangerous consequences." Uncertainty descended as new congressmen and senators arrived from North Carolina, which had recently ratified the Constitution. In the last week of April, the House abandoned assumption and turned to the rest of Hamilton's plan.[21]

Hamilton had been stymied on assumption, a key part of his plan. He needed a way to break the logjam of self-interested voting. To induce congressmen to change their votes, Hamilton needed to offer them something valuable in return. Only one issue before Congress was significant enough to serve that purpose: establishing the national capital, or the "residence" of government. The residence question had confounded Congress since it fled Philadelphia and the Pennsylvania militia in 1783. By late spring of 1790, most legislators understood that a final deal would combine assumption of state debts with the residence question. A few understood that Washington and Madison were acting together to promote the Potomac region as the future capital.

The struggle over the national capital was a geographic free-for-all, with shifting alliances backing multiple locations. The region that won the residence would benefit from major investments to build facilities, an influx of government workers who would buy products from local farmers and merchants, a surge of currency from tax payments, greater access to government information, and a heightened ability to influence policy. Consensus held that the residence should be centrally located, so all Americans could reach it, but consensus evaporated thereafter.

Some wished to place the capital in an existing city with an established infrastructure, while others proposed to build a new capital city free of the corruption that infected places like Philadelphia and New York.[22]

Before 1789, a variety of locations contended at least semiseriously to become the residence: New York City, the Falls of the Delaware River (near Trenton, New Jersey), Germantown (next to Philadelphia), Philadelphia, Baltimore, Annapolis, and unspecified locations on the Susquehanna River in Pennsylvania and on the Potomac River. In December 1784, the Confederation Congress approved a location near Trenton as the residence, but it never allocated money to build there. Most Virginians, particularly Washington, preferred the Potomac. They insisted that only a Potomac location would be accessible from America's western lands.

When the Constitution was released to the public in the fall of 1787, the residence battle resumed in Congress; Philadelphia lost by a single vote. After ratification the following year, the maneuvering began anew. Baltimore surged as a contender. As happened before, though, the scheming by different regions offset each other, producing stalemate.

The question roared back to life in September 1789. Eight House members from Pennsylvania, the most centrally located state, became the pivot for the politicking. They could form an alliance with New Englanders for a temporary capital in New York and a permanent one in Pennsylvania. Or they could join with southerners for a temporary capital in Philadelphia and a permanent one on the Potomac. Madison, looking at Potomac land for investment, dove into the sectional bargaining. His speeches in favor of the Potomac location were considerably more spirited than those he made for the Bill of Rights.[23]

Scheming over the residence spilled over into New York's lodging houses, drawing rooms, and taverns. In the spring of 1790, New Englanders and Pennsylvanians negotiated in secret. When those talks failed, both groups turned to the southerners. Madison, playing a waiting game, refused to make a deal. When the Pennsylvanians assembled a majority for placing the residence on the Susquehanna River, Madison stalled, amending the legislation to require that the location be on a navigable river (much of the Susquehanna was not) and calling the legislation unconstitutional.[24]

Although the House approved the Susquehanna bill, the Senate changed the proposed residence to Germantown. When the legislation came back to the House, Madison again played for time, staving off a vote one day, then amending the bill in a minor way. As he hoped,

Congress adjourned before the Senate could act on the amended bill for Germantown. Reviewing the carnage after six weeks of fruitless plotting, Madison predicted that only President Washington could resolve the residence question.[25]

Madison's unyielding support for the Potomac caused some to see him as a hard-nosed local politician, no longer a man of the nation. "In no one instance," wrote a Pennsylvanian, "has [Madison] lost so much reputation as on this business which has transported him far beyond his usual caution." A story of Madisonian payback made the rounds: When a nominee for federal office failed to support the Potomac, Madison arranged to reduce the man's salary. Whether the tale was true or not, the cerebral Madison was gaining a reputation as a political operator.[26]

His case for the Potomac site was not an easy one. Although it was at the geographic center of America's East Coast, it was not near the center of the nation's population, which was farther north in Pennsylvania. America's growth would be in the South and West, Madison answered, so the Potomac would become the population center—a prediction that did not come true. Only two small towns perched on either side of the Potomac: Georgetown in Maryland, Alexandria opposite. Roads were few, with the closest commercial center fifty miles away in Baltimore. The climate was thought unhealthy, and it lay in the heart of slave territory. A Potomac residence, Dr. Benjamin Rush of Philadelphia wrote, meant that "Negro slaves will be your servants by day, mosquitoes your sentinels by night, and bilious fevers your companions every summer and fall, and pleurisies every spring."[27]

During the congressional recess, Madison scrambled to build momentum behind the Potomac. He huddled in Philadelphia with Senator Robert Morris, the apparent leader of the Pennsylvania delegation. In a letter to Washington, Madison advised that Morris would again try to ally with New England, but if that overture failed, he would turn to the South. To arm Madison, the Virginia legislature authorized the donation of a ten-mile-square parcel for the residence, while Maryland and Virginia pledged $192,000 to construct government buildings. The labors of the Potomac Navigation Company seemed to be opening the river's upper stretches to navigation; by the wet season of 1789, ten-ton boats could clear Great Falls. The company gave Madison political support as well: Its board of directors included a former Maryland governor, two senators, and two congressmen. And, of course, President Washington, the trump card of American politics.[28]

Timing was another challenge. Madison had blocked the Susquehanna with delaying tactics, but he could not temporize forever. Time was not on his side. New Englanders would always oppose a Potomac capital, and John Adams of Massachusetts, as vice president, was the most likely successor to Washington. Adams would not support the Potomac, so Madison needed to win quickly. He distilled his strategy shortly after Congress adjourned in late 1789: If the Potomac was to win, "it must be under the auspices of the present Chief Magistrate and by some arrangement with PA [Pennsylvania]." And soon.[29]

When the House rejected the assumption of state debts in late June 1790, the residence question was the available tool for reviving Hamilton's pet program. Proposals and counterproposals swirled through Federal Hall. One senator reported "strange maneuvers" involving "the President's family," a term reserved for Washington's personal staff, including Major William Jackson and David Humphreys.[30]

Madison had to solve two simultaneous equations, each with multiple variables. The residence question would have two winners: a temporary capital and then a permanent one. Only existing cities like Philadelphia and New York had the infrastructure to serve as the temporary capital, but neither could be the permanent site; Pennsylvania's government had spurned the idea of housing the federal government in Philadelphia permanently lest it should demean the state government located there, while New York was considered to be too far north. Undeveloped locations like the Potomac and Susquehanna could serve only as the permanent capital, while locations like Baltimore and the Falls of the Delaware lurked as compromise choices.

The assumption issue could be plotted more precisely. Based on earlier votes, Hamilton knew exactly how many more he needed and which ones might be available. Luckily, several legislators from Maryland and Virginia had voted against assumption; if they switched—in return for a Potomac residence—both equations could be solved. Then again, a number of Pennsylvanians also had opposed assumption, so they too could swap their votes in return for bringing the residence to Pennsylvania.[31]

By mid-April, Madison called the chance of a Potomac residence "pretty much out of sight." Through an unseasonably cold May and June, Hamilton plunged into the bargaining. Madison led the Virginians, though another round of intestinal woes sidelined him for days. Even worse for the Potomac cause, Washington suffered a debilitating pneumonia that caused many to fear his death for the second time in a year. The dickering was intricate and fascinating. "Negotiations, cabals,

meetings, plots & counter plots," a South Carolinian wrote, "have prevailed for months past."[32]

A pivotal moment arose in mid-June, when Hamilton and Robert
Morris took an early-morning stroll around the tip of Manhattan. To
win assumption of state debts, the secretary explained, he needed one
vote in the Senate and five in the House. If Pennsylvania provided
those votes, Hamilton would deliver votes giving that state the permanent residence somewhere other than in Philadelphia, probably on the
Susquehanna. Morris agreed, but the deal crumbled when Hamilton
came up short on the residence vote and Morris's Pennsylvania colleagues rejected the bargain. The impasse continued. Madison thought
the Potomac site "stands a bad chance" but "it is not impossible."[33]

President Washington, recovering from his pneumonia, disliked the
congressional battling. Too many congressmen, he thought, acted with
"warmth and intemperance, with prolixity and threats," then wrote back
home "ascribing in letters . . . the worst motives for the conduct of their
opponents." Jealousy and mistrust were spreading within Congress.
Washington endorsed assumption of state debts, since the war was a
"common cause" among the states, all of which should share the costs.
And his enthusiasm for a Potomac capital never waned.[34]

The break came in the third week of June.[35] One evening, Jefferson
wrote, he encountered Hamilton outside his home on Maiden Lane.
The Treasury Secretary was "somber, haggard, and dejected beyond
description," and "uncouth and neglected" in his usually immaculate
dress. After pouring out his unhappiness over the failure of assumption,
Hamilton implored Jefferson to persuade his "friends from the South"
to pass the bill. Jefferson declined the appeal, then reconsidered. He
invited Madison and Hamilton to dine with him the next day to "find
some temperament for the present fever."

The Secretary of State's table featured the cookery of his slave chef,
James Hemings, who learned French cuisine while in Paris with his
master. Over Hemings's delectables, Madison and Hamilton reached an
agreement that included some fine shadings. Madison committed that
if assumption cleared the Senate, he would not block it in the House,
though he would cast his own vote against it. In Jefferson's phrase, Madison agreed to "leave it to its fate." In truth, Madison agreed to much
more. He would produce the House votes to pass it. In return, Hamilton
would find Pennsylvania votes to send the permanent residence to the
Potomac, with Philadelphia as the temporary capital for ten years.

The deal for the residence went relatively smoothly. Some northern-

ers probably voted for the Potomac in the belief that once the temporary capital was in Philadelphia, no one would move it to marshlands
in Maryland. Madison exhorted southerners to abandon any thought of
amending the bill. If it were not approved immediately, he warned, "the
prospect for obtaining a Southern position [may] vanish forever." By
mid-July, the president signed the legislation.[36]

Securing the southern votes for assumption required more sweeten-
ers. The Senate increased the value of all state debts to be assumed by
$2.2 million, more than one-fifth of which went to Virginia. In addition,
Madison won an extended deadline for submitting documentation on
settlements. In the following months, the federal board on settlements
lost its fervor for paperwork. It accepted such paltry documentary
evidence that Virginia's fiscal agent concluded that the state actually
profited from having bad records. In 1790, Virginia had presented only
$13 million in claims, many of them contested. By 1793, it had received
more than $28 million in final settlements.[37]

On August 11, Hamilton's public credit legislation was approved.
On the assumption question, four Maryland and Virginia congressmen provided the margin of victory by changing their votes from nay
to yea.[38]

The residence and assumption issues were resolved exactly according to
Washington's preferences. He engaged in neither jawboning nor arm
twisting, activities contrary to his idea of the dignity of his office. Yet
his influence determined the outcome. Afterward, Washington gave
executive jobs to two Maryland congressmen who lost reelection after
switching their votes to support assumption.[39]

From the president's perspective, perhaps the oddest feature of the
deal was the expectation of some northerners that Philadelphia would
become the permanent residence by inertia—that the new capital on the
Potomac would never be built. Those people seriously underestimated
Washington's commitment to the Potomac site and his executive abilities. Madison knew his fellow Virginian better than that, understanding
that Washington was the essential force in bringing the capital south.

For Madison, the 1790 deal was a triumph. He viewed winning
the capital for the Potomac as close to miraculous. The legislation, he
confided to Monroe, had "resulted from a fortuitous coincidence of
circumstances which might never happen again." He had steered the
Virginians into position to make the deal at exactly the right moment.

Despite voting against assumption, Madison acknowledged some uncertainty on the issue. He disliked increasing federal power, but he conceded that "the crisis demands a spirit of accommodation to some extent." He concluded that assumption was "an unavoidable evil, and possibly not the worst side of the dilemma." He also pointed out that its final form, including the settlements resolution, did not harm Virginia.[40]

Although both Washington and Madison achieved their goals in the 1790 deal, the episode reveals a transformation in their relationship. Madison no longer stood at the president's right hand. Now he sat across the table from Washington. With both Hamilton and Jefferson in his cabinet, Washington had less need for Madison on difficult problems; even if Madison gained the president's ear on a question, his voice was not the only one, and the other voices were intelligent ones. Their relationship remained cordial and marked by mutual respect, for Madison could disagree without being disagreeable. When Jefferson left the cabinet in late 1793, Washington wanted Madison to succeed him as Secretary of State, but Madison declined the office. By 1796, even after Madison had become a consistent opponent of the administration, Washington nevertheless asked him to care for the visiting son of the Marquis de Lafayette.[41]

By the end of 1790, Madison's political course was changing. His House colleagues now saw him as a Virginian first, dedicated to promoting his home state and region. Several forces pushed him in that direction. Congress was reverting to the pattern of sectional division that Madison had predicted for years. Also, Madison was protecting his political flanks back home from the likes of Patrick Henry.

Madison's confidence in his standing in Virginia was evident when he faced reelection in the second half of 1790. This time, he did not leave New York. He asked his father to place his name before the voters, and he enclosed letters to friends in his district that explained his position on the residence and assumption questions. He also asked his brothers Ambrose and William to attend the polling in two of the district's counties. With such minimal effort, he won easily.[42]

During the congressional recess between August and December 1790, Madison's physical movements foretold his political movement away from President Washington and toward Virginia. He left New York with Jefferson, passing a week in Philadelphia. Each man made living arrangements in the new temporary capital: The unassuming Madison reserved a room with his longtime landlady, Mrs. House, while the Secretary of State leased and began remodeling a fine home on Market

Street. After sailing down Chesapeake Bay, they stopped at Mount Vernon for conversation with the president. This time, though, Madison did not spend the night but rode on to the nearby home of George Mason. That simple act—leaving Washington and remaining with Jefferson to visit Mason, who had opposed ratification of the Constitution—confirmed Madison's evolving political and personal connections.[43] The tie between Madison and Jefferson was ripening into a potent political alliance, while his connection with Washington was thinning.

The partnership with Washington had become the foundation of Madison's national career. Together they won great victories, though Madison's command of events should not be exaggerated. He was central in the drafting of the Constitution, its ratification, forming the new government, and placing the nation's capital on the Potomac. He was essential to the adoption of the Bill of Rights. But most of those achievements were built on Madison's partnership with Washington; without the general, any or all of them might have been unattainable. There was no more powerful political ally than Washington, and Madison had made that proposition the guiding star of his political journey.

With his partnership with the president waning, Madison needed new political strategies. When he had strayed from Washington's preferences—pressing for discrimination in the public credit plan and opposing assumption of state debts—he had failed. Opposing Washington would place him on difficult political terrain, so he needed to develop ways to influence public opinion and to create a new political force.

When the reelected congressman headed to the temporary capital in Philadelphia in November 1790, he left at Montpelier a document that reflected a change in his personal situation as well. Since Madison had entered politics, his father and his brother Ambrose had operated the family plantation and businesses. Madison had nearly reached his fortieth birthday without taking much responsibility for the family's fortunes or his own livelihood. He knew no home other than his father's house.

In late 1790, in a lengthy set of instructions addressed to "Montpelier Overseer and laborers," Madison directed the management of lands at Montpelier that his father had placed in his name. He specified the fields to be tilled, the crops to be planted (corn, oats, and Irish potatoes), the agricultural methods to be followed, and the schedule for repairs and construction. Madison also prescribed the food for the slaves, ordering that they be treated "with all the humanity and kindness consistent with their necessary subordination and work." The sentence is a jarring one. "Humanity and kindness" were no part of enforcing "necessary subordination and work." Madison added that in his absence, his father would address those questions that should ordinarily go to Madison.[44]

He was no longer the restless young man who ached to be free of Virginia, its slaves, and attitudes he found narrow-minded. The familiar scenes and familiar faces of Montpelier were gaining power over him. The soaring view across the Blue Ridge, the quiet forests he rode and tramped through, the comforts of his lifelong home, and the needs of aging parents—all drew him back to Montpelier. Both personally and professionally, James Madison was becoming as much a Virginian as an American.

III

JEFFERSON

11

FIRST, FRIENDSHIP

They were the long and the short of it—Jefferson a lanky six feet two inches, and Madison at least eight inches shorter. They were best friends who held the presidency in turns, each serving for eight years from 1801 to 1817. Through their forty-year partnership, they transformed American politics. Which was exactly what they intended to do.

They first met in the Virginia General Assembly in the early years of the Revolution, after Jefferson had drafted the Declaration of Independence. Jefferson, eight years older, noted Madison's "habit of self-possession" and "the rich resources of his luminous and discriminating mind, and of his extensive information." Jefferson particularly recalled that the younger man was "soothing always the feelings of his adversaries by civilities and softness of expression." When Jefferson was Virginia governor in 1779, Madison served on his executive council. Their friendship became "intimate" during those months, according to Madison, yet when Madison went to Congress in 1780, he corresponded with Governor Jefferson mostly on public matters, often signing his letters formally, as "your humble and obedient servant." He addressed Jefferson in some letters as "your Excellency."[1]

Beginning in late 1782, the connection between the two men spread beyond the political and professional and into the personal and philosophical. In early September of that year, Jefferson's wife, Martha, died in childbirth. Jefferson's grief seemed to have no limits. For three weeks he paced his room, his daughter recalled, "night and day, only lying down occasionally." Then came weeks of riding on horseback through Monticello's woods and back roads, bursting into sobs when the pain was too great. "This miserable kind of existence," he wrote, "is really too burdensome to be borne." Jefferson's despair was so violent, a friend wrote to Madison, that he was reported to be "swooning away whenever he sees his children."[2]

As Jefferson pulled out of his spiral of grief, friends in Congress named him to the commission that was negotiating peace with Britain. The Virginian's term as governor had ended bitterly. He resented criticism of his conduct when British troops pillaged the state and drove him from the state capital in Richmond, then from Monticello. Easily bruised, Jefferson suffered through whispers that he had been caught unprepared or lacked manly courage. The experience, he wrote, "inflicted a wound on my spirit which will only be cured by the all-healing grave."[3] In late 1782, Jefferson embraced the chance to reenter the public arena and leave Monticello, now for him a place of sorrow. He brought his daughter Patsy to Philadelphia as he prepared for his mission to France. There they joined Madison, who was serving in Congress, at Mrs. House's establishment.

The bond between the two Virginians swiftly strengthened. Perhaps for the first time, they met as peers despite their age difference. Madison was a respected member of Congress and steeped in national politics, while Jefferson had been in Virginia for the last six years. Madison knew much that Jefferson wanted to learn.

The quarters were close. They shared meals and slept under the same roof. With Patsy Jefferson in tow and the warmhearted Houses all around, the Virginians formed a surrogate family, one that included the Floyds from New York as Madison lost his heart to young Kitty Floyd, who was only five years older than Patsy.[4]

Jefferson had ginger hair and a ruddy outdoor look. According to one of his longtime slaves, he was a "straight-bodied man as ever you see, right square-shouldered. . . . [As] Neat a built man as ever was seen in Virginia." At ease in society, Jefferson's appeal grew from his gentle grace, lively intellect, and relentless commitment to being pleasant. "It is a charming thing to be loved by everybody," he later wrote to his grandchildren, "and the way to obtain it is, never to quarrel or be angry with anybody." A vivid description of Jefferson's manner came from a woman who thought his politics terribly wrong:

> [Sitting down] in a free and easy manner, and carelessly throwing his arm on the table near which he sat, he turned towards me a countenance beaming with an expression of benevolence and with a manner almost femininely soft and gentle, [and he] entered into conversation . . . from which, before I was conscious of it, he had

drawn me into observations of a more personal and interesting nature. . . . [T]here was something in his manner, his countenance and voice that at once unlocked my heart.[5]

Many found Jefferson's intellect his most remarkable quality. Everything interested him, and he knew something about most subjects. A Frenchman described him as an "American, who without ever having quitted his own country, is at once a musician, skilled in drawing, a geometrician, an astronomer, a natural philosopher, a legislator, and statesman."[6]

For five weeks, until the Jeffersons left for Baltimore to board a ship for France, the two men were inseparable. Change suffused the moment. America's long and bitter war was ending. Jefferson was clawing back from the abyss of depression; he needed diversion and human warmth. Having pledged to his dying wife never to remarry, he needed a stimulating and sympathetic friend. For his part, Madison was at the brink of an emotional flowering, at least on his constrained terms. Smitten by young Kitty Floyd and delighted by Jefferson, the world was opening new vistas to him.

In January 1783, the bookish Madison was preparing a report recommending the books that Congress should acquire for its library. At the same time, Jefferson was drafting a shopping list of books for his own library, a list that paralleled Madison's report to Congress, with 550 titles comprising 1,300 volumes. The projects were catnip to bibliophiles like Jefferson and Madison. Collaborating on both lists, those two passionate readers each eagerly named titles that the other should read.[7]

Jefferson and Patsy left Philadelphia for Baltimore in early February, but patrolling Royal Navy ships delayed their transatlantic journey; then the Baltimore harbor froze. After a month of waiting, they returned to Philadelphia. For six more weeks, the two men spent more time at Mrs. House's table, prowling bookshops and taking country rambles when the weather permitted. They talked about everything—the Revolution, European politics, how to build a just government, the nature of man, curious animals and plants, farming, and America's future. Abruptly, when the preliminary peace treaty with Britain arrived in Philadelphia, Congress canceled Jefferson's mission to France.

By mid-April, when the Jeffersons left for Virginia, the friendship between the two men had advanced. Waiting to cross the Susquehanna River, Jefferson wrote with an emotional directness bound to gladden Madison. He hoped Madison and Kitty Floyd would marry, he wrote, because "it would give me a neighbor whose worth I rate high, and as I know it will render you happier than you can possibly be in a single state." Jefferson signed it, "your sincere friend."[8]

The warmth between the two men sprang from a wealth of common interests and experiences, beginning with the Revolution, which had vaulted them into political careers. Both hailed from western Virginia's hills, their homes only thirty miles apart. Both were eldest sons of wealthy plantation owners. Both professed to love liberty and detest slavery, yet both depended on the labor of people they owned. Both were unassuming in public, preferring conversation to formal entertainments. Neither inclined toward military pursuits, cherishing the life of the mind. Each was likely the smartest person the other ever met (with the possible exception of Alexander Hamilton).

Though the significance of their age difference had receded, Jefferson was more accustomed to being in charge. He had been fourteen when his father died, leaving him thousands of acres of land. Madison was nearly fifty when he inherited Montpelier, and he lived with and honored his mother until he was seventy-eight. By 1783, Jefferson had three daughters and cherished the paternal role. The childless Madison had never married. Jefferson rarely denied himself an intriguing book, a fine wine, a new gadget, or an architectural improvement to Monticello. Madison, supported by his father through much of his adulthood, often worried about money. His friend's epicurean, self-indulgent side was a revelation.

When Jefferson reached home in the spring of 1783, he immediately grew fidgety. Monticello held too many painful memories. He wrote to Madison in Philadelphia, trying to coordinate their upcoming travel schedules, but was still restless for public service. In June, the Virginia legislature selected him to succeed Madison in Congress.

For Madison, the second half of 1783 turned purgatorial as Congress huddled in its temporary quarters in Princeton. Spurned romantically by Kitty Floyd, Madison sank into his own depression. Jefferson, expressing surprise over the end of the romance with Kitty, offered his sympathy. "Of all machines," he wrote, "ours is the most complicated and inexplicable." By late October, Jefferson was back at Mrs. House's in Philadelphia, preparing to serve in Congress. He spent five weeks there and in Princeton with Madison. The two friends traveled together to Annapolis in late November, where Congress would convene anew. Madison did not linger but hurried home to Montpelier.[9]

They had been together for only three months of the preceding twelve, yet their sprawling, probing conversations would continue for the next four decades. Their subsequent correspondence included long, contemplative letters with homely details about weather and crops alongside challenging ideas about economics and trade, scientific curiosities, and the fate of nations. Their exchanges offer not only a window into each man's life but also into why they enjoyed each other so much. John Quincy Adams, who knew and worked with both, wrote with uncharacteristic awe of their collaboration: "[T]he mutual influence of these two mighty minds upon each other is a phenomenon, like the invisible and mysterious movements of the magnet in the physical world."[10]

Jefferson fired Madison's curiosity about science. Shortly after leaving Annapolis in late 1783, Madison wrote excitedly that he was testing a theory of the heat of the earth's core by calculating the planet's diameter. After Jefferson offered some corrections, Madison resolved to suspend his calculations until he could read the theory in the original version. Several months later, he related a report of a subterranean city discovered in Siberia. Jefferson urged Madison to take twice-daily observations of weather, wildlife, and plant growth so they could compare climate patterns between different locations. Jefferson specified twelve data fields to capture in chart format. Madison acquired the equipment necessary for the effort.[11]

When Jefferson became American Minister to France in 1785, he sent pamphlets to Madison about exciting European innovations, including "phosphoretic matches" (which could be extinguished with urine), animal magnetism, and the craze for hot-air ballooning.[12] Madison joined Jefferson's crusade against the writings of the Comte de Buffon, who argued that animal species in the Western Hemisphere were degenerate and thus smaller and more feeble than comparable versions in Europe. To disprove Buffon, Jefferson commissioned a New England expedition to gather horns and skeletons of moose, caribou, and elk. In 1786, Madison wrote an extended challenge to Buffon's theory as applied to American deer, rats, foxes, badgers, and rabbits ("extremely prolific and libidinous"). He obsessed over the number of teeth in moles and tried unsuccessfully to preserve a family of eight opossums to send to Jefferson in Paris. In 1792, when Madison was the leading member of the House of Representatives and Jefferson was Secretary of State, they were still at it. With both men scheduled to dine out one evening,

Jefferson invited Madison to stop by early to compare a "Northern hare" with a "common hare" acquired in the market.[13]

Wherever Jefferson went in France, he hunted up books to send to Montpelier. "In the purchase of books," he promised, "old and curious, or new and useful, I shall ever keep you in my eye." Madison asked for a French dictionary, treatises on international law and on "ancient or modern federal republics," plus "the Greek and Roman authors where they can be got very cheap." He craved a book on China.[14]

The openhanded Jefferson scoured Paris for nonliterary treats too. He ordered a special watch for Madison and found a pedometer for clocking Madison's walks around Montpelier.[15] In return, Madison sent New World products to Paris, including pecans, apples and cranberries, and a pamphlet on the Mohegan language.[16]

Jefferson also demonstrated his abiding trust in Madison. Before leaving for Paris, he asked his friend to superintend the education of his nephews, sons of his sister and Dabney Carr, "the dearest friend I knew." Madison faithfully paid the Carrs' bills and reported regularly on their progress.[17]

When Jefferson in early 1785 produced the only book he ever published, *Notes on the State of Virginia*, he sought Madison's judgment on whether southerners would resent his criticism of slavery. Jefferson developed the habit of seeking Madison's view when he had second thoughts about a step. "I ask your advice on it," he wrote from Paris, "and no one else's." Madison called the book "too valuable not to be made known," an opinion bound to gratify any author.[18]

Their correspondence across the Atlantic took on an unusual range and depth. In October 1785, Jefferson reported an encounter near the royal palace at Fontainebleau. Chatting with a woman on the road, he learned that she supported her children from day to day. If she found no work, they went without bread. When Jefferson gave her twenty-four sous, she "burst into tears of gratitude." Shaken, Jefferson reflected on economic realities and class structure.

"I ask myself," he wrote, "what could be the reason that so many should be permitted to beg who are willing to work, in a country where there [are so many] uncultivated lands?" French aristocrats kept land idle for the sport of game hunting. Jefferson thought that should not be permitted while people starved, since the "earth is given as a common stock for man to labor and live on." Americans should ensure that as many people as possible should have "a little proportion of land. The small landholders are the most precious part of a state."[19]

Three years later, during the opening weeks of the French Revolution, Jefferson again pondered property, government, and the rights of man. Beginning with the principle that "the earth belongs to the living," he theorized that property rights should die when a generation dies, as should all of its laws and debts. Society should not remain imprisoned by the decisions of people now vanished, he reasoned, people whose world vanished with them. Working out his idea, Jefferson urged Madison to assume a generation reaching the age of twenty-one at the exact same moment and expecting to live another thirty-four years (a number derived from actuarial tables): "Each successive generation would, in this way, come on, and go off the stage at a fixed moment, as individuals do now. . . . The second generation receives it clear of the debts and encumbrances of the first, the third of the second and so on."

All debts, Jefferson argued, including public debts, would then die with each generation. Laws and constitutions also would expire every nineteen years; if they were worthy, the new generation would reenact them. Asserting that "by the law of nature, one generation is to another as one independent nation to another," Jefferson, possibly influenced by his own chronic struggle with personal debts, proclaimed that his scheme was "solid and salutary." But, he continued, perhaps not. "Turn this subject in your mind, my dear sir," he asked Madison, "and develop it with that perspicuity and cogent logic so peculiarly yours."

Fresh from the Constitutional Convention, from writing *The Federalist*, and from his showdown with Patrick Henry at the Richmond ratifying convention, Madison made short work of Jefferson's vision of a social contract that expired every nineteen years. Politely declaring Jefferson's idea "a great one," Madison confessed his "skepticism." For one thing, Jefferson's world would be "too mutable and novel," depriving society of stability. Worse, if the laws vaporized every nineteen years, "the most violent struggles [would] ensue between the parties interested in reviving and those interested in reforming" the previous laws. The uncertainty would undermine the value of property and breed licentiousness.

Moreover, Madison rejected Jefferson's basic premise. There are, he insisted, valid debts between generations; they are *not* independent nations to one another. If a public effort benefits later generations—say, a canal or a road or a war for independence—it is only fair for later generations to pay some of the debt incurred in the effort.[20]

The exchange typifies how the two men complemented each other. Jefferson was a gifted polemicist and visionary. His facility with language and metaphor was a marvel. Rather than say simply that Congress could not agree on an adjournment date, he wrote, "The day of adjournment walks before us like our shadow."[21] Yet Jefferson's thinking was rarely systematic, and his creative impulses could lead him astray, a limitation that led him to avoid the cut and thrust of debate. "During the whole time I sat with him in Congress," John Adams recalled, "I never heard him utter three sentences together."

Madison understood his friend's qualities of mind and disposition. "[A]llowances," he pleaded after Jefferson's death, "ought to be made for a habit in Mr. Jefferson as in others of great genius of expressing in strong and round terms, impressions of the moment." Through their long partnership, as in this exchange over Jefferson's utopian vision, Madison would strain to protect Jefferson from this habit.[22]

Madison, in contrast, was relentlessly systematic; his reasons ordinarily had reasons. Despite his reserve in public settings, that turn of mind made him adept in debate, surefooted when countering an adversary's claims. Unlike Jefferson, Madison did not avoid disagreement. Ever courteous, he was happy to explain the error in an adversary's thinking. As a literary stylist, Madison was rarely more than a journeyman, yet his clanking prose could dismantle Jefferson's soaring visions.

The exchanges between Madison and Jefferson over America's new Constitution are equally revealing. Through the mid-1780s, both expressed dissatisfaction with the Articles of Confederation. The states had too much power and too many currencies, while trade foundered. Confining himself to "strong and round terms," Jefferson recommended that a new constitution should "make us one nation as to foreign concerns, and keep us distinct in domestic ones," while separating executive, legislative, and judicial functions. He feared, above all, a government modeled on European monarchies, "a government of wolves over sheep." He applauded the turbulence of republics and shrugged off the tumult of Shays' Rebellion: "I hold it that a little rebellion now and then is a good thing and as necessary in the political world as storms in the physical." In Jeffersonian fashion, the metaphors were powerful but the details thin.[23]

Like most of the delegates to the Philadelphia Convention, Jefferson disliked Madison's favorite proposal: that Congress should have the power to veto state laws. On that question, Jefferson provided the perfect metaphor. Madison's veto proposal, Jefferson wrote, violated the principle that "the hole and the patch should be commensurate." Instead, Madison's proposal would "mend a small hole by covering the whole garment." Only bad state laws, not every state law, should be reviewed. Court review of specific state laws, he added, would be "as effectual a remedy, and exactly commensurate to the defect."[24]

Because of the delegates' rule that Convention proceedings were secret, Madison could not share with Jefferson in France the process of Constitution writing as it was happening. Five weeks after the proposed Constitution was published, Madison sat down to send a full report to his friend. The difficulty of writing the Constitution, he insisted, made "the degree of concord which ultimately prevailed [no] less than a miracle." Designing the executive had been difficult, he continued, while the Senate would be "the great anchor of the government." Dividing power between the states and the national government was, "perhaps of all, the most nice and difficult." Madison defended his proposal for a congressional veto over state laws, complaining that the nation could devolve into a "feudal system of republics" riven by "continual struggle between the head and the inferior members." That veto, he added, also would protect individuals, as the "injustice of [state laws] has been so frequent and so flagrant as to alarm the most steadfast friends of republicanism."[25]

Jefferson did not mince words about two shortcomings of the Constitution. The omission of a bill of rights troubled him. It was, he insisted, "what the people are entitled to against every government on earth . . . and what no just government should refuse." He also did not care for the president's ability to serve multiple terms. The president would become an officer for life, Jefferson feared, because he would always be reelected. Rather than pursue the thought, though, Jefferson retreated into generalizations, denouncing "energetic government" as "always oppressive." As for rebellions, America's thirteen states had seen only one over an eleven-year period, which was "but one for each state in a century and a half. No country should be so long without one." Seven months later, Jefferson "sincerely rejoiced" at news of ratification, then employed another metaphor to press again for a bill of rights: "It is a good canvas, on which some strokes only want retouching."[26]

Fresh from the year-long battle for ratification, Madison could not quite match Jefferson's graciousness. He replied that he would consider amendments but added grumpily, "I have never thought the omission a material defect."[27] For the next thirty years Madison repeatedly stooped to explain constitutional provisions to Jefferson. Despite his regard for Jefferson's genius, Madison never deferred on constitutional issues to the views of one who, as Madison pointed out to the Richmond Convention, had not been in Philadelphia when the Constitution was written.

•   •   •

In the autumn of 1789, Jefferson sailed home from France. He was eager to see Madison, writing to his friend, "I particularly hope for much profit and pleasure by contriving to pass as much time as possible with you." He issued a blanket invitation for Madison to stay with him. "I will camp you at Monticello," he wrote, "where, if illy entertained otherwise, you shall not want that of books."[28]

In view of the limited time the two men had spent together—some months of professional engagement in Virginia politics, three months of companionship in 1783—the strength of Jefferson's feelings is striking. The five-year separation had only reinforced their connection.

Although Madison looked forward to Jefferson's return, he had always evaded his friend's more effusive overtures. In early 1784, Jefferson had pressed him to buy land even closer to Monticello, as James Monroe was doing.

> What would I not give [if] you could fall into the circle. With such a society I could once more venture home and lay myself up for the residue of life. . . . Life is of no value but as it brings us gratifications, among the most valuable of these is rational society. It informs the mind, sweetens the temper, cheers our spirits, and promotes health.[29]

Flattered, Madison nevertheless deflected the invitation. "I cannot altogether renounce the prospect," he replied, but "still less can I as yet embrace it." Perhaps, he added, sometime in the future.[30] Madison may have seen Jefferson's proposal as an invitation to a sort of permanent bachelorhood, or he may have felt his obligations to his parents had to override the proposal. Perhaps he lacked the cash for the move. Perhaps, also, he instinctively protected his own identity from being submerged in that of such a charming and fascinating friend.

At the end of 1784, Jefferson once more pressed Madison to purchase land near Monticello. "Agreeable society is the first essential in constituting the happiness and of course the value of our existence," Jefferson wrote. At least, he continued, Madison should visit him in France. He provided a detailed estimate of the journey's costs, then offered to advance the funds to his sometimes cash-strapped friend.[31]

Madison again demurred, beginning with two unpersuasive objections: A European journey would be too brief and would "break in upon a course of reading which if I neglect now I shall probably never resume." Few Americans have declined a European trip in order to complete some reading. More compelling was Madison's suspicion, in his words, that crossing the sea "would be unfriendly to a singular disease of my constitution." As for relocating near Monticello, he again begged off, pleading vaguely that "my situation is as yet too dependent on circumstances to permit my embracing it absolutely."[32]

As both men anticipated their reunion in late 1789, the surprising truth was that they were near neighbors, fast friends, and leading American politicians, yet they had not much collaborated on political matters. For years, they had shared political news, analyses, and gossip. They knew and worked with many of the same people. They achieved a sequential collaboration over legislative proposals that Jefferson developed for the Virginia General Assembly in the 1770s. One was a law protecting freedom of religion; a more ambitious effort was to rewrite and reform Virginia's laws. Jefferson, never adept in legislative bodies, failed to secure enactment of either. When Madison joined the legislature in 1784 and 1785, he steered the religion guarantee into law. "I flatter myself," he wrote to Jefferson, that the new law "extinguished forever the ambitious hope of making laws for the human mind." Through dogged persistence, Madison won approval of about half of the system of revised statutes despite Patrick Henry's opposition.[33]

Beginning with Jefferson's return to America in late 1789, the two Virginians would embark on the most influential political partnership in the nation's history. In autumn that year, Madison tried to meet Jefferson's ship in New York, then in Philadelphia. By mid-November, he learned that Jefferson had landed in Norfolk. Madison's pursuit of Jefferson was not solely due to sentiment, however. He was on a mission from President Washington: to persuade Jefferson to serve as Secretary of State in the new government of the United States. The time for their most direct political collaboration was upon them.[34]

12

THE HAMILTON PROBLEM

B y mid-March of 1790, Jefferson was en route to New York as the nation's first Secretary of State, ever more enthusiastic about his friend Madison. He raved to a friend that Madison was "the greatest man in the world." The two Virginians resumed their intimacy, beginning with Jefferson's request that Madison find him "temporary and decent" lodgings in New York. Soon Jefferson was leasing a house on Maiden Lane, a few doors away from the boardinghouse where Madison sheltered more simply. The two men could see each other constantly. As their political and personal bond grew stronger, their influence on each other's thinking increased.[1]

Through 1790, Madison and Jefferson were largely loyal supporters of the Washington administration, of which Jefferson was a senior officer. In that role, they struck the bargain that resolved the controversies over assumption of state debts and a permanent capital. All parties made the deal with eyes wide open. Jefferson proclaimed it "the least bad of all the turns the thing could take."[2]

But that bargain papered over a fundamental disagreement over the nation's future. Hamilton envisioned America as a New World colossus triumphantly taking its place among the great nations of the globe. Madison and Jefferson dreamt of a virtuous agrarian republic, modeling liberty for the despotisms of Europe and chatting peacefully with the new French republic. Though President Washington sought to harness both visions within his new government, they could not coexist quietly for very long.

After spending more than five years in France, including the first exhilarating months of that country's revolution, Jefferson was shocked by the aristocratic attitudes of upper-class New Yorkers. Dinner-table conversations, he later recalled, revealed "a preference of kingly over republican government," which left him "for the most part, the only advocate on the republican side of the question." Jefferson and Madison came to fear that Hamilton's vision of the nation would so ape British institutions and so embrace raw commercial values that America would lose its Revolutionary integrity.[3]

In December of 1790, Hamilton released proposals for new excise taxes and a new Bank of the United States. Madison disliked the tax proposal, but he knew the federal government had to raise revenue to pay the nation's debts.[4] The bank, he detested.

Hamilton first advocated a national bank when he was a twenty-five-year-old officer in the Continental Army. His proposed bank, like national banks in England, Holland, and Italy, would gather taxes and distribute revenues for the government, would issue bank notes that would serve as currency, would make loans for economic expansion, and would lend to the government in crises. It would be, Hamilton reported to Congress, "an institution of primary importance to the prosperous administration of the finances, and . . . of the greatest utility in . . . support of the public credit."[5]

Everything about the bank disturbed most Virginians. As chronic debtors, southern plantation owners naturally mistrusted banks. A national bank would enhance federal power at the expense of the states. If based in Philadelphia or New York, it might attract the national capital away from the Potomac, unraveling the recent bargain in Congress. Finally, it blatantly mimicked the Bank of England. Would it speed a drift to monarchy? Madison studied the Bank of England and central banks in Venice, Genoa, and Amsterdam. He concluded that they were not essential institutions. Instead of a central bank, he resolved, sound policy should foster competition among multiple lenders. Madison saw no need for a centralized financial system like Britain's. He produced a memorandum detailing that, over the previous century, the British had endured forty-two years of war. If the vaunted British financial structure merely made it easier for government to wage war, Madison wanted no part of it.[6]

The bank legislation sailed through the Senate, reaching the House in early February. Madison opposed it on two grounds: that it would centralize economic power and that the Constitution did not authorize Congress to grant a bank charter. When the bill's sponsors argued that Congress could act through "implied" powers granted by the Constitution's "necessary and proper" clause, Madison answered that the national government possessed only those powers named in the Constitution; the states and the people held all others.

The key constitutional provision appears in Section 8 of Article I, after a list of specific legislative powers, such as borrowing money and laying taxes. It states that Congress may "make all laws which shall be necessary and proper for carrying into execution the foregoing powers, and all other powers vested by this Constitution in the Government of the United States." Madison insisted that the clause could not authorize the bank, which was merely convenient, not "necessary." Other bodies could perform the same functions as a national bank. He also stressed that the Philadelphia Convention had specifically decided *not* to empower Congress to issue corporate charters.[7]

Madison's constitutional argument has echoed down the centuries, fueling the debate over the allocation of powers between federal and state governments. In early 1791, however, Madison's view commanded little support. For the previous two years, New Englanders retorted, Congress had repeatedly exercised implied powers. After all, nothing in the Constitution specifically authorized Congress to create governments in territories, but Congress had created them. Madison himself had argued that the president could discharge executive officials, despite the Constitution's silence on the subject; Madison had embraced that implied power.[8]

A bank supporter even quoted the passage from Madison's *Federalist* No. 44 that squarely endorsed implied powers: unless powers could be implied whenever "necessary and proper," Madison had written, the Constitution would have to include "a complete digest of laws on every subject to which the Constitution relates."[9]

Over Madison's opposition, the House passed the bank bill by a nearly two-to-one margin.[10] That dropped the constitutional question squarely into the lap of the president, who had ten days to sign the bill or veto it.

Washington asked his cabinet for advice. Jefferson and Attorney General Edmund Randolph sent memoranda arguing for a veto. The president was not satisfied. He called Madison in for "several free conversations" on the bill. Madison found that although Washington favored "a liberal construction of the national powers," the president knew firsthand that many at the Philadelphia Convention and the state ratifying conventions intended a limited national government. Washington, though still undecided, asked Madison to draft a veto message. He also asked Hamilton for a final written opinion on the question.

Working at breakneck speed, Hamilton produced a lengthy memorandum that boldly demanded a broad reading of the government's powers, no matter what the Philadelphia delegates intended. "Nothing is more common," he insisted, "than for laws to express and effect more or less than was intended." If a power could be discerned "by fair deduction" from the constitutional language, he concluded, appeals to the intentions of the Framers were irrelevant. Hamilton's avalanche of argument carried the issue. On the last possible day, Washington signed the bill.[11]

The bank bill demonstrated just how dangerous Hamilton was. As Jefferson complained several years later, "Without numbers, he is a host unto himself."[12] Harboring what Jefferson and Madison saw as a wrongheaded admiration for the British government and the British financial system, Hamilton was using his growing influence with Washington to replicate them in America. As Madison well knew, having Washington's support was the surest way to victory.

Madison's political realignment at this point prompts nagging questions. After years of cultivating Washington as a political mentor and ally, how did Madison end up on the wrong side of the president? And how was Madison, the advocate of a stronger national government throughout the 1780s, transformed into an urgent opponent of the federal government's powers? In *Federalist* No. 44, he agreed that the Constitution implied many powers. Yet now he denied such implied powers. What had changed?

Madison's own explanation, offered in old age, was simple, perhaps too simple. Hamilton, he said, intended to "*administer* the Government into what he thought it should be," while Madison wished the government to conform to the Constitution.[13] Omitted from Madison's explanation was a more embarrassing truth: that he did not foresee that the Constitution, in the hands of a powerful advocate like Hamilton, could accommodate more powers than Madison had imagined. In 1787 and 1788, Madison fought for a government with enough powers to be respectable, to address America's debts, to regulate trade, and to defend her foreign interests. He did not expect that government to preside over a centralized financial system. After only two years under the Constitution, Hamilton was making that happen. Anti-Federalists like Patrick Henry and Melancton Smith may have been right when they warned that the Constitution would allow a consolidation of government powers.[14]

Madison's opposition to Hamilton grew from other factors as well. Madison was appalled by the speculative frenzies that Hamilton's poli-

cies unleashed. Only a month after Washington signed the bank legislation, Madison railed against "speculators and tories," citing a scheme to
cheat former soldiers as "among the enormities produced by the spirit
of speculation and fraud."[15] He was not comfortable with raw capital-
ism, with insiders enriching themselves by trading pieces of paper—
unmoored promises to pay at some indefinite time in the future—with
hapless common folk who lacked inside information. Hamilton's policies seemed to multiply the opportunities for speculation. Madison
supported a growing trade for the United States, but he blanched at
Hamilton's financial system.

As the divide with Hamilton grew, Madison and Jefferson portrayed their adversary as pining for monarchy. Jefferson coined the term
"monocrats" to express this idea. From a distance of two centuries, their
fear can seem extreme, even delusional. Washington never aspired to
kingship. Events did not bring the nation close to monarchy.

But monarchy was not a theoretical proposition in 1791. Most Eu-
ropeans were subjects of hereditary rulers. Every native-born American
adult had been born a subject of the British king. Many blamed the
British Parliament, not the king, for the policies that brought on the
Revolution. In June 1789, some New Yorkers ostentatiously celebrated
the birthday of King George III.[16]

Moreover, the specter of monarchy was easy to find in the new
American government. At the Philadelphia Convention, Hamilton ar-
gued for a president and a Senate who served for life. Though the
Constitution had no such provisions, it also had no term limits. Could
Hamilton be trying to achieve those results through "administration"?

Jefferson continued to hear pro-monarchy talk. Shortly after the
bank was approved, he hosted a dinner attended by Hamilton, Vice
President Adams, and Attorney General Edmund Randolph. When
the guests touched on the British constitution, Adams said if the British could eliminate corruption and improve its representative features,
it would be the "most perfect constitution ever devised by the wit of
man." Hamilton went Adams one better, proclaiming the British system "the most perfect government which ever existed" without any
reforms. On another occasion, according to Jefferson's notes, Hamilton
stated that the American government would be unstable, so it "will
probably be found expedient to go to the British form." A year later,
Hamilton's father-in-law, General Schuyler, insisted to Jefferson that
choosing public officials based on hereditary descent would be better
than electing them.[17]

It was not just Hamilton. Many leading Americans seemed to as-
pire to the trappings of royalty and aristocracy, beginning with the
vice president's affection for pompous official titles.[18] Madison grumbled over Adams's "monarchical features," including his recently published *Discourses on Davila*, which included profoundly antidemocratic
passages. Madison disliked the president's weekly levees, which were
starchy, formal affairs. He complained that Washington's "satellites and
sycophants . . . have wound up the ceremonials of the government to a
pitch of stateliness which nothing but his personal character could have
supported." The United States Senate met in secret, its deliberations
haughtily concealed from public view.[19]

Madison's dislike for Hamilton's system was reinforced by Jefferson,
who was an even sharper critic of the government's financial policies.
Unlike Madison, Jefferson had no history of working with Hamilton and thus no residue of warm feelings for the New Yorker. When
Hamilton was ill with yellow fever, Jefferson scorned him as "timid in
sickness." Hamilton's bank scheme, Jefferson insisted, was designed to
"strengthen himself" by providing "corrupt services to many."[20]

Some have denied that Madison revised his constitutional views in
the early 1790s, while others have attributed his shift to political oppor-
tunism, or to Jefferson's seductive influence. None of these explanations
meets Madison on his own terms. His attitudes evolved in the political
world.[21] Having ended the national government's impotence under the
Articles of Confederation, the Constitution was spawning a government more centralized and powerful than Madison expected. Strict
construction of the Constitution was his response to Hamilton's deft
stretching of that document. Madison began to exalt state governments
as he defended what he thought was the true spirit of the American
republic against the Hamiltonian threat. In that cause, Madison did not
worry that his arguments might contrast with earlier statements. He
was a working politician fighting daily battles, not a theorist refining
pristine principles. Constitutional arguments were tools for gaining his
goals. He would employ those that best did so.

With both Congress and the president following Hamilton, Madison and Jefferson had to find a way to change the nation's politics.

When the national government moved from New York to Philadelphia
in early March 1791, Jefferson invited Madison to move into his house
on Market Street. "I have four rooms of which any one is at your ser-

vice," he wrote. "To me it will be a relief from a solitude of which I have too much." Madison, ensconced three blocks away at Mrs. House's, offered a thin excuse for declining. "My papers and books are all assorted around me," he replied, and "a change of position would necessarily give some interruption." In addition, with another lodger moving into Mrs. House's, Madison feared that "my leaving the house . . . might appear more pointed than may be necessary or proper" (an arch reference to the "necessary and proper" clause of the Constitution). He promised, however, to dine more frequently at Jefferson's, "being never more happy than in partaking that hour of unbent conversation."[22]

Soon the two Virginians were planning a northern tour. Their expedition, which spanned four weeks in late May and early June of 1791, entered history as the conspiratorial "botany trip." While posing as students of nature, some accounts claim, they schemed with New York politicians to undermine the Washington administration. This tale, though colorful, overlooks their lively interest in America's natural world.

For much of the trip they were with no one but each other—plus one personal slave for each—as they admired lush scenery, fished, chatted, and examined farming practices. They tried to identify trees and plants that did not grow in Virginia. In a moment of whimsy, Jefferson wrote letters on birch bark from the Adirondacks. They sailed on Lake Champlain and Lake George and visited battle sites around Saratoga and Long Island. Their correspondence and notes never refer to politics. Certainly no conspiracies were hatched during their visits with sturdy Federalists like Rufus King in New York and General Schuyler in Albany.[23]

They also encountered political friends. In Bennington, Vermont, they called upon a newly elected United States senator. In New York, they met with two future Republican allies, Aaron Burr and Chancellor Robert R. Livingston. Though those encounters were brief, Madison recalled that national events "entered of course into our itinerary conversations." Politicians will talk politics.[24] Their most important meetings in New York were with Philip Freneau, a Princeton classmate of Madison's and a talented newspaper editor.

Freneau, who had skippered coasting ships and published undistinguished poetry, recently had crashed into the rough-and-tumble world of New York journalism with slashing denunciations of Hamilton's policies.[25] He seemed the perfect editor for a new journal in Philadelphia that could counter the Hamiltonian *Gazette of the United States*.

In February 1791, Madison and Jefferson offered Freneau a part-time State Department position that would allow him to edit an anti-Hamilton newspaper that would circulate throughout the nation. Neither was troubled about offering public funds to support a critic of the Washington administration. Freneau declined. They made the same offer twice more in May, but Freneau would not budge.[26]

Madison extended a better offer to Freneau in July: Jefferson also would grant him access to State Department correspondence and its foreign newspapers, along with a contract to do the department's printing. Freneau relented. On the last day of October 1791, his *National Gazette* first appeared.[27]

Madison immediately seized upon the *National Gazette* as a tool for influencing public opinion. Through its first five months of operation, he contributed eighteen unsigned essays to it. In these articles, Madison abandoned the learned tone of *The Federalist*. His new articles were shorter and more accessible.

Madison's third essay in the series, "Public Opinion," explained the insight behind the founding of the *National Gazette:* that the true sovereign in a republic is public opinion, so long as the people's representatives follow that opinion. "The larger a country," Madison wrote, "the less easy for its real opinion to be ascertained, and the less difficult to be counterfeited." To ensure broad discussion of public issues, the nation needed "good roads, domestic commerce, a free press, and *particularly a circulation of newspapers through the entire body of the people.*" As he wrote in a later essay in the series:

> All power has been traced up to opinion. The stability of all governments and security of all rights may be traced to the same source. The most arbitrary government is controlled where the public opinion is fixed.[28]

Having embraced public opinion as the bedrock of republican government, Madison's next essay addressed political parties. Though he would not yet defend them, he admitted that parties unavoidably "arise out of the nature of things," so he offered a classic Madisonian response: "[T]he great art of politicians lies in making [parties] checks and balances to each other." Another essay preached the same principle for dividing power among the branches of government and between the states and the central government.[29]

As the series progressed, Madison's message grew sharper. He extolled the virtues of those who generate the products of the earth and stressed

the instability of commercial activity. He praised the American government for protecting "the rights of property and the property in rights."[30]

After five months of essays, Madison was ready to deliver a partisan
diatribe. In "The Union, Who Are Its Real Friends?" he described those
who were *not* friends of the union as a cartoon version of Hamilton:
They "pamper the spirit of speculation," promote "unnecessary accu-
mulations of the debt," seek to "pervert the limited government of the
Union, into a government of unlimited discretion," and support "principles of monarchy and aristocracy."[31]

The American republic, founded by men who uniformly denounced
political parties, was entering a period of partisan vituperation. Madison
and Jefferson, whose denunciations of partisanship had been as thump-
ing as any, would pitch into the battle.

The two Virginians faced two major challenges in vindicating their
"republican interest" against the "monocrats." Their opposition to Hamilton would be doomed if it became a challenge to Washington, whose
stature remained unassailable. The best course would be to win Washington's support. Also, they needed to invent a political party while
seeming to remain above partisan squabbling. With Freneau's newspaper in place, they pressed ahead.

Through the early months of 1792, Jefferson pursued an inside strategy, mounting a campaign to woo Washington to their side. He did not
confront Hamilton in cabinet meetings, something he hated to do and
never did well. Instead, he tried to undermine the president's confidence
in the Treasury Secretary.

Madison became the public face of the challenge to Hamilton. As the
Second Congress convened in late 1791, Madison completed his transition from the president's prime minister to leader of the opposition. He
spoke less often, since he no longer presented the government's proposals.
He commanded a natural constituency among southerners who disliked
the government's fiscal policies, about one-fourth of the representatives.
Another fifth of the congressmen almost always opposed him. Madison
needed to find supporters in the large group of unaligned members, or
else to cause the election of more men who agreed with him.[32]

Events provided rallying points for the Virginians' effort. When the
Bank of the United States sold its initial shares in July 1791, another
speculative frenzy erupted. Predictably, Madison found the scramble
disgusting. "Nothing new is talked of here," he wrote from New York.

"In fact stockjobbing drowns every other subject." A month later, his dismay over the "daring depravity of the times" had hardened into fury. "The stockjobbers will become the praetorian band of the Government," he wrote to Jefferson, "at once its tool and its tyrant, bribed by its largesses, and overawing it, by clamors and combinations."

Similar scenes played out in Philadelphia, which Dr. Benjamin Rush described in August as "a great gaming house," where men ignored their jobs to trade shares. At every street corner, he complained, "you hear citizens talking of nothing but Script [stock], 6 per cent, 3 per cent, deferred debt, etc. . . . Never did I see so universal a frenzy." The bubble burst in midmonth. "Many hundred villainous transactions came to light this morning," Rush recorded. "Long faces appeared in every street." Credit dried up, paralyzing economic activity. "Ships are lying idle at the wharfs," Jefferson wrote to a friend, "buildings are stopped, capital withdrawn from commerce, manufacturing, arts, and agriculture."[33]

Only nine months later, the country spiraled into a fresh financial crisis when a leading speculator, William Duer, defaulted on his debts. The panic spread with alarming speed. Express coaches between Philadelphia and New York carried market updates two or three times a day. Men wept in the streets and fistfights broke out in the New York coffeehouse where traders gathered. Bankruptcies mushroomed, beginning with Duer, an intimate of Hamilton's who served as his Assistant Secretary of the Treasury. Mobs outside Duer's Manhattan mansion bawled for his scalp; he ended his days in debtors' prison.[34] Madison and Jefferson concluded that Hamilton's system was rotten through and through.

"Every day exhibits new victims," Madison wrote to a friend at the height of the panic, "and opens new scenes of usury, knavery and folly." The economic distress gave greater force to Madison's critique of the government's policies. "The train of circumstances which has led to these evils [is] obvious," he wrote, "and reflections must soon force themselves on the public mind, from which it has hitherto been diverted by a fallacious prosperity."[35]

Madison and Jefferson thought Hamilton corrupted greedy congressmen by granting them the opportunity to make money on government debt and bank shares. Madison assured a friend there was a connection "between the speeches and the pockets of all those members of Congress." The following year, Jefferson had a list prepared of the "paper men" in Congress—those who owned public debt or stock in the national bank—so he could correlate their votes to their financial interests. Freneau's *National Gazette* relentlessly accused congressmen and speculators of gorging on "vast blessings" from the Treasury. Hamilton's tentacles seemed to reach everywhere. His department dwarfed other government offices and included postmasters, revenue collectors, and customs officials in every state.[36]

The mad gyrations of financial markets doomed two new initiatives urged by Hamilton and opposed by Madison in late 1791. First, Hamilton's Report on Manufactures proposed direct assistance from the national government to American businesses. The funds, to be raised through higher tariffs, would be paid in the form of "bounties." Hamilton also proposed federal support for a model manufacturing business that would foster technological innovations. The corporation—the Society for Establishing Useful Manufactures (SEUM)—was already located on the Passaic River in New Jersey. With William Duer promoting it and selling its stock for an insider's profit, its reputation became pestilential.[37]

There could be no mistaking Hamilton's purpose: to transform the infant republic into an industrial power to rival Britain, one that would use public revenues to build private businesses. Madison and Jefferson viewed Hamilton's latest proposals with horror. If the Constitution could be stretched so far, Madison wrote, "the parchment had better be thrown into the fire at once."[38]

In February 1792, while opposing a Hamilton initiative to pay bounties to cod fishermen, Madison was blunt: The program would "transmute the very nature of the limited government established by the people of the United States." For Madison, this was the ultimate distortion of the necessary-and-proper rationale, allowing its advocates "to do whatever they think fit, provided it be for the general welfare, of which they are to judge." He painted the consequences in dark shades, warning against a nameless, faceless "they":

> They may take the care of religion in their own hands; they may establish teachers in every state, county, and parish, and pay them out of the public treasury; they may take into their own hands the education of children . . . they may assume the provision for the poor; they may undertake the regulation of all roads other than post roads.[39]

In February 1792, Jefferson made his move behind the scenes. He asked Washington to transfer the post office and all of its lush patronage appointments from the Treasury to the Department of State. Hamilton's department, Jefferson warned, "possessed already such an influence as to swallow up the whole executive powers." Jefferson insisted that the Treasury Secretary's plans were "a species of gambling, destructive of morality, . . . which had introduced its poison into the government itself." Congressmen "feathered their nests" with government shares, he said, then they perpetuated Hamilton's system. Washington, however, was noncommittal.[40]

In any event, Hamilton's latest initiatives were going nowhere. Congress had no interest in the bounty program of the Report on Manufactures or in SEUM. With financial panics becoming regular events, SEUM expired slowly from lack of both capital and congressional support.[41]

When Congress adjourned in early May 1792, Madison and Jefferson had made some progress. Freneau's paper was broadcasting ever more strident attacks on Hamilton. Their political efforts, abetted by financial panics, had broken the momentum of the Treasury Secretary's seemingly endless store of new initiatives. Jefferson renewed his private campaign against Hamilton. In a letter to the president in late May, he accused his cabinet colleague of working to change "the present republican form of government to that of a monarchy."[42]

At the same time, Hamilton wrote a long and revealing letter about his battles with the Virginians. His confidant was Edward Carrington, the chief revenue collector in Virginia, an ally of Madison's during the ratification battle. Perhaps Hamilton expected Carrington to share the letter with Madison; he certainly did not ask that Carrington keep his remarks confidential.

When he became Treasury Secretary, Hamilton wrote, he expected Madison's support. Without that expectation, he said, he would not have taken the job. After all, Madison had previously agreed with him on funding the debt, on federal assumption of state debts, and on the principle of not discriminating between previous and current debt holders. Madison, in Hamilton's view, then changed his position on each question and now, "cooperating with Mr. Jefferson, is at the head of a faction decidedly hostile to me and my administration." The Treasury Secretary now saw Madison in a new light:

> The opinion I once entertained of the candor and simplicity and fairness of Mr. Madison's character has, I acknowledge, given way to a decided opinion that it is one of a peculiarly artificial and complicated kind.

Hamilton speculated on how he had lost his friend and ally. Perhaps, he suggested, it was Jefferson's malign influence. Madison always held "an exalted opinion of the talents, knowledge and virtues of Mr. Jefferson." He also suggested that Madison was "seduced by the expectation of popularity and possibly by the calculation of advantage to the state of Virginia." Hamilton did not mention the possibility that Madison disagreed with Hamilton's policies and hated their consequences.[43]

Regardless of Hamilton's sore feelings, the falling out among America's leaders was unsurprising. After gaining power, revolutionaries often clash with each other. Differences that seem unimportant while fighting a common foe will sharpen and become intolerable after the foe has been vanquished. There was no conventional power struggle in 1792 because President Washington was beyond challenge. But what would come *after* Washington was up for grabs. The initial battle would be over the ideas and government structure that would shape the nation, a battle that the former revolutionaries were especially well suited to fight. That Madison's partnerships with Hamilton and Washington would suffer was unavoidable.

The president and Congress would face the people's judgment in the 1792 elections, a prospect that revived Washington's longing for retirement. In early May, the president turned again to Madison, asking his opinion on the best time to announce it. When Madison protested that the nation could not afford to lose him as president, Washington answered that he had never been competent to manage public business. Age, he continued, was making him both less able mentally and physically and less able to tolerate the strain of office. He also cited "the spirit of party" and the disagreements between Hamilton and Jefferson in the cabinet.

Still objecting that Washington was essential, Madison advised that a retirement announcement should come at the last possible moment, while still leaving time for the nation to choose a successor. At the president's request, Madison drafted a brief retirement statement. In September, Washington said he had not yet decided what to do, but he never released the announcement. He was reelected, again unanimously.[44]

The vice presidency was another matter, especially under the Constitution's clumsy system of awarding the office to the runner-up in the electoral vote. Because Vice President Adams was not on a party ticket with Washington or really a "running mate," an elector could express dissatisfaction with government policies by not casting his second vote for Adams. Although there was not yet anything like a party structure, Freneau and Madison and Jefferson were using the term "Republican" to describe their policies. Madison defined anti-Republicans, who preferred the honorable title of Federalists, as those who were "more partial to the opulent than to the other classes of society . . . having debauched themselves into a persuasion that mankind are incapable of governing themselves."[45] In 1792, some in the nascent Republican "interest" began to discuss an anti-Adams strategy.

Voting for president was very much a state-centered affair in 1792. Each state had its own method for choosing presidential electors. In some, like South Carolina and New York, the legislature picked them. In others, like Virginia, voters made the choice directly, with some states choosing electors by statewide vote while others chose them by congressional district. In 1792, Republicans in Pennsylvania, New York, and Virginia resolved to push an alternative to Adams as vice president. Senator Aaron Burr of New York was a leading contender until Madison and James Monroe hurriedly insisted that New York Governor George Clinton would command greater support. When the votes were counted, Adams defeated Clinton by a 77–50 vote; Adams received no votes at all in Virginia.

With almost no organization or even a formal candidate for vice president, the Republicans had made a respectable showing. The congressional elections were equally encouraging. With the House of Representatives expanding from 65 to 105 members, Jefferson pronounced that the results provided "a decided majority in favor of the republican interest."[46]

There was no question who led that interest. Toward the end of 1792, a South Carolina congressman referred to Madison as the "general" of the Republicans and to Jefferson as the "generalissimo." A Massachusetts congressman recognized Madison as the opposition's legislative voice: "Virginia moves in a solid column, and the discipline of the party is as severe as the Prussian. Deserters are not spared. Madison is become a desperate party leader."[47]

When Madison wielded his pen for the Republican cause, he was no longer the thoughtful philosopher of *The Federalist*. In late December, he published in Freneau's paper an imagined dialogue between a Republican and an anti-Republican. The Republican proclaims that the people themselves will best keep their own liberties, while the anti-Republican dismisses the people as "stupid, suspicious, licentious." When the anti-Republican denounces his adversary as "an accomplice of atheism and anarchy," the virtuous Republican does not answer in kind because "Liberty disdains to persecute."[48]

Though Hamilton's policies would continue to define the emerging political alignments, soon foreign affairs would be even more divisive. On the other side of the Atlantic, the French Revolution was veering into a bloody phase that triggered a world war lasting twenty years, one that would help define the America that Madison and Jefferson hoped to shape.

13

BECOMING REPUBLICANS

In 1789, many Americans thrilled at the news that the French people had taken to the streets against their government. America's allies against the British, whose troops and fleet had been essential to winning independence, were claiming their own liberty. Lafayette, a hero to Americans, was a leader of the French rising. America seemed to be showing the world the way to freedom. In Paris, Jefferson embraced the revolution and advised its early chiefs.[1]

By 1792, the French Revolution was sinking into violence. The Austrian emperor, concerned for the fate of the French monarchy and of his sister, Queen Marie Antoinette, marched on France. War energized the revolutionaries and weakened King Louis XVI. In August, French mobs killed many of the king's Swiss guards, dethroned the king, and proclaimed a republic.

Unexpectedly, the French revolutionary soldiers prevailed over professional armies from Austria and Prussia. The upheaval grew bloodier. By February 1793, Louis and many aristocrats had been guillotined as enemies of the people. France declared war on Britain. A year before, the British prime minister had predicted fifteen years of peace. He reduced that nation's military by two thousand sailors and five thousand soldiers. His prediction proved to be very wrong.[2]

Americans celebrated the French victories. Despotism would die with the eighteenth century, wrote one of Madison's friends, because America "made the rent in the great curtain that withheld the light from human nature." With Europe's monarchies ganging up on the lone beacon of liberty on that continent, Madison feared that the failure of the French republic could ruin America too. In April 1793, he accepted the title of honorary citizen of France and sent his "anxious wishes for . . . a victory over the minds of [France's] adversaries."[3]

The execution of King Louis and the grisly revolutionary Terror complicated the situation for Americans. By the middle of 1792, Hamilton already scoffed at Madison and Jefferson for their "womanish attachment to France and a womanish resentment against Great Britain." Some Americans recoiled from the violence in France, but Jefferson did not. Rather than see that revolution fail, he wrote, "I would have seen half the earth desolated. Were there but an Adam and Eve left in every country, and left free, it would be better than it is now."[4]

War between Britain and France posed profound policy challenges for the United States that could not be resolved on the simple basis of pro-French or pro-British sympathies. Though many American hearts sided with the French, some heads favored the British. As Madison had lamented for years, the British dominated American trade with their extensive merchant fleet, their trading network, and their deep capital. Between 1787 and 1790, almost 90 percent of America's imports of manufactured goods came from Britain. In addition, the six hundred warships of the Royal Navy commanded the Atlantic. For more than a century, that navy was the most effective tool for projecting power on the planet. America, with a few ill-kept ships in a neglected naval service, could not challenge it. Even the French navy, less than half the size of Britain's, heavily outgunned the Americans. If the United States supported either of the combatants, America's merchant fleet would be at the mercy of the other.[5]

In late April, President Washington issued a proclamation that America would "pursue a conduct friendly and impartial towards the belligerent powers." Called the Neutrality Proclamation, Washington's statement warned that any American taking active part in the conflict would face punishment.

Jefferson and Hamilton agreed that the United States should not enter the war, but they differed sharply on related questions. Hamilton insisted that America's 1778 treaty with France was void because the revolution swept away the monarchy that signed it. Jefferson, in turn, opposed Washington's proclamation because he thought the congressional power to declare war included the exclusive power to declare that there was "no war." Madison agreed that the president had exceeded his powers, calling the proclamation an "unfortunate error." It "wounds the national honor," he wrote, by failing to support France, and it also gave the executive too much sway.[6] The emerging division at the top of the American government held some ironies. Madison and Jefferson had fought the Revolution in meeting rooms, not on battlefields, but they were implacably opposed to the British; Washington and Hamilton, who had faced death from British arms, were more readily reconciled with their former enemies.

Jefferson now openly opposed Hamilton during cabinet meetings; he later recalled being "daily pitted like two cocks." Disdainfully, he described Hamilton in one meeting as delivering a "speech of ¾ of an hour as inflammatory and declamatory as if he had been speaking to a jury." Jefferson resented that Secretary of War Henry Knox steadfastly supported Hamilton while Attorney General Edmund Randolph waffled, leaving Jefferson outnumbered. At one session, Jefferson related, Randolph "found out a hair to split, which, as always happens, became the decision."[7]

From the spring of 1793, the budding contest between Republicans and Federalists spread to foreign policy. Though public opinion would vacillate with events, over the long run the pro-French Republicans held the high ground. Only the French had supported American independence. Only the French spoke a common language of liberty and opposition to monarchy. The romantic image of valiant France, surrounded by monarchist jackals, appealed to Americans. And the British, through the Royal Navy, posed an immediate threat to American trade and self-respect.[8]

First, however, the Republicans had to survive the brash new emissary from France, Edmond-Charles Genet.

Genet was young, barely thirty. His country faced enemies on every border and at sea. A pro-royalist rebellion churned in the Vendée region, food shortages pinched French bellies, and inflation sapped the economy. A bloody slave revolt raged in one of her richest colonies, the sugar island of Saint-Domingue (now Haiti and the Dominican Republic). France needed help. She expected it from her sister republic across the Atlantic.

In early April 1792, Genet received a hero's welcome from crowds that thronged the harbor when he landed in Charleston, South Carolina. He made a triumphant overland procession to Philadelphia, enjoying public dinners and receptions along the way. Crowds sang the "Marseillaise" to him while French flags fluttered alongside the Stars and Stripes. Well-spoken and good-looking, Genet made a good first impression. Philadelphians greeted him in mid-May with a huge reception and festivities hosted by the French Benevolent Society, the German Republican Society, and other groups.[9]

In meetings with Washington and Jefferson, however, Genet stumbled badly, showing himself ignorant of or indifferent to American concerns. Both Americans rejected the Frenchman's demand that the United States accelerate its repayment of debts owed to France. While in Charleston and Norfolk, Virginia, Genet had commissioned French privateers, which were already bringing captured British ships into American waters as prizes. Few actions could so swiftly destroy American neutrality and bring conflict with Britain. When Genet reached Philadelphia, he commissioned more privateers, then dispatched an agent to Kentucky to recruit Americans to invade the Spanish territories of Louisiana and Florida. Genet was "calamitous," Jefferson wrote to Madison: "hotheaded, all imagination, no judgment, passionate, disrespectful and even indecent towards the P[resident]." Genet threatened to appeal over Washington's head to Congress and the American people.[10]

While Jefferson wrestled with the impetuous French diplomat, he longed to leave office. The disputes in the cabinet were wearing him down. In a letter, Madison insisted that no matter how unpleasant the cabinet sessions were, "every consideration private as well as public require[s] a further sacrifice of your longings for the repose of Monticello." His decision to retire, Jefferson answered tartly, "will rest on my own feelings alone." He did not owe perpetual service to the nation, "for that would be to be born a slave." Jefferson's wish to escape Philadelphia produced a lyrical passage:

> The motion of my blood no longer keeps time with the tumult of the world. It leads me to seek for happiness in the lap and love of my family, in the society of my neighbors and books, in the wholesome occupations of my farms and my affairs, in an interest or affection in every bud that opens, in every breath that blows around me.

After descending into self-pity—portraying himself as "giving [up] everything I love, in exchange for everything I hate, and all this without a single gratification"—Jefferson delivered a stiff warning to Madison: "So never let there be more between you and me on this subject."[11]

After only two months of dealing with Genet, Jefferson knew that the Frenchman was hopeless. "I saw," he wrote, "the necessity of quitting a wreck which could not but sink all who should cling to it." The cabinet unanimously agreed to demand that France recall Genet. Jefferson called it "true wisdom in the Republican party to approve unequivocally of a state of neutrality."[12]

Hamilton defended Washington's neutrality policy in a series of powerful newspaper essays under the name "Pacificus." Jefferson pleaded for Madison to respond to Hamilton's pro-British message. "For god's sake, my dear sir," he wrote, "take up your pen, select the most striking heresies, and cut him to pieces in the face of the public. There is nobody else who can and will enter the lists with him."[13]

Madison accepted the challenge, though he called the effort "the most grating one I ever experienced." He produced five essays under the name "Helvidius." Sometimes displaying an unrefined partisanship, they were not his best work. Nonetheless, Madison produced a stern warning against the growth of executive powers during foreign crises. "War," he wrote, "is in fact the true nurse of executive aggrandizement." He explained:

> In war the public treasures are to be unlocked, and it is the executive hand which is to dispense them. In war the honors and emoluments of office are to be multiplied; and it is the executive patronage under which they are to be enjoyed. It is in war, finally, that laurels are to be gathered, and it is the executive brow they are to encircle.[14]

The Genet controversy erupted in public demonstrations. Moving to capitalize on Genet's blunders—Madison called him a madman in a private letter—Federalists organized protest meetings in New York, Richmond, and twenty other towns. When those sessions adopted resolutions condemning the French government, Madison recruited James Monroe to help him organize a response. In eight Virginia counties, countermeetings adopted resolutions recalling France's support for American liberty and decrying efforts to model American government on British monarchy.[15]

Though the Genet episode was a setback for Madison and Jefferson, they hoped it would be temporary. The people, Madison insisted, were "averse to monarchy and to a political connection with that of Great Britain."[16] Then a plague descended on the nation's capital and washed away most thoughts of Genet's offenses.

"At first three out of four died," Jefferson wrote from Philadelphia in early September. "Now about one out of three. It comes on with a pain in the head, sick stomach, then a chill, fever, black vomiting and stools, and death from the second to the eighth day." Dr. Rush, who treated hundreds during the epidemic, provided a similar chart of the disease: chills and fever, then languor and nausea, then "stupor, delirium, slow pulse, bloodshot eyes, yellowness," and finally, "a bleeding at the nose, from the gums and from the bowels, and vomiting of black matter."[17]

It was yellow fever. It settled on the city for two months, killing many and terrifying the rest. Close to half the residents fled. Hamilton fell ill but recovered. "Deaths are now about 30 a day," Jefferson wrote in mid-September. "All flying who can."[18]

Jefferson's estimate of the death rate proved low. More than a hundred deaths a day were recorded into October. The young Todd family was cut in half when the pestilence carried off attorney John Todd and the younger of his sons, leaving his widow, Dolley, a single mother with an infant boy. For two months, most of civic Philadelphia, including the national government, simply stopped.[19] Roughly four thousand died, about 10 percent of the population.

Madison, staying at Montpelier, avoided the epidemic but not the hand of death. In early October, his younger brother Ambrose died at thirty-eight, the early death Madison had expected for himself. Ambrose, who managed the plantation with their father, left a widow, a daughter, and more responsibility for his eldest brother. With James Sr. now seventy, Madison was drawn deeper into his family's orbit.[20]

The president planned for Congress to convene in Germantown, near Philadelphia, to avoid the epidemic. In mid-November, Jefferson secured lodgings with a Germantown family for both Madison and Monroe, who was now a senator from Virginia. But the fever was receding and the city rebounded quickly, so Madison and his colleagues met in Philadelphia.[21]

Signs of change were evident as the Third Congress began. Though party affiliations were still casual, Republicans held rough majorities in both houses. The Speaker of the House, Frederick Muhlenberg of Pennsylvania, identified himself as a Republican. In a few months, the Senate would open its deliberations to the public. In the fifth year of the Washington administration, the cabinet would turn over. Jefferson carried out his long-threatened resignation and was succeeded by Attorney General Edmund Randolph.

Jefferson's valedictory was a report on America's commerce. He stressed Britain's domination of it, which coincided with disturbing news from that land. King George's government issued "Orders in

Council" authorizing the Royal Navy to seize the ships of neutral nations like the United States if they traded with France or its colonies. Anti-British sentiment flared, further obscuring Genet's offenses.

This back-and-forth pattern would continue for the next twenty years. First one of the major powers would inflame American opinion with high-handed disregard for American rights, then the other would. The pattern was likely unavoidable. Both nations, the superpowers of the day, were locked in a fight to the death, desperately scrabbling for ways to injure their enemy. For both, the United States was a minor concern: a small nation, an ocean away, with a tiny navy. America mattered only as a source of goods. Each superpower wished to have those goods and to deny them to its adversary. With America's commercial fortunes in the hands of powerful nations indifferent to its interests, it became a diplomatic shuttlecock.

Jefferson's retirement left Madison the unquestioned Republican leader. Their partnership gave a unique strength to the emerging Republican Party: The two men trusted each other so completely, and agreed so closely on the central issues of the day, that they could take turns as opposition leader. This extraordinary depth allowed each to retire for several years without any material setback to their cause.

Soon Federalists were calling the Republicans "Madison's party"; one termed Madison "the great man of the party." He had, a Connecticut congressman wrote, "unquestionably the most personal influence of any man in the House of Representatives," which he exercised with "infinite prudence and industry," applying his reason "upon everything with the greatest nicety and precision."[22]

Brandishing Jefferson's report on trade and riding the wave of public anger against the British, Madison once more demanded that trade policies discriminate against Britain, which still had no commercial treaty with the United States. The United States, he insisted, could be neutral in the European war while still favoring French trade, since France had signed a commercial treaty with America. After buttonholing individual congressmen to muster support, he presented resolutions raising import taxes and vessel duties for nations having no commercial treaty with the United States (that is, Britain). His goal, he told the House, was for America "to make her enemies feel the extent of her power," though not her military power.[23]

On January 14, Madison rose in the House to renew his challenge to British trade. America's ships carried the vast majority of its trade with other nations, he stressed, but British ships monopolized Anglo-

American trade. America's agricultural products were vital to Britain while British manufactured goods were mere "superfluities" to America. Retaliation against Britain would impose some costs on Americans, but Britain would be brought to heel:

> Her merchants would feel it. Her navigation would feel it. Her manufactures would feel it. Her West Indies would be ruined by it. Her revenue would deeply feel it. And her government would feel it through every nerve of its operations.[24]

Though his voice was low and his manner modest, Madison had learned to command the chamber. "Madison engaged our attention for two hours and a half," a Massachusetts congressman wrote home. "[I]n a full House and thronged with spectators there was such perfect silence that you might almost have heard a pin fall. In short, eloquence which baffle[s] everything I had ever heard and almost beyond description."[25] But Madison had no greater luck on the specific issue before that House than he had before; Congress took no action to discriminate against British shipping.

By March, Americans learned the extent of the Royal Navy assault on American merchantmen. The nation's ships "have had a terrible slam in the West Indies," Madison wrote to Jefferson. "About a hundred vessels have been seized by the British for condemnation." That total soon doubled. Madison briefly became the darling of the merchants for his hostility to Britain. American ship captains detained in Jamaica by British seizures adopted a petition endorsing Madison and greeted his January resolutions "with universal applause." Jefferson wrote from Monticello that Virginians, remembering "their ancient hatred to Great Britain," stood with Madison. But public opinion rushed past Madison's measured policies. A rueful Madison noted that those who had opposed his efforts to discriminate against British trade were now demanding more drastic anti-British measures, including creation of a "provisional" army—one that would exist only on paper but could be summoned in an emergency. Such rash steps, he thought, could provoke war.[26]

President Washington had no wish for war. He resolved to send a special envoy to Britain to negotiate a peaceful resolution. He asked the Supreme Court's chief justice, John Jay, to undertake the mission. Jay, whose judicial duties were light, sailed for London in May.[27]

With Jay's departure, the war clamor subsided. Congress could not muster the will to approve a mere thirty-day embargo on foreign trade. Madison reported to Jefferson that since Washington opposed commercial retaliation against Britain, it would not happen. "The influence of the executive on events," he wrote, "and the public confidence in the P[resident], are an overmatch for all the efforts Republicanism can make." The Senate's Republicans, he added, were "completely wrecked," and in the House they were "in a much worse condition."[28]

Through the country, however, Republican political sentiment was spreading in controversial new forms. America's first grass-roots political clubs blossomed in the form of "democratic-republican societies." Starting with the German Republican Society of Philadelphia in April 1793, the organizers were inspired by the French Revolution to gather together and express their opposition to monarchy, financial speculation, and taxes. The societies were not formally interconnected, but they corresponded with and visited each other. They adopted resolutions and issued addresses on public issues. They sponsored educational programs. They believed, as did Madison, that the people must be vigilant over government. At their peak, at least forty societies flourished from Massachusetts to South Carolina and west into Kentucky. The societies were a largely urban phenomenon; the majority of their members were mechanics and workmen, small merchants and tradesmen.[29]

As the societies grew, an antitax movement took root in the West, in the lands of the Appalachian Mountains and beyond. Westerners alternately felt neglected and oppressed by the distant government on the Atlantic coast. They complained that no troops protected them from hostile Indians and that trade through Spanish New Orleans remained throttled. At the same time, westerners particularly resented Hamilton's excise on whiskey, a key product for western farmers. Because it was expensive to send grain to market down the Mississippi or over the mountains, western farmers often distilled it. Whiskey sometimes served as a medium of exchange in the West. Collecting the whiskey excise could be a dangerous business for tax men bold enough to try.[30]

The democratic-republican societies in western Pennsylvania became centers of the antigovernment sentiment. Discontent boiled over in the summer of 1794. A mob burned down the home of a Pennsylvania tax collector. On August 1, the antitax agitators mustered six thousand men in a "grand review" near Pittsburgh. Six days later, President Washington called out more than ten thousand militiamen to meet the threat to the government. Though the episode was called the Whiskey Rebellion, not a great deal happened. Washington assumed command of his army at Carlisle, Pennsylvania, then returned to Philadelphia, with Hamilton serving as his conspicuous second. As the armed force traveled west, the rebels melted away. In Jefferson's skeptical phrase, "insurrection was announced and proclaimed and armed against, but could never be found." A few supposed ringleaders were arrested.[31]

Madison shed no tears for the whiskey rebels. They were, he wrote, "doing the business of despotism" because they gave Hamilton a pretext for creating an army. When public opinion repudiated the tax resisters, Madison was relieved there would be no calls for a large standing army.[32]

The not-quite-rebellion spawned a political sideshow. In his annual message to Congress at the end of 1794, the president referred with some asperity to the democratic-republican societies as "self-created societies." By the standards of political discourse in America, it was a fairly tepid remark, but it was the first time the great Washington had betrayed a partisan sentiment in public. Republicans pounced. What was the problem with self-created societies? they asked. After all, wasn't the Society of the Cincinnati, the organization of Continental Army officers, also self-created? Madison saw the president's statement as a crass ploy by Hamilton to trade on Washington's popularity (a ploy Madison knew well), which was "perhaps the greatest error in [Washington's] political life." Jefferson agreed, calling it an act of "boldness . . . from the faction of Monocrats."[33]

Jefferson's withdrawal to Monticello in no way weakened his connection with Madison. They knew how to sustain their intellectual engagement when apart. Politics, of course, was their principal shared concern. Whichever of them resided at the center of affairs took the burden of relating news and developments. In the spring and summer of 1793, Jefferson in Philadelphia wrote weekly to Madison at Montpelier. When their positions were reversed in March 1794, Madison wrote regularly to Jefferson from Philadelphia—seven times in a single month.[34]

Their correspondence went beyond politics. They reported on weather patterns and the progress of crops. Always searching for improved yields, they speculated on crop rotation and the potential of new plant strains like Jamaica corn or African upland rice. Their mechanical speculations included designs for the moldboards of plows and threshing machines, Jefferson's drop-leaf table system, and locks and hinges that Madison could not seem to describe to Jefferson's satisfaction.

When younger brother William was designing a new home, Madison sent the plans for Jefferson to review.[35]

Jefferson's letters bubbled with bonhomie and affection. In one, he burst out, "I long to see you."[36] On the page, Madison did not easily reciprocate such frankness. At no time was this emotional asymmetry more conspicuous than in the spring of 1794, as Madison fell in love with Dolley Payne Todd.

The family account holds that in the spring of 1794, Congressman Madison passed the young widow on a Philadelphia street and was "struck with her charms." Slightly taller than Madison, Mrs. Todd had an hourglass figure, a ready smile, and a merry disposition. Philadelphia was not so large that it was difficult to learn more about her; indeed, the Virginian may already have known her story. Mrs. Todd's first husband had been a rising lawyer from a Quaker family; her mother rented rooms to congressmen and other government officials, including Senator Aaron Burr of New York. Though she had lived in Philadelphia for a decade, Dolley Todd spent her formative years on Virginia plantations—Madison's world.

Burr, Madison's acquaintance from college days in Princeton, was the go-between. Mrs. Todd wrote a friend that "the great little Madison has asked [Burr] to bring him to see me this evening." Her phrase conveys a clear-eyed appreciation of Madison's stature, in every sense of the term. Her caller was a great man in the American republic, and he came from a wealthy family. He also was small, balding, far from dashing, and over forty. Mrs. Todd at twenty-five combined vitality and charm, and she had inherited some property from her husband. In an era when courtship and marriage were practical enterprises, she knew her worth. She also knew she could do much worse than "the great little Madison."[37]

The courtship advanced largely behind the veil of history, though two glimpses reveal Madison as an ardent suitor. On June 1, as Congress finished its session and he prepared to return to Virginia, he recruited Mrs. Todd's cousin to write a letter on his behalf. In a note that he approved "with sparkling eyes" before it was sent, the cousin wrote to Dolley that Madison "thinks so much of you in the day that he has lost his tongue, at night he dreams of you and starts in his sleep calling on you to relieve his flame for he burns to such an excess that he will be shortly consumed." Madison added his wish that Mrs. Todd's "heart will be callous to every other swain but himself."

To underline the seriousness of his intentions, the letter said that

Madison had rented James Monroe's house in Philadelphia while Monroe left for France to serve as American Minister, adding: "[D]o you like it [the house]?" Madison was rushing pell-mell upon the citadel.[38] This was not the calculating, cerebral politician seen by much of the world.

Madison's letter to Jefferson at Monticello on that same day included no reference to Mrs. Todd, nor did any earlier letter to Jefferson. Madison's silence on that subject could have been due to anxiety about the fate of his courtship, or to delicacy about romantic matters, or to a reserve that Madison could not overcome.

By August, matters with Mrs. Todd had progressed sufficiently that she came to Virginia, ostensibly to visit her relatives. Answering a letter that has not survived, Madison's ardor was undiminished: "I cannot express, but hope you will conceive the joy [your letter] gave me." Illness evidently had delayed her travels, which "filled me with extreme disquietude," but Madison was relieved by news of her resumed journey. The letter included the hope that "the sentiments of my heart can guarantee those of yours."[39]

The wedding came quickly. They exchanged vows on September 15, the anniversary of the wedding between Madison's parents. Like most Virginia weddings of the time, it was a family affair, held at the western Virginia home of Dolley's sister Lucy and George Steptoe Washington, the president's nephew. The clergyman who presided was married to a cousin of Madison's.

On the day of the ceremony, Mrs. Todd slipped away to write to her best friend. Her version of the event was not that of an excited bride but of a woman of the world. She was giving her hand that day, she wrote, "to the man who of all others I most admire." Their union would provide "everything that is soothing and grateful in prospect—and my little Payne [her surviving son] will have a generous and tender protector." After describing the property settlement for her son, she signed, "Dolley Payne Todd." The final writing on the sheet, entered after the wedding ceremony, struck a slightly rueful note as she recorded her new name: "Evening. Dolley Madison! Alas!"[40]

Her besotted bridegroom did not announce his marriage to Jefferson until weeks later, his syntax stiffening with the news. His entire description of the event was that on the fifteenth of the month "I had the happiness to accomplish the alliance which I intimated to you I had been some time soliciting."[41] For three weeks after the wedding, the newlyweds lingered at the homes of different relatives. In October they began their return to Philadelphia, where they occupied the Monroes' modest house on North Eighth Street.

Madison had dramatically changed his personal life. For so long a bachelor in boardinghouses and the extra man at social events, he now had a household: a vivacious and outgoing wife, her teenage sister, Anna, and a stepson aged two and a half. The tranquillity of his days and evenings would be but a memory. So too would any loneliness.

Soon John Jay would report the results of his diplomatic mission to England, which would transform Madison's political life.

14

PARTY WARRIOR

I n London, Jay signed a treaty with the British in November 1794, though President Washington did not receive the document until the following March. The president kept the treaty secret until the Senate could take it up in June. After ratifying all but one paragraph of Jay's treaty, the Senate still did not release it publicly. Not until mid-summer 1795 did Republican senators funnel it to the press. The text, as Madison put it, "flew with an electric velocity to every part of the Union." Not many liked it.[1]

Jay had little leverage in the negotiation. Alarmed by French military power, the British were in no mood to be generous. They did not fear America's few hundred soldiers nor its creaky warships. Madison had long preached that trade retaliation would bring Britain to heel, but most Americans doubted it. As Hamilton wrote to Washington, a trade war would eliminate imports "necessary to us in peace, and more necessary" in wartime; it also would dry up import taxes.[2]

Jay secured only slight advantages. The British renewed the promise made twelve years earlier to vacate their forts around the Great Lakes. Commissioners from both nations would address boundary disputes, the pre-1776 debts owed by Americans to British merchants, and British seizures of American ships. But American maritime rights as a neutral went unprotected, permitting the British to seal off trade with France and its colonies. The British could continue trading with the Indian tribes in America's West and could travel the Mississippi River to do so.[3]

Calling the treaty a "ruinous bargain," Madison blamed it on Jay's politics. The Federalists, he fulminated, were "a British party, systematically aiming at an exclusive connection with the British government and ready to sacrifice . . . the dearest interests of our commerce [and] the most sacred dictates of national honor." Virginians, he reported, were universally disgusted with the treaty. Even in New England and the middle states, the public response was negative. Protesters burned Jay in effigy in Philadelphia, Boston, and New York. Hamilton, having resigned as Treasury Secretary months before, tried to speak for the treaty at a street meeting in New York. He was stoned.[4]

Despite the outcry against the treaty, the president signed it. It was better than war. The Republicans should have had a golden opportunity to capitalize on public discontent, but as soon as anti-British feelings flashed through the nation, they began to ebb.

It started with Hamilton, always Hamilton. With characteristic energy, he defended the treaty in twenty-eight newspaper essays under three separate pseudonyms. Some of his essays answered others of his essays. Peace with Britain was essential, he argued, and would bring prosperity. From Monticello, Jefferson bemoaned Hamilton's onslaught. "There is nobody but yourself who can meet him," he wrote to Madison. "For god's sake take up your pen and give a fundamental reply."[5]

This time, Madison passed. As he had learned two years before, dueling with Hamilton in the public press was a thankless task. No one could match the New Yorker's output, much less his incisive reasoning and sharp rhetoric. Among a generation that bristled with "gladiators of the quill," Hamilton stood alone. Far better, Madison resolved, to challenge the treaty on his home ground, in the House of Representatives.[6]

Before Congress convened at the end of 1795, Republican prospects waned. Rapprochement with Britain brought prosperity as Europe gorged on American goods. American exports rose by 50 percent, as did the prices they commanded, while import prices declined. Rage over the treaty melted away as Americans remembered, again, how much they trusted President Washington.[7]

When Congress met in early December, Madison could feel the tide running against him. He predicted that the Federalists would argue "it is too soon now to meddle with [the treaty], as they will hereafter pretend it is then too late." The treaty's defenders, he wrote to Jefferson, were planning "to blazon the public prosperity, to confound the treaty with the president, and to mouth over the stale topics of war and confusion."[8]

Madison would not let them off so easy. He would press the fight, though the ground might not be especially favorable. He was a party leader now and would not back down.

• • •

In framing his attack on the Jay Treaty, Madison explored another inconsistency in the Constitution. Under the charter, the executive negotiates a treaty, which becomes the law of the land if two-thirds of the Senate concurs in it. But that means that binding federal law is created without any participation by the House of Representatives.

That outcome, Madison argued, was wrong. Article I of the Constitution states that "all legislative powers . . . shall be vested in a Congress of the United States, which shall consist of a Senate and House of Representatives." If *all* lawmaking includes the House, then what of treaty-created law, which the House never touches? In conversations at Monticello in October 1795, Madison and Jefferson resolved to use this argument to attack the treaty. Jefferson insisted that the House actually could reject a treaty, but Madison chose a more modest position: that the House could decline to adopt measures needed to implement a treaty.[9]

As Congress gathered in Philadelphia, Madison thought a majority in the House opposed the treaty. He feared, however, that some would not vote their convictions. "The name of the P[resident] is everywhere used with the most wonderful success by the Treaty partisans," Madison wrote. The president did not officially transmit the treaty to the House until early March 1796, ensuring it did not come up before the announcement of a very popular treaty with Spain. Under that agreement, Americans gained the right to deposit trade goods in New Orleans as well as full use of the Mississippi.[10]

The legislative fight began with a resolution asking the president for the diplomatic papers relating to the Jay Treaty. Madison plunged into the constitutional contradiction he had identified. If the House must enforce a treaty ratified by the Senate, he said, then treaties could be used to exclude the House from all lawmaking: "If, by treaty, . . . the president and Senate can regulate trade, they can also declare war, they can raise armies to carry on war, and they can procure money to support armies." Yet the Constitution gave those powers to *both* houses of Congress. If the House "must carry all treaties into effect," he said, "it would no longer exercise a legislative power; it . . . would have no will of its own."[11]

By late March, the president refused the House's request for the treaty papers. To determine their next step, House Republicans caucused as a party for the first time ever. On April 2, they decided to present resolutions asserting the House's power not to enact a law that would implement a treaty.[12] In doing so, Madison had to confront an uncomfortable precedent: The Philadelphia Convention had rejected a proposal that a treaty should not become law unless implemented by statute. That rejection—which was known to all who were at the Convention—certainly implied that treaties become law without any involvement of the House of Representatives.

Though he might have explained that Convention episode away on other grounds, Madison dismissed it with a thoroughly unpersuasive argument. The intentions of those at the Philadelphia Convention, he told the House, were no "oracular guide" to the Constitution, which was a "dead letter" until the state conventions ratified it; by those ratifications, "life and validity were breathed into it by the voice of the people." Thus the state conventions were the true guide to constitutional meaning, and amendments proposed in the state conventions were even "better authority."[13]

In coming years, Madison would repeat that the ratifying conventions provide important guidance for constitutional interpretation. The contention is an odd one, since the ratifying conventions provide, at best, wildly inconsistent guidance. Most obviously, the ratifying conventions merely cast up-or-down votes on the entire Constitution. They could not change a single word in the document. Only when former delegates in Philadelphia spoke in the state meetings do those debates provide insight into why certain phrases in the text were chosen or others rejected. Moreover, there were thirteen ratifying conventions, but only nine had to act in order to create the new government. Does that mean that the last four state ratifications (including Virginia's) were irrelevant? What if a single delegate in a single ratifying convention offered an interpretation of a provision—what weight could that statement have had when hundreds of delegates in the other twelve conventions neither heard him nor raised a similar point? To be accorded authority, should an interpretation have been discussed in at least seven of the thirteen conventions? Or five of the first nine? Even those remarks that were recorded are of doubtful importance: they were simply the views of a single delegate, or a few, unratified by any action by the state conventions.

The amendments proposed by the ratifying conventions were even less useful. For example, Madison triumphantly noted that two state conventions proposed amendments to limit the treaty power. But those proposed amendments were never adopted, so they prove only what the Constitution does *not* say. Moreover, eleven other state conventions adopted no such proposals. By exalting the ratifying conventions as constitutional authority, Madison clung to an incoherent system of constitutional interpretation.

Madison's performance in the treaty debate disgusted many Federalists. His conduct, one wrote, "will serve to plunge him in infamy—and ruin his hard-earned and long-continued reputation." A Massachusetts congressman considered the Virginian "irrevocably disgraced, . . . devoid of sincerity and fairness."[14]

Madison could feel the antitreaty votes melting away. Through "mercantile influence and the alarm of war," he wrote to Monroe, treaty advocates persuaded "seven or eight of the stiffest antitreaty men [to take] a wrongheaded course." Still, he did not back down, speaking in support of the resolution to the end, when it lost by a narrow margin.[15]

By pressing a misbegotten constitutional argument in the treaty debate, Madison again showed that he cared more for political victory than for consistent constitutional interpretation. For him, constitutional construction was a means for achieving political ends. A cynic might argue that exalting the state ratifying conventions would shift attention away from inconvenient statements Madison himself made at the Philadelphia Convention.[16] It also would free him (and everyone else) to scavenge for authoritative precedent from among the two hundred amendments proposed by the state conventions and statements by scores of state delegates. More likely, Madison was grasping for the best argument he could contrive to defend a position that was fast eroding. At a minimum, the inglorious episode demonstrated his partisan feelings overpowering his constitutional judgment.[17]

Strain was showing in Madison's appearance as well as in his arguments. "Mr. Madison," wrote Vice President Adams, "looks worried to death. Pale, withered, haggard." A Federalist editor pronounced him finished: "As a politician he is no more; he is absolutely deceased, cold, stiff, and buried in oblivion for ever and ever." Madison confessed to Jefferson both his fatigue and his frustration with his fellow Republicans:

> The progress of this business throughout has to me been the most worrying and vexatious that I ever encountered; and the more so as the causes lay in the unsteadiness, the follies, the perverseness, and the defections among our friends, more than in the strength or dexterity, or malice of our opponents.

His consolation, he wrote, was that he would soon withdraw from public life.[18]

Since Jefferson's retirement more than two years before, Madison had carried the Republican banner largely on his own. He was bone-weary from the effort. He also had responsibilities to a young wife, a stepson, and his parents. His father, after a life of labor, had developed painful sciatica; brother Ambrose, who had borne many family responsibilities, was gone.

One more challenge stood between Madison and his escape from public service: steering the Republicans through the election of 1796, when the nation would choose Washington's successor. The Jay Treaty debacle, he wrote to Jefferson, "ought to have been so managed as to fortify the Republican cause," but instead "left it in a very crippled condition."[19]

Everyone expected the president to retire after two terms. Washington made no secret of his wish to return to Mount Vernon. In mid-May 1796, before any official statement had come from Washington, Madison wrote that Jefferson was the expected presidential candidate "on one side" and "Adams apparently on the other."[20]

Washington had demonstrated the power of the presidency. Madison wished that power to reside in Republican hands. As the party's national leader, Madison's first problem involved his own candidate. Jefferson, entrenched at Monticello for the preceding thirty months, would not say out loud that he wanted to be president. Indeed, Jefferson insisted that it was Madison who should be the next president. In December 1794, with newlywed Madison groaning back into his congressional harness in Philadelphia, Jefferson urged him to continue serving until he moved on "to a more splendid and a more efficacious post"—the presidency.

> There I should rejoice to see you: I hope I may say I *shall* rejoice to see you. I have long had much in my mind to say to you on that subject. But double delicacies have kept me silent.[21]

Anticipating Madison's objection that Jefferson was the natural Republican choice for president, Jefferson declared he would not leave retirement "for the empire of the universe."

Madison was not fooled. He knew that only Jefferson could lead the Republicans. He replied impatiently that "reasons of every kind, and some of them of the most insuperable as well as the most obvious kind, shut my mind against the admission of any idea such as you seem to glance at." Reserving the subject for a time when they might have "a free conversation," Madison gave fair warning: "You ought to be preparing yourself however to hear truth which no inflexibility will be able to withstand."[22]

Jefferson persevered. A month later he insisted that he had proposed Madison for president "with entire sincerity":

> [T]here is not another person in the United States who being placed at the helm of our affairs, my mind would be so completely at rest for the fortune of our political bark. The wish too was pure and unmixed with anything respecting myself personally.

Jefferson added a long protest that his health was "entirely broken down," his love of family and farming beyond measure, and that "the little spice of ambition, which I had in my younger days, has long since evaporated."[23]

Madison still was not buying it. Jefferson, not Madison, was the Republicans' best candidate. The "insuperable" and "obvious" reasons went well beyond their eight-inch height differential, though that was a fair place to start. Leadership is personal. A leader inspires confidence and loyalty. Tall, square-shouldered, amiable, and nimble-witted, Jefferson inspired both with an air of relaxed command. Short, skinny, pale, and reserved, Madison's slightly anxious and remote manner took more time to appreciate. In 1795, Napoleon Bonaparte was demonstrating that height is not essential for a great leader. Madison too had found ways to project himself as a leader. But a choice between him and Jefferson was not a difficult one.

Other factors amplified Jefferson's stature. He was eight years older, with greater claim to the patriotic myth of 1776, having served in the Continental Congress and written the Declaration of Independence. (His authorship of that document, however, was not widely known until the presidential election of 1800.) As American Minister to France, he had met with kings and revolutionaries. Perhaps equally important, he had little public role in the partisan bloodletting of the last several years. Hamilton and Madison had exchanged broadsides in the press, while Madison daily sparred with opponents in the House of Representatives. Jefferson seemed to float above the struggle, first opposing Hamilton in the privacy of the cabinet and then retiring to Monticello. In addition, despite his insistence to the contrary, Jefferson was a gifted politician with a zest for political combat.[24]

Madison applied a simple solution to his reluctant-candidate problem: He ignored his candidate. Throughout the summer and early autumn of 1796, while political maneuvering proceeded around the nation, Madison avoided traveling the thirty miles between Montpelier and Monticello. "I have not seen Jefferson," he confided to a friend in late September, "and have thought it best to present him with no opportunity of protesting . . . against being embarked in the contest." From June 1 until December, no letter passed between the two friends. It was a novel campaign arrangement and not far from ridiculous: Jefferson knew that Madison and other Republicans were pressing his candidacy; Madison knew that Jefferson knew. Yet by ignoring each other, Jefferson could preserve the fiction that he did not want the office and Madison could get on with the business of winning it for him. "The Republicans," he had written early in 1796, "knowing that Jefferson alone can be started with hope of success, mean to push him."[25]

Madison's next problem was how to win the election. The young nation had never had a contested presidential election. Parties existed only as loose groupings in the Congress and among the politically engaged in some states. The electoral process was still completely decentralized. In seven states, the legislature chose the presidential electors; four others allowed voters to choose electors by district; in two states voters chose electors on a statewide ballot, while three states used systems that blended different elements.

Madison and Jefferson began the election season with a signal advantage: Virginia, by far the most important state, was the most solidly Republican. According to the 1790 census, one out of five Americans lived in Virginia, which comprised about 20 percent of the nation's land area.[26] In 1796, Virginia would cast 21 electoral votes. With only 70 needed to win, a clean sweep of Virginia would give Jefferson 30 percent of a winning total. No other state could provide such a solid base.

A second advantage came from a happy combination of ideology and talent. Though wealthy landowners themselves, Madison and Jefferson were fashioning a political party that claimed to speak for the common people. The best political operatives, it quickly emerged, were common types who gravitated to the Republicans. These ambitious men pioneered electioneering techniques—including the creation of political tickets and local organizations—that aristocratic Virginians might find unseemly. Prominent among the innovators was John Beckley, who earned a reputation for energy and political craft from his Philadelphia base. In 1795, when Madison had no stomach for the newspaper war over the Jay Treaty, Beckley stepped forward as the Republican champion. In September 1795, he sent circular letters to

Republicans to rally opposition to the treaty, making sure that "all our movements are kept secret." For the 1796 presidential contest, Beckley sent out thirty thousand handbills in Pennsylvania alone, instructing one rider to follow close behind a Federalist operative and destroy any Federalist handbills left behind before passing out the Republican sheets.[27]

Though Republican leaders supported Jefferson for president, there was no consensus on a vice presidential choice. Republican congressmen caucused on the question but could not agree. The choice devolved upon party members in each state. Pennsylvanians and New Yorkers favored Aaron Burr, but southerners mistrusted the New Yorker.[28]

The public phase of the campaign began with the release of Washington's Farewell Address in mid-September. To prepare his address, Washington worked from a draft by Hamilton. Famously, the departing president counseled Americans to "steer clear of permanent alliances with any portion of the foreign world." He warned against the "baneful effects of the spirit of party," a spirit he called the "worst enemy" of popular government. In an apocalyptic passage, he predicted that party rivalry would produce "the most horrid enormities" and "the ruins of public liberty."

As one Federalist wrote, Washington's farewell served as "a signal, like dropping a hat, for the party racers to start." Washington's cautions against party spirit evaporated, though the campaign was a relatively muted affair by later standards. Neither Jefferson nor Adams gave a public speech or issued a public statement. Their surrogates campaigned for them and did so with little concern for the disputes of the preceding four years, largely ignoring the Jay Treaty, Genet's misconduct, the Bank of the United States, and the funding of the debt. Instead, they framed the contest as one of personalities.

Republicans identified Jefferson as a friend of the people and Adams as a monarchist. Federalists claimed Adams was the proper successor to Washington and denounced Jefferson as opposed to the Constitution and slavishly devoted to France. Because many candidates to be electors proclaimed which man they supported, most voters and legislators could vote for the elector candidates who would then vote for their preferred presidential candidate. Beckley led the Republican effort in Pennsylvania and coordinated with Republicans in other states. Burr devoted six weeks to electioneering through New England, though Beckley warned that Burr's efforts "are more directed to himself." Tracking the Republican leaders' efforts is difficult. Because they believed that Federalist postmasters read their mail, they communicated largely through couriers; little of their correspondence has survived.[29]

By December 1796, with the votes mostly cast but not yet counted, Madison was back in Philadelphia and resumed his correspondence with Jefferson. Since late September, the two friends had discussed the election, along with the prospect that Jefferson would finish second to Adams and become vice president. "You must reconcile yourself," Madison wrote, "to the secondary as well as the primary station, if that should be your lot." After his usual denial of any wish for the presidency, Jefferson authorized Madison to concede the election to Adams if there should be a tie vote: "He has always been my senior from the commencement of our public life," Jefferson wrote, and "this circumstance ought to give him the preference."[30]

Jefferson had good reasons for deferring to Adams. The president who succeeded Washington would always compare unfavorably to the departing hero. Moreover, Jefferson wrote, "The president is fortunate to get off just as the bubble is bursting, leaving others to hold the bag." He predicted that Washington's successor would be blamed for any problems, while Washington "will have his usual good fortune of reaping credit from the good acts of others."[31]

Jefferson toyed with the idea of extending an early olive branch to Adams. He drafted a letter wishing that any Adams administration "may be filled with glory and happiness to yourself and advantage to us." Unsure whether to send the note, he forwarded it to Madison, asking him to send the letter on to Adams if it seemed a good idea. Madison thought it was a terrible idea. The letter, Madison worried, could offend Republicans who supported Jefferson. It also might offend Adams. "You know the temper of Mr. A better than I do," he wrote, "but I have always conceived it to be rather a ticklish one." Madison's final objection was unanswerable. Since Republicans might have to oppose Adams's actions as president, "there may be real embarrassments from giving written possession to him of th[is] degree of compliment and confidence." Jefferson accepted his friend's judgment.[32]

The final vote totals were close: Adams nosed out Jefferson, 71–68. The Federalist Thomas Pinckney came in third, with 59 votes, while Burr totaled only 30 votes. The party divisions followed sectional lines. Adams received only two electoral votes from the six states below Maryland; Jefferson won no electoral votes east of the Delaware River. All of the Republican electors from Virginia cast their second votes for someone other than Burr. Under the flawed constitutional provision then in force, Adams would be the nation's second president and his opponent, Jefferson, would be his vice president.

The new president faced large challenges. Prosperity was slackening. Though the threat from Britain had receded, trouble was brewing with France. A less revolutionary government in Paris had reacted angrily to the Jay Treaty; it proposed to void the Franco-American treaty of 1778. "They had rather have an open enemy," Monroe wrote from Paris, "than a perfidious friend." By January 1797, it was French ships that were preying on American merchantmen. Madison wrote with concern of the "sweeping system of captures adopted by the French, particularly in the West Indies." Adams summoned Congress for a special session to address a crisis.[33]

Washington's retirement was a milestone. Some twelve hundred gathered at a Philadelphia ball to celebrate his birthday in February 1797. Two weeks later, a public dinner marked the end of his presidency. Madison had remained on cordial terms with the president. Washington even considered appointing Madison to a mission to France in the winter of 1796–97, a move that Hamilton himself recommended. Madison, now a staunch partisan, could not accept the post from his political opponents.[34]

The intimacy and partnership between Washington and Madison were long over, submerged by political disagreements. Though Madison certainly felt sadness at the great man's departure from the scene, as a Republican leader he could only welcome it. Republicans would no longer have to contend with Washington's tremendous stature in policy disputes.

Madison too was entering a major transition. The new vice president, Jefferson, would succeed him as the everyday leader of the Republicans. Madison had carried the party banner through difficult struggles. The experience had toughened him. When Jefferson complained about Madison's support for federal construction of postal roads, Madison dismissed the objection. "I was not unaware of the considerations you suggest," he wrote, "but do not consider my proposition as involving any dangerous consequences."[35]

Above all, Madison was eager to go home. His thoughts were increasingly of Montpelier. Managing the plantation from afar, his scrutiny included how many wagonloads of manure should be applied to each field. His letters betrayed a near-mania for the use of clover to restore worn-out soil; he insisted on "the absolute necessity" of rotating crops with red clover, "with all the help that manures can supply." Through his last three months in Philadelphia, he wrote seven times to his father on matters ranging from the construction of a new stable to the shingling of a barn to the purchase of woolens and linens and a watch for family members. He also feared that he and Dolley would not reach Virginia in time to see brother Ambrose's widow, who was gravely ill. He and Dolley were, he wrote, consumed with "hurry and confusion" in moving their household.[36]

Yet no one on the national political scene thought James Madison was leaving for good. In a puckish letter to his wife, President-elect Adams noted Madison's departure:

> Mr. Madison is to retire. It seems the mode of becoming great is to retire. Madison I suppose after a retirement of a few years is to be president or V.P. . . . It is marvelous how political plants grow in the shade.[37]

NO TIME FOR QUALMS

Bringing his small family back to Virginia in the early summer of 1797, Madison's mind filled with domestic matters. For more than a decade, he had spent less than a third of his time at Montpelier. Great affairs had claimed his passion and his presence. As a young man, Madison deprecated Montpelier as "an obscure corner."[1] Now, with Jefferson taking over as Republican leader, Montpelier and Virginia would be the center of his world.

Madison's birthright included not only Montpelier but also his father's position as Orange County's leading citizen. His next-eldest brother, Francis, married and living on a nearby farm, took no role in Montpelier affairs and left almost no footprint in family records. His next brother, Ambrose, was gone and much missed. The youngest brother, William, was also settled on a local farm with his own family.[2]

Madison's first priority was the house. Perched on a ridge that looked over rolling hills to the west, its eight rooms had held as many as nine Madisons at a time, plus enslaved servants. Now it must accommodate three generations: the elder Madisons, plus James Jr., Dolley, Dolley's sister, and five-year-old Payne Todd.

James had a plan for expanding the residence. Adapting urban ideas to a rural setting, he designed a city row house that would abut the existing structure, but the two dwellings would look like a single house. The new addition held two rooms downstairs and two upstairs. It had a separate entrance, stairwell, common rooms, and bedchambers. The only connection to the elder Madisons' residence was a door into the second-floor library, where James could conduct business and political work. The design achieved an artful compromise between multigenerational living and the need for private space—a compromise that reflected Madison's personality as much as the ingenious contrivances of Monticello expressed Jefferson's. Madison added a two-story portico to the housefront to take advantage of the soaring western views; in warm months, the portico became a living space. With pillars, he created a neoclassical look.[3]

Like most home improvements, the expansion took longer than planned. By late summer, Madison had to delay a visit to Monticello because he was "so completely plunged into necessary occupations." Workmen arrived and left as Madison juggled foremen and plasterers. In April 1798, he declined Jefferson's exhortation to write a political essay, explaining, "There is really a crowd and weight of *indispensable* occupations on my time." By early 1799, Madison finally could invite the Monroes to visit, but six months later he was still supervising the project's last steps.[4]

Montpelier's farms demanded attention too. Madison applied his agricultural theories, strewing red clover with abandon and enforcing crop rotation. Farming was suffering in Virginia. Low tobacco prices were driving Virginians to plant new crops, especially wheat; Madison implemented a seven-year crop cycle, with five years of wheat, corn, peas, and potatoes followed by two years of all-healing clover, punctuated with traditional farmer's despair over drought, frost, and pests. He managed a large labor force, with a few white foremen and occasional skilled workers plus roughly a hundred slaves, several of whom were skilled artisans. The household help and skilled slaves lived near the big house; the rest resided near the fields they tended.[5]

Despite his labors, Madison could enjoy the slower pace of country life, cushioned with flotillas of relatives and friends. In Orange County, neighborly visits might extend for several days. Madison could take guests on his morning tour of the fields, then retire to his study for several hours. Dinner in the late afternoon would precede cards or chess with conversation, then supper. Though he and Dolley never had children of their own, they often were overrun by young people. On the Madison side alone, their nieces and nephews numbered fifty, while numerous Taylors (Madison's grandmother's family) lived nearby. In Philadelphia and now in Virginia, Dolley's teenage sister Anna lived with them. Her sister Lucy was in western Virginia, sister Mary near Richmond—plus Dolley's ten cousins in the Coles family.[6]

From his study, Madison monitored political developments and resumed his correspondence with Jefferson in Philadelphia, the roles in their partnership now reversed. During the 1780s and after Jefferson's resignation from the cabinet, Madison had kept his friend informed while Jefferson offered reflections from afar. Now Jefferson dwelt at the center and it was Madison who served as a sounding board for ideas. Occasionally Jefferson exhorted Madison to reenter politics, or at least draft a sharp response to some Federalist diatribe. In January 1799, he demanded Madison's opinion on a constitutional question, calling it "a set off against the sin of your retirement."[7] Between congressional sessions, when Jefferson returned to Virginia, the two friends exchanged visits, resuming conversations on agriculture, science, and politics.

Despite Jefferson's pleas, Madison did not leave Virginia for four years. Through that time, their partnership never flagged.

America's confrontation with France, which ripened into an undeclared naval conflict called the "Quasi-War," dominated Adams's presidency. Madison and Jefferson opposed any hint of alignment with Britain. The rise of authoritarian government in France disappointed them, of course; Madison admitted that France demonstrated that popular representatives "are not incapable of violating the trust committed to them." Indeed, France seemed a Madisonian object lesson that a weak central government is an invitation to despotism. For all of France's faults, however, the Republican partners could not imagine Britain as America's friend; they blamed the rupture with France on the folly of Jay's treaty.[8]

By 1797, France was riding high. Its armies were victorious in Europe, the Royal Navy was riddled with mutiny, and the Bank of England was failing. America's first ally grew arrogant and dismissive of America. French policy toward America, as a leading history puts it, became "one irritably absent-minded scheme after another." In late 1796, France refused to receive the diplomat sent to replace Monroe. Adams tried sending a three-man negotiating commission instead.[9]

While awaiting word from those commissioners, Congress dithered over proposals to strengthen port fortifications and build warships. Party rivalries grew more rancorous. A Virginia senator complained to Madison that "the insolence and scurrility of the British faction here can scarcely be borne." A Tennessee senator quarreled with another, then challenged him to a duel. A federal grand jury investigated whether a Republican congressman's letter to constituents expressed "unfounded calumnies against the happy government of the United States." Madison and Jefferson feared the Adams administration soon would move to throttle communications between congressmen and their constituents.[10]

At the end of 1797, Monroe poured kerosene on the flames by issuing a pamphlet denouncing government policies. "Our national honor is in the dust," he wrote. "We have been kicked, cuffed, and plundered all over the ocean; our reputation for faith [demolished]; our government and people branded as cowards." In January 1798, a Vermont Republican and a Connecticut Federalist engaged in a literal spitting contest on the floor of the House, then squared off with wooden cane (the Federalist) versus fireplace tongs (the Republican). The combatants thrashed across the floor until separated by colleagues. President Adams, prone to jittery nerves in good times, did little to calm the roiling waters.[11]

Only a foreign outrage could quiet America's corrosive political sniping. While French privateers continued to seize American merchant ships, French diplomats supplied the outrage. When Adams's commissioners arrived in Paris, French officials promptly demanded bribes from them. Large ones. The official report, which reached America in April 1798, referred to the French officials as "Monsieur X, Monsieur Y, and Monsieur Z," so the event entered history as the "XYZ Affair." It was a catastrophe for Republicans. The French demand was "scarcely credible," Madison wrote to Jefferson: "I do not allude to its depravity, which however heinous, is not without examples. Its unparalleled stupidity is what fills one with astonishment."[12]

From Philadelphia, Jefferson confirmed the political damage to the Republican interest. Previously unaligned congressmen, he wrote to Madison, "have chiefly gone over to the war party." Philadelphia Federalists festooned their hats with black cockades—decorative ribbons—so Republicans responded with cockades of the French tricolor (red, white, and blue). When a Philadelphia street gang wearing black cockades clashed with another sporting the tricolor, cavalry had to restore order. War rumors swept the city and the party presses stoked the fires. A Republican paper described Adams as "unhinged" in his drive for war with France, while a Federalist editor castigated Republicans as "scum of party filth and beggarly corruption." From the eye of the storm, Jefferson kept his head, counseling that the "reign of witches" would subside.[13]

Not, however, right away. As patriotic feeling surged, Congress approved funding to fortify harbors and build cannon; it authorized the arming of merchant ships and the seizure of French privateers in American waters. Following Jefferson's advice, congressional Republicans worked to soften the war measures. A bill established a "provisional" army, to be called up when needed, but only for ten thousand men, not the twenty-five thousand initially proposed. Another bill established a new executive department to oversee the navy. President Adams called for a national day of "solemn humiliation, prayer and fasting" on May 9.[14]

Detached from the daily arm wrestling in Philadelphia, Madison drew lessons from the crisis. Foreign policy, he told Jefferson, was the governmental function "most susceptible of abuse," because it "can be concealed or disclosed, or disclosed in such parts and at such times as will best suit particular views." Worse still, he added, the people cannot judge foreign policy questions. "Perhaps it is a universal truth," Madison concluded, "that the loss of liberty at home is to be charged against danger real or pretended from abroad."[15]

The Alien and Sedition Acts, adopted in June and July of 1798, proved Madison's point. The Alien Act allowed the president to deport any foreigner deemed "dangerous to the peace and safety of the United States." The intended targets were Irish immigrants, who were seen as dangerous and pro-French (most were anti-British). Adams, doubting the law's wisdom, never applied it in a deportation. It expired in 1800.[16]

The Sedition Act, however, was a more serious matter. It prohibited any "false, scandalous, and malicious writing" that targeted the government or a federal official. More startling, it barred writings that would bring the government, the president, or either house of Congress "into contempt or disrepute," or "excited against them . . . the hatred of the good people of the United States." That last provision would have banned most American political jokes over the last two centuries, along with much political discourse. Adams liked the Sedition Act. Chafing under the scourging that Republican editors regularly applied to him—one referred to him as "blind, bald, crippled, toothless [and] querulous"—Adams authorized fourteen prosecutions of Republican editors under the new statute.

Adams used the Sedition Act to settle political scores, beginning with Matthew Lyon, the Vermont Republican who wielded the fireplace tongs on the floor of Congress six months earlier. The Lyon indictment targeted an article claiming that Adams demonstrated "an unbounded thirst for ridiculous pomp, foolish adulation, and selfish avarice." Lyon's words indisputably were intended to bring Adams "into contempt or disrepute," so off Lyon went for six months in jail. The conviction did not hurt him politically. From his jail cell, Lyon won reelection to Congress. Indeed, imprisoning Republican editors only drew attention to their messages.[17]

Madison and Jefferson concentrated on wringing political advantage from the Alien and Sedition Acts.

As a political issue, the 1798 legislation was made to order for the Republicans. After years of complaining about dangerous monocrats, about threats to public liberty and personal rights, now they could point to national laws that threatened all of those things. If Americans could go to jail for speaking their minds, Republicans asked, why had they fought for independence? Had they merely exchanged British oppressors for homegrown ones? And how could the Sedition Act be reconciled with the First Amendment's guarantee of a free press?[18]

Madison and Jefferson led the attack. Jefferson stopped at Montpelier in early July, on his way home from Philadelphia, to work out their strategy.[19] Many avenues were closed to them. Congress was controlled by Federalists. The Supreme Court too. That left state governments as a political platform for challenging the Federalist statutes.

Jefferson naturally turned to the states as bulwarks of liberty. From the first time he read the Constitution, he feared the charter's centralizing tendency and advocated state autonomy. The tactic was less congenial for Madison. Under the Articles of Confederation, he had castigated narrow-minded and self-serving state governments. Yet during the first decade under the Constitution, watching Hamilton and Washington expand national powers, Madison had grown more willing to assert state rights.

Through the summer of 1798, public meetings in Virginia and Kentucky condemned the Alien and Sedition Acts. To translate that energy into action, Jefferson drafted resolutions for the Kentucky legislature. His effort, largely adopted in November 1798, included two explosive assertions. First, Jefferson claimed that the Constitution was adopted by the states, each of which retained the power to judge for itself the constitutionality of federal actions. This "compact theory"—that the Constitution was a compact among the states—contradicted Madison's insistence in 1787 and 1788 on the importance of ratification by "the people," which made the Constitution an agreement among "We, the people."

Jefferson's draft also asserted that the Alien and Sedition Acts were "altogether void, and of no force." With that phrase, he claimed for states the power to suspend federal laws within their borders, even though the Constitution states that federal statutes are the supreme law of the land. If states can declare that certain federal laws do not apply within their borders, then there is no national government. Coming from the pen of the sitting vice president, this was dangerous doctrine. Jefferson took pains to conceal his authorship of the resolution, but over the years such secrets have a way of becoming known.[20]

Madison harbored reservations about Jefferson's aggressive language and adopted a softer tone for resolutions he drafted for the Virginia legislature. He declared Virginia's "warm attachment to the Union of the states" and expressed regret that federal laws had exceeded constitutional limits. Madison echoed Jefferson's "compact theory," but rather than declare federal laws "void," he offered the murky assertion that states should "interpose for arresting the progress" of unconstitutional federal laws. Madison did not explain what it meant for a state to "interpose."

Madison's opaque prose was intentional, a choice not to replicate Jefferson's clarion call to the states. The Virginia Resolution concluded with an exhortation for other states to join in declaring the Alien and Sedition Acts unconstitutional, but it stopped short of any claim that the laws themselves could be declared null and void.[21]

The Virginia and Kentucky Resolutions immediately commanded nationwide attention, little of it positive. Ten states specifically declined to join the positions announced by Virginia and Kentucky; four states took no action at all. Federalists, buoyed by war fever, prospered in the 1798 elections. Even in Republican Virginia, they gained four congressional seats. When General Washington assumed titular command of the provisional army and installed Hamilton as his second, Republicans feared the dangers of combining Washington's political magic, Hamilton's thirst for power, and armed men in uniform.[22]

Yet Madison did not relent. He aimed to renew the Republican attack on the Alien and Sedition Acts but to turn public debate away from Jefferson's controversial state-rights views. He would refocus the public on the repressive laws. First, though, he had to cool off his partner. In August 1799, Jefferson wrote to Montpelier to propose a new resolution that would inflate state-rights theory even further. The new document, Jefferson wrote, should announce that if the other states would not condemn the federal statutes, Virginia would "sever ourselves from that union we so much value."[23]

Here was true dynamite: The vice president proposed to announce that Virginia was willing to dissolve the union. Madison dropped everything and rode to Monticello. He insisted that neither Virginia nor Republicans could even hint at secession. As Jefferson explained to a third member of their effort, because Madison had opposed any reference to secession, "from this I recede readily."[24]

Madison had just won a seat in the Virginia House of Delegates, which allowed him to reframe the Republican position. He had run for the office because his old nemesis, Patrick Henry, also was returning to the legislature. In one of the strange political minuets of the era, Henry had become a Federalist as Madison evolved into a Republican.[25] Regardless of Henry's political label, Madison would never trust him; he had ample reason to mistrust him now. General Washington had urged Henry to join the legislature in order to roll back Madison's Virginia Resolution. Before Henry and Madison could tangle one more time, however, the older man died. With Henry finally removed from the scene, Madison moved to defend Virginia's attack on the Alien and Sedition Acts. His "Report of 1800," adopted by the legislature, completed his revision of Jefferson's initial position.[26]

Madison's report featured the careful and sober analysis that was his strength. It distilled much of his constitutional thinking through nearly a decade of opposition—through campaigns against the Bank of the United States, against Hamilton's "Report on Manufactures," and against the Alien and Sedition Acts. He began with a quick linguistic somersault to escape Jefferson's "compact theory" of the Constitution. When the Virginia Resolution used the term "states," he explained, the term did not mean "states" but meant "the people composing those political societies, in their highest sovereign capacity." Thus, "states" actually meant "people," he continued, landing smoothly on both feet. Accordingly, the Virginia Resolution recognized that the people had approved the Constitution through their state conventions—just as Madison had said twelve years before.

Madison still made no effort to clarify when or how a state (that is, its people) could "interpose" its constitutional judgment about a federal law. Those mysteries would persist in Madison's analysis. States should not interpose—whatever it meant to interpose—"in a hasty manner, or on doubtful and inferior occasions," but should do so only on occasions "deeply and essentially affecting the vital principles of the political system."

He decried the Alien and Sedition Acts as beyond the federal government's powers and specified the constitutional violations worked by each provision of each statute. In arguing that the Sedition Act violated the First Amendment guarantee of a free press, he anticipated doctrines the Supreme Court would not embrace for more than a century:

> Some degree of abuse is inseparable from the proper use of everything; and in no instance is this more true than in that of the press. It . . . is better to leave a few of its noxious branches to their luxuriant growth, than by pruning them away to injure the vigor of those yielding the proper fruits. . . . [T]o the press alone, checkered as it is with abuses, the world is indebted for all the triumphs which have been gained by reason and humanity over error and oppression.[27]

Madison connected a free press to an informed electorate. The Sedition Act, he wrote, would "repress that information and communication among the people which is indispensable to the just exercise of their electoral rights." If editors faced prison for criticizing an official, voters would be denied the information they need to decide how to cast their votes.[28]

When Madison reached the all-important question whether the Virginia Resolution invalidated the federal statutes, he wrote mildly that Virginia had issued a "declaration that proceedings of the Federal Government are not warranted by the constitution." Though Virginia would oppose "the first symptoms of usurpation," he affirmed its commitment to retaining the union. Madison wrote no word suggesting that a state might suspend or otherwise thwart a federal law.[29]

Madison's report was a soothing, twenty-thousand-word shower designed to wash away the extreme positions in Jefferson's Kentucky Resolution. Who could deny Virginia's right to lodge a protest against a federal statute, especially a protest written as cogently as the "Report of 1800"? Madison's effort directed public attention toward the Alien and Sedition Acts and away from Jefferson's state-rights excesses. Madison had retrieved the political issue for the Republicans for the coming campaign while shielding Jefferson from his own impulsiveness.

Though Madison intended the "Report of 1800" to provide the authoritative rendition of the Kentucky and Virginia Resolutions, the state-rights genie could not be stuffed back in the bottle. It would continue to erupt for decades and even centuries, often in ways that Madison never intended. In battles over the federal tariff in the 1830s, John C. Calhoun of South Carolina contrived a theory of state "nullification" or "interposition," conflating the terms to claim that a state can suspend federal law within its borders. Madison, many years retired at that point, sternly opposed Calhoun's theory. Nullification and interposition reemerged in the slavery debates of the 1840s and 1850s. Northern leaders cited the ideas to justify refusing to return runaway slaves. In a weird symmetry, nullification simultaneously provided the ideology for southern secession and for the abolitionist actions that drove the southern states to secede.

A century later, interposition flickered to life a third time, when it was deployed to resist the school integration ordered by the 1954 Supreme Court ruling in *Brown v. Board of Education.* Several southern states adopted interposition statutes to block integration. In decisions involving the Fugitive Slave law in the 1850s and school desegregation in the 1950s, the Supreme Court rejected any state power to nullify federal law. The idea, however, lives on.[30]

In 1798 and ever since, Jefferson's Kentucky Resolution has tended to drown out Madison's more measured words in the Virginia Resolution and the "Report of 1800." Madison confused his own legacy by using the enigmatic term "interposition" and appearing to embrace Jefferson's "compact theory" of the Constitution. To herd Jefferson back onto a safe political path, Madison ended up taking a stronger state-rights posture than he did at other times in his career. Such was the price of riding intellectual shotgun for Jefferson.

While Madison and Jefferson were concentrating on the Alien and Sedition Acts, Adams began to doubt the wisdom of war with France. The two nations could scarcely reach each other to fight. With the Royal Navy patrolling the Atlantic, the French could mount no serious attack on America; the United States could do little damage to France, which had six times the population. The two nations' ships might fight isolated actions on the seas; American captains and sailors acquitted themselves brilliantly in several bloody encounters. Each nation could prey on the other's merchant shipping. Yet neither posed a serious threat to the other, nor had much to gain from war.[31]

Adams resolved to try again for peace in early 1799. He proposed to send three new commissioners to France. The Senate agreed to the step, perhaps the greatest of Adams's public career. His timing, for once, was good. With France's European wars taking a turn for the worse, it had a new appetite for conciliation.[32]

Also, the election of 1800 loomed on the calendar. It promised to be a bruising contest. In late 1799, as political actors anticipated the clash, staggering news arrived: General Washington was dead at sixty-seven, victim of a throat infection and the limited medical skills of the day.

Before Virginia's House of Delegates, Madison paid unqualified tribute to the fallen leader, his former partner. "Death has robbed our country of its most distinguished ornament, and the world of one of its greatest benefactors," he said, adding that Virginia legislators would "pay to his memory the tribute of their tears." Though his partnership with Washington had withered, his regard for the general's integrity was unchanged. After a year of the Adams presidency, Madison wrote nostalgically of Washington's thoughtful style: "[C]old, considerate and cautious . . . ever scrutinizing into the public opinion, and ready to follow where he could not lead it: . . . A hero in the field, yet overweighing every danger in the cabinet . . . pursuing peace everywhere with sincerity."[33]

The electoral battle of 1800 would have dismayed Washington. Both sides viewed the contest as a fight for the nation's soul. That it was a rematch between Adams and Jefferson only sharpened the bitterness, as did the preceding years of verbal broadsides, street riots, taxpayer rebellions, angry public meetings, and effigy burnings.

Republicans denounced Adams as a monarchist and tool of the British. They argued that the nation's taxes were too high, its military spending unnecessary, its foreign policy recklessly hostile to France. The controversial newspaperman James Callender, who was supported by Jefferson, wrote that "[t]he Reign of Mr. Adams has, hitherto, been one continued tempest of malignant passions" that succeeded in "extinguish[ing] the only beam of happiness that glimmers through the dark and despicable farce of life."[34]

Federalists replied by calling Jefferson a godless infidel and dangerous "Jacobin" devoted to all things French. New England newspapers, Jefferson sighed to Madison during the campaign, were filled with "the old stories of deism, atheism, antifederalism, etc." According to a New York newspaper, victory by Jefferson would bring a bloody civil war led by Frenchmen, Irishmen, and southern slaves. Privately, Martha Washington called the Republican leader "one of the most detestable of mankind."[35]

In a 1799 newspaper essay titled "Enemy to Foreign Influence," Madison pitched into the fight. His immediate target was Britain—which "above all nations, ought to be dreaded and watched"—but also those Americans who urged pro-British policies. Such policies, he argued, were a "foreign poison vitiating the American sentiment, re-colonizing the American character, and duping us into the politics of a foreign nation." He summoned the spirit of the Revolution to vindicate American independence.[36]

Paranoia ran rampant. Both Jefferson and Charles Pinckney of South Carolina stopped signing their letters; if their correspondence was intercepted, they would deny writing it. Leading Republicans, as they had during the 1796 election, sent letters by the hand of trusted colleagues, avoiding Federalist postmasters. When Jefferson and Madison proposed to confer on election strategy, Monroe argued that news that they had met would become "a subject of some political slander, and perhaps of some political injury."[37]

Eighteen months before votes were cast, partisans maneuvered over how the states would choose presidential electors. In Republican-leaning states, Madison's friends pressed for winner-take-all systems that would maximize the number of Republican electors. When Adams won in 1796, his three-vote victory margin came from single electoral votes won in each of three otherwise Republican states. In every state east of the Delaware River, in contrast, Jefferson had won no electoral votes.

In a letter to Madison, Charles Pinckney recommended that Virginia and North Carolina adopt the winner-take-all approach. "The success of the republican ticket depends upon this act," he wrote. "This is no time for qualms." A Virginian agreed, insisting that a "single vote may be everything." Madison supported the change, which Virginia enacted.[38]

In the third week of January 1800, Madison joined Virginia's Republican caucus in Richmond. Party organization was the order of the day. The caucus selected a blue-ribbon slate of elector candidates, led by Madison, and appointed five-man committees for each county. Monroe, the newly elected governor, integrated the Republican Party structure with the electoral process; of three hundred election officials throughout the state, two-thirds also served on Republican county committees. Republicans in New Jersey and Pennsylvania established similar organizations. John Beckley of Philadelphia again organized the canvass. He distributed party pamphlets from South Carolina through New England, along with five thousand copies of a profile of Jefferson, the first campaign biography in history.[39]

New York and New Jersey were hotly contested. Aaron Burr directed the Republican campaign for the New York legislature, which would choose the presidential electors. If that local election went Republican, Jefferson thought it would decide the presidency. When Burr managed a clean sweep, a Virginia Republican exulted to Madison: "The Republic is safe."[40]

The celebration was premature. In Maryland, Federalists plotted for the legislature to seize the power to choose electors, which spread the battle to that state's legislative elections. According to a Baltimore Republican, the Federalists aimed to prevail "either by fair or foul means"; he feared "their arts and villainy."[41]

Like Virginia, Massachusetts adopted the winner-take-all system, ensuring that no stray Republican elector could be chosen from that state. Federalists in Congress proposed a national election commission of six members appointed by each house, plus the chief justice of the United States. The commission would rule on any "irregularities" in voting. With Federalist majorities in Congress, and with Federalist Oliver Ellsworth as chief justice, Federalists could expect the commission to sympathize with them. Republicans, including Madison, objected that the Constitution gave the states unrestricted power in choosing electors. John Marshall, then a Federalist congressman, agreed with Madison and helped defeat the bill.[42]

The Federalists also continued to prosecute Republican editors. In the summer of 1800, a federal jury convicted James Callender under the Sedition Act and sentenced him to nine months in prison. Republican editors in Connecticut, New York, and Pennsylvania followed Callender to jail. Madison thought the Federalist campaign self-defeating. By such repressive measures, he told Jefferson, the Federalist Party was "industriously cooperating in its own destruction."[43]

Madison's prediction proved true, though the election's finale included considerable drama. Hamilton issued a pamphlet denouncing Adams, the candidate of his own party. The pamphlet simultaneously injured Adams, sullied Hamilton's reputation, and undermined Hamilton's scheme for vaulting vice presidential candidate Charles Cotesworth Pinckney past Adams under the Constitution's odd balloting system. Madison applauded Hamilton's mad course.[44]

The deciding votes came from South Carolina, where Charles Pinckney (*not* Charles Cotesworth Pinckney, his Federalist cousin) brought home every electoral vote for the Republicans. In the final tally, Jefferson and Burr each won 73 votes; Adams had 65, and C.C. Pinckney 64.[45]

Which led to one more crisis: With Burr and Jefferson tied, there was no winner. At least one Republican elector should have thrown away his second vote on a noncandidate, so Burr would have finished second to Jefferson. But none did.

The contest went to the House of Representatives, where each state delegation would cast a single ballot. Monroe warned Madison that even though Jefferson was plainly intended to be the party's candidate for president with Burr the candidate for vice president, Burr might lunge for the higher office in the House balloting. Madison refused to believe his college acquaintance capable of such perfidy. On a House vote, Madison assured Monroe, "the candidates would certainly I think be arranged properly." Based on confidential assurances from a friend of Burr's, Madison wrote to Jefferson that he expected no effort "to strangle the election of the people, and smuggle into the chief magistracy the creature of a faction."[46]

Madison was wrong. After indicating he would defer to Jefferson in the House vote, Burr issued a statement that he would accept the presidency if the House chose him. House Federalists embraced Burr, thereby denying Jefferson a majority through thirty-four deadlocked ballots in February 1801. With Adams's term expiring, the constitutional confusion was acute. If the House deadlock persisted, it was not clear who, if anyone, would be president. Madison, still in Montpelier, offered an ingenious solution: Jefferson and Burr should jointly convene the new Congress after March 4; since one of them would eventually be president, their joint action would undeniably be legitimate. Then the new House of Representatives, dominated by Republicans, could select Jefferson as president. Madison's plan proved unnecessary, though, when Burr tardily sent word that no one should vote for him for president. Two ballots later, the Federalists broke ranks. Jefferson won.[47]

Thomas Jefferson's inauguration was a pivotal moment, though perhaps not the "revolution" he would later call it. The messy election represented a critical achievement under the Constitution: the peaceful transfer of executive power between contending parties. Madison had labored for a government controlled by the people's will as expressed at the ballot box; here was the triumph of those efforts.

On March 4, 1801, the unpretentious Jefferson walked from his boardinghouse to deliver his inaugural address at the unfinished Capitol in the raw emptiness of Washington City. The incompleteness of both the building and the city were powerful metaphors for a republic that had not reached adolescence. Those at the ceremony strained to hear the new president's mumbles. But when his words were printed, they struck a conciliatory note that warmed most Americans: "We are all republicans, we are all federalists. . . . I believe this [is] the strongest government on earth."

On that day of triumph, Madison, the partner who helped Jefferson conjure the Republican Party out of nothing, was missing. He had troubles of his own.

Five weeks before the inauguration, James Madison, Sr., died at the age of seventy-seven. The old squire had been failing gradually. While Madison was preparing to become Jefferson's Secretary of State, his father's health grew "sensibly worse"; then, Madison wrote, "very gently the flame of life went out."[48]

For two more months, Madison remained in Virginia to settle his father's estate. When he set off for Washington in late April, he was followed by dark memories from the previous year. Not only had his father died, but in September 1800, James and Eliza Monroe lost their infant son to fever. At almost the same time, Virginians faced their deepest anxiety: Near Richmond, an abortive slave revolt called Gabriel's Rebellion was foiled at the last moment. For Madison, whose grandfather was poisoned by his slaves and who lived on a plantation where slaves outnumbered whites by ten to one, the failed rebellion must have unlocked a cabinet of fears. Its psychic impact would linger over the South for decades.[49]

Despite such gloomy thoughts, Madison should have approached Washington City with real eagerness. His partnership with Jefferson had borne remarkable fruit.

They had created the first national political party, then led it to victory. The Republicans had seized the presidency and a solid majority in the House. The Federalist edge in the Senate was down to two votes. Madison would hold the most prestigious cabinet office, steering foreign policy in a critical period. He would sit at the right hand of the new president, his most trusted adviser and political confidant. The Sedition Act expired on the last day of John Adams's term in office. The conflict with France had been resolved by Adams's final peace commission. The times seemed promising.

For Madison and Jefferson, the election of 1800 was more than a partisan victory. They had founded a party to speak for the common man while exalting public opinion as the true sovereign. They saw their mission as nothing less than rescuing the American experiment in self-government from the wealthy aristocrats behind Hamilton and the Federalists. In the struggle for the meaning of the Revolution, in their view, the people had won; America, unlike France, would remain republican. The political party they had founded would dominate the nation's public life for the next six decades and would thrive—in ever-changing form—into the twenty-first century.

Yet there was irony in this signal achievement. Neither Madison nor Jefferson valued political parties, fearing them as the tools of self-interested persons, often a means for corrupting political life. In a truly virtuous republic, they believed, parties would not be necessary. In *Federalist* No. 10, Madison wrote that parties "inflamed [people] with mutual animosity, and rendered them much more disposed to vex and oppress each other than to cooperate for their common good." But the two Virginians discovered they had to form a party, despite its evils. Confronting the American political scene in the 1790s, Madison and Jefferson abandoned their ideology to establish a political party that changed the nation's course.

Madison's small family rode to Washington with him in the late spring of 1801. They would stay in the Executive Mansion with Jefferson until their house was ready for them. Madison made one further adjustment for this new phase of his life. Following the custom of the time, he dropped the designation "Jr." from his name. Going forward, he would be "James Madison."

IV

—◆—

JAMES MONROE

16

FRIENDS AND RIVALS
AND FRIENDS

When Madison's term in the Confederation Congress expired at the end of 1783, he already knew about the twenty-five-year-old James Monroe, a former Continental Army officer who was one of the new delegates from Virginia. Madison's closest congressional colleague was Monroe's uncle and mentor, Joseph Jones. Madison and Jones lodged together in Philadelphia and in Princeton, while Jones was working to smooth his nephew's entry into the world of politics and government.[1]

Monroe needed a doting uncle. Orphaned at fifteen, Monroe inherited his father's modest assets: some acres in Westmoreland County, Virginia, on the tidewater side of the state, plus a few slaves. He assumed responsibility for his three younger siblings. Monroe's fortune was his childless uncle, who sponsored him for the College of William and Mary. In the spring of 1776, revolutionary fervor brought Monroe into the Continental Army.

A solid six-footer, Monroe was only eighteen when he saw combat in the Battle of New York City. At the Battle of Trenton, Lieutenant Monroe led the capture of enemy artillery, suffering a bullet wound in the shoulder. After failing to recruit a regiment he could command, he signed on as aide to General William Alexander. He soldiered with luminaries who would lead the future nation: General Washington, of course, and also Alexander Hamilton, John Marshall, and Aaron Burr. He survived the winter at Valley Forge and more fighting. After a second attempt to recruit his own regiment and a second failure, then-Colonel Monroe shed his uniform.[2]

In embarking on a career in politics, Monroe's principal advantages were an honorable war record, his uncle, and an affable earnestness that inspired trust. Having shouldered family duties and military command at a young age, Monroe seemed older than his years, though he was eight years junior to Madison. He read law with Thomas Jefferson. A bachelor, the gregarious ex-officer frequented Richmond's taverns with Marshall, a former schoolmate and leading bon vivant. A female admirer described Monroe as having eight "perfections of person or mind," a list which included "every perfection that a female can wish or a man envy."[3]

In the spring of 1784, as Jefferson prepared to leave on his diplomatic mission to Paris, he told Madison that Monroe wished to begin a correspondence with him. Jefferson endorsed Monroe, writing that, as an individual, "a better man cannot be." Madison agreed to the arrangement, beginning forty-six years as friends, business partners, political allies, and sometime rivals.

Madison's early letters to Monroe included some of the philosophical speculation that ran through his exchanges with Jefferson. But Monroe tended to ignore such musings, focusing instead on political matters, often with practical insights, shrewd judgments, and rueful references to his financial condition. Monroe usually lived at or beyond the limits of his means, which were relatively slender. Madison learned to omit literary or theoretical subjects when writing to Monroe.[4]

No one ever accused Monroe of intellectual brilliance. One British official, after months of negotiating with the Virginian, described him as "plain in his manner and somewhat slow in his apprehension," but "a diligent, earnest, sensible, and even profound man." A fellow member of the Virginia bar offered a similar assessment:

> Nature has given [Monroe] a mind neither rapid nor rich, and therefore he cannot shine on a subject which is entirely new to him. But to compensate him for this he is endued with a spirit of restless emulation, a judgment strong and clear, and a habit of application which no difficulties can shake, no labors can tire.[5]

Monroe wrote advocacy pieces for the newspapers, but his efforts had more partisan bite than flourish or power. No volume of Monroe's political essays has been published.[6] Monroe had few illusions about his literary talents. In 1788, as the nation puzzled over the proposed Constitution, Monroe wrote a pamphlet opposing ratification. Dissatisfied with his own effort, he withheld it from public view, giving copies only to a couple of friends.[7]

Monroe was frank about his emotions. During a period of friction with Madison and Jefferson, he wailed that his erstwhile friends had "hurt my feelings," an admission that few statesmen of the era confided to paper. Such emotional directness can disarm adversaries and charm friends. "Turn [Monroe's] soul wrong side outwards," Jefferson wrote to Madison, "and there is not a speck on it."[8]

Monroe's open manner included a hypersensitivity to criticism. Intensely ambitious, he took offense over any slight or rebuke, sometimes firing off a self-justifying diatribe. He nearly fought a duel when Hamilton wrongly accused him of leaking scandalous disclosures about Hamilton's love life. As a diplomat, he quarreled with colleagues and superiors. While Madison seemed to have the hide of a rhinoceros when it came to public criticism and private disputes, the bluff and hearty Monroe was easily wounded and nursed grudges for years. A New Yorker offered a brutal comparison of the two Virginians: "Madison is quick, temperate, and clear. Monroe slow, passionate and dull."[9]

At one point, Monroe's combination of ambition and sensitivity seemed to sever his partnership with Madison for good. Yet when Madison's presidency foundered, he reached out to his old friend Monroe. Together, they helped bring the nation through the War of 1812, a conflict that rarely went well. Monroe's reward was his own two-term presidency, which completed the extraordinary twenty-four-year Virginia Dynasty, when the nation's highest office was held by three friends who lived within fifty miles of one another.

Early on, Madison and Monroe found they shared the passion for fron tier lands that fired so many leading Virginians. In 1784, each traveled to the frontier, passing through the same upstate New York fort a week apart. Monroe's journey was the more adventurous one, ranging as far west as Niagara and north to Montreal. In the following year, Madison proposed they visit New England and Canada, but Monroe set off in the other direction, descending through the Ohio River Valley with members of a commission sent to negotiate with Indian tribes.[10]

Their shared enthusiasm for the West had political implications. Both opposed a potential agreement with Spain to forgo trade down the Mississippi for twenty years. Monroe feared the pact would undermine the union, prompting formation of "a union of the southern states."[11]

They pooled their resources to speculate in land in New York's Mohawk Valley, though they were hardly highfliers. Madison lived on his public salary and family handouts, while Monroe faced even more acute limitations. In scrambling lurches, they acquired almost a thousand acres, then asked Jefferson to find European investors to underwrite a broader effort. In early 1786, Monroe announced that he hoped to introduce Madison "to a young lady who will be adopted a citizen of Virginia in the course of this week." He referred to his new bride, the twenty-year-old Elizabeth Kortright, a stylish New Yorker who would acquire a reputation for reserve and snobbishness.[12]

For the newlyweds, Madison undertook a chore that especially flummoxed him. Before the Monroes moved back to Virginia, they ordered furniture from a New York cabinetmaker. While the order was in production, Mrs. Monroe's sister visited the workshop and fled in horror. She pronounced the items "vile." Monroe asked Madison, who was attending Congress in New York, to investigate.

Madison was the wrong man for the job. At age thirty-six, he had never lived in his own residence, shuttling between his parents' home and boardinghouses in distant cities. Having never selected furniture, he admitted to "having little confidence in my own judgment of cabinet workmanship." So Madison sought assistance from two married friends. After the trio visited the workshop en masse, Madison reported that neither friend thought Monroe had a basis for canceling the order. Madison unhelpfully added that the furniture did not "entirely please my eye," though "no particular defect appears in the workmanship." His ambivalent report was not likely to put the Monroes' minds at rest.[13]

On the burning issue of the day, the two Virginians agreed that the Articles of Confederation should be replaced, though Monroe feared a strong national government. Based on his experience in Congress, he saw public issues as contests between different sections of the country, and he did not trust New Englanders. "I earnestly wish," he confided to Madison, "the admission of a few additional states into the confederacy in the southern scale." Nevertheless, Monroe supported the call for the Annapolis Convention of September 1786 and for the Philadelphia Convention thereafter.[14]

The first hiccup in their friendship came when Monroe was not named to Virginia's delegation to Philadelphia. He resented the omission, singling out Edmund Randolph for having "a disposition to thwart me." Monroe also blamed Madison for making "arrangements unfavorable to me" even though Madison was someone "upon whose friendship I have calculated."[15]

Madison and Monroe resumed their correspondence after the Philadelphia Convention, though not with the same easy familiarity. While Madison urgently advocated for the Constitution in Congress, the younger man offered only wary support. Admitting he had "strong objections" to parts of the new charter, Monroe initially wrote that these were "overbalanced by arguments in its favor." Gradually, as prominent Virginians criticized the document publicly, Monroe swung to a more negative view. By April, on the cusp of the Virginia ratifying convention, Madison knew Monroe was leaning against the Constitution. Monroe ran for a seat in the Richmond ratifying convention from King George County but lost; he won a second race in Spotsylvania County. Finally, Monroe would be on the inside.[16]

To sort out his views on the Constitution, Monroe drafted the pamphlet he never issued publicly. His draft acknowledged that the national government under the Articles "must always be void of energy, slow in its operation, sometimes oppressive, and often altogether suspended." Yet Monroe questioned whether a single government could govern a territory that extended along the entire Atlantic coast. He thought the Senate would be too aristocratic and the federal judiciary too powerful. The congressional power to impose direct taxes terrified him. During convention sessions in Richmond, Monroe's remarks drew heavily on the analysis in his unpublished pamphlet, though the true Anti-Federalist leaders were Patrick Henry and George Mason. Monroe's opposition to ratification was not so extreme that he alienated Madison.[17]

In the convention's aftermath, though, Monroe became a central part of Henry's scheme to derail Madison's career, first by denying him a seat in the new United States Senate and then by arranging his defeat in a race for the House. After placing Madison's home county in a congressional district with other counties known for Anti-Federalist views, Henry induced Monroe to run against Madison.

Monroe never mentioned Henry's maneuvers in his letters to Madison in New York. Others, however, sounded the alarm. "I have already apprised you of the political hostility of Monroe," one wrote, "and it will be well for you to pay some regard to it." Another warned that the "beau" (Monroe) would oppose him.[18]

The 1789 campaign in Virginia's Fifth Congressional District was the only contest for lower office that has ever pitted two future presidents against each other. That the contenders were friends and business partners made it even more compelling. Though Madison found his friend was willing to be a cat's-paw for Henry, his great political enemy, there is no record that Madison complained about Monroe's candidacy. Perhaps he concluded that Henry was bound to find a tough candidate to run against him, so it might as well be Monroe.[19]

Monroe wrote to Jefferson in Paris to explain his course. He did not, he said, wish to disappoint friends who had "pressed" him to run against Madison, and he hoped his effort would encourage constitutional amendments. A simpler explanation is more credible: Monroe disagreed with Madison over whether, how, and how soon the Constitution should be amended, and he thought he just might win the race.[20]

Henry had set a dangerous trap for Madison. Of the eight counties in the district, only two had shown strong support for the Constitution when they chose delegates for the Richmond Convention. Madison could not expect to run well in Amherst County, which was staunchly Anti-Federalist, or in Monroe's home county, Spotsylvania. Moreover, Madison hated campaigning. He did as little of it as he could get away with. This time, he knew he had to run hard.

Madison launched two efforts to reach the district's roughly five thousand male voters. The first involved enlisting support from leading citizens in each county. Local luminaries often guided the votes of those who lacked the leisure or the inclination to follow public events. Madison wrote careful letters to prominent figures, intending that the letters be shown widely through each community or even published in local newspapers. In three of the four letters that have survived, he confronted the major question before the voters: whether the Constitution required a bill of rights. Anti-Federalists were loudly proclaiming that Madison would not back amendments to the document he had supported so fiercely.

Madison pledged to promote certain types of amendments but only if they were adopted by Congress and then ratified by the states. He opposed a second constitutional convention, and he opposed amendments that would restrict the government's powers to tax and to regulate trade. On those terms, his support for amendments was unqualified, and his position counteracted much of the Anti-Federalist anger against him.[21]

A second campaign technique was less to Madison's liking: speaking to public meetings in local towns, even sharing the podium with his opponent. The physical contrast between the two candidates was stark.

Monroe, vigorous and athletic, with a full head of auburn hair, loomed over the pale, slender Madison and his receding hairline. Monroe was more outgoing and convivial, though not a gifted orator.

As the two men jointly addressed voters in Culpeper, Louisa, and Orange Counties, bitter winter weather transformed the campaign into a trial by ordeal. Temperatures plunged through January, while sleet and snow made travel grueling. On one occasion, the candidates spoke outdoors to a congregation of Lutherans who stood in the snow. "[They] seemed to consider it a sort of fight," Madison said later, "of which they were required to be spectators." Riding twelve miles home from that snowy meeting, Madison suffered a frostbitten nose. He later mocked his frostbite scar as a wound suffered fighting for his country.[22]

Conditions were worse on election day, February 2. Three days before, ten inches of snow fell. The dawn temperature at Montpelier was an arctic 2 degrees; Fredericksburg recorded ten below. To cast their ballots at their county seats, voters risked icy country roads in freezing carriages or perched on suffering horses. Nearly half of the electorate braved the conditions, handing Madison a comfortable win, 1,308–972.[23]

After the votes were counted, both candidates declared that their friendship was unaffected. Neither had made the sort of disparaging campaign remarks that are difficult to forgive or forget. To Jefferson in Paris, Madison affirmed his goodwill toward his vanquished opponent, admitting concern about Monroe's sometimes delicate feelings.

> It was my misfortune to be thrown into a contest with our friend, Col. Monroe. The occasion produced considerable efforts among our respective friends. Between ourselves, I have no reason to doubt that the distinction was duly kept in mind between political and personal views, and that it has saved our friendship from the smallest diminution. On one side I am sure it is the case.

Monroe provided a comparable assurance to Jefferson. "It would have given me concern," he insisted, "to have excluded" Madison from Congress, and he harbored no resentment over his defeat: "As I had no private object to gratify so a failure has given me no private concern." Barely thirty years old, Monroe had time to make his way. Losing to the prominent Madison was no disgrace.[24]

Claims of goodwill between adversaries can ring hollow, but Madison and Monroe meant what they said. Within ten weeks of the election, they were exchanging friendly letters about public issues. While

Madison went off to New York to help President Washington form the new government, Monroe turned to private law practice in Virginia. He purchased four tickets for Madison in the Fredericksburg Academy lottery; one was a winner.[25]

The loss to Madison did not hold Monroe back. In 1790, the Virginia legislature awarded him one of the Senate seats that Patrick Henry had denied to Madison. Serving in Philadelphia, where Jefferson was now Secretary of State, Monroe resumed his close connection with both men. Unlike Madison, who dodged Jefferson's invitations to buy land near Monticello, Monroe had embraced the idea. In 1788, he purchased eight hundred acres in Albemarle County, a few miles from Monticello. He moved his family there a year later.[26]

With Madison and Jefferson, Senator Monroe helped form the core of the emerging "republican interest." Madison and Monroe published newspaper commentaries, traveled together to Philadelphia and back, and visited in each other's homes. When Citizen Genet's excesses fired anti-French feeling in 1793, Madison and Monroe organized events to show public support for the French Revolution.[27]

Monroe's 1794 appointment as the American Minister to France powerfully underscored the trust between the two men. The moment was a sticky one for President Washington and his policy of neutrality. France's revolutionary government had requested the recall of the previous American Minister, Gouverneur Morris, a Federalist who generally held revolutionaries in low esteem. Needing a minister more friendly to France, Washington reached out to Republicans. He started with Madison, who declined the post. Two other candidates also did not work out.[28]

On a morning in late May, Secretary of State Edmund Randolph offered the prestigious position to Monroe. Surprised, Monroe asked for time to reflect. Randolph replied that if Monroe did not accept within an hour, the president would move on to his next choice. Called to the Senate floor for legislative business, Monroe sent an urgent note to Madison; after explaining the situation, he surrendered his future to his friend:

> May I request you to go to Mr. Randolph, and settle the matter with him. I promised him you would in the course of ½ an hour. If [the appointment] has not the approbation of my few friends and yourself in particular, [I] certainly will decline it. Weigh

therefore all circumstances and paying as little regard to private circumstances as should be, tell him for me what answer to give.

Madison accepted the job for Monroe.[29]

A few weeks later, Madison traveled to Baltimore to see Monroe onto his ship for France. He also took over the lease on Monroe's house in Philadelphia. Madison, then courting Dolley Payne Todd, was ready to abandon the boardinghouses he had frequented for the previous decade and a half.

With Monroe on the far side of the Atlantic, the two men kept their personal and professional ties as close as distance permitted. At the end of 1794, Monroe greeted the news of Madison's marriage by offering to buy French goods for the newlyweds. "Clocks, carpets, glass, furniture, table linen, etc.," he wrote, were "cheaper infinitely" in France. The Madisons returned a lengthy shopping list, including curtains for beds, windows, and parlor, carpets, and a china tea set and service. Deferring to the Monroes, Madison added that they should pick up any items "which you may know to be acceptable to a young housekeeper" so long as they were purchased "at second hand, cheap."[30]

The Monroes shipped back a bed, damask, mattresses, curtains, carpets, and "very cheap" china, along with twelve to eighteen chairs, two to three tables, one or two sofas, a clock, and a chimney piece. Knowing Madison's literary passion, Monroe asked for a list of books his friend would like. When the goods began to arrive, Madison acknowledged his "very great obligations to your kindness," but he noted that the damask had been switched for an "inferior and cheaper sort of silk." In reply, Monroe advised his provincial friend that styles had changed: "They never make curtains here of late of damask and that sent [to Madison] is the best and most costly kind of silk next [to] damask. It costs always near as much."[31]

Monroe arrived in Paris at a key moment. Only the week before, with the guillotining of Robespierre and Saint Just, the political pendulum had begun to swing away from the radical Jacobins. Monroe, who spoke good French, embraced his hosts. In an address to the National Convention's seven hundred members, he did not follow Washington's careful neutrality but voiced unabashed enthusiasm for France. After reciting America's revolutionary trials, he applauded the "fortitude, magnanimity and heroic valor" of French armies and "the wisdom and firmness of her councils."[32]

Monroe found the occasion overpowering. It was, he wrote home to Madison, a highly emotional event "of not merely interesting but distressing sensibility."[33] For months, his infatuation with France flourished. Back home his National Convention address made Monroe a darling of Republicans and a whipping boy for Federalists. More concerning, Secretary of State Randolph sent him a sharp reprimand. The rebuke, Monroe told Madison, "hurt." Madison counseled restraint and caution, sending examples of how Monroe's remarks in France were being used against Republicans in election campaigns.[34]

Over the winter of 1794–95, Monroe grew anxious that John Jay's mission to London would sour America's relations with France. When he acquired Jay's treaty, Monroe denounced it to Madison. If ratified, he warned, the treaty would be "one of the most afflicting events that ever befell our country"; it was making his position in France "a bed of thorns." Monroe expressed contempt for his own government's policies.[35]

As Monroe predicted, the Jay Treaty curdled French attitudes toward America, while Monroe's standing at home also deteriorated. Rumors, Madison warned, were linking him to land speculation in France; the president might recall him. Matters grew worse when Monroe attended a Fourth of July celebration where French officials hissed during a toast to President Washington. The American Minister was caught between an increasingly conservative Washington administration and a French government growing disenchanted with its fellow republic. When the president recalled Monroe, Madison claimed to be shocked, but it should have been no surprise. Diplomats who oppose their own government's policies do not long hold their posts.[36]

In late June 1797, with Adams installed as president, Republicans lustily welcomed Monroe home. Vice President Jefferson, Burr, and Congressman Albert Gallatin of Pennsylvania met Monroe's ship on the Philadelphia docks. When Monroe reached Virginia, he swiftly resumed his intimacy with Madison, already back at Montpelier after leaving Congress. Both now were out of public office.

By the end of the year, Monroe was borrowing money from Madison and inviting him for visits. "We are very lonesome and very desirous of seeing you," he wrote, warning that his Charlottesville dwelling was modest. They shared craftsmen and building supplies for their respective home-construction projects. In midwinter, Dolley raided Montpelier's larder to send the Monroes "a few pickles and preserves with half a dozen bottles of gooseberries and a bag of dried cherries." In return, the Monroes sent mattresses, napkins, and tablecloths. After Monroe moved into his new home in Albemarle County, he invited the Madisons to visit, adding, "Your skill in architecture and farming would be of great use to me at present."[37]

The friendship between the two men did not involve the same sort of intellectual communion Madison found with Jefferson. Monroe's warm nature was direct and less prone to theorizing; he was more of a soldier than the other two Virginians ever could be. Yet he and Madison sprang from the same plantation world, were political actors of the first rank, and agreed on most political subjects. They also were contemporaries in their family lives. Madison acquired a family in 1794, marrying the much younger Dolley and taking on her two-year-old son. The Monroes were at a comparable stage: They had an eight-year-old daughter at the time and would have two more children. The commonplaces of daily life knitted the two families together. The widower Jefferson, already with three grandchildren, was at a different stage of life. Indeed, Dolley's good friend in the Jefferson household was Patsy Jefferson Randolph, Jefferson's daughter, who was near Dolley in age.

Monroe and Madison talked and wrote regularly of public events while Monroe drafted a lengthy defense of his conduct as Minister to France. Both men supported Jefferson in extending the Republican cause and worked on the Kentucky and Virginia Resolutions. Monroe resisted encouragement to run for Congress, but his career received a shove when Madison returned to the Virginia legislature.[38]

On December 6, 1799, Madison rose in the House of Delegates to nominate Monroe as Virginia's next governor. His proposal, according to a newspaper report, "produced such a general rustling in the House that, for several minutes, we could not hear one word which he said." Opponents objected that Monroe's mission to France had failed; they called for an investigation of it. Madison rejected the idea as "entirely superfluous." Then, the newspaper report continued, Madison "spoke highly of [Monroe's] character as pure, and of his public character as unimpeachable." Madison knew he had the votes. With his forceful push, Monroe was elected governor by a nearly two-to-one margin.[39]

Monroe's first year as governor was rocky. Through the summer of 1800, he worked to contain unrest over the federal prosecution of Republican editor James Callender. More alarming was the discovery in September of Gabriel's Rebellion, the conspiracy in which hundreds of slaves had agreed to gather and march on Richmond. Governor Mon-

roe organized a harsh response to the conspiracy, which had been betrayed before any action was launched. He hanged twenty-seven slaves
and deported others to the West Indies.[40]

At the end of the summer, Monroe's only son died in infancy. In-
forming Madison of the tragedy, he opened himself on paper in a way
that Madison rarely could:

> An unhappy event has occurred which has overwhelmed us with
> grief. At ten last night our beloved babe departed this life after
> several days sickness. . . . I cannot give you an idea of the effect
> this event has produced on my family, or of my own affliction. . . .
> Many things have occurred my friend, in these late years that
> abated my sensibility to the affairs of this world, but this has
> roused me beyond what I thought it was possible I could be.
> Knowing the interest you take in our welfare, I perform a painful
> task in communicating to you and family this great calamity.[41]

The loss did not distract Monroe from pitching into the effort to
elect Jefferson president. Inclined to suspect the worst in others, Monroe proved prescient when he anticipated trouble from Aaron Burr after
Jefferson and Burr finished in a tie in the 1800 election. When Jefferson
prevailed on the thirty-sixth ballot in the House of Representatives, the
Virginia Dynasty began. It would dominate the nation's politics for the
next quarter-century, through strife and war and prosperity. It would
not be a smooth ride for Madison or Monroe.[42]

17

DISTANT DIPLOMACY

Jefferson mingled truth and self-congratulation when he called his election the "Revolution of 1800." The new century brought fundamental change to America, though Jefferson's administration reflected those changes as much as it led them. The Republicans embodied shifts that brought America closer to the revolutionary ideal of popular self-government.

Many states and local governments dropped or lowered property requirements for voting, though the franchise still was confined to white males except for New Jersey, where women could vote until 1807. Voting rates skyrocketed. In some parts of the nation, voter turnout rose from 20 percent to 80 percent. As Americans spread westward, national traits of independence and self-reliance grew stronger and regard for central authority declined. Social stratification weakened in frontier settlements, where few enjoyed inherited wealth, where talent and determination usually determined prosperity.

Newspaper circulation exploded. In 1790, America had only ninety-two newspapers, eight of them printed daily. Twenty years later, four times as many newspapers circulated more than 22 million copies a year. The United States had the largest newspaper circulation in the world, even though it was far from the most populous nation; France had six times the population.[1]

Jefferson's second inaugural address, delivered in March 1805, outlined an elysian vision of a republican nation that honored individual liberties, imposed low or no taxes, and rested at peace with the world. Americans, Jefferson said, "breath[e] an ardent love of liberty and independence, and occupy a country which left them no desire but to be undisturbed," especially by their government. "It may be the pleasure and pride of an American," he boasted, "to ask what farmer, what mechanic, what laborer, ever sees the tax-gatherer of the United States?"

Relying solely on import taxes, he promised, the nation soon would pay off its war debts and devote its resources to building canals and roads, to developing education, the arts, and manufacturing. America could preserve this utopia while Europe was at war, Jefferson insisted, because the nation's material interests were "inseparable from our moral duties; and . . . a just nation is taken on its word"; less virtuous nations had to rely on "armaments and wars to bridle others."

The international scene posed far more peril than Jefferson admitted. Napoleon's imperial ambitions, propelled by France's revolutionary energy, were setting Europe and the North Atlantic ablaze. As a trading nation, the United States hovered close to the flames of the global conflagration. For the next decade, Madison and Monroe would strain to keep America safe while vindicating its rights. Some of the greatest obstacles to that effort were their own Republican doctrines.

As Jefferson's Secretary of State, Madison had many responsibilities beyond diplomacy, including supervising the territorial governments for the lands that would become Ohio, Indiana, Illinois, Michigan, Wisconsin, Alabama, and Mississippi. He also managed the nation's legal officers and ran the post office, the patent office, and the census.

To perform these tasks, his agency had a budget of $11,910, of which $5,000 was Madison's salary. The balance paid for eight clerks who copied correspondence and preserved official papers. Madison's greatest responsibility was serving as the president's principal adviser on any issue of significance. After leaving office, Jefferson acknowledged his heavy reliance on Madison, insisting that his friend "is justly entitled to his full share of the measures of my administration. Our principles were the same, and we never differed sensibly in the application of them."[2]

To deal with his father's estate, Madison stayed at Montpelier through the first two months of the new administration. His father's outdated and incomplete will vastly complicated the job. Not until early May of 1801 did he, Dolley, her sister Anna, and nine-year-old Payne arrive in the nation's grubby new capital.

Washington's residences clustered around the unfinished Capitol building, the unfinished Executive Mansion, and the navy yard. Tree stumps stubbled the sweeping boulevards that looked nothing like the architect's drawings. In wet weather, mud made them virtually impassable. On dry days, choking dust swirled. The not-quite-city matched the infant republic, which also was being hewn from the North American forest, its soaring ideals often mired in the scramble of the day. Piles of stones and bricks and wood marked building sites where the presence of slave workers refuted the high-flown aspirations of the statesmen who glided by on horseback and in carriages.

Travel to Washington was no casual matter, even from neighboring Virginia. Jefferson had to cross eight rivers to reach the capital; five had neither ferry nor bridge. On one journey to Montpelier, Madison found the Rapidan River so high that he had to disassemble his carriage and float it across in three separate trips. Then the horses swam over.[3]

At the State Department, Madison found an overwhelming backlog of work. After two months on the job, Madison apologized to a friend for not answering a letter. His duties had prevented him from writing a personal letter since reaching Washington. Always diligent, Madison burrowed through heaps of correspondence. As Washington settled into its sulfurous summer, the effort took its toll on his health.[4]

The pace of trans-Atlantic diplomacy matched Madison's temperament. Messages took from four weeks to three months to pass to and from London, Paris, or Madrid. The long gaps allowed for deep reflection about each initiative and response; taking an extra day to think over a question did not much prolong an exchange. Madison used the time to play out in his mind the likely countermoves he would face and to recommend the responses that American Ministers should make. Diplomacy, often compared to a chess match, closely resembled one in Madison's era. At a dizzying pace, European nations went to war with Napoleon and made peace with him. From the far side of the ocean, Madison was playing chess by mail against adversaries who were in much closer contact with each other.

Socially, Madison played chess frequently. His drawing room always held a chessboard, pieces arrayed in opening positions. In March 1802, a British diplomat tried to enlist Madison's support for an English translation of a manual by the French chess master Francois-André Philidor. Madison's "passion for chess," the Englishman wrote, made him a natural sponsor of the project.[5] Madison's diplomatic practices bore traces of the game. He strived to be logical, deliberately weighing potential moves and responses. Confronting a problem, his first instinct was to gather all the written material that might shed light on it and retreat to his study. Because most diplomatic negotiations unspooled at a measured pace, he could map the interests and goals of the parties and select his course. Madison's written instructions to American diplomats bristled with analytical discipline.

Chess, however, is a streamlined contest of largely rational analysis; most players aim to keep emotion from clouding their play. Madison's diplomacy shared that trait, which meant he could miss the emotional forces driving policy. He sometimes complained that his adversary—most often Britain—was allowing political passions to dictate illogical policies that were contrary to its true interests. That emotion can trump reason is hardly a revelation in politics, yet Madison could find it maddening.

For Madison, the diplomatic chess matches were more difficult because he was anticipating moves by European leaders he had never met. Denied the critical information that comes from a person's tone of voice and body language, he often had only unreliable press accounts of the policies and actions of other governments. This lack of direct contact amplified the role of the diplomats on the scene. Ministers like Monroe and Robert Livingston sent Madison long accounts of negotiations, yet he could never have enough information. In 1807, when William Pinkney succeeded Monroe as Minister to Britain, Madison wrote that he and Jefferson regretted the "infrequency and scantiness of communications from our foreign ministers." He needed, Madison added, "to know what has not passed as well as what has." He wanted a report at least every two weeks, "if it were only to contradict by . . . silence, the falsehoods which sometimes arrive."[6]

Long delays in diplomatic exchanges created problems too. As sailing ships plowed across the Atlantic and back—a round-trip could consume six months—events might overtake Madison's rigorous instructions. Napoleon might vanquish an opposing army, or the British cabinet might tumble. Those delays placed a premium on the ability of the men on the scene to improvise. For that reason, America had always sent its ablest figures as Ministers to France and Britain: John Adams and Jefferson, Monroe and John Jay.

Madison pushed his nation's interests aggressively. The small man with an apparently mild disposition was a tenacious adversary. A British diplomat found Madison "a social, jovial, and good-humored companion full of anecdote" who was usually better informed than Jefferson. But he also found Madison "rather too much a disputatious pleader." Madison's pattern of pressing America's positions to the hilt could surprise Americans as much as foreigners.[7]

· · ·

For decades, foreign control of New Orleans had been a burr under America's saddle. That port provided the best trade outlet for farmers west of the Appalachian Mountains, but Spain often limited American trade through it. A bankrupt monarchy, Spain distrusted the bumptious American republic. The Spanish government, Monroe and a colleague wrote jointly in 1805, "despise[s] and hate[s] the principles and career of our government." Another American diplomat found the hidebound Spaniards impossible to deal with: "Pride and unpliancy of temper render them slow in remedying the most glaring faults, and constant in error."[8]

The 1795 treaty with Spain opened New Orleans to American trade, but in 1802 a colonial official revoked America's "right of deposit," closing New Orleans warehouses to American goods that were waiting for oceangoing ships. Outrage from the West prodded Jefferson and Madison into action. They turned to Monroe, who had just finished his third term as Virginia's governor. Through frontier travels and his time in Congress, Monroe had won a reputation as a friend of the West. Jefferson nominated him in January 1803 to be the American Envoy Extraordinary to resolve the New Orleans crisis.[9]

Monroe knew the job would strain his rickety personal finances. After a recitation of his money woes, he warned Madison that he might need a loan, "trespass[ing] on your friendship again in this respect." One expedient was to sell his household goods to the Madisons, including silverware, three dozen plates, candlesticks, beds and mattresses, and porcelain figures; Madison applied the proceeds to pay interest on Monroe's debts. The Monroes planned to replace the items with bargains bought overseas.[10]

Throughout Monroe's posting in Europe over the next four years, he and Madison continued private exchanges about politics, family, and Monroe's finances. Their official State Department correspondence included few personal references. Madison gave Monroe characteristically detailed instructions, which included authority to pay 30 million livres (about $5.6 million) to acquire New Orleans and Florida. Madison enclosed a draft treaty with seven substantive articles for a territorial acquisition, plus trade arrangements among two or three nations, depending on whether Spain and France both had to sign the treaty. Madison explained each treaty article, the rationale for the language he used and how it might be modified during negotiations. He admitted, however, that the instructions "will necessarily leave much to your discretion

Which proved to be the case. When Monroe arrived in Paris in mid-April of 1803, the political planets were aligned perfectly. France, nearing the end of the single year of peace it enjoyed between 1793 and 1813, was preparing for renewed war. The army Napoleon had sent to suppress the slave rebellion on Saint-Domingue had been annihilated by disease and battle. Napoleon concluded that French destiny lay in Europe, not the New World, so he resolved to convert the Louisiana Territory to cash.

Monroe, joining the American Minister to France, Robert Livingston, quickly struck a bargain to buy Louisiana for $15 million. Six weeks after Monroe arrived, the treaty was on its way back to Washington. In early July, most of the nation gleefully celebrated the Louisiana Purchase, the signature achievement of Jefferson's presidency. In official correspondence, Madison brushed aside concerns that the treaty was beyond the authority of Monroe and Livingston, or beyond the government's constitutional powers. Doubling the size of the nation, he pointed out, was "highly advantageous."[12]

Madison, however, admitted two problems with the treaty. First, the government had to find the funds to pay for it. "The unexpected weight of the draft now to be made on the treasury," he admitted, "may possibly be inconvenient." Monroe and Livingston arranged for a London bank to raise the money but then bickered for months over how those arrangements had grown snarled. Their disagreement morphed into an acrimonious dispute over who received credit for the purchase. "The most difficult, vexatious, and embarrassing part of my labor," Monroe moaned in a letter to Madison, "has been with my associate." A year after the treaty, the two envoys were still denouncing each other in nasty letters home.[13]

The second problem was whether the purchase included West Florida, which extended east from the Mississippi River to the Perdido River on the Gulf Coast and included the port of Mobile. Because the Mobile River drained a significant portion of the Mississippi Territory, the Americans wanted to control it. The treaty with France described no boundaries at all, stating simply that the United States was acquiring whatever land France had earlier acquired from Spain. Monroe and Livingston insisted that the treaty covered West Florida, and that even if it did not, the United States should take the land.[14] Madison was more cautious. He directed Monroe to acquire West Florida from Spain advised him not to hurry, since the province "now more certainly ever must drop into our hand."[15]

Monroe had achieved one of America's greatest diplomatic successes in a few weeks. With a single accomplishment, he became the nation's leading diplomat, the man who euchred Napoleon out of an empire, paying four cents per acre when federal lands in the West were selling for fifty times that price. Madison and Jefferson rewarded Monroe by appointing him Minister to Great Britain, the nation's most sensitive diplomatic post. The challenges in London would be considerably more difficult.

In 1804, the Anglo-American relationship was deep and emotionally fraught. Culturally and linguistically, the two peoples were as close as nations separated by an ocean can be. They read each other's writings. They shared a legal system and notions of representative government. Yet wounds from the Revolution festered on both sides: Many Americans still bristled at British arrogance and presumption, while many Englishmen thought of Americans as traitors predisposed to bite any hand that fed them. Economically dependent on trade with each other, they also were commercial rivals around the globe.

American merchants were growing rich from the European wars. While the French and English slaughtered each other and burnt each other's ships, neutral Americans traded with both sides. Between 1793 and 1805, America's merchant fleet more than doubled; by 1810, it had tripled. The British resented America's prosperity, which seemed to flourish behind the shield of the Royal Navy. In their view, the British served mankind by battling the French devils while Americans became wealthy and fat. A leading British pamphlet complained that Britain's enemies were trading "under the neutral [American] flag, cheaply as well as safely, taking away Britain's markets, injur[ing] our manufacturers, and threaten[ing] our colonies with ruin."[16]

The nature of the war increased the friction between Britain and America. With the Royal Navy the master of the seas, particularly after its smashing victory at Trafalgar in September 1805, Britain gravitated to a war of blockade and economic strangulation. The toll on American shipping was heavy. By one calculation, between 1805 and 1808 the British seized an American merchant ship every other day. In 1808, they seized one out of every five American merchantmen on the ocean. Those seizures provided an ample basis for war between Britain and America.[17]

Britain's dependence on seapower led it to the practice of impressment, or forcing seamen into service. The Royal Navy needed a huge labor force to staff more than six hundred warships. In 1792, it had required only 36,000 seamen; the number nearly quadrupled by 1805, to 120,000. To replace deserters fleeing the Royal Navy's harsh discipline and low pay, as well as those sailors falling to disease or combat, the British had to add 10,000 new seamen each year.[18]

They could find sailors in only so many places. Press gangs roamed British ports, grabbing deserters and the unwary alike. The British also looked to American ships, which were a lure for dissatisfied British tars. On American ships, British seamen well knew, discipline was easier and pay was higher. Whenever a Royal Navy ship docked at an American port, it risked desertions by sailors seeking a better berth. In the British view, Americans seduced their seamen from their duty.[19]

Yet the act of impressment was highly provocative. It denied the sovereignty of the nation whose ship was boarded and stripped of its seamen. Arrogant British captains made the practice not only insulting but infuriating. They loitered at the entrances to American ports and demanded to search every passing vessel. Outrages committed by British ships were a constant irritant. Often within sight of shore, the British humiliated the nation. Accidents would happen. When a British warship fired a warning shot in New York Harbor, the cannonball hit a merchant ship by mistake and killed an American sailor. Furious New Yorkers rioted in response.[20]

Equally offensive was the English doctrine for determining who could be impressed. Under English law, every individual born in the king's realm was his subject forever. Should an Irishman or Scot acquire American citizenship, the British deemed him still a subject of King George III and still obligated to serve him. Americans, by contrast, freely granted citizenship to immigrants. For Americans, the contrasting views of citizenship captured the difference between a republic where an individual chose his destiny and a monarchy that enslaved the individual to the nationality of his birth. When a British officer snickered at the notion that an Irishman had become an American, he denied America's legitimacy.[21]

The impressment issue resonated within American hearts because of its ideological content. The American Revolution glorified liberty. Impressment denied it. British captains impressed many British subjects and deserters, but they also impressed between five thousand and ten thousand American citizens, sometimes knowingly. In the language of the day, the British "enslaved" those Americans.[22]

Although impressment waxed and waned as a political issue, often depending upon the flagrancy of British seizures, Madison considered the practice intolerable. American sailors, he wrote in 1801, were impressed illegally, then "menaced or maltreated into enlistments," subjected to harsh floggings, and placed at risk of becoming battle casualties or prisoners of war. In detailed instructions to Monroe in early 1804, Madison explained that British policy also was contrary to Britain's interests because of "the jealousy and ill will excited among all maritime nations," which "may threaten the good understanding" between Britain and the United States.[23]

British officials did not agree. One told Monroe that "the question of the seamen was all important." To fight Napoleon, British captains needed crews. They were not squeamish about how they got them. In London, Monroe thought he might soften British practices and lay the groundwork for more improvements in the future. Madison was not so patient. United States policy, he wrote to Monroe, was "to get rid of impressments altogether on the high seas."

Madison's instructions included the draft of a thirteen-article treaty covering impressments, the rights of American merchant vessels, and the definition of blockades and contraband. Like any good chess player, Madison spelled out fallback positions and his reasons for choosing the language in each article.[24]

Turmoil in the British government delayed Monroe's London negotiations for more than two years. First the cabinet turned over. Then Prime Minister William Pitt fell ill and died. The delays signaled a fundamental truth that Madison and Jefferson never quite accepted: that America's complaints were not very important to Britain. The war with France, which consumed British attention for two decades, was paramount, followed closely by Irish unrest and rebellion. King George's periodic fits of dementia, which began in 1788 and recurred in 1804, could dwarf everything. America was well down the list.[25]

Moreover, America's tiny military posed little threat. For European nations with hundreds of thousands of men under arms, American threats seemed laughable. Monroe tried to explain that, in Europe, the "respect which one power has for another is in the exact proportion of the means which they respectively have of injuring each other." European leaders, he wrote another time, "understand the science of pushing things to the last point . . . they are at it daily with many powers, and have no more feeling in the business than wood or marble."[26]

Jefferson's America preferred the smallest possible army and navy.

The Republican view held that a strong military brought repression at home and adventurism abroad. An American diplomat wrote from Paris that the French correctly considered the United States "a government which abhors war and regards fleets and armies as nuisances or scourges." The American Minister to Spain suggested that Republican doctrine be loosened to permit at least a few more warships.[27]

British contempt for American weakness translated into galling incidents. When British warships camped at the entrance to New York Harbor in the summer of 1804, they trapped two French warships at New York's piers. New York was, Madison wrote in a testy note to the British Minister, "absolutely blockaded by a foreign armed force." Such high-handed actions inflamed Americans. Madison instructed Monroe to complain about the incidents in "a manly tone" but also to strike a conciliatory note in search of an agreement. That approach would never work. Nothing would be gained, Monroe wrote in 1805, "without an attitude of menace and an evident ability . . . and determination to execute it if necessary."[28]

The British tended to discount Jefferson and Madison's policies, believing that they did not accurately express the pro-British sympathies of most Americans. The British government, Monroe explained to Madison, "has been accustomed to view us as a divided people, [in which] the greater and more respectable portion" favored Britain over France.[29]

Frustrated by the delays in London, Monroe traveled through France to Spain, attempting in both places to win support for the American claim to West Florida. He failed, for familiar reasons. "They know the pacific temper of our government and country," Monroe explained; they did not fear the United States. Disappointed, his Louisiana triumph now two years in the past, Monroe trudged back to London.[30] The frustrations prompted more of Monroe's periodic complaints to Madison of his ever-strained finances and his vagabond life, moving from Paris to London to Paris to Madrid to Paris to London, sometimes with his wife and daughters but often without them.[31]

Troubled by the apparent stalemate with Britain and beset with domestic criticism, Jefferson appointed an additional envoy to join Monroe: William Pinkney, a Federalist lawyer from Baltimore who had negotiated commercial claims with the British. Monroe resented Pinkney's appointment, thinking it undercut his stature. In May 1806, Madison sent with Pinkney his customary detailed instructions. An agreement on impressments, he directed, was "indispensable" and "a necessary preliminary" to any American concession. Madison also insisted that the British loosen restrictions on American trade, particularly with British colonies in the West Indies.[32]

Two British negotiators finally began talks with the Americans in the fall of 1806. Early on, the Americans made a pivotal concession. The British, Monroe wrote later, flatly rejected any change in impressments. No treaty could even mention them. As a sop, the British offered to provide a private letter stating their intention not to impress American citizens. If the Americans would not accept that, the negotiation was over.

Monroe and Pinkney blinked. They agreed to the British nonterms on impressment. In a letter to Madison, they acknowledged that they took the step "on our own responsibility," but "in full confidence that our conduct and the motives of it will be approved." Monroe understood that instructions should yield in the face of changed circumstances. Several years before, Madison had instructed him to purchase New Orleans and Florida from the French. When he and Robert Livingston leapt at the opportunity to buy all of Louisiana, their deviation from instructions was celebrated. In the current situation, Monroe and Pinkney accepted that Britain would not bend on impressments and that toothless America could compel no other course; rather than cut off the talks, they forged ahead. Their decision reflected the change that can come over a negotiator who spends months and years away from home. This was not, however, a mere deviation from instructions; rather, it was an abandonment of them. In so doing, Monroe and Pinkney had overlooked their government's rage over impressments.

On January 1, 1807, the negotiators signed final treaty terms. Monroe and Pinkney wrote to Madison that although the British would not abandon impressment, the private note from the British government on the subject meant that "its practice would nevertheless be essentially if not completely abandoned."[33] Monroe had high hopes for the treaty. An understanding with Britain could shelter the United States from war for a generation. Only Britain could truly threaten its safety: France lacked the navy to do so; Spain was too weak; Prussia, Austria, and Russia were too far away. The prize of peace was a great one. An ambitious man who secured such a triumph, after winning the Louisiana Purchase, might see himself as a future president, even as the next president.

For Monroe, a great deal was riding on the treaty with Britain that he and Pinkney sent back to Washington City.

18

THE RUPTURE

In early February 1807, Madison wrote to Monroe that British impressments had "at no time been more numerous or vexatious." The United States would sign no agreement, he added, without British concessions on impressments. His message crossed in midocean with the Monroe-Pinkney treaty, which contained no British concessions on impressments.[1]

When the British Minister presented the treaty to Madison, the Secretary of State immediately asked what its terms were on impressments. The Minister replied that the document never mentioned the subject. Madison, the Englishman reported, "expressed the greatest astonishment and disappointment . . . he did not think it would be possible to ratify the treaty."

Madison's original instructions to Monroe, and his later instructions to Pinkney, could hardly have been more clear. There could be no agreement without British concessions on impressment. And yet here was a treaty signed by Monroe and Pinkney that simply ignored his instructions. Madison had no political maneuvering room. A decade earlier, he had denounced the Jay Treaty as a craven surrender to Britain. He could not embrace a comparable submission now. Jefferson agreed. On the evening of that same day, the president told a delegation of senators that he would reject the treaty. "Our best course," Jefferson wrote some weeks later, "is to let the negotiation take a friendly nap."[2]

As Jefferson and Madison studied the treaty, they liked it less and less. They invited comments from Republican merchants, who uniformly concluded that it failed American interests. A New Englander said he preferred no treaty at all. Objections from Senator Samuel Smith of Maryland, whose family ran a Baltimore trading house, filled three letters. Smith also raised a political problem with rejecting the treaty:

This 1794 portrait shows Madison in a jauntier outfit than the basic black he ordinarily preferred for everyday wear. *Gilcrease Museum, Tulsa OK. Photo by Kevin Winter/Getty Images*

Kitty Floyd's delicate beauty won Madison's heart in 1783, though he was twice her age. The pain of that failed engagement still smarted for Madison many years later. *Library of Congress*

Alexander Hamilton's intellectual brilliance and high spirits made him a compelling figure. Though he and Madison had different backgrounds and personalities, they joined together in the fight for a stronger national government. *Library of Congress*

Philadelphia's State House, renamed Independence Hall, was the home of the Confederation Congress during Madison's service from 1779 to 1783, and home of the Constitutional Convention of 1787. *Library of Congress*

Lining up by state, the delegates signed the draft Constitution, with Madison, portrayed in a light-colored suit, in his customary place next to Washington at the head of the room.

Courtesy of Independence National Historic Park

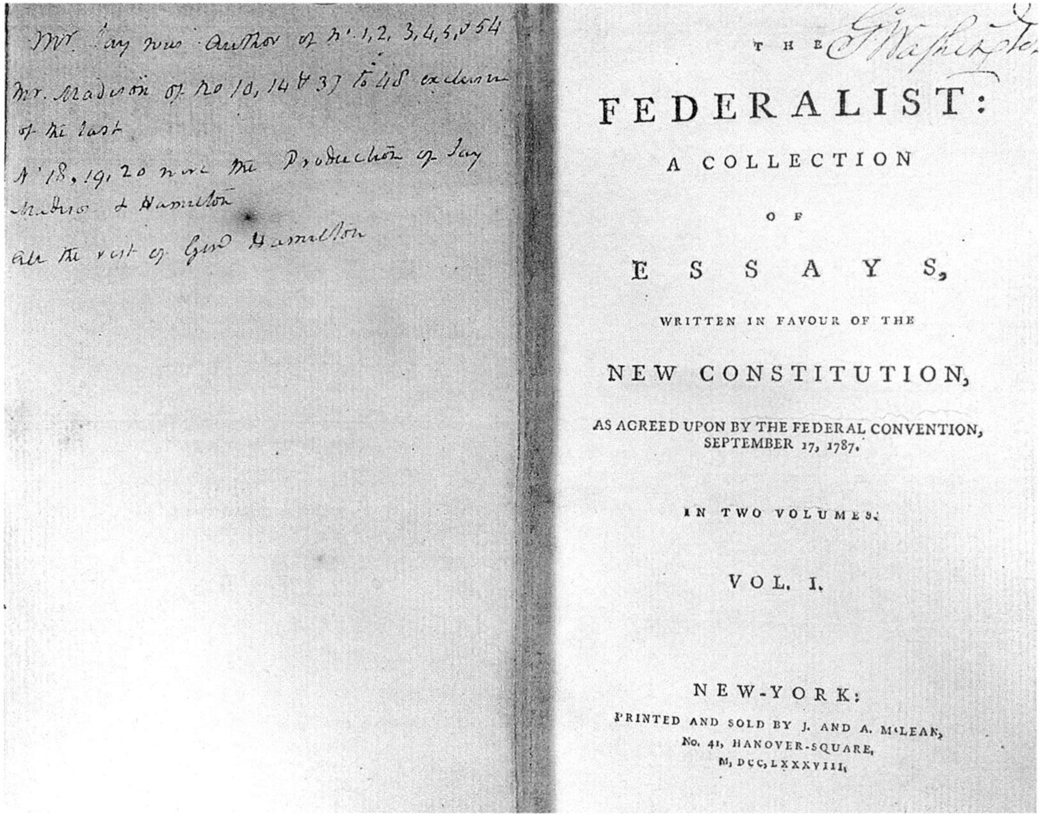

THE

FEDERALIST:

A COLLECTION

OF

ESSAYS,

WRITTEN IN FAVOUR OF THE

NEW CONSTITUTION,

AS AGREED UPON BY THE FEDERAL CONVENTION,
SEPTEMBER 17, 1787.

IN TWO VOLUMES.

VOL. I.

NEW-YORK:

PRINTED AND SOLD BY J. AND A. M'LEAN,
No. 41, HANOVER-SQUARE,
M,DCC,LXXXVIII,

Hamilton shipped bound volumes of *The Federalist* throughout Virginia
and New York, including several to General Washington, who signed
this copy in the upper right-hand corner.
Chapin Library of Rare Books, Williams College

Patrick Henry, a brilliant orator and canny politician, was Madison's political nemesis for more than a decade. They clashed for weeks at Virginia's ratifying convention in June 1788.
Library of Congress

New York's Governor George Clinton was no match for Hamilton's oratory in New York's ratifying convention, but his Anti-Federalists enjoyed an overwhelming majority there.
Library of Congress

Melancton Smith, a New York lawyer, led the Anti-Federalist faction that finally joined in that state's grudging ratification of the Constitution. *Collection of the New-York Historical Society*

When New York City celebrated the new Constitution, its parade featured the "Federal ship *Hamilton*" in honor of the only New York delegate who signed the national charter. *Collection of the New-York Historical Society*

General Washington's duties as presiding officer at the Constitutional Convention in Philadelphia in 1787 did not prevent him from sitting for this portrait through the summer.
Courtesy of Independence National Historic Park

Washington was acclaimed through his journey from Mount Vernon to New York City to take the oath as America's first president. This drawing captures the ladies of Trenton, New Jersey, greeting him with garlands of flowers.
Library of Congress

New York renovated its City Hall into a grand "Federal Hall" for the new Congress that met in the spring of 1789, with Madison as the undisputed leader of the House of Representatives. *Library of Congress*

The chamber of the House of Representatives in New York's Federal Hall was two stories high, with vaulted windows. *Library of Congress*

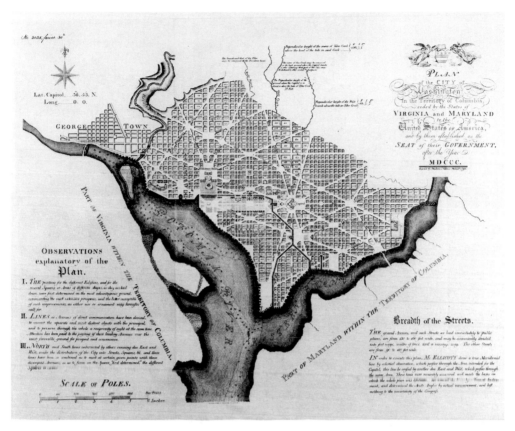

For more than five years, several Congresses struggled to choose the proper location of the nation's capital. Through a subtle political bargain, Madison achieved Washington's powerful wish to place the capital on the Potomac River, very near the president's home at Mount Vernon. *Library of Congress*

Madison strongly opposed creation of the First Bank of the United States, which he thought was unconstitutional, but lost the battle to Hamilton when President Washington signed the bank legislation in February 1791. The bank was established in this Philadelphia headquarters. *Library of Congress*

After Congress moved to Philadelphia in December 1790, it met in Congress Hall, adjacent to Independence Hall. In this House of Representatives chamber, Madison moved steadily from spokesman for the administration to leader of the opposition. *Federal Hall, Historical Society of Pennsylvania*

Thomas Jefferson and Madison saw each other only sporadically through many years of their friendship, but became constant companions when Jefferson became Secretary of State in 1790. *Courtesy of Independence National Historic Park*

After eight years as the nation's chief executive, Washington's weariness with the political world was unmistakable. *Library of Congress*

In the 1790s, when construction began on the new national capital on the Potomac, the town of Georgetown was a sleepy river port. *Library of Congress*

Only the north wing of the Capitol building was completed when Congress arrived in Washington in 1800, so both the Senate and the House of Representatives met there, with commanding views of the rural countryside. *Library of Congress*

RICHMOND, *August* 9th, 1800.

SIR,

WE have taken the liberty to advise you, to have the Tickets for Electors of President and Vice-President of the United States written; and have thought proper to recommend to you the following form. We think it advifeable that the Committees in the different Counties fhould procure to be written, a fufficient number of Tickets to be diftributed among the Freeholders. In the formation of the Ticket, particular attention fhould be paid, in difcriminating between the Republican Candidate William H. Cabell, and the Federal Candidate William Cabell.

WE are happy to inform you, that we have received poffitive affurances from Colonel Ellzey, that he will with pleafure ferve as an Elector, if he fhould be honored by the fuffrages of a majority of his fellow citizens.

We are Sir, very refpectfully,
Your fellow citizens,

P. N. NICHOLAS, CHAIRMAN.
MERIWETHER JONES,
SAMUEL PLEASANTS, *Jun.*   } COMMITTEE.
JOSEPH SELDEN,
GERVAS STORRS,
JOHN H. FOUSHEE, SECRETARY.

Form of the Republican Ticket.

The following persons are selected by the Voter, whose name is written on the back of this Ticket, for Electors of President and Vice-President.

George Wythe,	of the City of Richmond.
William Newfum,	of Princefs Anne.
Edmond Pendleton, fen.	of Caroline.
William H. Cabell,	of Amhurft.
James Madifon, jun.	of Orange.
John Page,	of Gloucefter.
Thomas Newton, jun.	of Norfolk Borough.
Carter B. Harrifon,	of Prince George.
General Jofeph Jones,	of Dinwiddie.
William B. Giles,	of Amelia.
Creed Taylor,	of Cumberland.
Thomas Read, fen.	of Charlotte.
George Penn,	of Patrick.
Walter Jones,	of Northumberland.
Richard Brent,	of Prince William.
William Ellzey,	of Loudoun.
Andrew Moore,	of Rockbridge.
General John Brown,	of Hardy.
General John Prefton,	of Montgomery.
Hugh Holmes,	of Frederick.
Archibald Stuart,	of Augufta.

Madison retired from politics from 1797 to 1800, when he took up a seat in the Virginia Assembly and ran as a presidential elector pledged to vote for Jefferson. *Library of Congress*

As president, Jefferson set an informal air while relying heavily on Madison, his political partner for twenty years. *Library of Congress*

This 1804 portrait, painted while Madison was Secretary of State, conveyed the sobriety and reserve that Madison displayed on public occasions. *Library of Congress*

Also painted in 1804, this portrait of Dolley Madison in an empire-waisted gown captured her appeal but not her energy and vivacity. *Library of Congress*

With a background as a soldier, James Monroe was persuaded by Patrick Henry to run against his friend Madison in the first congressional election in January 1789. Madison won comfortably. *Library of Congress*

When elected president, Madison began the final expansion of Montpelier, adding wings on both sides of the house. *Photograph by Kenneth Wyner, courtesy of The Montpelier Foundation*

LEFT: An immigrant from Switzerland, Albert Gallatin became a leading Republican congressman, then the influential Secretary of the Treasury in both the Jefferson and Madison administrations. *Library of Congress*

BELOW: America teetered on the brink of war with Britain when HMS *Leopard*, in search of sailors who had deserted, opened fire on the unprepared *Chesapeake*, a U.S. Navy frigate. In response, Jefferson and Madison persuaded Congress to declare a controversial embargo on trade with Britain. *The Mariners' Museum, Newport News, VA*

After repeated military failures during the early months of the War of 1812, Madison recruited John Armstrong of New York, a former officer in the Continental Army, as his Secretary of War. The appointment ended unhappily. *Courtesy of Independence National Historic Park*

The British set fire to the public buildings in Washington, leaving both wings of the Capitol as burnt-out husks. *Library of Congress*

During the dark days at the end of 1814, New Englanders met at the Hartford Convention to consider withdrawing from the union to make their own peace with Britain. *Library of Congress*

General Andrew Jackson's smashing victory in the Battle of New Orleans, which occurred in January 1815 after the Treaty of Ghent was signed, gave most Americans the sense that they had won the war. The treaty returned the two countries to *status quo ante bellum:* a classic draw. *Library of Congress*

Serving as Secretary of State and Secretary of War—sometimes as both at once—James Monroe provided essential ballast to an administration locked in a military struggle with a far stronger opponent. *Library of Congress*

Dolley Payne Todd, raised a Quaker, wore Quaker bonnets through the early years of her marriage with Madison. She abandoned them when Madison was elected president. *Library of Congress*

Nearly 68 years old, Madison in 1817 embraced retirement to his lifelong home at Montpelier, after two terms as president. *Library of Congress*

John Payne Todd was Dolley Madison's sole surviving son from her first marriage. Known as "Payne," he never settled down and caused great heartache to his mother and stepfather, Madison. *Image copyright © The Metropolitan Museum of Art. Image Source: Art Resource, NY*

Madison, Monroe, and Chief Justice John Marshall served as distinguished senior delegates to the 1829 Virginia Constitutional Convention. Madison argued for somewhat wider voting rights, but without success. *Collection of the New-York Historical Society*

In 1824, the Marquis de Lafayette traveled to America for a reunion with his revolutionary colleagues from forty-five years before. When he stayed at Montpelier, Lafayette urged Madison to oppose slavery publicly. *Library of Congress*

The Nat Turner slave rebellion in 1831 in southeastern Virginia claimed the lives of more than 60 whites and more than 100 slaves, terrifying white Virginians and underscoring for the Madisons the perils of slavery. *Library of Congress*

Edward Coles, Dolley Madison's cousin and James Madison's secretary, freed his own slaves and established them on farms in the Illinois Territory. Coles repeatedly urged Madison to take steps to free his slaves, without success. *Edward Coles, Historical Society of Pennsylvania*

Madison grew so feeble that he spent his final years in two rooms at Montpelier, usually wearing gloves and nightcap to keep warm. Nevertheless, his mind remained sharp and he talked with visitors for hours. *Library of Congress*

Dolley lived for thirteen years after Madison's death, most of the time in Washington, D.C., where she sat for this unretouched photographic image. Though she resumed her status as a social fixture in the capital, she struggled to make ends meet. *Library of Congress*

And is it not probable that sending back the treaty may be attributed to hostility against Mr. Monroe? May not Mr. Monroe so consider the subject? May he not think it necessary to defend himself in the public prints?[3]

Smith made good points. Monroe could be touchy. Nevertheless, Madison and Jefferson would have nothing to do with the treaty.

Anticipating trouble, Madison tried to placate Monroe with soft words. "All of us," he wrote in a private letter, "are fully impressed with the difficulties which your negotiation had to contend with, as well as the faithfulness and ability with which it was supported." Madison tried to demonstrate confidence in Monroe by asking that he and Pinkney resume negotiating under new instructions, once more demanding concessions on impressments; Madison conceded that the issue was one "altogether of thorns."[4]

Madison's gestures, however, were obvious window dressing. Monroe knew that the treaty would have been a mixed blessing, but he thought it a necessary step. The United States, Monroe feared, was too weak to stand alone in a world at war. As he wrote in an earlier letter, "it is important for us to stand well with some power," and Britain was the power that could do America the most harm. After nearly four years in Europe, Monroe took a practical view of America's risks, prospects, and values. Better to reach a partial accommodation and coax the British toward future friendship. Yet Madison and Jefferson, unwilling to compromise their commitment to liberty and free trade, took Monroe's work and briskly deposited it in the rubbish bin.[5]

Despite Madison's new instructions, resuming the negotiation had to seem like a fool's errand. Nothing had happened to soften British attitudes. The Royal Navy still needed sailors. American merchants still traded with Britain's enemies. The American military had grown no more impressive.

Moreover, the European war was growing more bitter. Britain and France increasingly targeted American ships, which typically flitted between British and European ports, trading their way through multiple stops. In November 1806, Napoleon's Berlin Decree responded to Britain's blockade by proclaiming that neutral ships would not be welcome in French-controlled ports if they also traded with Britain. Two months later, Britain retaliated with an "Order in Council" authorizing the seizure of any ship trading between European ports. Most American merchantmen would violate the British order or the French decree; many would violate both.

The prospects for renegotiation were grim. When the British Foreign Minister learned that Jefferson was likely to reject the treaty, he suggested the entire effort be dropped.[6] Nevertheless, Madison and Jefferson would not give up. They struggled to concoct an alternative negotiating strategy. What if, they wondered, the United States pledged that its ships would hire no foreign seamen? With British sailors excluded from American ships, Britain could abandon impressment. The idea was capsized by statistics from the Secretary of the Treasury, Albert Gallatin. Without British seamen, America's merchant fleet could not sail; by one estimate, 30 percent of its seamen were British. Lacking an innovative new proposal, Madison set to work on new instructions to Monroe and Pinkney. The task, he told Jefferson, proved "more tedious as well as more difficult than was at first supposed."[7]

Madison's new instructions were immense, extending for more than ten thousand words of sometimes withering criticism of the treaty, a critique that was bound to mortify the American negotiators. Once again, Madison insisted that the United States would enter no treaty that did not limit impressments. A single passionate passage cried out that abandoning American sailors to impressments would deliver up "their lives, everything in a word that is dearest to the human heart." Nevertheless, Madison authorized his envoys to pledge that American ships would discharge British seamen with fewer than two years in the American service; he did not explain how such a pledge could be enforced on ships that cruised the globe for months and even years.

Madison added a sentence-by-sentence dissection of the Monroe-Pinkney treaty. The treaty's provisions on East Indies trade created "insuperable objections." A separate British note addressing Napoleon's Berlin Decree was "inadmissible." Conditions had to be removed on trade with Europe and on the vital reexport of produce from non-British colonies in the West Indies. The United States must be able to grant equal trading status to nations opposing Britain. Britain must revoke its taxes on exports to the United States. In all, Madison directed that two dozen treaty provisions be renegotiated.[8]

When the instructions reached the all-important question of why Britain would grant concessions it had already refused, Madison offered lame threats. The British, he warned, had "vulnerable possessions in our neighborhood"; true enough, but without a viable American army or navy, Britain could hardly fear for its Canadian or Caribbean possessions. Madison also pointed out that the president could ban imports from a foreign nation that abused American trading interests; by renegotiating the treaty, the British could avoid such a "nonimportation" order. Madison had been urging economic retaliation against Britain for fifteen years, but his countrymen always avoided that course. Even if that threat were credible, it was a small fright for a British government locked in a death struggle with Napoleon.

The baleful effect of Madison's instructions on the sensitive Monroe was predictable. Madison's willingness to offend his friend likely was due to several factors, beginning with real frustration that Monroe and Pinkney had ignored his unmistakable instructions. Madison's obsessive nature probably played a role, compelling him to produce a detailed catalog of error without regard to its impact on Monroe. Madison also may have thought the instructions would enlighten the American envoys on key considerations—though he had been involved in politics far too long to expect others to welcome being lectured about their errors.

Several newspapers speculated that Madison's hostility to the treaty was a strategy to saddle Monroe with a political debacle that would keep him from succeeding Jefferson as president. The speculation seems unfounded. Madison did not scheme for office at any other point in his career: not when battling for his political survival in the 1788 congressional campaign, or in the presidential campaigns of 1808 and 1812. It seems even less likely when the target would have been a close friend. In May 1807, Madison was not aiming to block Monroe from the Executive Mansion.[9]

Yet he knew that his new instructions had the power to wound. Madison sent a private note to Monroe professing to be pained that he could not affirm Monroe's efforts. His own actions, Madison protested, involved "the same conscientious discharge of duty which is stamped on your proceedings." Madison added the wish that the new instructions "may yet close our common labors with success and satisfaction." He closed effusively, signing with "assurances of the great esteem and regard with which I remain Dear Sir your friend and servant."[10]

When news of the treaty's demise arrived in London in the spring of 1807, Monroe and Pinkney halted talks with Britain over Canadian trade and boundaries. Monroe began to draft a protest to Jefferson but never sent it, choking back his disagreement until he could speak with the president in person. Under Madison's new instructions, which arrived in July, Monroe and Pinkney dutifully asked the British to resume negotiations. The British Foreign Minister suggested they put their request in writing, but events overtook the effort.[11]

In late June, USS *Chesapeake,* one of the handful of U.S. Navy frigates, sailed from Norfolk for a Mediterranean patrol aimed at North

African pirates. A British squadron had lingered off the Virginia coast for weeks, its sailors deserting whenever they could. The squadron, led by HMS *Leopard*, demanded to search *Chesapeake*, known to be a destination for deserters. It was a momentous request. The British routinely searched American merchantmen, but they had never before stopped an American warship.[12]

Chesapeake's captain was spectacularly unready. The United States, after all, was not at war. Cables and lumber were stacked on the decks. The gunpowder needed on deck was still in the hold. Lashes immobilized most of the thirty-eight cannon. The Americans stalled, but *Leopard* would not wait. Three broadsides killed four Americans and wounded many more. *Chesapeake* surrendered. The British claimed four of its crew as deserters.[13]

Reporting the news to Jefferson, Madison called the incident "not merely without provocation or any justifiable cause [but] committed with the avowed and insulting purpose of violating a ship of war under the American flag." The four impressed sailors, he insisted, were Americans. A few weeks later, Madison complained that British ships off Norfolk still acted in a "hostile and insolent spirit," their actions amounting to "an invasion and a siege."[14]

War talk swept the nation. "Never since the battle of Lexington," Jefferson observed, "have I seen this country in such a state of exasperation." The Virginia militia marched to Norfolk's defense. "A tame submission," warned Madison's brother-in-law, "will disgrace the nation." But Jefferson wanted no war; the nation was no better prepared for conflict than *Chesapeake* had been. Though Madison struck a combative pose with the British, he knew that war was not an option.[15]

The *Chesapeake* incident washed away any thoughts of a commercial treaty with Britain, particularly after the Royal Navy hanged one of the four seized sailors (he was, in truth, a British deserter, though the other three were not). Anglo-American misunderstandings were at a peak. Relieved of any duty to resume talks, Monroe could finally return home, leaving Pinckney as the American Minister in London. Arriving in Washington City in late December, Monroe reported to Madison and Jefferson, then withdrew, his unsuccessful treaty already forgotten by most, though not by him.[16]

As Congress convened in late 1807, Britain had made no reparations for *Chesapeake*. In fact, it had issued a new Order in Council requiring

that neutral ships acquire a British license before stopping at any European port. In response, Napoleon issued the Milan Decree, claiming as
a French prize any ship that had submitted to British search or called
at a British port. With American trade increasingly the target of the
European belligerents, the United States had to act. Its only weapons
were economic.

Economic warfare has undoubted virtues, principally that it re-
taliates against adversaries without bloodshed. That retaliation, however, can easily fall flat. If a determined adversary is willing to absorb
financial losses over the short or even medium term, economic warfare
will fail. Moreover, economic weapons also inflict losses on the nation
deploying them. Blocking your adversary's trade interrupts your own. If
the boycotting nation is determined, it will endure those costs. Whether
the policy succeeds, then, turns on the wills of the contending parties.

A trade embargo is an extreme form of economic warfare and a
policy of last resort. In late 1807, nothing else was working and war was
impossible. Nearly two years before, the venerable Elbridge Gerry of
Massachusetts had proposed an embargo to Madison, mostly to protect
American ships from seizure. Americans, Gerry argued, should stop
sending their "property to sea, with almost the certainty of its sacrifice"
to the Royal Navy or to French customs agents; an embargo would
"preserve their immense capitals from depredations." After the *Chesapeake* affair, the American Minister to France endorsed an embargo as a
wise defensive measure and also an offensive weapon that would teach
America's enemies a lesson.[17]

With surprisingly little debate, the Jefferson administration proposed an embargo and Congress adopted it. Over the Christmas holiday, Madison promoted the policy in two unsigned editorials in the
National Intelligencer, the Washington newspaper that spoke for the
administration. The embargo, he wrote, would dispel the European view
that "we are a divided people, or that our republican institutions have
not the energy to defend us."[18] It was wishful thinking. Within a year,
the embargo had succeeded only in confirming those propositions.

The law included so many holes that Congress amended it four
times over the next year in a frantic attempt to make it effective. The
initial law had perverse features. It did not bar imports in foreign vessels, which often were paid for in specie, so trade shifted to foreign
ships while hard currency drained out of the country. The embargo law
allowed American vessels to leave port to retrieve property from the
West Indies. An impressive number of merchants instantly discovered

the need to send such missions. Some six hundred merchantmen set off on that voyage, free to sail wherever economic opportunity beckoned.[19]

The embargo depended on public acceptance of the privations it caused at home, but Americans had no stomach for sacrifice. Opposition to the embargo blazed immediately, then spread. Federalist newspapers and officials denounced the policy as punishing Americans for British sins. Seaport communities suffered, especially in New England. In Salem, Massachusetts, three shipyards shut down; unemployment spread so swiftly that the town's soup kitchen had to feed twelve hundred people daily. American seamen left for Halifax to find work on foreign ships. By 1809, New York's debtors' prison held a thousand men, more than one percent of the population.[20]

An epidemic of smuggling erupted. Amelia Island in Spanish East Florida became an entrepot for inbound British goods and outbound lumber, rice, and indigo. Illegal shipments there doubled, then redoubled, then expanded exponentially. The northern border with Canada was a sieve. Ports in Maine harbored Canadian and British vessels, while American coastal ships crept northward in search of profits.[21]

The St. Lawrence River became a bloody border with Canada as government agents chased smugglers. A Vermont shootout left three smugglers dead and an army lieutenant wounded; seven smugglers were captured. Smugglers tried to kidnap customs officials and killed at least two of them. In one incident, a troop of army dragoons drove off sixty armed smugglers in ten boats. When smugglers faced criminal charges, sympathetic juries often set them free. Massachusetts juries returned guilty verdicts in only twelve of sixty-five smuggling trials. A Gloucester mob destroyed a government cutter that patrolled for smugglers.

Conversely, the embargo brought such prosperity to Canada that British army officers drank toasts to Jefferson. The embargo's failures caused tempers to rise in Congress. In a duel over remarks made during an embargo debate, a Tennessee Republican wounded a New York Federalist. The Republicans, however, could not shoot all of the embargo's opponents.[22]

Foreign developments also undermined the embargo. When Spain rebelled against Napoleon in early 1808, Spanish officials in the Americas flung their ports wide open to British goods. Delirious to have a new market, the British flooded Spanish America with goods they could no longer sell into the United States. The embargo took a toll on the British economy, but the impact was not enough. From London, William Pinkney reported that smuggling was muting the embargo's effect. The

American Minister in Paris was more discouraging. "Here the embargo is not felt," he wrote in late August, "and in England . . . it is forgotten." He added that in Europe "[i]t is believed that we cannot do much, and even that we will not do what we have the power of doing." The fundamental problem was that the British government was willing to absorb whatever injury the embargo inflicted, while the American government was not.[23]

The unpopular embargo threatened to make 1808 a treacherous political year for Republicans in general and for James Madison in particular. Positioned as Jefferson's successor as president, Madison was tied to the despised policy. Federalists hoped that opposing the embargo would revive their moribund party. The Republicans were breaking into factions because the fading Federalists no longer provided what Madison called "the cement" of a viable political opposition. On top of all that, Monroe was planning to make his own political statement in the 1808 election.[24]

As a presidential contender in 1808, Madison had political liabilities beyond the embargo. He had never run for office beyond his Virginia congressional district. Over the previous thirteen years he had faced voters only once, when elected to the Virginia House of Delegates in 1799. Many saw him as Jefferson's partner and helpmate, not as a vital leader in his own right, a problem exacerbated by his studious manner. As one Republican wrote, he could seem "too timid and indecisive." His Republican credentials were tarnished by his connection to Hamilton in *The Federalist* essays. He would never rival Jefferson's popularity.[25]

Madison's road to the presidency began with the Republican members of Congress, who would select the party's candidate. Two factions within that caucus mistrusted him: the "Old Republicans," a group of conservatives who longed for the supposed ideological purity of earlier eras, and the "Invisibles," a powerful group of senators who often acted in a self-interested manner.

Initially, the implausible John Randolph of Roanoke led the Old Republicans. Tall, slender, beardless, and with a high-pitched voice reminiscent of a *castrato*, the Virginian entered House debates carrying a riding crop and accompanied by his hunting dogs and slave attendant. His brilliance overcame his odd qualities. Though a powerful congressional figure for a time, his savage and erratic personality eventually marginalized him. Based on little more than ill will, Randolph blamed

Madison for accommodating a massive land scam in the Mississippi Territory called the "Yazoo fraud"; in fact, Madison's only connection with that scandal was to work with two other cabinet members to settle conflicting claims long after the fact. Nevertheless, Randolph's hostility toward Madison was deep-seated. In 1806, Randolph declared that "most of the evils which the US now suffered proceeded from the . . . weak, feeble, and pusillanimous spirit of the keeper of the Cabinet—the Secretary of State."[26]

The Invisibles, true to their name, were more difficult to trace and characterize. Leading senators like Samuel Smith of Maryland and William Branch Giles fell in with this group when it suited them, even joining forces with Federalists at times. Though Giles supported Madison in 1808, Smith enlisted with seventeen Republican congressmen who signed a newspaper statement in March that bitterly denounced the Secretary of State:

> We ask for energy and we are told of his [Madison's] moderation. We ask for talents and the reply is his unassuming merit. We ask for his services in the cause of public liberty and we are directed to the pages of the Federalist, written in conjunction with Alexander Hamilton and John Jay, in which the most extravagant of their doctrines are maintained and propagated. We ask for consistency as a Republican. . . . We ask for that high and honorable sense of duty which would at all times turn with loathing and abhorrence from any compromise with fraud and speculation. We ask in vain.[27]

Some Republicans cast longing eyes at Monroe as an alternative to Madison. As early as 1806, Randolph and others urged Monroe to seek the presidency. Randolph despaired of Madison's "cold and insidious moderation" and his "unfortunate matrimonial connection." Monroe, referring to the appointment of Pinkney as his co-envoy in London, blamed Jefferson and Madison for actions "calculated to hurt my feelings and [they] did actually hurt them." But in 1806, Monroe demurred to the suggestion that he seek the presidency. "There are older men," he wrote, plainly referring to Madison, "whom I have long been accustomed to consider as having higher pretensions to the trust than myself."[28]

By early 1808, angry over rejection of his treaty, Monroe took a different view. Monroe partisans in the Virginia General Assembly plotted to make him the party's presidential candidate. "The friends of Col.

Monroe here are very numerous," the state's governor wrote, "and many of them are very violent. . . . The opposition of many of them to Mr. Madison is virulent in the extreme." Federalists began to consider Monroe's merits as a candidate. A New York Federalist thought Monroe would be a "powerful antagonist" to Madison, adding: "The Federalists here feel a strong partiality for him."[29]

Because Madison commanded support among congressional Republicans who would name the party's nominee, Monroe enthusiasts organized a Virginia caucus in Richmond that could endorse their man first. When news of the Richmond scheme reached Washington, Madison supporters accelerated their timetable.

Monroe's forces won the race against the calendar. Their Richmond caucus met on the evening of January 21 and voted 57–10 for their candidate; Madison's Virginia partisans met separately to vote unanimously for elector candidates pledged to Madison. In Washington, only Madison's caucus met, and it gathered two days later. Madison won with 83 votes, with three going to Monroe and three to old George Clinton of New York. Although more than fifty congressional Republicans avoided taking up sides by staying home, Madison emerged from the jockeying as the unquestioned Republican candidate.[30]

Monroe could have restrained those pressing his candidacy but he chose not to do so. On the day after the Washington caucus, he wrote that when choosing its president, the nation should act "at perfect liberty [and] without any the slightest interference" from candidates. He had not offered himself as a candidate, he stressed, but added that he would never "withhold my services from my country should they be called for." He thereby struck the carefully calibrated pose that prevailed in early American politics, professing disinterest in the tawdry business of office seeking while signaling his eagerness for office. Jefferson, alarmed by the struggle between his closest political friends, wrote to Monroe that he watched "with infinite grief a contest arising between yourself and another, who have been very dear to each other, and equally so to me." Monroe would not budge, not even for Jefferson. He replied that he would be an "inactive spectator" of the presidential election, adding: "Should the nation be disposed to call any citizen to [the presidency] it would be his duty to accept it. On that ground I rest."[31]

Monroe's willingness to contest the nomination seems to have blindsided Madison, though their correspondence in early 1808 reflects the slow-motion fraying of a friendship. On January 5, shortly after welcoming Monroe home from France, Madison's note to Monroe reflected no tension. He enclosed a draft for three hundred dollars, of-fered news about the British Minister, and reminded Monroe that he should designate those of his diplomatic papers that should be withheld from Congress as confidential. Madison closed with customary good wishes from his family to Monroe's. Monroe's response from Richmond two weeks later—only two days before the nominating caucuses met in that city—was equally casual. Monroe related news of his lodgings and professed to be unsure whether Madison really owed him three hundred dollars; he signed with the usual family wishes.[32]

Two weeks later, after the caucuses, Monroe's tone changed. He crisply reminded the Secretary of State to return certain papers that Monroe needed to compose his self-defense over the rejected treaty. Madison's slowness in returning those papers was understandable, since he now knew that Monroe was preparing a written challenge to Madi-son's official actions. Monroe's signature was a frosty "very truly yours." Madison returned Monroe's papers promptly, blaming the delay on the press of business. He signed his letter "sincerely your friend and servant" but omitted family references.[33]

Monroe worked hard on his self-defense over the British treaty, which he forwarded to Madison in early March. His rebuttal, he ex-plained, was triggered by Madison's harshly written instructions of May 20: "To write anything in vindication of my conduct is most distressing to me, but it was impossible to avoid it after receiving your letter." Mon-roe had devoted fifteen thousand words to the distressing task.

He responded to each point raised in Madison's May 20 instructions and several times insisted that Madison's criticisms of the treaty were contradicted by the government's previous and subsequent actions. He and Pinkney accepted the British terms on impressments, he wrote, because the alternative was war, and "I knew the United States were not prepared for war." Monroe concluded his disquisition by wishing the administration success and pledging his willingness to serve the nation again "in foreign war or domestic trouble." For Monroe, it was a moder-ate document, mostly free of sharp language. In a cover note, Monroe proclaimed his friendship to "the administration"; he closed with best family wishes, then a cool "sincerely."

Madison was expecting Monroe's document, but he could not have welcomed it. He was entering a presidential campaign and still arm wrestling with Britain as Secretary of State. Monroe's extended critique of the year-old decision to reject the treaty would aid neither effort.[34]

The two men exchanged businesslike letters for the next six weeks concerning confidential documents to be withheld from Congress. Madison hazarded a "your friend" in closing one note, but the atmosphere grew steadily colder. After Madison's letter of April 18, all was ice. Though they continued to be neighbors in Virginia for the next two years, they neither met nor exchanged letters.[35]

A third Republican was thinking about the Executive Mansion. George Clinton of New York, longtime governor and vice president during Jefferson's second term, was angling for the position, pushed by his ambitious nephew and political heir, DeWitt Clinton. Though never a shining intellect and now approaching seventy, George Clinton hoped to draw on northern resentment of both the embargo and the Virginia ascendancy in the national government. He also flirted with an alliance with the Federalists. But Republicans in the key states of New York and Pennsylvania stood with Madison, while Clinton's proposed Federalist alliance evaporated when that party nominated one of its own for president, Charles Cotesworth Pinckney of South Carolina. Through convoluted scheming, Clinton ended up on the New York ballot as a candidate for both president and vice president; in other states, he was the Republican vice presidential candidate.[36]

Madison made no campaign speeches, appearances, or statements. His extensive correspondence in 1808 includes neither discussion of campaign planning nor political instructions from him. Though Madison must have discussed the contest with allies, no record survives of it. His "friends," surrogates in each state, organized electoral tickets to support him and maintained a steady flow of newspaper commentary touting his virtues. Their task became lighter in March with the public release of Madison's official dispatches concerning Great Britain. The pugnacious tone of his correspondence gave voice to American frustrations and helped answer the charge that he was weak.

Monroe, on the ballot only in Virginia, played a shadowy role in the election. He had little prospect of winning yet refused to withdraw, even sketching out a labyrinthine road to final victory. Despite his claims to have done nothing to promote his candidacy, Monroe consulted with members of his campaign committee. In a letter to a supporter, he admitted that his situation required "a great deal of care and circumspection": He wished to stand apart from Jefferson and Madison without actually opposing them. He dictated that his committee should not attack the administration and should treat Madison "with tenderness," but should support neither. He was treading a narrow path. He was cordial with the Clinton forces but never joined them either. A Virginia newspaper aptly described him as "indignantly mute."[37]

Despite the efforts of Monroe, the Clintons, and the Federalists, Madison won handily, defeating Pinckney 122–47. Clinton won six electoral votes from his home state, plus the vice presidency. Madison lost only in Delaware and four New England states. Federalism was a spent force, an aristocratic party that could not thrive in a democratic republic. Madison swamped Monroe in Virginia, winning every electoral vote and carrying the popular vote, 14,665 to 3,408.[38]

Monroe had an unorthodox response to his electoral drubbing: He suggested that Jefferson reappoint him as American Minister to Britain. Jefferson declined, but Monroe clung to a surprising hope for high office in the new Madison administration.[39]

That winter, Madison had more pressing concerns than Monroe's relentless ambition. With Jefferson increasingly detached from events, Congress was deciding what to do about the hated embargo. Treasury Secretary Gallatin argued for an end to a policy that could not be enforced, a charade that threatened "to prostrate the law and government itself." But if the embargo were abandoned, did that mean war with Britain? Months before, Jefferson had reached that conclusion. Gallatin actually preferred war to displaying "our impotence to enforce our laws."[40]

Congress's deliberations zigzagged crazily. A few weeks after enacting a substantial toughening of the embargo, Congress began to consider revoking it entirely. Madison noted the difficulty "in collecting the mind of Congress to some proper focus"; its ideas had never been "so mutable and so scattered." Though Madison would not become president until March 4, 1809, many in Congress expected him to resolve the impasse.[41]

With barely two weeks left in Jefferson's presidency, Congress passed the Non-Intercourse Act, which replaced the embargo with a ban on trade with Britain and France, since those two countries were attacking American trade. The new law could not really be enforced, however, since America's merchants were skilled at misrepresenting the source of goods arriving in the country and at misstating a ship's destination when it left. In the first four months under the statute, seventy-nine ships left New York harbor with the declared destination of the tiny Azore Islands; the flummery was transparent. As a prominent English newspaper writer put it, Americans "know that their cargoes will come to England. . . . Aye, and they intend they shall come here, too; only their silly, their empty pride, will not let them acknowledge it." The British Minister in Washington agreed. "The whole measure is a subterfuge," he wrote, "to extricate [the government] from the embarrassments of the embargo system."[42]

On March 4, 1809, the new president would take office. The nation's condition was fragile. Incoherent public policies reflected a fundamental contradiction: The United States disdained all things military while the most powerful nations in the world waged war on its sailors and its shipping.

Small wonder that Jefferson left office with undisguised glee. "Never," he wrote, "did a prisoner, released from his chains, feel such relief as I shall in shaking off the shackles of power."[43]

19

RECLAIMING A FRIEND

Madison entered the House chamber at noon on March 4, 1809, twelve days before his fifty-eighth birthday, to take the oath as the fourth president of the United States. As he assumed the nation's highest office, he retained the ability to underwhelm. One spectator recalled that the new president "trembled excessively when he began to speak." He "seemed scarcely able to stand," according to this account, and his voice was "feeble." John Quincy Adams could not hear Madison at all. Another observer thought the new president looked embarrassed. Writer Washington Irving dismissed Madison as "but a withered little apple-john."

Madison seemed ill at ease all day, beginning with a crowded reception at his home on F Street (Jefferson had not yet vacated the Executive Mansion). At the equally thronged evening ball at Long's Hotel, the new president entered to the strains of "Madison's March," a stately air written for him as Secretary of State. Partygoers stood on benches to catch a glimpse of the chief executive, whose slight form was difficult to pick out in the crowd. Adams found the room's heat "oppressive, and the entertainment bad"; when windows would not open, sweltering guests smashed the glass panes to let in fresh air.

Trying to be convivial, Madison greeted a friend at the ball with bantering remarks, then confessed, "I would much rather be in bed." As usual, Mrs. Madison shone more brightly, dressed in a buff velvet gown with a long train, bedecked with pearl necklace, earrings, and bracelets, and crowned with a satin and velvet turban with two plumes. "She looked a queen," one woman wrote.[1]

Madison's inaugural address applauded republican institutions as the "true glory" of the United States, but he did not sugarcoat the nation's problems. Though he preferred to "cultivate peace by observing justice," such an honorable course "could not avail against the injustice and violence" of Britain and France "in their rage against each other." Madison pledged to respect core republican doctrine: preserving the rights of conscience and a free press, reducing the debt, and limiting the military. He would always remember, he promised, that a militia is "the firmest bulwark of republics; that without standing armies their liberty can never be in danger; nor with large ones, safe." Humbly, he asked his fellow citizens to "supply my deficiencies."

Nor did Madison sugarcoat the nation's problems in private. He expected the Non-Intercourse Act to have no impact on Britain or France; a Federalist critic compared it to "a child running at a man with a wooden sword from a toy shop." But the nation neither wanted nor was prepared for war. From Monticello, Jefferson acknowledged the quandary. "I know of no government which would be so embarrassing in war as ours," he told Madison. On military matters, a friend moaned, "we are mere children."[2]

Madison stumbled in appointing his cabinet, particularly when it came to his successor at the State Department. For that key position, Madison wanted Treasury Secretary Gallatin, a supremely talented native of Switzerland. Through eight parsimonious years at the Treasury, however, Gallatin had said no to enough Republicans that the Senate's Invisibles threatened to ally with Federalists to defeat his transfer to the State Department. Confronting this opposition, Madison flinched. He settled for retaining Gallatin at Treasury and chose instead Robert Smith, formerly Navy Secretary and brother to the powerful Maryland senator Samuel Smith. The episode left hard feelings between Gallatin and the Smiths that would bedevil Madison's first term in office. Robert Smith would prove a maladroit diplomat and disloyal to boot.

To head the military departments, Madison chose nonentities. War Secretary William Eustis of Massachusetts had little experience of arms; he had been an army surgeon during the Revolution. Navy Secretary Paul Hamilton of South Carolina was gracious, bibulous, and inept. Careful geographic balance was intended to restore Republican unity, but the cabinet performed the work of government poorly.[3]

In a public career as long as Madison's, missteps happen. No political leader gets everything right. Nevertheless, Madison's unwise cabinet selections—surprising in one so experienced—suggested to contemporaries that he could be pushed around. They showed other limitations as well. Madison was a gifted political theorist and writer of constitutions, an effective polemicist and legislative leader, and a successful Secretary of State. As president, though, his reflective style could make him seem indecisive, though Gallatin disputed the charge. "Mr. Madison . . . is slow in taking his ground," the Treasury Secretary conceded, "but firm when the storm arises."[4]

Yet a president's role is not primarily cerebral; often it is instinctive and symbolic. Presidents need to be visible, to move briskly among political figures and congressmen. They often have less need to think deeply than to choose wisely between often-unattractive options while inspiring confidence. Madison, at an advanced political age, needed to master new skills.

Back in Virginia, Monroe's hopes for a high place in Madison's cabinet had crashed to earth. The new president, Monroe later wrote, might have "avail[ed] himself and the public of my services" by appointing him Secretary of State, which "would have displayed some magnanimity." In another letter, Monroe admitted that his presidential candidacy made such magnanimity difficult. Jefferson, now back at Monticello, began months of work to heal the rift between his longtime colleagues and neighbors.[5]

The Madisons moved into the Executive Mansion a week after the inauguration, bringing with them Dolley's son, Payne, now a teenager. The household included Dolley's sister Anna, her congressman-husband Richard Cutts, and their three sons. Over the next eight years, two more Cutts children would be born in the mansion, joining a shifting cast of nephews, nieces, and children of friends, plus Dolley's sister Lucy and her children. The Madisons, superficially a childless couple, were surrounded by children.[6]

On April 19, 1809, only six weeks into his presidency, Madison triumphantly announced the end of non-intercourse with Britain. The British Minister to the United States, David Erskine, declared that on June 10 his government would withdraw the hated Orders in Council and its restrictions on American trade would end. In anticipation of that happy event, Madison proclaimed that on the same day the United States would lift its limits on British trade.

The public response was ecstatic. Church bells rang, cannon fired, and candles illuminated windows. The French Minister left Washington to avoid "riotous celebrations." Even Madison's enemies joined a chorus of praise for him. According to a Philadelphia publisher, Madison's achievement demonstrated Jefferson's failure: "In proportion as one rose, the other sunk. Mr. Madison was raised among the celestials—Mr. Jefferson sunk among the infernals."[7]

The agreement with the British Minister would relieve Americans from the Sisyphean struggle against Britain's naval might. With America's freedom of the seas restored, the resulting prosperity would quickly redeem the embargo's sacrifices and illustrate the wisdom of rejecting the Monroe-Pinkney treaty. The softening British position could be traced to world events. The French were winning battles in Spain. The British economy was staggering, in some part due to the American embargo. Then, as quickly as it had thrilled Americans, the agreement with Erskine turned to dust.

Erskine, only thirty-two, had been sent to Washington City with instructions to offer compensation for *Chesapeake* plus revocation of the Orders in Council; in return, he was to secure America's agreement not to trade with France and to limit trade with French colonies. Most important, the United States had to agree that the Royal Navy was authorized to enforce those restrictions. That last condition, had Erskine troubled to mention it to Madison, would have infuriated the president. Although the Non-Intercourse Act barred trade with France, it would be humiliating to grant Britain the right to enforce the ban—to deputize British warships to police compliance by boarding American vessels on the high seas. Madison later called that condition "absurd and insulting."[8]

Erskine evidently took the same view, so he never brought it up during the negotiation. He insisted later that he acted in accord with the spirit of his instructions, if not with their letter. Based on Erskine's partial presentation of Britain's offer, he and Madison readily reached an agreement that was signed in mid-April. It provided that on June 10 the hated Orders in Council would dissolve and America would begin to trade with Britain. When the date came, some six hundred American ships sailed for British ports.[9]

Madison played out in his mind the next moves in the diplomatic chess match. He expected Napoleon to match the British initiative and relax his limits on American trade. Perhaps France would cede the Floridas to the United States. Jefferson reported that the Erskine Agreement was "the source of very general joy" and added his own highly optimistic predictions: that the national debt soon would be extinguished, that Republicans would sweep upcoming elections, and that America would acquire both Cuba and Canada, creating "such an empire for liberty as she has never surveyed since the creation."[10]

In mid-June, news arrived of a British blockade of Holland. Madison became suspicious. How could Britain revoke the Orders in Council yet impose a new blockade? The British move, he fretted to Jefferson, was "meant to be trickish." His suspicions were well founded. When Erskine's masters in London received his American agreement, they speedily disavowed it, then recalled him. To illustrate the extent to which Erskine had exceeded his authority, the British government published the instructions he had flouted. The crushing news reached America in late July, when Madison was already at Montpelier for his late-summer escape from Washington's fevers and heat. Gallatin and Robert Smith urged the president to return to the capital to deal with the crisis.[11]

Madison's triumph had evaporated. Without the Erskine Agreement, much of America's merchant fleet was naked on the seas, exposed to British seizure. If the ships succeeded in reaching Britain, the supplies they delivered would ensure that any new trade restrictions would be ineffective. Madison was furious. He fumed that such "an outrage on all decency was never before heard of."[12] Reluctantly, he returned to Washington to deal with what he called Britain's "mixture of fraud and folly." Though Secretary of State Smith argued that Madison had no legal power to restore non-intercourse with Britain, Madison did so on August 9.[13]

The parallels between the Erskine Agreement and the Monroe-Pinkney treaty are vivid. In both situations, senior envoys ignored their instructions after developing a greater appreciation of their adversary's situation. In both instances, the home government summarily rejected the resulting agreement.[14]

The failure of the Erskine Agreement helped destroy any shred of trust in American-British relations. Britain rubbed salt in America's wound by replacing Erskine with Francis James Jackson, an overbearing aristocrat with a sneering contempt for all things American. Jackson swiftly alienated both Smith and Madison, whom Jackson described as "obstinate as a mule." Madison directed Smith to stop meeting with Jackson. Jackson responded by traveling in New York and New England, where he received fawning attention from Federalists; then he returned to Britain. For many months, Britain went without a Minister in Washington. In early 1811, Madison allowed William Pinkney, his Minister in London, to come home. With neither nation having a fully accredited envoy representing it, misunderstanding and conflict became even easier.[15]

While America's foreign policy foundered, the nation's most experienced diplomat, James Monroe, remained home in Virginia. He was beginning to take steps, however, to end his political exile.

In the aftermath of the Erskine Agreement, Madison's government received little cheerful news. Napoleon, happy to see Britain and America at loggerheads, imposed yet more repressive measures against neutral ships. French seizures of American ships rivaled, then exceeded, those by the British. Madison described himself as "equally distrustful" of both major powers.[16]

When Congress convened near the end of 1809, Madison's annual message urged it to protect the nation's rights as a neutral, but the Eleventh Congress was by no means equal to the task. Few Congresses are held in high esteem, historian Henry Adams wrote later, but "seldom if ever was a Congress overwhelmed by contempt so deep and general as that which withered the Eleventh." As the world's two superpowers pillaged American shipping, Congress slashed military spending. Challenged by Madison to reorganize the nation's militia—he called it "the great bulwark of our security"—Congress did nothing. The Republican majority was roughly 28–6 in the Senate and 94–48 in the House, but it was too riven by faction and indecision to act on any major issue.[17]

Madison's official family left its own ill-tempered stamp on the legislative branch. Isaac Coles, Dolley's cousin and Madison's secretary, horsewhipped a congressman in the Capitol building. Madison's brother-in-law, a congressman from Virginia, suffered a serious hip wound in a duel with a Federalist colleague. But it was on trade policy—specifically the weird career of Macon's Bill No. 2—that the Eleventh Congress most earned its woeful reputation for unwisdom.[18]

Madison's annual message, deferring to Congress, recommended no specific trade policy, though only something less drastic than the embargo would be politically feasible. When no one in Congress moved to address the question, Madison and Gallatin drafted pure protectionist legislation: Their bill would have allowed British and French goods to enter the country, but only if carried in American ships. No British or French vessel would be allowed to call at American ports. Former House Speaker Nathaniel Macon of North Carolina agreed to sponsor the bill. Like most halfway measures, it was denounced as both too strong and too weak. Madison distilled the problem as "the frustration of the intermediate courses." After weeks of debate, the bill cleared the

House; the Senate passed an eviscerated version, triggering another month of legislative tailchasing. No agreement emerged.[19]

By early April 1810, it seemed that Congress would do nothing about trade. In this muddle, a South Carolinian presented a complex alternative that became known as Macon's Bill No. 2 (though Macon himself would vote against it). The bill proposed to invert American policy. Instead of brandishing an ineffective stick against Britain and France, this legislation proposed to offer carrots. Non-intercourse denied access to American markets unless the foreign power abandoned its restrictions on American shipping. The new proposal would open American markets to all comers while increasing import taxes; *but* if either France or Britain stopped harassing American traders, the United States would restrict the *other* nation's shipping—unless the other nation *also* relaxed its limits on American trade, which would result in open trade for all.

Congressmen puzzled over the proposal. Was it an innovation? Or was it the same old policy turned inside out? Or was it simply dumb? One member from Connecticut despaired that "a more completely bewildered, disorganized set of men hardly exists." Madison described Congress as in an "unhinged state."[20]

Whether due to confusion or exhaustion, Congress approved Macon's Bill No. 2 in May 1810. "After the hurricane of passion in which the Congress opened their session," a British diplomat snorted, "it is truly laughable to witness the miserable, feeble puff in which they evaporated." Though skeptical of the statute, Madison resolved to make the best of it, "however feeble it may appear." He thought Napoleon might seize the initiative by granting concessions that would prompt the United States to close its markets to Britain.[21]

That was exactly what the French emperor did. Sort of. In early August the French Foreign Minister, the Duke of Cadore, issued a letter appearing to state that Napoleon's Milan and Berlin Decrees against American shipping would be revoked on November 1 if either the United States restored its ban on British trade, or if the Americans "cause their rights to be respected by the English." News of Cadore's letter reached America in late September. It seemed like it might be the breakthrough Madison needed. At least, he wrote to Jefferson, it would give Americans "the advantage . . . of having but one contest on our hands at a time." As the sponsors of Macon's Bill No. 2 had hoped, the British responded to Cadore's statement with their own hedged, not-entirely-solid implication that they too would cancel restrictions on American trade.[22]

With the November 1 date looming, Madison had to decide. He could accept the French declaration, despite its ambiguities, or he could accept the British statement, despite its conditions. Or he could accept neither. After nearly ten years of managing America's foreign policy, he could have no illusions that either nation bore good intentions toward the United States. Each sought only its own advantage in the global chess match. Having played so long with only pawns, though, Madison wondered if he might have a chance to steal a victory.

He resolved to accept the Cadore statement. He knew it was risky. Napoleon was a treacherous megalomaniac. His word was not his bond. But Madison felt strongly that doing nothing would mean war, and he could not bring himself to trust Britain, America's principal adversary for most of his adult life. In the choice between trusting Britain or trusting France, he would trust France. If the French honored Cadore's statement, peace might be possible. On November 2, 1810, he accepted the Cadore letter and restored non-intercourse with Britain. Lacking definitive evidence that the French decrees were repealed, he wrote anxiously to the American Minister in Paris: "[I]t is to be hoped that France will do what she is understood to be pledged for."[23]

It was a mistake. On the day the Cadore letter issued, Napoleon had secretly imposed confiscatory taxes on American imports into French-controlled ports. He also had directed the sale of previously seized American ships and cargoes. Madison knew none of this when he made his calculation that Napoleon would see the advantage in enlisting American support against Britain; to Madison, that was the logical policy for France to follow. But Napoleon followed a different logic. Locked in a war to extinction, he saw no reason to make concessions to the United States, which could do him little harm and was already on a collision course with his enemy. When American diplomats asked whether his antitrade decrees were still in effect, Napoleon did not answer.

That Napoleon's decrees remained in effect emerged as early as the week after Madison's proclamation of November 2. New statements by Cadore undermined the implications of his earlier letter. France still excluded many American goods. Only a month after Madison's daring proclamation, his annual message to Congress admitted at least partial failure. Referring to "the embarrassments which have prevailed in our foreign relations," he stated that France was refusing to release American ships and cargoes. He again urged Congress to revisit America's trade policies. He again asked for Congress to reorganize the nation's militia. But for many more months he refused to concede that the Cadore letter was the false trick it turned out to be.[24]

The Cadore letter episode took another chunk out of Madison's political stature. The acerbic John Randolph called it "a bargain which credulity and imbecility enter into with cunning and power." The president, sometimes characterized as timid and weak, had taken a high-risk plunge, heedless of the cost to his reputation if it failed. He never expressed regret over that decision. He had sought to turn the nation away from a war for which Americans refused to prepare. When the gamble failed, Madison's expectation of war grew stronger.[25]

Expecting war, sadly, did not mean arming for it. Since 1801, Treasury Secretary Gallatin had enforced the Republican abhorrence for government spending and government debt. Gallatin applied large annual surpluses to reduce the country's debt, paying it down by $38 million (or 40 percent) between 1801 and 1812. After nearly two years in office, Madison had paid off the purchase price for Louisiana. Both Jefferson and Madison paid down debt rather than build up the army or navy, even though America's weakness thwarted their diplomacy. They held paramount the Republican principles of government frugality and disdain for a peacetime army. As Nathaniel Macon expressed it, "I scarcely know which is worst, war or an army without war."[26]

First, however, Madison had to address the feud between Gallatin and the Smith brothers, which was making cabinet meetings intolerable and paralyzing the government. Maryland's Senator Samuel Smith had never been an admirer of James Madison. In the 1790s he opposed the Virginian's calls for trade retaliation against Britain. In 1806, he expected to be named Monroe's partner for the London negotiation, then was insulted when William Pinkney, a Federalist, was selected. Smith may have disliked Madison, but he despised Gallatin. In 1809, the Treasury Secretary questioned a transaction with public funds by the Smith family's trading business. Calling it "most extraordinary," Gallatin told the senator that the transaction "left very unfavorable impressions on my mind." Smith and his brother bitterly resented the attack on their integrity.[27]

The bad blood spread through the wives of the adversaries. Mrs. Robert Smith and Mrs. Gallatin refused to attend the same social events. After one unpleasant encounter, Secretary Smith said that, except for appearances, he gladly would have shot Gallatin the next morning. Madison favored Gallatin, who was both competent and an old friend. But he tolerated Smith, even though he had to draft much of

Smith's official correspondence for him, and even though the man reck-lessly revealed to the public the confidential discussions in the cabinet.[28]

The Smith-Gallatin situation came to a head in early 1811, when the twenty-year charter for the Bank of the United States—Alexander Hamilton's creature—was scheduled to expire. Two decades before, Madison had opposed the bank on constitutional grounds, but its suc-cessful operations in the interim had changed his mind. In practice, Gallatin emphasized, the bank was an excellent tool for managing gov-ernment finances. Hamilton's idea had turned out to have considerable merit.[29]

The bank renewal pitted pragmatism against Republican orthodoxy, which viewed the bank as a monster of central government. The House approved an extension of the bank, but the measure stalled in the Senate, with Samuel Smith leading the opposition. When the Senate divided evenly on the bill, Vice President Clinton cast his tie-breaking vote against the bank, contrary to the wishes of his own president.[30]

Gallatin took the defeat hard. First he had lost the appointment as Secretary of State to Robert Smith. Then he had to endure serving in the cabinet with that smug bumbler. Now he had to shut down the Bank of the United States, an institution he thought important to the nation's prosperity and its ability to finance a war. Gallatin's frustra-tion bubbled over in a resignation letter submitted to the president on March 7, 1811. He stressed the damaging strife within the cabinet:

> Measures of vital importance have been and are defeated: every operation even of the most simple and ordinary nature is pre-vented or impeded: the embarrassments of Government, great as from foreign causes they already are, are unnecessarily increased: public confidence in the public councils and in the executive is im-paired; and every day seems to increase every one of those evils.[31]

Gallatin's letter forced Madison's hand. The president could no lon-ger indulge Robert Smith's failings at the cost of losing Gallatin, his ablest aide. Madison told Smith he must leave office. He offered to appoint Smith Minister to Russia, which was as far away as he could send the Marylander. Smith accepted the new post. Upon reflection, his anger building, he then declined it.[32]

Smith's departure presented Madison with an opportunity to bolster his government, which had been shaken by the twin embarrassments of the Erskine Agreement and the Cadore letter. A new Secretary of State with political heft could revive public confidence as the confrontation with Britain evolved. Equally important, Madison needed a foreign policy adviser who commanded the respect of foreign diplomats and provided a reliable sounding board for Madison's thinking. It was time to patch things up with Monroe.

Since the 1808 election, Jefferson had been trying to bring Madison and Monroe together. Less than a month after leaving office in March 1809, Jefferson reported to Madison that, after a decent interval, Monroe would seek "a cordial return to his old friends."[33]

In November 1809, Jefferson seized upon a report that Monroe would accept appointment as governor of the Louisiana Territory. He rode to Monroe's nearby home for a candid talk. If Monroe would take the post, the former president advised, it "would be a signal of reconcilia-tion on which the body of republicans . . . would again rally to him." The prideful Monroe replied that he was not "un-ready to serve the public," but the Louisiana position was "incompatible with the respect he owed himself"; he would consider only jobs that reported directly to the presi-dent. Jefferson reported to Madison that Monroe would accept a posi-tion that satisfied the man's "close attention to his honor and grade."[34]

In April 1810, Monroe started his comeback by standing for a seat in Virginia's House of Delegates. "I have always been a Republican," he proclaimed in an election-day speech. "I have fought and bled for the cause of republicanism." He offered a qualified endorsement of the na-tion's leading Republican:

> Mr. Madison is a Republican and so am I. As long as he acts in consistence with the interests of his country, I will go along with him. When otherwise, you cannot wish me to countenance him.[35]

It was a start, albeit a grudging one.

A month later, Monroe took a larger step. He traveled to Washing-ton City and spoke with Madison for the first time in two years. Though the journey was nominally to resolve his diplomatic expense accounts, it plainly represented a peace gesture. Monroe described his reception as "kind and friendly." Jefferson was delighted. Monroe, he wrote to Madi-son, was achieving "the most perfect reconciliation and cordiality . . . towards yourself. I think him now inclined to rejoin us with zeal." Over the summer of 1810, while Madison was back at Montpelier, he and

Monroe resumed neighborly relations, sharing the services of a French gardener. The thaw was progressing.[36]

Monroe assumed a leadership role in the Virginia legislature, but he needed a more prominent position. Madison could help. When a federal judgeship became vacant in January 1811, Madison swiftly appointed Virginia's governor to the post, opening the governor's chair for Monroe. Less than two months after Monroe became governor, Gallatin wrote his resignation letter, forcing Madison to dismiss Robert Smith from the State Department.

At first, Madison moved deliberately. Before meeting with Smith, he asked a go-between to determine whether Monroe was willing to take over as Secretary of State. Monroe was willing, but he asked the intermediary if the president would consider revising his foreign policy according to circumstances. Before Monroe's reply arrived, Madison grew impatient. He wrote directly to his old friend, asking him to take the job "as soon as possible," preferably within two weeks.[37]

At the threshold of returning to high national office, Monroe could not entirely conquer his pride. He asked Madison to acknowledge that, as Secretary of State, Monroe would not be expected to abandon his views on foreign policy. Also, feeling some embarrassment to be leaving the governor's office after only a few weeks in it, he asked Madison to request his resignation as governor. By return post, Madison complied with both requests. His answer on the foreign policy issue was a masterpiece of slippery verbiage, subject to widely varying interpretations. This time, Monroe chose not to quibble. Pronouncing Madison's statement "liberal and manly," Monroe began packing for Washington.[38]

Smith and the other Invisibles delayed Monroe's appointment in the Senate but could not defeat it. As they had after the congressional election contest of 1789, Madison and Monroe picked up their friendship as though it had not been interrupted. By Monroe's account in late April, President Madison

> is perfectly friendly, and corresponding with our ancient relation, which I am happy to have restored. On public affairs we confer without reserve, each party expressing his own sentiments, and viewing dispassionately the existing state, animated by a sincere desire to promote the public welfare.[39]

Finally, Madison had won a key victory. Monroe's stature reinforced an administration that had seemed wobbly. As a favorite of the Old

Republicans, he brought support from that faction. An experienced diplomat, he had spoken directly with French and British leaders over the last fifteen years and had lived in war-torn Europe. He also brought the judgment of a seasoned political operator who had been senator and governor. "He unites," one younger official wrote of Monroe, "the ease of the courtier to the honesty of an old Roman." Not least important, the president's closest adviser would now also be his friend.

From retirement, Jefferson expressed the emotion for both men. "I know," he wrote to Monroe, "that the dissolutions of personal friendships are among the most painful occurrences in human life." For Madison and Monroe, the pain was ended. For the second time, they had collided politically yet avoided destroying their relationship. When the wounds healed and their interests warranted a reunion, they resumed their partnership.[40]

Through the summer of 1811, both men concluded that America had to resist Britain. That meant war. Monroe's warlike inclinations impressed even Madison's valet, a young slave, who remembered the new Secretary of State as "always fierce for it [war]." To bring the country to the same conclusion, Madison called Congress into session a month early. His annual message of November 5 reviewed carefully the insults and oppression from British ships "hovering on our coasts." He accused Britain of making "war on our lawful commerce" and added: "With this evidence in trampling on rights which no independent nation can relinquish, Congress will feel the duty of putting the United States into an armor and an attitude demanded by the crisis."[41]

The small man in the Executive Mansion, supposedly a quailing, bookish soul, was telling the nation to don its armor. To reinforce the message, he now had a tough former soldier as his principal adviser.

THE REPUBLICAN WAY OF WAR

Though he possessed neither military experience nor martial inclinations, Madison was cajoling and hauling the nation into what would become the War of 1812. That contradiction applied to the Republican Party as well. Republicans embraced war but refused to create a military to fight it. They believed in militia, citizen-soldiers who would drop their plows to pick up their muskets, then return to peaceful pursuits when the fighting was over. Moreover, Madison was going to war in 1812, a national election year, which would place the question of war and peace directly before the voters. No other American war has begun in a presidential election year.

No single event triggered the fighting. The greatest British outrage, the *Chesapeake* affair, had occurred five years earlier. The Erskine Agreement had imploded three years before. Rather than a response to exploding events, the War of 1812 was a howl of wounded pride, fueled by injuries that still rankled years later. As Monroe wrote in 1811, "War, dreadful as the alternative is, could not do us more injury than the present state of things, and it would certainly be more honorable to the nation, and gratifying to the public feelings." A Virginia Republican called it a metaphysical war, one fought "not for conquest, not for defense, not for sport," but "for honor, like that of the Greeks against the Trojans."[1]

Although Madison's commitment to war was clear when he called Congress into session early in the fall of 1811, then urged it to place the nation in armor, Republican doctrine dictated that Congress, not the executive, should initiate war. Accordingly, Madison limited his public statements on the subject, though in private he made his view entirely clear. "I believe there will be war," Dolley wrote to a sister in December 1811, "as M sees no end to our perplexities without it." According to an account of a February 1812 dinner:

The President, little as he is in bulk, is unquestionably above others in spirit and tone. While they are mere mutes, . . . he on every
occasion, and to everybody, talks freely . . . [and] says the time is
ripe, and the nation, too, for resistance.

Madison sent Monroe to assure congressmen of his commitment to
war and had a key ally in Henry Clay of Kentucky, the thirty-six-year-
old Speaker of the House, who also chose war.

Congress, however, continued its fractious ways, unable to seize the
lead that Madison urged on it. Jefferson thought it impossible that "a
body containing 100 lawyers in it should direct the measures of a war."
When Congress finally adopted a tax increase to pay for war preparations, Madison called it "the strongest proof . . . that they do not mean
to flinch from the contest to which the mad conduct of Britain drives
them." Madison applauded congressional moves to prepare an American attack on Canada and began rudimentary planning for such an
offensive.[2]

Frustrated by Congress's delays, Madison and Monroe tried a daring
gambit to jolt the nation into war. Their ploy relied on a French confidence man masquerading as the fictitious Comte Edouard de Crillon.
In the winter of 1812, Crillon approached both the president and the
Secretary of State about John Henry, an Irishman with ties to New
England Federalists and to some British officials. Three years earlier, the
British had paid for Henry to travel through New England and report
on Federalist discontent. When Henry's reports included little that did
not appear in daily newspapers, the British declined to support him
further. Henry and Crillon resolved to use the situation to fleece the
American government.

They led Madison and Monroe to believe that Henry's letters to his
British masters would reveal a conspiracy between traitorous Federalists
and perfidious Albion. When Crillon dangled the bait, the Americans
rose like trout. Monroe offered the nation's entire secret service budget,
$50,000, to buy Henry's letters, then sweetened the deal by throwing
in free passage to Europe for Henry and his two daughters. By early
March, Monroe and Madison had the papers and Henry was sailing to
Europe on *Wasp*, a twenty-two-gun sloop that cost as much to build as
the government had just paid for Henry's papers.

With a flourish, the president sent the papers to Congress. They
revealed, he proclaimed, British intrigues with Federalists "for the purpose of bringing about a resistance to the laws, and eventually, in

concert with a British force, of destroying the Union and forming [New England] into a political connection with Great Britain." Monroe called release of the Henry papers "a last means of exciting the nation and Congress."[3]

After an initial spasm of public anger against Britain, a congressional investigation uncovered the princely payment to Crillon and Henry. Henry's reports to the British proved to be gossipy, not incriminating. Public opinion turned. The president seemed a gullible mark for flim-flam artists, yet also deceitful in his unveiling of the Henry papers. He and Monroe had blundered.[4]

Nevertheless, they did not relent in their campaign for war. In early April, Madison called for a thirty-day embargo on British trade as a step toward war. Some Americans proposed to fight *both* Britain and France, but Madison thought that course presented "a thousand difficulties." When the latest dispatches from Europe arrived in mid-May, they showed no promise of British concessions. A few days later, Madison sent a war message to Congress.[5]

The message began by denouncing the "crying enormity" of British impressments. British ships, he continued, "hover over and harass our . . . commerce," had "wantonly spilt American blood," and "plundered [American ships] in every sea." Madison recited the repudiated Erskine Agreement, brandished the Henry papers as proof that Britain attempted "a dismemberment of our happy union," and accused the British of sponsoring Indian attacks on western settlers. "We behold," he concluded, "on the side of Great Britain a state of war against the United States; and on the side of the United States, a state of peace towards Great Britain." Congress, he said, should take appropriate action.

Three days later, the House voted for war, 79–49. The Senate delayed for almost two weeks, then approved the war resolution by a 19–13 vote. The president recognized that he should perform some symbolic act to rally the nation, yet had little instinct for such public theater. He chose to visit the Navy and War Department offices, where he exhorted the assembled clerks to act to secure "a speedy, a just, and an honorable peace." He marked the occasion by donning a "little round hat [with] a huge cockade," a patriotic decoration of ribbons. The event prompted more derision than patriotic fervor.[6]

The nation's response to the war mirrored the divisions in the congressional vote. Many New England towns shrank into something like mourning. In Rhode Island, ships flew flags at half-mast, shops closed, and the bells of the meetinghouses rang dolefully for an entire day.

When a Providence merchant began to outfit two privateers to prey on British shipping, his pro-British neighbors sank one of them. In Massachusetts, the state legislature and numerous town meetings considered resolutions opposing the war; the governor refused to call out the militia. "As Mr. Madison has declared war," declaimed a Boston pastor, "let Mr. Madison carry it on." Opponents began to call it "Mr. Madison's war." Madison lamented that opposition to the war "has the double effect of crippling [the army's] operations and encouraging the enemy to withhold any pacific advances."[7]

War controversy plunged Baltimore into weeks of street battles. Republican mobs sacked a Federalist newspaper office, then branched out into antiblack violence, then demolished a schooner that was leaving to trade in the Caribbean. The rioting crested with an attack on the city jail, where prominent Federalists were being held for their own protection; many were beaten and tortured with candle grease dripped into their eyes; one died. Militia with cannon finally drove the rioters off.[8]

Secretary of State Monroe was buoyant, blithely predicting American success with "little annoyance or embarrassment in the effort." Because Britain would accept only "unconditional submission," he explained to a Virginia friend, "the only remaining alternative was to get ready for fighting."[9]

But the country was nowhere near ready. The British army included almost a quarter-million battle-hardened veterans, most of whom opposed Napoleon in Europe. The American army, numbering less than seven thousand, was scattered among twenty-three forts and posts. It could hardly confront the British across a thousand miles of Canadian border while defending New Orleans and the East Coast and controlling aggrieved Indian tribes across the West. The U.S. Navy had five frigates and a handful of smaller vessels, but no ships of the line (those with at least two gun decks). The Royal Navy had grown to nearly a thousand warships, including more than one hundred ships of the line; by one calculation, the Royal Navy had three fighting *ships* for every *cannon* in the U.S. Navy. The British squadron for North America boasted thirty-three frigates and six ships of the line.[10]

Years later, Madison admitted that he "knew the unprepared state of the country, but . . . esteemed it necessary to throw forward the flag of the country, sure that the people would press forward and defend it." The effort, however, would have benefited from competent war leaders, both civilian and military. With Eustis as War Secretary and Hamilton as Navy Secretary, the nation stumbled into combat. In truth, Madison's only hope was that Napoleon would distract the British long enough for America to don its armor in earnest.[11]

Two months after adoption of the war resolution, bitter news arrived from London. On the day before the Senate vote, the British government suspended the Orders in Council that had limited American trade for the previous five years. Had that action come earlier, it might have prevented war. Now it was too late. Madison and Monroe had their war for America's honor.[12]

In the summer of 1812, after Congress adjourned, a weird quiet descended on Washington City. It was "as if we were at peace with the world," one resident wrote. On the northern border, little went right. American generals, mostly Continental Army veterans, displayed neither energy nor resolve. A junior officer called them "ignoramuses and imbeciles." The worst disaster came when General William Hull surrendered Detroit and two thousand men without a fight, setting off cries of treachery and puncturing American fantasies of a swift conquest of Canada. General Henry Dearborn, commanding in the northeast, had no appetite for combat. When the news arrived that Britain had withdrawn its Orders in Council, Dearborn agreed to an armistice with the British forces facing him; Madison, annoyed, canceled the truce. Despite his evidently mild disposition, one government official noted, the president possessed "a great deal of close-mouthed zeal, latent fire, and dormant genius."[13]

Madison did not lead a unified nation. The greatest problem was New England, where merchants and Federalist leaders thought it was insane to fight with Britain. To Jefferson, Madison complained of "the seditious opposition in Massachusetts and Connecticut, with the intrigues elsewhere cooperating with it, [which] have so clogged the wheels of war." A college friend of Madison's warned that his New England neighbors would prefer a civil war against their sister states to fighting against Britain. Not only New Englanders were uncertain about the war. An invasion of Canada in the Niagara region stalled when New York militia refused to cross the border.[14]

With the nation's attention shifting from diplomacy to fighting, Monroe wanted to move with it. He longed to mount a steed and lead troops to smashing victories. Madison agreed to send his old friend to a command in the West at the highest possible military rank. Monroe could hardly perform worse than the current generals. On reflection, though, Monroe sniffed political danger. Most western troops were Kentucky militia led by William Henry Harrison, who would not be under Monroe's command. Moreover, army rules defined Monroe's seniority according to his final rank in the Continental Army, so others would outrank him. Doubtful that he would have an independent command, Monroe chose to stay in the cabinet.[15]

The American army had little infrastructure for procurement and distribution of supplies, not even an accounting system. The Quartermaster Department had been created two months before the war began; the Ordnance Department two weeks before; the Commissary General ten weeks after. Confusion prevailed. The navy provided the lone bright spot. Resourceful captains and crews in well-built frigates fought three early duels with British warships and won each time. The naval victories had no strategic value but were powerful morale builders; they also dismayed the British, long accustomed to controlling the sea.[16]

In the presidential election that autumn, Madison's opponents could point to military failure in an unpopular war, but the president still made no time for campaigning. He recognized the importance of the vote. "The current elections," he wrote in mid-October, "bring the popularity of the war or of the administration, or both, to the Experimentum Crucis." (Literally, "the crucial experiment.") In two paragraphs sent to the South Carolina legislature, he insisted that the war was based "neither in ambition nor in vainglory," but was "forced by persevering injustice on exhausted forbearance."[17]

Madison profited from the weakness of his political opposition. The decaying Federalist Party slid into support for DeWitt Clinton, then Republican mayor of New York City. Clinton tried to appeal simultaneously to New Englanders who opposed the war and to westerners who wanted to fight the war with greater energy. To finesse such a contradictory appeal, his principal campaign document did not even mention the war. The strength of the Republican Party dictated the result. Clinton carried all but one of the states northeast of Pennsylvania but Madison held the rest, winning the electoral vote by 128–89.[18] Because Vice President George Clinton (DeWitt's uncle) had died in April 1812, Madison's new vice president was Elbridge Gerry of Massachusetts.[19]

In his annual message in early November, Madison stressed that America had to add naval strength on the Great Lakes to gain control of the Canadian border. He called for higher pay for soldiers and stronger militia laws (yet again), noting the refusal by Massachusetts and

Connecticut to use their militias to defend American coasts. He also reaffirmed the war's purpose to vindicate America's sovereignty. Not fighting, he insisted, would have been an admission that "the American people were not an independent people, but colonists and vassals."[20]

Madison acted to energize his cabinet. For Secretary of the Navy, he recruited William Jones of Philadelphia, a successful merchant. War Secretary proved a difficult position to fill; with the army so unprepared, the job could easily torpedo a political career. Madison offered it to Monroe, but his friend developed cold feet again, worried that failure might cripple his presidential ambitions. Monroe agreed to serve as act-ing War Secretary while Madison searched for a permanent choice.[21]

In ten weeks at the War Department, Monroe planned the 1813 campaign, once again aiming at Canada.[22] Embracing that goal, Madi-son underscored that control of the Great Lakes "is the hinge on which the war will essentially turn." He urged a national commitment to that effort, which required the building of ships to fight on the lakes. If the British "build two ships, we should build four. If they build thirty or forty gun ships, we should build them of 50 or 60 guns."[23]

The acting Secretary of War agreed. Monroe planned an attack across the Niagara frontier and then northeast into the heart of Canada. A separate American force would march on Montreal and Quebec through the Champlain Valley or the St. Lawrence Valley. A senior colleague applauded Monroe's plan for aiming at "grander deeds" with "energy becoming the times." Monroe was perfecting the plan when the new permanent War Secretary, John Armstrong of New York, took of-fice in early February 1813.[24]

Armstrong was Madison's fourth choice for the job. In Armstrong's favor, he was intelligent and had military experience from the Revo-lution. Also, he was a prominent Republican in New York, the most populous state in the union. Geography dictated that New York serve as a bulwark against New England's disloyalty and as a springboard for any invasion of Canada.

But Armstrong had substantial liabilities, beginning with his repu-tation as an intriguer. In 1783, as a young officer, he drafted the near-mutinous complaints about the failure to pay the Continental Army. As American Minister in Paris, he quarreled with most American diplomats. Having married into New York's powerful Livingston clan, he had taken up Robert Livingston's feud with Monroe over who was entitled to credit for the Louisiana Purchase. His appointment as War Secretary would increase his national profile and make him a potential rival to Monroe for the presidency. Far worse than any of these concerns, Armstrong's military judgment was erratic: Before the war, he had recommended fighting both France and Britain at the same time.[25]

Monroe opposed Armstrong's appointment, then objected to Armstrong's initial military plans, particularly his proposal to travel to New York to oversee operations against Canada. Armstrong retaliated by blocking a renewed move by Monroe to gain a military command. Strife was returning to Madison's cabinet.[26]

The army's performance did not improve with the turning of the calendar to 1813. Bloody fighting on the Niagara frontier produced more failures. A feeble push up the Champlain Valley, led by the sometimes treasonous and always incompetent General James Wilkinson, achieved nothing. Militia, despite Republican dogma, proved unreliable, sometimes refusing to follow orders. Few militia companies would stand against either British regulars or Indians. Inept generals were an equal challenge. "The creator," Jefferson wrote, "has not thought proper to mark those in the forehead who are of stuff to make good generals. We are first therefore to seek them blindfold, and then let them learn the trade at the expense of great losses."[27]

New England's hostility to the war prevented any attempt to attack Halifax in Nova Scotia, the Royal Navy's home port in North America. It also restrained enlistment in the army, which never numbered as many soldiers as Congress authorized. Although the nonslave population of the United States was fourteen times that of Canada, American armies rarely enjoyed a numerical advantage on the battlefield, never one large enough to compensate for poor training and limited ardor. Due to weak leadership and ambivalence about the war, one out of every eight American soldiers deserted. Soldier executions were more common than in other American wars, rising to 146 in 1814.

The navy, after its early victories, was largely trapped in port by a British blockade. Robert Fulton, inventor of the steamboat, pestered Madison with proposals for submarine warships and steam-powered battleships; Congress actually approved funds for steam-powered warships, but the new craft could not be developed fast enough to make a difference.[28]

News of a triumph on Lake Erie arrived in the second half of the year. Commodore Oliver Hazard Perry's flotilla destroyed a British fleet, freeing Harrison's Kentucky militia to move into Canada. At the Battle

of the Thames, the Kentuckians won a key victory and also killed Tecum-
seh, the Shawnee leader who had rallied northwestern tribes against the
United States. Though the northwestern frontier would not be entirely
quiet until the war's end, Harrison had broken Indian resistance there.[29]

With America's military still struggling, Monroe's frustrations built.
In April, when a British naval squadron spread mayhem on the shores
of Chesapeake Bay, Monroe complained that Armstrong had planned
no defense of the region. When the British ships returned in July, Monroe could sit at his desk no longer.

Disregarding his diplomatic duties, Monroe set off on horseback
to undertake a personal reconnaissance. For several days, he shadowed
the British ships from hilltops and the edge of forests. When a British
detachment landed on an island to retrieve fresh water for the seamen,
Monroe breathlessly proposed an American attack. Madison rejected
the proposal, noting dryly that it "would seem to require more celerity
and secrecy than might be attainable." The president added that only
militia would be available: "The militia I learn from Mr. M[onroe] are as
nothing on such an occasion." When the British did not move against
Washington, Armstrong felt vindicated. Navy Secretary William Jones
muttered that his cabinet colleagues were spending their time running
for president and were "intent only on each other," not on the British.[30]

With the war against Napoleon entering a critical stage in Europe,
1813 brought no major British attack. The greatest threat to America
came in June, when Madison fell gravely ill with a "bilious fever," the intestinal ailment that periodically afflicted him. Dolley nursed him night
and day, "sometimes in despair." After two perilous weeks, Monroe wrote
that the doctors thought the president would recover. Two months after
Madison's fever first struck, Dolley wrote that "even now, I watch over
him as I would an infant, so precarious is his convalescence."[31]

Madison's illness surely derived in part from his punishing work
habits, first formed as a college student. While at the College of New
Jersey, Madison had experimented with what he recalled as "a minimum
of sleep and a maximum of application," a schedule that broke his health
for a time. He never lost the compulsion to work harder and longer than
his constitution would permit.[32]

A young Virginian who stayed in the Executive Mansion described
the president sometimes napping in a chair after dinner, "for I frequently found him there upon my return from an evening party." Awak-
ened, Madison would retreat into his study "and he would be at his
desk by candlelight in the morning." Madison's officials and secretaries

sometimes stayed with him through evenings of work. When Dolley scolded him for not resting, "he declared that the pressure of the war business allowed him no alternative." Dolley blamed those pressures for his illness, bewailing "the disappointments and vexations heaped upon him by party spirit."[33]

After resting in Montpelier for several weeks, Madison returned to the capital in October. In his absence, with Armstrong in upstate New York, Monroe had shanghaied the War Department's files, directing that all army correspondence be sent to him. According to the department's chief clerk, Monroe's usurpation left Madison "more in a passion than [the clerk] ever saw him"; the president "thought that Mr. Monroe had been meddling with the affairs of the War Department."

Yet Madison forgave the bureaucratic poaching, just as he overlooked Monroe's passionate demand at the end of 1813 that Armstrong be dismissed. "This man," Monroe fumed, "if continued in office, will ruin not you and the administration only, but the whole republican army and cause." While Robert Smith had been Secretary of State, Madison had developed a high tolerance for bickering within his cabinet. He took no immediate action against Armstrong, who had been War Secretary for less than a year. Madison did not want more turnover in that office.[34]

The best news of 1813 had come early, in late February, as the president was about to take the oath of office for his second term: Tsar Alexander of Russia offered to mediate peace talks between Britain and the United States. Though Madison doubted Britain would accept the offer, he leapt at it. Going to war to defend the nation's honor did not require that the nation keep fighting indefinitely. The appointment of American peace commissioners, however, bogged down in political sniping.

Madison's first two choices went through the Senate easily: John Quincy Adams was already in Russia as the American Minister; naming Federalist senator James Bayard was a prudent gesture of bipartisanship. But some senators gagged on the nomination of the controversial Gallatin, who was eager for new duties after twelve years at Treasury. Gallatin's talents and experience would make him the natural leader of the American peace commissioners. While Madison lay desperately ill in June, the Senate debated the nomination. Gallatin, critics insisted, should not serve as both Treasury Secretary and peace commissioner, though American diplomats (including John Jay) had held dual appointments in the past. Madison stuck to his nomination, but the Senate rejected it. Madison complained that the Senate had "mutilated" the peace mission, though the vote had little real impact: Gallatin already had left for St. Petersburg.[35]

By year's end, the war's toll showed on the president. An Englishman described Madison as having "the air of a country schoolmaster in mourning for one of his pupils whom he had whipped to death." Yet the president's fighting spirit was undiminished. "The little president is back," wrote one Republican in late October, "and as game as ever." Madison spoke in "a very sanguine way of the conquest of Canada" and extolled his nation's "future greatness and the genius and virtue and general intelligence of the people."[36]

Madison's determined spirit was essential. The British, as he expected, rejected Russian mediation. They offered, instead, one-on-one peace talks. Although Madison and Monroe expected little from such talks, since no third party would be present to support American claims, they accepted the invitation.

The war would continue.[37]

The year 1814 began with a budget crisis. Before Gallatin left for Europe, he had secured enough loans to carry the nation through the end of 1813. Navy Secretary William Jones, filling in as acting Treasury Secretary, outlined a grim reality for the new year: The government had to borrow $29 million to pay war expenses, but there were no lenders. New Englanders controlled much of the nation's wealth but would not underwrite a war they opposed; in fact, they were slow to pay even the taxes they owed. The Royal Navy shrewdly relaxed its blockade of New England ports, which meant that even more of the nation's commerce funneled through them, drawing hard currency from the rest of the country. With the Bank of the United States shuttered, the government had no vehicle for borrowing. State-chartered banks flooded the nation with bank notes of doubtful value. The war had suspended public land sales, cutting off more federal revenue. "The whole system," Jefferson predicted, "must blow up before the year is out."[38]

In March, Jones warned that the needed loan might fail entirely. The government could try ending the trade embargo and imposing double customs taxes; that would increase revenues but also would allow the sale of American food and supplies to British forces in Canada. Then again, American smugglers were already supplying the British. Though he disliked the step, Jones recommended repealing the embargo. For once, Congress adopted administration policy. The move was only a partial success. With the government's credit weakened, it could not borrow all it needed, even when it paid high interest rates and accepted deep discounts.[39]

In April, the British occupied harbors in eastern Maine, an advance that brought a third of Maine under British control by the end of 1814. America's situation worsened on the beleaguered Niagara frontier. In a raid in late December 1813, British forces burned Buffalo and Black Rock to the ground. Some twelve thousand American settlers fled the region, now a charred wasteland.[40]

Neither did the peace talks seem to hold much promise. By resigning from the Treasury to satisfy congressional opponents, Gallatin was able to take his place as a peace commissioner with Adams, Bayard, House Speaker Henry Clay, and Jonathan Russell, American Minister to Sweden. The parties agreed to meet at Ghent, in Belgium. More than offsetting that pale glimmer of hope, however, was Napoleon's military collapse. British, Prussian, Russian, and Austrian armies were bearing down on Paris. If Napoleon fell and British forces were released from Europe, America's prospects would be grim. "The English people," Gallatin warned from Europe, "eagerly wish that their pride may be fully gratified by what they call the 'punishment of America.'"[41]

In March, a dejected Monroe, still believing that Armstrong was mismanaging the military, considered resigning from office to avoid being swept into the looming debacle. He concluded, though, that the political cost of resignation would outweigh that of enduring what promised to be a terrible crisis.[42]

By late May 1814, Madison's nightmare arrived: Peace had broken out in Europe. The news, he wrote to Navy Secretary Jones, "ought to prepare us for the worst." A new wave of terror came when British Admiral Cochrane invited America's slaves to rise and join British forces that had again moved into Chesapeake Bay. Cochrane's statement, Madison sputtered, reflected "the most vindictive purposes" and "the most inveterate spirit against the Southern states." The British were reviving a strategy from the Revolution, when many slaves fled to British warships. As they had a generation before, slaves in the Chesapeake region fled when they could; some enlisted with the Royal Marines. "I can see and feel," wrote a leading Pennsylvania Republican, "the general gloom of our national prospects."[43]

Madison resolved to press ahead on both the war and peace fronts. In June, he led the cabinet to approve a new attack on Canada. He also proposed, however, softening the American negotiating position on impressments. The cabinet agreed that the question could be deferred to a separate and later negotiation with Britain. If the European war truly was over, Britain probably would abandon the practice of impressments on its own.[44]

Within days of that decision, a more disturbing report came from Gallatin and Bayard in Europe. They had heard that Britain would demand draconian peace terms, including dissolution of the United States. Britain, they added, would never concede on impressments. Madison reconvened his Cabinet, which revised its negotiating position again: A peace agreement, they agreed, could ignore impressments entirely. America would abandon the most important reason for declaring war, a war it could not win.[45]

Madison's doubts about his Secretary of War, doubtless reinforced by Monroe's hostility to Armstrong, grew stronger when William Henry Harrison resigned his commission because Armstrong had inserted himself between Harrison and his subordinates. Though Harrison's military record was mixed, his resignation was unwelcome. He was popular with his men and had won a significant victory, a claim few American generals could then make. Then Armstrong promoted General Andrew Jackson of Tennessee without consulting the president.

Rather than confront Armstrong, Madison undertook an investigation of his own Secretary of War. He began to review Armstrong's correspondence files, an effort that further undermined his confidence in the man. The exercise led Madison down an odd path in the midst of a war that was going badly. After days of examining the records, Madison prepared a detailed memorandum analyzing problems with the War Department's accounting procedures. Though Madison's ideas on the accounting issues may well have been correct, it was hardly a subject worthy of his attention at that pivotal moment in the nation's life. Though Madison's grasp of the war's larger strategy was solid, this minute exercise represented oddly misdirected effort.[46]

Madison and Armstrong sharply disagreed over the proper response to the British naval squadron sailing in the Chesapeake Bay. The year before, a similar squadron plundered and terrorized coastal towns and plantations for months without threatening either Washington or Baltimore. The warships resumed the work in February 1814. By May, Madison was warning War Secretary Armstrong that when the British officers chose targets, "the seat of government cannot fail to be a favorite one."

To defend his capital, Madison created a military district for the Chesapeake region. The commander was William Winder, whose principal qualification was that his uncle was governor of Maryland. Armstrong disparaged the president's moves, arguing that the British had ignored Washington a year before because the city held little strategic importance. They would strike at Baltimore, Armstrong said, because it was a trade hub and home to privateers that were attacking British merchant ships.

Nevertheless, Madison directed Armstrong to make "systematic provision against invading armaments for both cities," then followed up by demanding copies of instructions sent for the new military district of Washington. The president and his friend Monroe conducted a personal inspection of the defenses at Fort Washington on the Potomac. The War Secretary reinforced the defenses of neither Baltimore nor Washington, preferring to launch one more campaign on the Niagara frontier. According to a cabinet memorandum, Washington's defenders numbered three thousand regular troops and ten thousand militia, but not that many were actually available for service against the four thousand British veterans arriving on fifty Royal Navy ships. Dolley wrote to a friend in late July that Washington was "in a state of perturbation" because the British had closed to within twenty miles of the city. To calm public fears, the Madisons delayed their annual late-summer retreat to Montpelier. In a letter dashed off in a stolen moment, the president assured his mother that they would leave Washington as soon as feasible.[47]

In mid-August, the British again moved up the Chesapeake. For Madison, their timing was awkward. He had finally concluded that War Secretary Armstrong was entirely unsatisfactory. In a curt note, he cited several actions taken by Armstrong without his knowledge, then "lay down some rules" for army business. He specified ten steps that Armstrong could take *only* with Madison's approval. With the British hammering on Washington's door, he did not fire the War Secretary, though he plainly wished to do so.[48]

On August 18, when the alarm sounded that the British were moving, Monroe again reached for his sword and spyglass. He persuaded the president that he should lead a scouting expedition, then rode out at the head of two dozen dragoons. He remains the only sitting American Secretary of State to lead armed men during war. Two days later, he was sending Madison urgent reports about the British progress. Madison, desperate for information, passed Monroe's reports on to the army commanders and peppered Monroe with observations about the military situation, sometimes on an hourly basis. Monroe had the sharp pleasure of declaring that Armstrong was wrong: The British were going to attack Washington. Energized by days on horseback, Monroe cheered on his colleagues: "I have much confidence in our success but the trial will be great, and I trust the exertion equal to it."[49]

Madison directed the removal of government records to the countryside. He still hoped the British, without cavalry and having a relatively small land force, would turn away. When they kept coming, Madison and three cabinet members joined General Winder's camp. Armstrong arrived late. Winder's militia, plus a few hundred sailors, were planning to confront the invaders at Bladensburg, northeast of the city. Armstrong predicted an American loss. The president's party rode to the expected battlefield.[50]

At Bladensburg, the scene was both poignant and ridiculous. Evidently hoping to inspire the American soldiers and their commanders, the sixty-three-year-old president and his cabinet officers mostly got in the way. Indeed, they unhelpfully brought their own dysfunctions onto the battlefield. Madison asked Armstrong if he had advised Winder on tactical matters. In a classic passive-aggressive response, the War Secretary answered that he would if the president ordered him to do so. When the two men rode over to join Winder, Madison's horse reared and bucked while Armstrong made desultory conversation, offering no military advice. The president, struggling with his horse, said little. Arguably worse, though, was Monroe's contribution before the battle. Addressed as "Colonel Monroe" while in the saddle, the Secretary of State imperiously rearranged American defensive positions, to the dismay of American officers. When the battle began in early afternoon, Madison viewed the fighting until the outcome was clear.[51]

With such confused leadership, the American resistance could not last long. The militia outnumbered the British by nearly two to one, but it broke and ran early. A contemporary described it as a mismatch between Britain's "conquering veterans" and "young mechanics and farmers, many of whom had never before carried a musket." The detachment of American sailors fought hard, but they were surrounded and captured en masse. The Americans suffered about eighty casualties, the British four or five times that number. In honor of the militia's swift departure, the encounter was dubbed "the Bladensburg Races."[52]

Madison hurried back to Washington, a city in chaos, reaching it after an hour's ride. A mass flight was under way. At the Executive Mansion, Dolley had left dinner out while taking away the silver and official papers. Amid the furor, she remembered the power of symbols, ordering that Gilbert Stuart's portrait of George Washington be torn from its frame and spirited out of the city.

Madison too had to stay out of British hands. He would be a great prize for the enemy, but there was little plan for keeping him safe. He had intended to meet his senior officials in Frederick, Maryland, but the road was jammed. After ensuring that Jones was destroying the war supplies at the Navy Yard, Madison improvised. He remounted his horse and led a small group to cross the Potomac. Riding with two friends, Madison spent the night in a private home in Virginia.

Next day, Madison scoured the countryside until he found Dolley at a Falls Church inn. After a short rest, he left early to recross the river into Maryland. He spent the next night in Brookeville, north of the city, in the home of a prosperous Quaker merchant. Despite the confusion and disappointments, Madison retained his signature calm and self-possession. A friend there described the president as "tranquil as usual, and tho' much distressed by the dreadful event which had taken place, not dispirited." Soldiers and civilians straggled through the small town, many spending the night in the woods. Monroe joined Madison in Brookeville in the morning.[53]

While the president wandered country lanes, the British burned most of the public buildings in Washington. The only resistance consisted of a few potshots taken from behind buildings. The invaders first burned the Capitol and the Treasury. When they reached the Executive Mansion, they found that local looters had already helped themselves. The British soldiers took more souvenirs, including letters from the president to his wife and a ceremonial dress sword. They also gleefully wolfed down the meal that Dolley had left for the president.

A violent thunderstorm struck in the early morning, turning ashes into sludge. The British resumed their destruction when the sun rose, burning the War and State Department offices. They also destroyed the offices, printing press, and type of a newspaper that had annoyed Admiral Cockburn. Smash all the "C"s, he cheerily told his men, so the editor could not attack him personally again. They put to the torch only those private buildings that had housed snipers. After little more than a single day, the British withdrew to Bladensburg.[54]

The burning of Washington will always be the central event of Madison's presidency. No occasion rivaled the drama of a capital in flames, enemy soldiers in its streets, and a government in flight. The tableau encapsulates the quandary of a small nation challenging the world's leading power, and of a government that struggled to manage its military. Yet the aftermath of the ignoble event illustrated a quality of Madison's that can be overlooked: his tenacity and determination. On this occasion, they were matched by Monroe's.

Less than forty-eight hours after the British marched away from Washington, the two Virginians rode together into the capital. The nation they led had absorbed a mortifying insult. Whatever their personal feelings, they had to find a way back from the destruction that lay around them.

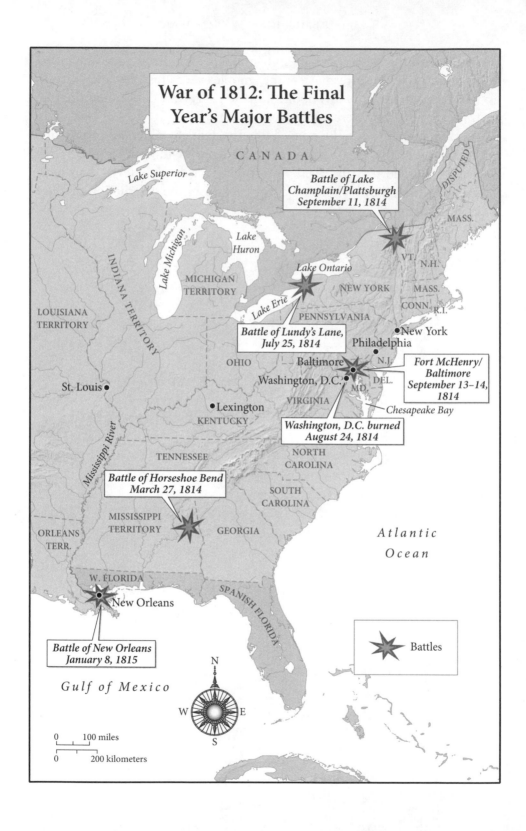

War of 1812: The Final Year's Major Battles

CANADA

Lake Superior

Lake Michigan

Lake Huron

Lake Ontario

Lake Erie

DISPUTED

MASS.

Battle of Lake Champlain/Plattsburgh September 11, 1814

VT. N.H.

MICHIGAN TERRITORY

NEW YORK

MASS.

CONN. R.I.

INDIANA TERRITORY

LOUISIANA TERRITORY

PENNSYLVANIA

New York

Battle of Lundy's Lane, July 25, 1814

Philadelphia

OHIO

Baltimore

N.J.

Fort McHenry/ Baltimore September 13–14, 1814

St. Louis

Washington, D.C.

MD.

DEL.

Lexington

KENTUCKY

VIRGINIA

Chesapeake Bay

Washington, D.C. burned August 24, 1814

TENNESSEE

NORTH CAROLINA

Battle of Horseshoe Bend March 27, 1814

SOUTH CAROLINA

MISSISSIPPI TERRITORY

GEORGIA

Atlantic Ocean

ORLEANS TERR.

W. FLORIDA

New Orleans

SPANISH FLORIDA

Battle of New Orleans January 8, 1815

Gulf of Mexico

N

W   E

S

Battles

0   100 miles

0   200 kilometers

Mississippi River

21

NEAR TO A MIRACLE

Madison never wrote down how he felt that evening, August 27, 1814, as he and Monroe rode past the smoldering ruins of their government. The looters were gone, but the roar of cannon told him that the Royal Navy was bombarding nearby Fort Washington. He had toiled ceaselessly for five years as the leader of the world's only republic, the best hope of mankind, yet now an enemy army had reduced its public buildings to rubble. The humiliation, visible everywhere, could never be erased. Washington had never resembled the aspirations of its founders. Twenty years after its founding, one cabinet member wrote, it was still only "a meager village, a place with a few bad houses and extensive swamps." But it also "was the capital of the nation, and six thousand troops have laid its best parts in ashes."[1]

Madison was exhausted. He had spent much of the last several days in the saddle, far from his usual sedentary routine. There was time neither for rest nor for questioning the decisions and indecision that had led to the depressing sights around him. The care of the republic still lay in his hands.

"Prompt measures," Monroe later wrote, "were indispensable." Madison asked his old friend again to take command of the War Department and of the Washington military district. Colonel Monroe agreed.

In the morning, they toured the destruction together. From Greenleaf Point they watched British warships attack Alexandria on the river's far shore. The Executive Mansion was a burned-out husk: "unroofed, marked walls, cracked, defaced, blackened with the smoke of fire." The State, War, Navy, and Treasury offices were ashes. The Capitol was a smoking wreck, "the most magnificent and melancholy mien you ever beheld," with thousands of volumes in its library incinerated while "the meadows and sheep walks in the plain below look as green as ever." Near the Capitol, a friend rushed up to Madison. The city's residents, he related, were "violently irritated at the thought of . . . more futile resistance" so a delegation soon would surrender the city to the British.

Angrily, Madison forbade the "dishonorable" mission. He would not abandon Washington a second time. He would, he declared, "defend the city to the last." Colonel Monroe chimed in. Any effort to capitulate, he added, would be met with the bayonet. Then he began to place cannon to repel the British ships if they turned their guns on Washington. The British, though, preferred to plunder the wealth contained in Alexandria warehouses.[2]

Madison had unfinished business with his other War Secretary. It was time for plain speaking with John Armstrong. In a long meeting on August 29, the president explained that "violent prejudices" were held against both Madison and Armstrong for failing to defend Washington. Soldiers were refusing to serve so long as Armstrong was War Secretary. When Armstrong attempted to defend himself, Madison snapped back. The New Yorker, he said, had failed to appreciate the danger to the city and "had never himself proposed or suggested a simple precaution or arrangement for its safety, everything done on that subject having been brought forward by myself." Though Madison expressed his utter dissatisfaction with Armstrong, he inexplicably did not fire him. Nevertheless, the War Secretary understood that he would never have the president's confidence. A few days later, he submitted his resignation.[3]

On September 1, barely a week after the British entered Washington, Madison issued a proclamation that the United States had been injured but not beaten. Emphasizing that Britain controlled Washington "for a single day only," he called upon his countrymen to "unite their hearts and hands" in "manful and universal determination to chastise and expel the invader." To demonstrate that the American government was unimpaired, he called Congress into emergency session on September 20, in less than three weeks.[4]

Madison greeted Congress with an address that disparaged the burning of Washington as a "transient success." Happily, he could point to an unprecedented cluster of American victories elsewhere, beginning with the successful defense of Baltimore's Fort McHenry against the same force that burned Washington, the encounter that inspired lawyer Francis Scott Key to write the words of "The Star-Spangled Banner." Commodore Thomas Macdonough's triumph on Lake Champlain was even more important, as it blocked a dangerous British thrust from Canada. General Andrew Jackson had subdued the Creek Nation on the southern frontier, a victory that brought great swaths of Indian land. And Generals Jacob Brown and Winfield Scott had won battles in bleeding Niagara. After two years of war, Madison had found able military leaders. To support the war effort, Madison continued, Congress must approve more financing and (yet again) reform the militia. The Bladensburg Races convincingly demonstrated its inadequacy.[5]

The nation's financial condition was dire. The British blockade had destroyed most trade except for smuggling. Exports that stood at $108 million in 1807 had sunk to $7 million in 1814. Imports shrank from $138 million in 1807 to less than $13 million. The financial system was collapsing. Banks from New York to Georgia had stopped circulating hard money, leaving everyone but New Englanders with only doubtful paper money. Even though Congress had raised taxes several times, government revenue plunged from $13 million in 1811 to $6 million in 1814, while war expenditures mushroomed. The government needed $23 million to pay for the last three months of 1814 and another $50 million to keep fighting. The Treasury Secretary could raise none of it. Navy Secretary Jones described his department as "destitute of money," with seamen unpaid and no funds for recruiting. "[I]f the salvation of a city depended upon the prompt transportation of a body of our seamen," he added, "I have not a dollar." At the end of the year, the government defaulted on scheduled debt payments.

Many mocked the president who fled while the capital city burned. Several years later, graffiti on the burned-out Capitol still proclaimed: "James Madison is a rascal, a coward, and a fool," and "The capital of the Union lost by cowardice." A tavern song included the bitter verse:

> Our capital you lost, Jim, much wealth with it likewise,
> Your fame has fled, your honor's dead, your minions be despised,
> In wisdom you're deficient, Jim, in energy also,
> Most manfully, you ran away, James Madison, my Jo.[6]

A leading Federalist summarized the situation: "Without money, without soldiers and without courage, the president and his Cabinet are the objects of very general execration."[7]

Confronting this mountain of troubles, Madison went to work with his customary calm and focus. As his secretary through the war years recalled, "amidst all the troubles and excitement attendant on a foreign war, and provoking feuds at home," Madison never "utter[ed] one petulant expression, or gave way for one moment to passion or despondency."[8] He stabilized his cabinet by recruiting a new Treasury

Secretary, Alexander Dallas of Philadelphia. He left Monroe atop the War Department and as interim Secretary of State. His old friend was the administration's main pillar.

Focusing on the peace talks, Madison and Monroe decided to give Gallatin and his colleagues even greater freedom. The peace in Europe meant that the question of America's maritime rights was no longer pressing. If America could only come to terms with Britain, no nation would care to seize American cargoes, ships, or seamen. New instructions confirmed Gallatin's recommendation that America accept the status quo ante bellum: Both sides would stop fighting; the war would have resolved nothing.[9]

After those instructions were dispatched in early October, bad health and bad news besieged Madison in the makeshift presidential residence. Dolley complained that the fragile Madison grew ill as soon as they moved into the Octagon House near the Executive Mansion. An American diplomat returning from Ghent reported that the British were presenting impossible demands: that the United States relinquish most of Maine, level the forts on its northern border, give up fishing rights in the Atlantic, and establish an Indian "buffer state" in the Northwest Territory comprising 15 percent of the nation's land. The American commissioners expected the talks to end in failure. To rally support for his government, Madison took the unusual step of sending to Congress both the British demands and his conciliatory instructions to the American commissioners.[10]

New England, with Britain still occupying eastern Maine, seemed ready to dissolve the union. Earlier that year, the British extended their blockade to that region and launched raids on the New England coast. In mid-October, Massachusetts invited its sister states to a convention in Hartford. Vermont and New Hampshire refused the invitation, but Connecticut and Rhode Island accepted. Antiwar Federalists swept fall elections in the northeast. The president, a visitor reported, "looks miserably shattered and woe-begone. . . . His mind is full of the New England sedition." In November, the Massachusetts governor sent a representative to Canada to explore a separate peace with Britain; the island of Nantucket actually made one. Madison ordered two veteran regiments to winter quarters near Hartford, where they could keep a close watch on the New England convention. He ordered other troops on alert to "put rebellion down."[11]

New England's antiwar feelings, Madison wrote in a letter, created "our greatest difficulties in carrying on the war; as it certainly is the greatest, if not the sole inducement with the enemy to persevere in it." Madison blamed the region's leaders, "aided by the priests," for misleading the people into a "delusion scarcely exceeded by that recorded in the period of witchcraft." He hoped for the best but added that "the worst ought to be kept in view."[12]

A large British force was sailing to attack New Orleans. Madison and Monroe hurried troops and supplies to Andrew Jackson's army there. British seizure of that key port city could threaten the entire Mississippi Valley and shake American control over its western lands. The British knew that New Orleans was "our most distant and weakest point," Gallatin warned from Europe, "and that if captured it could not be retaken without great difficulty."[13]

The peril was acute. The vindictive foreign enemy, flush with victory over Napoleon, was bearing down with awesome military power. Madison's government had no money. The nation's wealthiest region was considering secession, its capital had been invaded, and its central buildings burnt. It would have been easy to fall into despair. In the temporary residence—afflicted by the bilious fever that never completely left him—the president continued to work through the night, every night.[14]

Then, in late November, Vice President Gerry died.

Madison's luck turned dramatically in the first month of 1815. The first good news came from Hartford. The gathered New Englanders were content to issue a report that complained about embargoes, slavery, and the reckless expansion of the nation. They called for repeal of the Constitution's three-fifths clause and for a new requirement of a two-thirds vote in Congress for declarations of war, embargoes, and admitting new states. But the New Englanders proposed no disloyal action. Remembering their ties to other regions, their own Republican neighbors, and the federal troops on their doorstep, they embraced neither disunion nor defiance. The secession threat vanished.[15]

Then Monroe received astonishing news from New Orleans. He cheerfully sent the president "an account of a victory truly glorious." Jackson's mismatched army of regulars, militia, and pirates had trounced the largest army Britain had sent to America. Placing his men behind barricades to face overconfident redcoats who advanced over open ground, Jackson produced shockingly lopsided results: more than two thousand British casualties, including three generals, compared to fewer than two hundred and fifty Americans killed or wounded. "History records no example," Monroe wrote to America's now-favorite general, "of so glorious a victory obtained with so little bloodshed." The threat to the Mississippi Valley evaporated as British troops straggled back to their ships. In Washington, crowds staged a torchlight parade, cheering lustily as they surrounded Madison's residence. "Glory be to God," exulted *Niles' Weekly Register* in Baltimore, "that the barbarians have been defeated."[16]

On the evening of February 13 came the most startling rumor of all: The Ghent negotiators, having predicted failure only three months earlier, had signed a treaty that Britain's Prince Regent already had ratified. Hearing the report, a Pennsylvania senator rushed to the Octagon House to determine what the president knew. He found the house dark, the president "sitting solitary in his parlor . . . in perfect tranquility, not even a servant in waiting." The senator asked if the report was true; Madison bade him sit down. "I will tell you all I know," he said, then confirmed that he thought there was peace but he had no official confirmation. The senator recalled with some wonder the president's "self command, and greatness of mind, [which] I witnessed on this occasion."[17]

On the next morning, Monroe delivered the treaty to Madison. The British had accepted a return to the status quo at the beginning of the war, terms Madison and Monroe already had approved. The Senate unanimously ratified the treaty two days later. In a panglossian statement, Madison proclaimed that peace was "the natural result of the wisdom of the Legislative Councils, of the patriotism of the people, of the public spirit of the Militia, and of the valor of the Military and Naval forces of the Country."[18]

For a month the news had been almost too good to believe, vanquishing the specters of invading redcoats, barren government coffers, and a disintegrating nation. In declaring a national day of thanksgiving, Madison reminded Americans that "no people ought to feel greater obligations to celebrate the goodness of the Great Disposer of events . . . than the people of the United States."[19]

The abrupt reversal in the British negotiating position had been spurred by that nation's great hero Arthur Wellesley, duke of Wellington, the general who conquered Napoleon. Offered command of British forces in America, Wellington had questioned the wisdom of continuing the war. The British, he noted, had neither gained control of the Great Lakes nor carried the war onto American soil in a meaningful way; he dismissed the seizure of eastern Maine as a temporary achievement. "You have no right from the state of war," the duke concluded, "to demand any concession of territory." When Wellington spoke, the British government listened. It soon decided that, after twenty years of war with France, continuing to fight with the United States was foolish.[20]

In retrospect, much about the War of 1812 can seem small, beginning with the president. In an era filled with military giants like Napoleon and the duke of Wellington, Madison would never cut a heroic figure. Even a supporter like Henry Clay deemed him "wholly unfit for the storms of war," finding that "nature has cast him in too benevolent a mold" for such duty. Moreover, America's defense of its honor can seem abstract, even flimsy, especially since the British had disrupted American trade and impressed American seamen for a decade before the war began. The blundering of America's military makes for depressing reading, and even the casualty numbers seem of marginal significance. In the entire war, Americans lost about two thousand men killed and four thousand wounded—less than a single day's slaughter in any of a dozen Civil War battles.[21]

Yet it was a watershed for the new nation. Despite sharp sectional differences, Americans had stood mostly together in defense of principles of personal freedom and liberty that were at the core of the nation's founding. Impressments and free maritime trade seem like antiquated notions two centuries later, but in 1812 the nation's sovereignty was wrapped up in them. That the war involved challenging Britain, the former mother country, gave it a coming-of-age quality that has led many to call it a second war of independence. In the middle of the fight, John Adams insisted that a "more necessary war was never undertaken."

> It is necessary against England: necessary to convince France that we are something: and above all necessary to convince ourselves that we are not nothing.[22]

America, stepping out on the world stage, had not distinguished itself, but it was still standing. One feature of the war had concrete consequences: It broke the power of the Indian tribes east of the Mississippi, speeding the seizure of most of their lands.

In important ways, the War of 1812 truly was "Mr. Madison's War." It was about principles, not gain. It was fought with a quiet tenacity, often ineptly, and with endless tolerance of those who opposed it. As a close friend wrote years later, the war was conducted "in perfect keeping with the character of the man, of whom it may be said that no one ever had to a greater extent, firmness, mildness, and self-possession." When peace came, Madison welcomed it in a darkened house, sitting alone with his thoughts.[23]

Madison and America had done no better than survive the war. The same could not be said for some of the doctrines on which Madison and Jefferson had built the Republican Party. Madison asked Congress in late 1814 to re-create Hamilton's Bank of the United States. The resulting legislation was so flawed that he vetoed it. Congress tried again. In 1816, he signed legislation creating the second Bank of the United States. His former Navy Secretary, William Jones, became its first president.[24]

Having had his residence burned down by an invading army, Madison became an advocate for a standing army and an effective navy. When proclaiming the Treaty of Ghent, Madison reminded Americans that peace did not mean an end to spending on defense: "A certain degree of preparation for war is not only indispensable to avert disasters in the onset, but affords also the best security for the continuance of peace."[25]

Peace unleashed America's economic development. Foreign trade quickly boomed. In 1815 alone, imports rocketed up by nearly a factor of ten, from $13 million to $113 million; exports rose from $7 million to $52.5 million. Settlers flooded into the lands taken from Indian tribes. Immigration from Europe soared. By 1830, the nation's population would grow by 50 percent.[26]

Economic development required building out the nation's transportation network. Canals and roads—"internal improvements"—became a national obsession. In December 1815, Madison asked Congress to develop a program to support them, though he cautioned that there might be a "defect in constitutional authority" for such a program. When Henry Clay pushed through an internal improvements program near the end of Madison's term, the president's Republican soul rebelled. The Philadelphia Convention, he insisted, did not give Congress the power to intrude on such state and local matters. A constitutional amendment was needed. On the day before he left office, he vetoed the improvements bill.[27]

Madison's republican beliefs framed one of the notable elements of his war presidency: his broad tolerance of opposition. New England governors had refused to provide militia while many ministers preached resistance to the war. In every state, newspapers published scandalous attacks on him. Public rallies denounced him. Madison endured it all. He instigated neither lawsuits nor prosecutions of printers. He launched no political retaliation against New England. He did not suspend habeas corpus rights or interfere with state courts that upheld refusals to send state militias to federal service. In contrast, both John Adams and Thomas Jefferson—in peacetime—had directed prosecutions that jailed their critics. Some saw weakness in his tolerance of dissent. Andrew Jackson called Madison "a great civilian" but added that his "mind of a philosopher" rendered him "not fitted for a stormy sea."[28]

For Madison, though, the highest value was preserving self-government, even if it made for messy politics and inefficient warmaking. He pointedly contrasted America's war years to those in Europe:

> [T]he difference between our government and others was happily this: that here the government had an anxious and difficult task at hand, the people stood at ease—not pressed upon, not driven . . . whereas elsewhere government had an easy time, and the people bear and do everything.[29]

Peace brought Madison a popularity he never before enjoyed. There seemed almost a national amnesia about the lean times just past. Though the war ended in no better than a draw, many Americans felt they had won a victorious peace. The last battle of the war was Jackson's smashing win at New Orleans. Both impressments and seizures of American ships came to an end, even though their end was caused not by American arms but by European peace.

Throngs clamored to squeeze into Dolley Madison's Wednesday-evening socials. After years of grumbling about "Mr. Madison's War," his taxes, and his diffident ways, Americans were discovering his quiet virtues. In February 1816, *Niles' Weekly Register* of Baltimore, then becoming the nation's largest newspaper, sang the president's praises:

> His style is chaste; his logic concise, cogent, and impressive. He argues without acrimony—replies without anger—exhibiting firmness without obstinacy—moderation without weakness— . . .
>
> At once cautious and sincere, he does not feel obliged to say all he thinks, though he would scorn to utter what he does not think. . . . A stranger to intrigue, he knows nothing of deceit and artifice; but to guard against them.

The gaudiest compliment came from old John Adams. In a letter to Jefferson, the second president wrote that, despite its many troubles, Madison's administration "acquired more glory, and established more Union, than all his three predecessors . . . put together."[30]

Though the pressures of the presidency did not vanish with the signing of the Treaty of Ghent, they subsided greatly. Madison faced neither hostile armies nor reelection. No embargo embittered merchants. Unaccustomed to leisure time, the compulsive president began digging through his unanswered correspondence. He found a letter from the English philosopher Jeremy Bentham, dated 1811. Apologizing for replying five years late, Madison addressed Bentham's proposal to assemble American statutes as a single code.[31]

Madison and Monroe, yoked in public office and in the public mind, both took extended leave of Washington in the summer of 1815. The strain of the war had worn on both men. Monroe's usual robust health faltered, then one of his daughters fell ill. For three weeks, he indulged the healing waters of White Sulphur Springs, but his condition only worsened. On his way home, he stopped at Montpelier for a visit.[32]

Monroe was the front-runner for the Republican presidential nomination in 1816. Following the course adopted by Jefferson in the election of 1808, Madison made no public comment on a successor, but all understood that Monroe was his choice. Monroe nearly stumbled when the Republican congressional caucus met. The new War Secretary, the large and vigorous William Crawford of Georgia, proved attractive to congressmen who were growing weary of presidents from Virginia. Monroe eked out a 66–54 win. In the fall contest, the Federalists could muster only token opposition. Monroe won resoundingly, 183–34. His Federalist opponent Rufus King observed peevishly that Monroe "had the zealous support of nobody, [but] he was exempt from the hostility of everybody."[33]

Madison's final message to Congress, delivered in December 1816, announced with pride that the budget had returned to surplus. He congratulated the nation on the fortieth anniversary of the Declaration of Independence and celebrated the constitutional government that "watches over the purity of elections, the freedom of speech and of the press, the trial by jury, and the equal interdict against encroachments and compacts between religion and the state."

Three months later, on an unseasonably warm day in early March, he joined a crowd of eight thousand to watch Monroe take the oath of office in the open air, in front of the temporary building that Congress was using while the Capitol was being rebuilt. Jefferson had passed the Republican torch to Madison, who now passed it to Monroe, their old conflicts long washed away. During the most difficult days of Madison's presidency, Monroe had stood with him, an indispensable support. Gallatin, longtime colleague of both, wrote to Madison from Europe that few statesmen "have the good fortune, after such a career as yours, to carry in their retirement the entire approbation of their fellow citizens with that of their own conscience."[34]

In the thirty-seven years since Madison entered the nation's public life, the United States had been transformed. Its population had nearly tripled to nine million. Having spread far past the old barrier of the Appalachian Mountains, Americans were served by 3,500 post offices. Steamboats plied the Mississippi River, and gaslights brightened the streets of Baltimore. Irish navvies were digging the Erie Canal across upstate New York and promoters touted a new form of transportation, railroads.[35]

Madison did not conceal his relief to be leaving office. He never, one cabinet member observed, "seemed so happy as now." A frequent visitor found that though Madison "is a confounded sensible fellow, and talks about everything like a professor," he also "enjoys a joke hugely" and sometimes laughs "in a manner altogether unbecoming a great man." After the inauguration, and a final month of receptions and parties, Madison eagerly set out for Montpelier on a steamboat from Washington. A companion described him as "playful as a child" who "talked and jested with everybody on board." The former president reminded his friend of "a school boy on a long vacation."

He had carried heavy public burdens for many years, sharing them at different times with Hamilton, Washington, Jefferson, and Monroe. He had fought for the Constitution and the Bill of Rights; he had been essential in building a self-governing republic that both worked for and respected its people's liberties; he had defended that republic through a bloody world crisis. Laying down those burdens, knowing that the great experiment in self-government would continue, made him positively giddy.[36]

V

DOLLEY

22

ALL THINGS TO ALL MEN

By the spring of 1794, when Aaron Burr introduced James Madison to her, twenty-four-year-old Dolley Payne Todd had endured as many reversals in fortune as a Dickens heroine. She was the second of eight children, the oldest girl. Born to Quaker parents in North Carolina and related to several eminent Virginia clans, she spent her early years on plantations owned or leased by her father. Though rural Virginia afforded few intellectual opportunities for young females, Dolley developed a taste for reading and always placed a high value on education. In a will prepared while her son was an infant, she directed that "no expense be spared" on his education, which was "to him and to me the most interesting of all earthly concerns."[1]

The first reversal came in 1782, when Dolley was fourteen: Virginia legalized the emancipation of slaves in 1782, and the Society of Friends resolved that Virginia Quakers should free their slaves. Her father, John Payne, dutifully emancipated his and moved the family to Philadelphia, the center of Quaker life in America.[2]

John Payne's business ventures wilted in the nation's metropolis, but Dolley bloomed. "She came upon our comparatively cold hearts in Philadelphia suddenly and unexpectedly," recalled a lifelong friend, "with all the delightful influences of a summer sun." He recalled her creamy complexion, blue eyes, and winning smile, which raised "to fever heat" the "thermometers of the heart."[3]

When John Payne's health failed along with his business, his wife converted their home to a boardinghouse for members of Congress. The family's greatest asset proved to be the four daughters, who easily attracted male admirers. The second eldest, Lucy, eloped with George Augustine Washington, wealthy nephew of the great general. In time, the sisters would marry two congressmen, a Supreme Court justice, and a president. In his final illness, Dolley's father arranged her marriage to a promising Quaker lawyer, John Todd. Dolley complied with her father's wishes and soon bore Todd two sons.

When yellow fever struck Philadelphia in early autumn, 1793, John Todd sent Dolley and their infant boys to the country. He stayed behind to nurse his stricken parents, who soon died, then so did Todd and his younger son. In a few weeks, Dolley became a widow with an eighteen-month-old. She inherited some property from the Todds, which provided a measure of independence and allowed her to continue to care for her youngest sister, Anna, but her personal losses continued. Her eldest brother, sent to Britain on business, had disappeared and was presumed dead. Two other brothers would die in 1795. Under the weight of these blows, Dolley clung to her remaining family. Her sometimes frantic anxiety for family members became the dark underside of her high spirits and love of life.[4]

Several suitors competed to be Dolley's second husband. "That I have not been insensible to your charms ought not, I think, be regarded as a fault," one wrote. "Few persons in similar situations would not have felt their irresistible influence." Her choice of James Madison was eminently practical. He was wealthy, smart, prominent, and genial, and pursued her zealously. That the bridegroom was seventeen years older was no barrier in that time, or any other. That his physical gifts were modest seems not to have fazed the young widow.

By marrying outside her faith less than a year after John Todd's death, Dolley ensured her expulsion from the Society of Friends. That did not trouble her. Ten years later, in Philadelphia for several months, she recalled with a shudder "the times when *our Society* [of Friends] used to control me entirely and debar me from so many advantages and pleasures." Although she was by then "entirely from their clutches," she wrote, she still felt "my ancient terror of them."[5]

Marrying James meant not only leaving Quakerism, but also re-entering the Virginia country life of her girlhood. That life, of course, rested on the labor of the hundred slaves who worked at Montpelier. John Payne's decision to free his slaves had begun his downward spiral. Dolley did not balk at accepting slavery back into her life.

James and Dolley shared a conviviality and sense of fun. When a friend sent stockings to Dolley that were too small, she mockingly wrote that "the hose will not fit even my darling little husband." At the age of sixty, she challenged a young girl to a footrace on Montpelier's front portico, assuring her that "Madison and I often run races here." Another visitor drew a vivid image of the Madisons at play:

Mr. and Mrs. Madison would in private sometimes romp and tease each other like two children, and engage in antics that would astonish the muse of history. Mrs. Madison was stronger as well as larger than he. She could—and did—seize his hands, draw him upon her back, and go round the room with him.[6]

Friends prized James's fondness for jokes and amusing stories. He was, one wrote, "an incessant humorist, and at home in Montpelier used to set his table guests daily into roars of laughter over his stories and whimsical way of telling them." The surviving samples of James's humor incline more toward whimsy than hilarity. When a friend disclosed she was having a well dug, James recalled the adage that "truth is at the bottom of a well," then added: "I expect when you get to the bottom of yours, you will discover most important truths. But I hope you will at least find water." In a letter, James recounted the tale of a Frenchman with an imperfect command of English. Discovering in his dictionary that to "pickle" meant to "preserve," the Frenchman bade his companion a good evening with the wish, "May God pickle you." Even if the wit was short of raucous, a warm disposition shone through.[7]

Dolley also saw in James, as she wrote on her wedding day, "a generous and tender protector" for her surviving son, John Payne Todd (always called, prophetically, "Payne"). James and Dolley both referred to Payne as "our son," and Payne called James "Papa." Coming to child-rearing in middle age while holding demanding public offices, James was a distracted parent. "I endeavor to keep him a little in the path of the student," he wrote of thirteen-year-old Payne, but official duties caused him to leave the boy "much to his own disposition." Dolley seems to have been the sterner figure. The year before, Dolley refused to send to her sister a letter written by Payne because "it is so bad that I tell him to write again." Payne's later career strongly suggests that he was an indulged only child.[8]

For James and Dolley's first decade of marriage, young Anna Payne was part of their household. She had lived with her sister Dolley through the terrible days of the yellow fever epidemic. Dolley described Anna as her "daughter-sister," calling herself "a sister who has ever loved you like her own child." Years later, Dolley despaired when illness struck Anna, "who have been since your birth the darling—the friend and the sister that lived most in my thoughts and affections." Another sister, Lucy, lived with the Madisons with her children for several years between the death of her first husband and her marriage to Supreme Court Justice Thomas Todd.[9]

That James never fathered a child with Dolley exposed him to barroom ridicule, which included references to the mismatch in size between husband and wife. One observer described Dolley as an Amazon while comparing James to "one of the puny knights of Lilliputia." The barest whiff of evidence suggests Dolley may have endured a miscarriage in their early years together, but their home was ordinarily far too full for the question to foster sadness. Over the years, some two dozen nieces and nephews, plus more distant relations, sported through the rooms at Montpelier and in Washington. On top of these came friends and political aspirants. A longtime friend observed of the Madisons, "They are seldom alone."[10]

Managing the household, even with slave labor to do the grinding daily chores, was a substantial job. Guests had to be fed at least three times a day, linens and clothes kept clean, and the house kept in order and good repair. Dolley did not complain about those duties, but she chafed occasionally at having to live where James chose to live. At one point she described herself as "the very shadow of my husband." At another, she complained that she had hoped to visit Philadelphia but "I deceived myself—Washington and Orange [Montpelier] forever rise up to impede my *fairer prospects.*" She was sensitive to the sacrifices women made for families and husbands, including the risks of childbirth. When one of Jefferson's daughters gave birth to her third son, Dolley confided that the new mother "hopes 'tis her last." When her sister Lucy's husband asked Lucy to leave Montpelier to keep him company, Dolley wrote that "she like her flexible sex gave up the rest of the winter for *his accommodation.*"[11]

She nursed James through his fevers, fits, and intestinal misadventures. During her own protracted illness in 1805, Dolley feared for James as much as for herself. While James was taking her to Philadelphia for treatment, Dolley wrote to her sister, he came down "with his old bilious complaint. I thought all was over with me, I could not fly to him and aid him as I used to do." She added simply, "I tremble for him." When fever nearly killed James during the summer of 1813, she reported his recovery in two exhausted sentences: "It has been three weeks since I have nursed him night and day—sometimes in despair! But now that I see he will get well I feel as if I should die myself with fatigue."[12]

Their public partnership was a singular one. James's career provided a platform on which Dolley built fame and celebrity unrivaled by any

American woman before her. In turn, she assisted his career in ways equally unprecedented.

For their first seven years of marriage, the Madisons drew little public notice. They lived principally in Philadelphia until early 1797, when James retired from Congress to Montpelier. He began the addition of a four-room section to the main house for him and Dolley, Payne, and Anna. Dolley was entering a house managed by James's mother, Nelly. Fitting together two households required hundreds of adjustments and accommodations, small and large, but Nelly Madison had a reputation for a disposition as mild as her eldest son's. Over the years to come, she and Dolley made the rearrangements work.

The slower pace in the country was an adjustment too. Social life included reciprocal visits with Jefferson and the Monroes. Frequent visitors included siblings, cousins, and other nearby relations, many of them country people with the interests of country people: weather, crops, hunting. Slavery was different in the country too. In Philadelphia, Dolley and James had a couple of slaves as household servants, or to manage horses and carriage. At Montpelier, black slaves outnumbered whites by a wide margin.[13]

The winter of 1801 brought both the death of James Sr. and the beginning of Jefferson's presidency. With James becoming the new Secretary of State, he and Dolley packed up again, this time for the raw national capital on the Potomac.

Official Washington had no social traditions and little female presence. President Jefferson and Vice President Burr were widowers. Since Congress met for only a few months at a time, most of the hundred or so congressmen and senators arrived without their wives. Dolley filled the social vacuum. Jefferson called on her and her sister to act as hostesses for formal events, making her the leading female figure in the capital, a standing that her animated personality reinforced. After a first meeting, the wife of the city's lone newspaper publisher was "highly pleased" with Dolley: "She has good humor and sprightliness, united to the most affable and agreeable manners."[14]

Dolley was, as a niece put it, "a foe to dullness." Her graciousness and cheer filled the Madison home on F Street. Jefferson's weekly dinners at the Executive Mansion were politically segregated—he hosted Federalists one week and Republicans the next—but the Madisons observed no such discrimination. Their home became a place where members of both parties could engage in the sort of informal exchanges that grease the wheels of government. Dolley was adept at building personal connections. "[H]er face expresses nothing but good nature," said one young woman. "It is impossible however to be with her and not be pleased, there is something very fascinating about her—yet I do not think it possible to know what her real opinions are. She is all things to all men."[15]

Dolley proved a natural complement to James. She enjoyed the spotlight and never grew flustered in its unforgiving glare. One of her oldest friends traced Dolley's "mind, temper, and manners" to her Quaker background. During James's cabinet years, she dressed with style, her figure evolving from hourglass to statuesque and beyond, but still wore a Quaker bonnet and kept a discreet handkerchief over low necklines. She plunged into social gatherings. With Dolley Madison there was no reserve or hauteur. She played cards with a beguiling lack of success and she liked to take snuff. "You are aware that she snuffs," wrote one female contemporary, "but in her hands the snuff-box seems only a gracious implement with which to charm." A possibly apocryphal exchange with Henry Clay of Kentucky, a snuff-taking friend, captured the essence of Dolley's success:

Clay: "Everybody loves Mrs. Madison."

Dolley: "That's because Mrs. Madison loves everybody."

Dolley's rejoinder was not strictly true, of course. Indeed, she was more likely than James to hold a political grudge. But she had the gift of appearing to love everybody, an invaluable talent for the spouse of a politician who was uncomfortable in large gatherings. At formal dinners, Dolley ordinarily sat at the end of the table and directed conversation as the occasion required. James sat midtable, where he could talk in a relaxed fashion, recount his anecdotes, and quietly contribute jokes and wordplay.[16]

In 1804, Dolley mourned when Anna, her cherished daughter-sister, married Congressman Richard Cutts, a Republican from the Maine district of Massachusetts. She admonished Anna to remember "the solitary being you left behind." Ten days later, she wrote that she still missed Anna, but she would "reflect on my own selfishness and strive to be reconciled."[17]

A greater crisis arose in the summer of 1805, when an infection grew on Dolley's knee. Every infection could be fatal in those pre-antibiotic times. When the malady worsened, James canceled their annual retreat to Montpelier and brought her to Philadelphia to be treated by the improbably named Dr. Physick. James and Dolley feared the seasonal fevers of Philadelphia, which had carried off Dolley's first husband and younger son. Yet James feared the infection more, so they took the risk.[18]

Installed in Philadelphia, Dolley's spirits sagged. She confided to Anna her fear of death and her "most immoderate grief" over her situation, but she rallied within a few days. James stayed by her side for three months. He was, she wrote, her "unremitting nurse." He was a nurse of a particular kind, however, using the time to dive into an analysis of English maritime law. His goal was to demonstrate that the British government's trade policies violated its own legal precedents and thereby to "overturn this colossal champion of belligerent usurpations."

The resulting 204-page pamphlet, *An Examination of the British Doctrine, Which Subjects to Capture a Neutral Trade Not Open in Time of Peace*, was dense and scholarly. Few who attempted it actually reached the end. A Federalist senator admitted that Madison's effort "very justly exposes the fallacy and inconsistency of the British Courts of Admiralty" but added that he had "never read a book that fatigued me more."[19]

As Dolley recovered slowly, James wrestled with the timing of his return to Washington. "She will be infinitely distressed at my leaving her," he wrote to Jefferson, "with the gloomy prospect of relapse," yet he also felt the call of his public duties. He delayed for several weeks as her condition wavered. Finally, reassured by her improvement, he left. As he had feared, she was immediately anxious, writing after only a few hours of her "grief . . . at even a short separation from one who is all to me." She wrote again on three of the next four days.[20]

For the next several weeks, James and Dolley experienced the longest separation of their marriage. They wrote frankly of their longings for each other and their anxiety for each other's welfare, Dolley lapsing into formal Quaker pronouns. "What a sad day!" she wrote in late October. "The watchman announced a cloudy morning at one clock, and from that moment I found myself unable to sleep from anxiety for thee my dearest husband." She signed another letter: "Our hearts understand each other. In fond affection thine." A third letter implored, "Think of thy wife! Who thinks and dreams of thee!" When she received a sentimental letter from James, she wept with joy.[21]

James's letters addressed her as "dearest" and "beloved," and he signed with "unalterable love." He wrote in early November that a letter from her gave him "much happiness, but it cannot be complete till I have you again secure with me." As the moment for reunion approached, he concluded a note with "repeated expressions of my anxiety to have you safe with me."[22]

James could be flirtatious. He sent his best love to Dolley in one note, adding "a little smack" for one of their friends, "who has a sweet lip, though I fear a sour face for me." A postscript to a letter he received from that friend, he wrote, "makes my mouth water." Another time he sent a kiss to the same woman and told Dolley to "accept a thousand for yourself." Such expressions evidently were standards in James's social repertoire. After Dolley's sister Lucy remarried and moved away, she sent her best wishes to James through Dolley: "Oh! And when he kisses you—he was always so fearful of making *my mouth water.*"[23]

Convalescing in Philadelphia, Dolley's conversations strayed frequently onto political topics. Beginning with the transparently false assertion that "I am not much of a politician," Dolley wrote that she was "extremely anxious to hear (as far as you may think proper) what is going forward in the Cabinet" about a possible war between Spain and England. James supplied a balanced view: Such a war might improve American relations with Spain and worsen them with England. He added that she could deflect questioners by pointing out that the power of declaring war resides in Congress, noting, "that is always our answer to newsmongers." Dolley's letters commented on newspaper stories and reported on French and Spanish diplomats who chose to live in Philadelphia rather than in Washington's rude environs.[24]

In the midst of the anxiety over Dolley's infected leg, good news arrived. Sister Anna delivered a baby boy in August and named him after James. This followed the birth earlier in the year of a more surprising namesake: James Madison Hemings, the son of Sally Hemings, a Monticello slave since recognized as Jefferson's longtime intimate. A Hemings family story recounts that Dolley promised Sally Hemings a gift if she named her child for James, though the promised gift never arrived. By naming her child for Jefferson's best friend, Sally Hemings implied that her connection with Jefferson went far beyond that of owner and slave. A year after Madison Hemings was born, Jefferson's daughter named a new son James Madison Randolph. That gave Madison two namesakes at Monticello: one slave, one free.[25]

In late November 1805, Dolley returned to the capital's modest social swirl. The death of her mother in 1807, and of her sister Mary the following year, caused deep pain. "What in this world," she wailed to

Anna, "can compensate for the sympathy and confidence of a mother and a sister?" She sounded the same note to an old friend from Philadelphia: "I used to think that I could not survive the loss of my mother and my sisters yet am I still here; and in all the bitterness of mourning striving to reconcile my heart to the greatest misfortune!"[26]

She remained intensely engaged with politics, which her letters mention in a familiar manner. Understanding that social connections influenced affairs of state, she puzzled over the standoffish manners of the wife of the British Minister. Widespread evasion of the trade embargo in 1808 vexed her. She and James talked politics. During the crisis over the Erskine Agreement in 1809, he sent her the recent newspapers on the subject, pointing out the different tone of a British Minister's speech compared to his formal diplomatic instructions. James promised a fuller report when he knew more.[27]

Dolley's prominence could make her a political target. When John Randolph was urging Monroe to seek the Republican presidential nomination, he derided Madison's "unfortunate matrimonial connection." More seriously and more preposterously, newspaper accounts claimed that Jefferson pimped out both Dolley and her sister Anna.[28] With an unbridled press, American politics was not a profession for those easily wounded.

As the presidential election of 1808 approached, other politicians admired Dolley's contributions to James's prospects. Commenting on the contest between Madison and George Clinton for the Republican nomination, a senator pointed out that Madison "gives dinners and makes generous display to the members," while Clinton "keeps aloof." Because Madison had "a wife to aid in his pretensions," the senator concluded, "in these two respects Mr. M[adison] is going greatly ahead of [Clinton]." After Madison won the presidency, his Federalist opponent, Charles Cotesworth Pinckney, insisted he "was beaten by Mr. and Mrs. Madison. I might have had a better chance had I faced Mr. Madison alone."[29]

23

THE LADY PRESIDENTESS

With her husband as president, some christened Dolley the "Lady Presidentess" (the term "First Lady" would not gain currency for decades). She began to wear finer gowns, though always with republican pearls, not aristocratic diamonds. She gave up Quaker bonnets in favor of silk turbans. Topped with feathers or plumes, they became a signature, irresistibly seizing attention at social events. In the crush of one inaugural party, the crowd swallowed up the slight president, "but not so with her ladyship," an admirer wrote. Dolley's "towering feathers . . . distinctly pointed out her station wherever she moved." Another friend wrote that Dolley "answered all my ideas of royalty." Indeed, during her years in the Executive Mansion she was repeatedly compared to a duchess, princess, or queen. In a nod to her elevated status, Dolley scaled back her card playing.[1]

She immediately began to redecorate the Executive Mansion, redeeming it from the genteel shabbiness of Jefferson's presidency. Working with architect Benjamin Henry Latrobe, Dolley replaced furniture and accessories, installed chimney pieces, and repapered the rooms. Deftly, she and Latrobe added candles and lamps along with large mirrors to reflect and magnify the light. Her sitting room was a striking yellow, a joyous cry in a drab city. When possible, new items were of American design and manufacture: This was, after all, the president's home. The result was a more stylish and comfortable space.[2]

In late May 1809, Dolley launched her Wednesday-evening "drawing rooms," receptions open to diplomats, Republicans and Federalists alike. Though Presidents Washington and Adams had staged weekly receptions, they were stiff, formal affairs. Dolley banished stiffness and formality.

Guests mingled and chatted, served by circulating waiters or elbowing each other to refreshment tables crowded with wine, punch, coffee,

tea, cake, fruit, and the ice cream that became a Dolley Madison trade-
mark. She wore gowns of buff and yellow—nothing dark that would
drag down the spirit. Sometimes musicians played. Dolley had an un-
canny skill for remembering people's names. "Her memory was so tenacious," wrote one friend, "that after a single introduction she could, like
Cato, name every gentleman and lady that had been introduced to her."[3]

Equally important, Dolley seemed to have a good time. Her pleasure
was infectious. "I never saw a lady who enjoyed society more than she
does," wrote one woman. "The more she has round her the happier she
appears to be." Her tact smoothed over rough places and relaxed the
nervous. She paid special attention to those guests who seemed most
awkward. "There was nothing in her manner that looked like conde-
scension, or bordered on haughtiness," wrote an admirer. "Everything
she did had the appearance of real kindness and seemed to spring from
a sincere desire to oblige and to gratify." She used props to break the
ice with guests. Asked why she was carrying a copy of *Don Quixote*, she
replied that she could employ it "to have something not ungraceful to
say, and, if need be, to supply a word of talk."[4]

Washingtonians came to her Wednesday soirees in numbers. "The
first one was very numerously attended by none but respectable people,"
wrote Latrobe. By the third week, he added with regret, the mansion
was overrun "by a perfect rabble in beards and boots." The Wednesday
drawing rooms grew so popular that they were renamed "squeezes"
because every movement involved navigation through a close-packed
crowd. The writer Washington Irving gushed that Dolley's drawing
room resembled a "fairy land":

> Here I was most graciously received, found a crowded collection
> of great and little men, of ugly old women and beautiful young
> ones, and in ten minutes was hand in glove with half the people
> in the assemblage.[5]

The Wednesday drawing rooms were only a portion of Dolley's social
regimen. She returned all visits made upon her, "and it gave her pleasure
to do so," according to a niece. She staged "dove parties" for the wives of
cabinet members and foreign Ministers when their husbands attended
formal events. Presiding over political dinners—mixing Federalists and
Republicans, men and women, foreigners and Americans—she guided
the conversation along agreeable lines. The food was ample and tasty
but plain, always characteristically American, usually with ice cream. "I

never felt more at home," Vice President Gerry wrote after a dinner at the Madisons', "or spent a more social time."

Some events were more challenging than others. In August 1812, Dolley wrote that they had received "29 Indians to dinner with us, attended by 5 interpreters and the heads of departments making 40 persons." After dinner, the entire company danced to band music. Dolley looked forward to a similar triumph a few days later when more of the "same terrific kings and princes" would arrive.[6]

During their late-summer retreats to Montpelier, Dolley and James entertained on a smaller scale. Beginning in 1809, James supervised a further expansion to make Montpelier a suitable home for a president. He added single-story wings on either side, leaving his mother undisturbed in the rooms she had occupied for nearly fifty years.

The Madisons' hospitality, as recounted by a Montpelier guest who arrived late one afternoon, was unpretentious. Dolley greeted her warmly. "She said I must lay down by her on her bed," then helped her guest loosen her outfit and take off her bonnet. Once reclining, "Wine, ice, punch, and delightful pineapples were immediately brought. No restraint, no ceremony. Hospitality is the presiding genius of this house, and Mrs. Madison is kindness personified." The Madisons had twenty-three for dinner that evening.[7]

Constantly on display, Dolley was always on the prowl for a new turban or other accessory, so long as it was striking. She asked a friend to keep an eye out for "a turban, or even anything brilliant . . . such as gauze or lace flowered with gold or silver." She asked another to find her "a fascinating headdress—It must be of large size," preferably with "some artificial flower or fruit." Asking a friend in Paris for "any pretty thing," she added that the bill should be sent to James. When the bill arrived, Dolley was aghast that it totaled two thousand dollars, a reaction that James presumably shared. "I am afraid," she wrote back to France, "I never shall send for anything more."[8]

The Madisons' entertaining was by no means frivolous. Social conversation softens political life and allows the exchange of news and ideas. At Dolley's Wednesday drawing rooms, dinners, and teas, James could engage in bridge building and information gathering. At the Wednesday receptions, he diligently shook hands with each guest, then stood to the side for serious conversations on pressing public matters. Dolley, at the center of the swirl, served as a second set of eyes and ears. It was a platform from which James could advance his policies. In the early months of 1812, the British Minister reported faithfully on the president's warlike remarks at a Wednesday drawing room. As a senior American official explained after attending a drawing room: "According to custom, I saw what was to be seen and heard what was to be said."[9]

The partnership between James and Dolley was central to his presidency. She spoke comfortably of current issues and unfailingly pressed the administration position. In late 1810, as relations deteriorated with Britain, Dolley predicted to one of James's allies that the English would yield to American demands after the French offered the illusory concessions of the Cadore letter; she enclosed a copy of the presidential proclamation on the subject. Six months later she wrote happily of Monroe's appointment as Secretary of State.

Dolley welcomed friends and foes to her events. As one guest observed, she "won a popularity for her husband which his cold and reserved manners never could have done." Though she shared her feelings only with those she trusted, her partisanship could be sharp. To one confidant, Dolley made clear her displeasure with the Smith brothers of Maryland. She told her sister Anna how she resented an anti-Madison pamphlet written by Robert Smith: "You ask me if we laughed over the Smith pamphlet: Mr. M[adison] did, but I did not—It was too impertinent to excite any other feeling in me than anger." As the election of 1812 neared, she complained about DeWitt Clinton, the Smiths, and various Federalists. In early 1813, her distaste for Congress spilled over in a letter to a Philadelphia friend:

> The city is more dissipated than I ever knew it, the week is too short for parties. The mornings are devoted to Congress, where *all* delight to listen to the violence of evil spirits—I stay quietly at home—as quietly as one can be who has so much to feel [at] their conduct.[10]

Dolley gravitated toward practical politics, the vital business of patronage appointments. In one letter she reported on likely nominees for judicial vacancies. She often was asked to help in securing federal jobs. Washington Irving sought her sponsorship for a federal sinecure, and others tried to enlist her support through a quiet word during a Wednesday squeeze or a dinner at the mansion. Although neither James nor Dolley left any record of their conversations about such requests, by 1816 a cluster of their relatives had spent time on the public payroll. That number included son Payne, a secretary to Gallatin on the peace commission; Dolley's brother John C. Payne, who held diplomatic posts despite his chronic dissipation; brother-in-law Richard Cutts, after losing his seat in Congress; and Samuel Todd, nephew of Dolley's first husband. Except for Dolley's cousins Isaac and Edward Coles, who each served as James's personal secretary, no family member held a particularly august position. All, however, were looked after.[11]

An 1810 letter from Dolley suggests that she worked on James's behalf in subtle ways. Demanding that her letter be kept secret, she confided to an unnamed recipient that she had deliberated for two weeks on whether to make contact with him. Having concluded that he would not otherwise learn of "the necessity for your aid," she had acted: "Come then, as soon as possible to my husband who will not call, though he wishes for you every day."[12]

Dolley might have posted that Machiavellian letter to the estranged James Monroe, coaxing him back from his self-imposed exile from the Republican mainstream. Regardless of the recipient, though, either Dolley was acting on her own in the political sphere, or James was using her as his agent. Either explanation accords with Dolley's prominent role in the Madison administration and moves her well beyond the role of gracious purveyor of ice cream and punch. That conclusion is reinforced by Dolley's question in 1814 to Hannah Gallatin, wife of Madison's longtime colleague. In peacetime, she asked, would the Gallatins "like to be in Europe, as *Minister?*" After the Treaty of Ghent was ratified, James indeed appointed Gallatin to be the U.S. Minister to France.[13]

For female relatives and friends, Dolley provided the sponsorship that could work to their greatest advantage: She placed them in social settings where they might make an advantageous match. When her sister Lucy became a widow, Dolley brought her and her three children into the Executive Mansion. Lucy was Dolley's equal in vivacity, described by a niece as "full of repartee and impulse"; after grinding cabinet meetings, James found "the hearty laugh which she caused him was as refreshing as a long walk." Within three years, Lucy married Supreme Court Justice Thomas Todd in the nation's first "White House" wedding.[14]

Dolley's looks faded—a British diplomat dismissed her in 1809 as "fat and forty, if not fair"—but her importance to James's career only grew. During the 1812 election season, a Federalist senator commented sarcastically that Dolley "made a very good president and must not be turned out." She tried to shield James from the fevers and illness brought on by his habitual overwork. One niece observed that Dolley ran a "cheerful and happy household," knowing that "sprightly conversation acted as a charm on Mr. Madison." Dolley's poise and humor created a world in which a weary chief executive, contending with powerful nations abroad and with political disarray at home, could relax. A guest at the Executive Mansion noted that with the president's wife, "'Tis not her form, 'tis not her face, it is the woman altogether whom I should wish you to see."[15]

Dolley's Quaker background did not inhibit her support for war against Britain. "I have always been an advocate for fighting when assailed," she wrote. "I therefore keep the old Tunisian saber within my reach."

Americans must, she urged her sister Anna, "fight for our rights." In the spring of 1812, she wrote to a friend in Europe of the short-term embargo, "to be followed by war!! Yes—that terrible event is at hand." Dolley's fighting spirit flared when incompetence brought the fall of Detroit in the war's early days. "Do you not tremble with resentment," she wrote to a cousin, "at this treacherous act?"

Most often it was Dolley who met with visiting American soldiers and sailors to applaud their courage while James worked in his office or conferred with his officials. When the British fleet rampaged through Chesapeake Bay in 1814, Dolley's letter to her son breathed defiance:

> The British on our shores are stealing and destroying private property, rarely coming to battle but when they do, are always beaten. . . . If the war should last 6 months longer the U.S. will conquer her enemies.[16]

Barely two weeks later, however, the British army was marching toward Washington City, prompting widespread panic. On the day before the Battle of Bladensburg, before James's vain attempt to inspire the militia and focus its generals, he instructed her to "be ready at a moment's warning to enter my carriage and leave the city," taking public and private papers with her. The British admiral had threatened that unless Dolley left the mansion, he would burn it down with her inside. After filling a carriage with papers, she sent servants to seek wagons, a scarce commodity in a town packing to flee. Dolley resolved not to leave until James rejoined her.

On the morning of battle, Dolley could only wait anxiously. Climbing to the top floor of the mansion, she used a spyglass to search for movements that would reveal the fortunes of battle. She was infuriated to see groups of soldiers, "wandering in all directions, as if there was a lack of arms, or of spirit to fight for their own firesides!" She regretted that there was not a cannon in each of the mansion's windows, primed to wreak havoc on the enemy. Lacking cannon, she ordered dinner prepared and the table set. Servants put ale, cider, and wine in coolers in the dining room.

At three o'clock in the afternoon, a free black man galloped up to the mansion. "Clear out, clear out!" he called. "General Armstrong has ordered a retreat!" Another messenger arrived from James, Dolley recounted later, "to bid me fly." Confusion replaced tension. "Tell me for gods sake where you are," sister Anna wrote from a few blocks away, "and what [you are] going to do." With a few slaves—including Paul Jennings, James's valet, and her own maid Sukey—plus the Frenchman who served as cook, Dolley waited for James as long as she could bear.

When word came that the British were expected in a moment, she decided to leave with sister Anna's family, sweeping the dining-room silver into a bag. She supervised the removal of the Stuart portrait of General Washington, which had to be unscrewed from the wall. "This process was found too tedious for these perilous moments," Dolley wrote later, so she ordered the frame broken and the canvas removed. Two New Yorkers accepted the precious painting for safekeeping. The cook saved Dolley's parrot.

Dolley drove to nearby Georgetown, then crossed the Little Falls Bridge into Virginia and comparative safety. She spent the night at a private home, then met James at a tavern where a woman balked at serving her, complaining that Dolley's husband had sent her own husband off to fight. Despite the indignities, Dolley's levelheaded management of the flight, including her attention to the portrait of George Washington, became a legendary moment in a war that produced few of them. Her self-possession and determination became a model of patriotism, happily obscuring the images of James fleeing the city and of Washington in flames. With Dolley portrayed in heroic poses, Americans were less likely to resent that their president seemed so much less heroic.[17]

Over the next three days, James and Dolley met only once; he needed to seize the reins of government, at least the ones he could reach. On August 27, he wrote to her that the British had left Washington:

> We shall accordingly set out thither immediately. You will all of course take the same resolution. I know not where we are in the first instance to hide our heads; but shall look for a place on my arrival.[18]

The return was difficult. A caller several days later thought the president looked heartbroken. Dolley, according to a friend, "could scarcely speak without tears." Nothing was left of the efforts she had poured into renovating the Executive Mansion. Clothes for the Madisons and their servants, their personal items, all had been stolen or burned. For months, Dolley scrounged for secondhand furniture.

They put the hurt aside. Moving temporarily into the Octagon House, a three-story building not far from the Executive Mansion, Dolley set herself to making it fit for entertaining. Less than a month after the British had left the capital in flames, Dolley greeted a record turnout for the season's first Wednesday drawing room. In reduced surroundings, Dolley filled the void, wearing ever more glamorous fashions. Like the swift convening of Congress, it was a statement that America may have been bloodied, but it was still in the fight.[19]

The Madisons were in Octagon House in early 1815 when they received the news of Jackson's victory in New Orleans and then of peace. The gloom of years lifted at once. "Our house is crowded with company," Dolley wrote when Congress adjourned in March 1815, "in truth ever since the peace my brain has been turned with noise and bustle. Such overflowing rooms I never saw before."[20]

The rebuilding of the Capitol and Executive Mansion proceeded slowly, but peace and prosperity sustained the Madisons. "This is D[rawing] Room evening," Dolley wrote in March 1816, "and we have such throngs, you never saw." James and Dolley had passed through a withering crucible. James, she added, "has been very well . . . his spirits are fine, and nothing can surpass the sweetness of his temper." Though James was publicly neutral about the presidential contest of 1816, Dolley was not so careful. She spoke for him when she wrote, "Me and mine still adhere to Colonel M[onroe] as the best deserving on every point."[21]

James greeted retirement at Montpelier with unfeigned delight. At sixty-six, he was ready to walk away from public office and its cares. "I am hastening my preparations to become a fixture on my farm," he wrote to an old friend, "where I anticipate many enjoyments which, if not fully realized, will be welcome exchange for the cares and anxieties of public life." Jefferson, already eight years into his retirement, applauded his friend's departure from public office and return to books, farm, and tranquillity. "A day of these," he added, "is worth ages of the former."[22]

Dolley's feelings were more complex. Leaving Washington meant leaving many friends. It also meant separation from sister Anna, sister Lucy, and her son Payne. Heading for an extended stay at Montpelier in the spring of 1815, she had written to a friend, "I leave Washington with sorrow."

Though Dolley had lived at Montpelier after James left Congress in 1797, and had been there for summer weeks ever since, it was still the Madison family's home, not entirely hers. Country life had undoubted charms, but she had dwelt primarily in cities for thirty years. More than James, she would miss the pulse of being at the center of the nation's life. Many in Washington would miss her a good deal more than they would miss James.[23]

24

ADAM AND EVE AT MONTPELIER

Arriving travelers first glimpsed Montpelier's gentle beauty through dense forest. The setting sun lit the front of the house, which faced west from the crown of a hill. The classical balance of the house design, its strong columns sparkling in the light, projected order and calm. Tulip trees, weeping willows, and silver poplars rose in clusters, concealing the outbuildings. A line of trees to the north led to a small, six-columned temple with a dome roof. The mistress of the house, one visitor wrote, led the welcome "with open arms and that overflowing kindness and affection which seems a part of her nature." Of an evening, James and Dolley and their guests often gathered on the broad portico, behind the columns.

The house and estate were large, but homey touches disclaimed grandiose pretentions. A tin cup hung on the front gate to keep track of rainfall. A telescope on the portico could scan the skies but was more often trained on mundane sights, including guests approaching through the woods. When foul weather kept James from walking the grounds, he paced the portico for exercise.[1]

On most days, James and Dolley kept a regular schedule, including hearty country breakfasts. James studied in the mornings. Early in retirement, he subscribed to periodicals that never seemed to arrive; he suspected they were being misdirected to Montpelier, Vermont. His correspondence was voluminous, sometimes oppressive. Americans thought it their right to correspond with the former president, and James labored to answer them. His letters reflect his curiosity about everything, from the origin of Greenlanders to the pseudoscience of phrenology to European views of South America. In later years, after rheumatism struck his hands and made holding a pen impossible, he dictated responses to Dolley or her brother John Payne.[2]

As long as he could, James toured the farm daily on his old horse Liberty, looking in on the four separate "quarters," each supervised by a foreman or overseer and worked by slaves who lived on that quarter. At two in the afternoon, James and Dolley called on his mother, who lived on her own side of the house, attended by her own slaves, and did so until her death in 1829. Nelly Madison was eighty-seven when James and Dolley moved back from Washington. She remained mentally alert to the end. Unfailingly referred to as "the old lady," she received guests while seated on the couch in her main room, often knitting gloves and stockings for grandchildren and great-grandchildren. She worked the child's name into the pattern of the garment. She took pride in her eldest son. James, she told visitors, "had never given her a moment's anxiety, save for his health."[3]

Dinner was later in the afternoon. The gentlemen lingered at table after the ladies left to corral scampering children. James dominated conversation while he freely passed around the wine ("of no mean quality," according to a guest from New England). No longer distracted by weighty responsibilities, James blossomed as a storyteller, as described by one visitor:

> [H]is conversation was a stream of history . . . so rich in sentiments and facts, so enlivened by anecdotes and epigrammatic remarks, so frank and confidential as to opinions on men and measures. . . . Every sentence he spoke was worthy of being written down. The formation and adoption of the Constitution. The Convention and the first Congress, the characters of their members and the secret debates. Franklin, Washington, Hamilton, John Adams, Jefferson, Jay, Patrick Henry and a host of other great men were spoken of and characteristic anecdotes of all related. It was living History![4]

Like many raconteurs, James sometimes reprised favorite anecdotes, but a niece insisted that even long-familiar stories were entertaining. Guests, she wrote, "watched the play of his countenance, the transition from brilliant mirth through to brilliant mirth [and] found equal interest in that, as in his story." Evening conversation, possibly sprinkled with chess or cards, continued until ten over coffee, tea, and supper.[5]

In retirement, with hundreds of acres of Montpelier land under cultivation for wheat, corn, and tobacco, James indulged his passion for agriculture. A visitor described him as "quite the farmer, enthusiastically fond of all its employments, and wearing pantaloons patched at the knees." A large garden contributed vegetables, pears, figs, grapes, and strawberries for the table. James experimented with decorative trees and fruits, many sent by friends, to see what might thrive in Virginia's hills. He corresponded widely about those experiments and about innovations in farm design and practices.[6]

Accepting the presidency of a newly formed Agricultural Society of Albemarle, Madison delivered an address to that group in May 1818 that announced a gospel of wise stewardship for the abundant lands that most Americans took for granted. A pamphlet of his remarks circulated across the country.[7]

Madison began by reciting some principles of Malthusian economics: that all species, including humans, propagate to excess until overpopulation brings on famine and disease. Residing in a huge, thinly populated nation, he still foresaw environmental calamities unless agriculture became more efficient.

Madison struck a profoundly conservationist note, enumerating many errors of American farmers. They thoughtlessly cultivated poor lands rather than making them fertile with manures, a resource "particularly neglected" in Virginia. They plowed in shallow furrows, and up and down hills, which encouraged topsoil erosion. They neglected irrigation, raised too many cattle, and used horses instead of oxen as work animals. (Oxen thrive on simple grass and hay while horses gobble expensive grain and corn.) The leveling of forests for timber and firewood, with no thought to restoring them, was madness. And Americans cut the trees around their homes, "where their shade would have been a comfort and their beauty an ornament." He decried the "inconsiderate and indiscriminate use of the axe."[8]

Despite his critical view of American farming, Madison thrived in the first decade of his retirement, suffering no more illness than usual for him. He enjoyed, one friend observed, "habitual cheerfulness." A New England visitor found that James in 1824 looked younger than he had ten years before, "with an unsuccessful war grinding him to the earth." The former president, the visitor continued, "is one of the most pleasant men I have met, both from the variety and vivacity of his conversation."[9]

Dolley too presented a smiling face to the world. Even in retirement, her social burdens were substantial. On one Fourth of July, the Madisons welcomed ninety neighbors to an afternoon barbecue, an affair that must have required days of preparation. The house still echoed with nieces and nephews. Dolley's brother John Payne lived nearby with a growing brood. Sister Anna and her children arrived for most summers. The families of James's brothers lived in Orange.[10] Nelly Madison Willis, daughter of long-dead brother Ambrose, was a special favorite. Old friends and perfect strangers visited through the spring, summer, and autumn. All received Virginia hospitality.

A longtime friend, visiting in 1828, exclaimed that Dolley "certainly has always been, and still is one of the happiest of human beings. . . . Time seems to favor her as much as fortune. She looks young and she says she feels so." Yet the slower life of Montpelier took a toll on her, especially through the winter months, when few visitors came and the bustle of farm life subsided. Dolley dreaded the shortening of days each fall, which promised "a rigid winter—now threatening us in no lover-like whispers." James devoted winter days to sorting and organizing his papers, a task she assisted but did not enjoy. "This is the third winter in which he has been engaged in the arrangement of papers," she wrote to a cousin, "and the business appears to accumulate as he proceeds—so that I calculate its outlasting my patience." She grumbled but did not abandon the task.[11]

Dolley greeted spring with relief, bidding farewell to "the dreary months." Gone from her life were brilliant parties with statesmen and diplomats, glittering events she commanded in regal turbans. James lived much in his mind, examining old papers and considering new issues raised by his correspondents. Every newspaper, every book, piqued his curiosity with something else. President Monroe and cabinet members consulted him on public matters; he dispensed advice cautiously, as was always his hallmark.[12]

Dolley retained a lively interest in current events. After the bitter presidential contest between Andrew Jackson and John Quincy Adams in 1824, she wrote that she feared "the license people take with their tongues and pens will blast the good of the country." When Americans donned the "cloak of politics," she continued, they were "not like Romans, but Goths and Vandals." When friction flared between France and the United States, she supported Henry Clay's attempts to calm the contending parties. But Dolley's engagement with the world had always risen through the interesting people she met, not so much through the written word. Montpelier brought many fewer fascinating people into her life.[13]

James's library held more than four thousand volumes of philosophy, history, and science, most not to Dolley's taste. She preferred contemporary novelists like Walter Scott, and enlisted her son and nieces to find for her "a clever novel, old or new." She sometimes composed verses and kept a pet bird that had learned French phrases. She cared for the garden, particularly the flowers. Her interest in clothes remained, and she relied on sister Anna and Anna's daughters in Washington to supply her with current fabrics and designs "of the present sleeve . . . and how turbans are pinned up, bonnets worn, as well as how to behave in the fashion." Her activities at Montpelier were pastimes, not passions. People had always been her passion. To a girlhood friend, she wrote, "Our amusements in this region are confined to books and rural occupations."[14]

Montpelier sharpened her yearning for the company of her sisters. After only a year of retirement, she wrote to Anna in a maudlin mood: "Even the cooing of the doves remind[s] me of you my sister! And the many scenes I have passed, never, I fear, to return!" Dolley could find Montpelier slow. "I am [a] poor dull creature," she complained, "and at such a distance that I must submit and live along as well as I can detached from others." A year later, she called herself a "poor isolated being, who cries to embrace" her sisters; Dolley referred to Montpelier as "the place she cannot leave."[15]

She was married to a frail man seventeen years older than she who was entirely dependent upon her to manage his life, beginning with the selection of his clothes in the morning. She ached to see other places and other people but knew she could not. "A spell rests upon me," she wrote in the winter of 1820, in the grip of cabin fever, "and withholds me from those I love best in the world. Not a mile can I go from home—and in no way can I account for it, but that my husband is also fixed there."

Despite her blue moods, Dolley's zest revived with the retreat of winter and always stirred when company called. After a visit to Montpelier in early spring, a friend reported on the Madisons: "Her soul is as big as ever and her body has not decreased. Mr. M is the picture of happiness. They look like Adam and Eve in paradise."[16]

During nearly twenty years of retirement, few events interrupted James and Dolley's routines. Those few came from James's service to the University of Virginia, the yearlong victory lap of America taken by the Marquis de Lafayette in 1824 and 1825, and the Virginia Constitutional Convention of 1829.

The University of Virginia in Charlottesville was Jefferson's dream. At Jefferson's particular request, Madison served on the board of trustees—called the board of visitors—for ten years from its founding in 1816. When Jefferson died in 1826, Madison succeeded him as rector for eight more years. Madison rarely missed board meetings or students' public examinations. As rector, he supervised all aspects of the nascent college: building the campus, recruiting professors, disciplining students, and jockeying for public funds.[17]

Dolley often accompanied him to Charlottesville, affording a break from Montpelier's duties. When James went by himself, they corresponded faithfully, assuring each other of mutual devotion after thirty years together. During an early separation, he promised not to "lose a moment in getting home." On a later trip, stranded in Charlottesville during student examinations that stretched interminably, he urged her to write so he would know she was well. "I cannot express my anxiety to be with you," James wrote in 1826. "I hope never again to be so long from you." Four days of separation, Dolley wrote, "seem so many weeks." The following year, the seventy-six-year-old James wrote her of "my greatest anxiety to hasten the moment of being where my heart always is."[18]

Lafayette's triumphal tour, instigated by President Monroe's invitation, also upended the Montpelier routine. The aging Frenchman remained a powerful symbol of the American Revolution, which he had joined as a teenage military commander. Lafayette's revolutionary struggles in France—first a rebel against monarchy, then hounded by the extreme Jacobins, finally imprisoned by the Austrians—enhanced his legendary stature. Though Lafayette's time in America had been largely devoted to military activities, he and James traveled together to New York's western frontier in the 1780s. On that journey, James offered an unblinking assessment of the Frenchman, noting both "very considerable talents [and] a strong thirst of praise and popularity." Almost forty years later, James greeted his old colleague's return with the sunny prediction, "You will be hailed by every voice of a free people."[19]

For thirteen months, Lafayette traveled the continent as "The Nation's Guest," bathed with acclaim wherever he passed. He came twice to the western Virginia hills, beginning with ten days at Monticello in November 1824. On the steps of the mansion, he and Jefferson wept in each other's arms. James arrived at the opening dinner in time for dessert, then sat on one side of the honored guest at a banquet in the rotunda at the University of Virginia.[20]

"My old friend embraced me with great warmth," James reported to Dolley. "He is in fine health and spirits." James, a stranger to weight gain, marveled at Lafayette's girth, finding him "so much increased in bulk and changed in aspect that I should not have known him."[21]

When Lafayette came to stay at Montpelier, Dolley wrote that she "was charmed with his society—and never witnessed so much enthusiasm as his appearance occasioned here and at our court house, where hundreds of both sexes collected together, to hail and welcome him." The mansion house was buffed to a high sheen for the occasion. James, who customarily owned one suit at a time, bought a new one. Lafayette resumed a conversation about slavery he had pressed decades before, urging James to oppose it publicly and to free his slaves. In dinners with James's neighbors, Lafayette repeatedly questioned the continuation of slavery in Virginia, then pointedly visited Montpelier's slave quarters.[22]

Nine months later, in 1825, Lafayette returned to Monticello. Madison and Monroe, who had recently left the presidency, joined Jefferson to extend a final farewell to their French friend. When those four men sat together, they embodied the democratic revolutions that upended the Atlantic world through the preceding five decades. All four felt the sadness of the gathering, wondering if they might see one another again.[23]

In autumn 1829, the Virginia Constitutional Convention in Richmond prompted the Madisons' longest absence from Montpelier. Madison's career began at Virginia's first constitutional convention in 1776, so the 1829 version provided a fitting bookend to his public duties more than a half-century later. The event joined him with two other lions of Virginia's first generation: his old friend Monroe and Chief Justice John Marshall. For Dolley, the occasion promised a return to urban society during the dreary months of late fall and winter. The Madisons stayed in Richmond with Dolley's cousin, whose husband, Andrew Stevenson, was Speaker of the U.S. House of Representatives.[24]

James approached the convention in his usual fashion: with study and memoranda. The burning issues concerned voting rights, representation, and slavery, a replay in some respects of the conflicts at the Philadelphia Convention of 1787. On voting rights, James preferred universal manhood suffrage but did not think Virginians were ready for it, so he endorsed extending the vote to male heads of households who paid taxes, which would end the property-ownership requirement.

The representation issue broke along geographic lines. The eastern, tidewater portions of Virginia featured large plantations worked by slaves. The areas west of the Blue Ridge were home to small farms with few slaves. Because slaves counted in population totals for allocating state legislative seats, eastern planters enjoyed disproportionate political power, which western Virginians resented. Those in the east demanded the status quo be retained. James hoped for a last-minute compromise.[25]

The pageantry of the event was powerful. In a choreographed opening ceremony, Madison nominated Monroe to serve as presiding officer, then joined with Chief Justice Marshall to escort the former president to the chair. As the debates moved into angry clashes, Monroe relinquished the chair to younger men better able to control them. Richmond residents watched for sightings of Virginia's great men. Every morning, Madison and Marshall walked together to Virginia's Capitol, the lanky jurist and the former president, whose small frame was further diminished with age and rheumatism. When Monroe and Madison entered a theater for an evening performance, the audience rose and cheered.[26]

Madison, the only surviving member of the 1776 convention, attended every convention session for two months, sitting at the very front so he could hear better. He, Monroe, and Marshall, he wrote later, were "mindful of the years over our heads," that their views might be dismissed as those of doddering old men. For weeks, he held his tongue, gauging the convention's rhythm. Such bodies, he wrote to a young friend, are characterized by "procrastination in the beginning and precipitation towards the conclusion." He waited for the optimal moment to present his compromise on the explosive apportionment question.[27]

On December 2, Madison rose to speak. He was a figure from another time, with powdered hair, short pants and hose, and shoe buckles. Fashion may have moved to long trousers with lace shoes, but Madison had not. Delegates clustered around his front-row seat, straining to hear his soft voice. They gathered, wrote one witness, "like children about to receive the words of wisdom from the lips of an aged father."

Madison's themes were familiar. In human hands, power "will ever be liable to abuse." Majorities will oppress minorities. Conscience is no protection against government wrongs. "The only effectual safeguard to the rights of the minority must be laid in the basis and structure of the government itself." To do so, the representation provisions in the state constitution should protect both eastern and western Virginians.

The solution, James urged, was to count each slave as three-fifths of a person for representation purposes, as the federal constitution did. That rule recognized that slaves retain "the character of men," and the rule's virtues included "its simplicity, its certainty, its stability, and its permanency." But James proposed that the three-fifths rule apply only in choosing representatives for one house of the legislature, thereby dusting off his unsuccessful proposal from the Philadelphia Convention that seats in one house of the legislature be allocated to favor slaveholders, with the other house free of that bias. This was his "structural" solution. He concluded with a profession of faith in his fellow Americans and their ideals:

> Other Nations are surprised at nothing so much as our having been able to form Constitutions in the manner which has been exemplified in this Country. Even the Union of so many States is in the eyes of the world a wonder: the harmonious establishment of a common Government over them all, a miracle. . . . I have now . . . a consoling confidence that we shall at last find that our labors have not been in vain.[28]

He finished his speech to wide applause, but Dolley was uncertain of its effect. "There will be compromises," she wrote, "but impossible yet to say to what extent."

Madison had little impact on the final results. Westerners felt betrayed by him. During earlier committee sessions, he had supported their proposal to count only white residents, then moved to his compromise proposal. The tidewater landowners, in no mood for compromise, ultimately preserved their decisive advantage in representation. On adjournment day, every delegate queued up to shake Madison's hand. Some shed tears. Madison had no illusion about the new constitution. With suffrage still limited, the state government would be one "resting on a minority, [which was] an aristocracy, not a republic, and could not be safe." He disliked the representation provision, apologizing to Lafayette that concessions were necessary to avoid "an abortion . . . inflicting a stain on the great cause of self-government."[29]

For Dolley, the Richmond sojourn was more successful. She still lit up in company, her blue eyes sparkling and her gift for making personal connections undiminished. She prized the "short interval" away from Montpelier, "in which I ought to be happy." After two months there, she wrote proudly, "the longer we stay the more attention we receive."[30]

She quickly caught up on political news and rumors, with special attention to scandals rocking the administration of President Andrew Jackson. Martin Van Buren, she proclaimed, was in position to be the next president, while John C. Calhoun's political star "is a little in the wane." Back in Montpelier, she declared that she preferred Richmond to Washington City. Too many of her former acquaintances in the nation's capital had moved on, and she disliked the sharp partisan edge there. Richmond had gaiety but also "quiet hospitality." She would like to spend winters there, she added, though she never would.[31]

When the Madisons reached home in January 1830, they faced severe financial troubles. Some were common to Virginia planters of the time. The soil, even when managed by a careful farmer like Madison, was playing out. With new lands opening in the west, Virginia property values stagnated or declined. Aging slaves could no longer work and must be supported. Jefferson had died deeply in debt. Monroe was trying to sell his lands to cover his debts. Madison could see calamity before him.

Some troubles were unique to Madison. To sustain the lifestyle of a president and then a former president, he had been spending all of Montpelier's income and then some. Close relations made the situation worse, beginning with stepson Payne Todd. As an aide to the American peace commission at Ghent in 1814, Payne distinguished himself by his drinking and gambling. He thereafter bounced from ill-considered ventures to gambling and drinking binges.[32]

By 1830, the thirty-eight-year-old Payne still had made no place in the world. Knowing that his stepfather's name could be converted into cash and that James would cover his debts, Payne avoided Montpelier. When Dolley could not bring herself to reprove her son, the chore fell to James. "It is painful to utter reproaches," James wrote in November 1825, when Payne failed to arrive for a promised visit.

> Weeks have passed without even a line explaining the disappointment, or soothing the anxieties of the tenderest of mothers, wound up to the highest pitch by this addition to your long and mysterious absence. . . . Let the worst be known, that the best may be made of it. . . . I must not conclude without imploring and conjuring you to hasten to the embraces of your parents, and to put an end to the uncertainties which afflict them.[33]

Payne was a sore that did not heal. Six months later, James chastised him anew for ignoring Dolley's letters, which "inflict[ed] new tortures." James predicted "the most mortifying consequences" from Payne's mounting debts and urged Payne to return to the "bosom of your parents who are anxious to do everything to save you from the tendencies of your past career, and provide for your comfort and happiness." A year later, James confronted almost three thousand dollars in fresh debts incurred by Payne, plus the fear that Payne would draw funds with a blank check that James had rashly given him. If Payne presented the check, James wrote to Edward Coles, "I need not speak of the calamity."[34]

Payne's downward slide landed him in debtors' prison in Philadelphia in 1829. Dolley wrote to sister Anna of her shame and alarm:

I received [a letter] from him in which he tells me that he was boarding within prison bounds! For a debt of 2—or 300$ he has submitted to this horrid—horrid situation—It almost breaks my heart to think of it. . . . My pride—my sensibility, and every feeling of my soul is wounded.

No matter how low Payne sank, James and Dolley would not give up on him. With James, Dolley added, "his anxiety and wish to aid and benefit P[ayne] is as great as a father's." Knowing that Dolley's greatest fears focused on Payne, James never said no to him.[35]

Through his retirement years, James spent roughly forty thousand dollars to cover Payne's debts (equivalent to more than a half-million of today's dollars). James succeeded in hiding from Dolley about half of those repayments. James's goal, according to Dolley's brother John, was "to ensure her tranquility by concealing from her the ruinous extravagance of her son."[36]

Payne was not the only drain on the Madisons. Richard Cutts, husband of Dolley's sister Anna, was broken by the financial panic of 1819, landing in debtors' prison. Having made loans to Cutts for a business venture, James could not pay off his own bank loans and was dragged into lawsuits against Cutts. James allowed the Cutts family to live in the Washington house he owned. The situation was a delicate one. When Anna and her children came to Montpelier for summers, Cutts stayed home.[37]

These financial demands came during years when James's luck as a farmer was all bad, his setbacks resembling the biblical plagues of the Egyptians. In asking for an extension on one loan, he reported "my crops of every sort having for several years, essentially suffered from insects and bad seasons." Some years brought too much rain, which destroyed crops, fostered disease, and triggered floods. Other years brought drought that withered the plants.[38]

When Jefferson agonized over his debts in early 1826, Madison replied sympathetically, based on his own experience:

Since my return to private life . . . such have been the unkind seasons, & the ravages of insects, that I have made but one tolerable crop of Tobacco, and but one of Wheat. . . . And having no resources but in the earth I cultivate, I have been living very much throughout on borrowed means.

Jefferson died a few months later, leaving his heirs little but woe. Monroe, in his turn, auctioned his land, then sold his slaves.[39]

Watching his friends' troubles, Madison began fresh efforts to collect on outstanding debts but with little success. He sold off land in Kentucky and stock in a turnpike company. Finally, in the early 1830s, he began selling land in Virginia, though prices were low. He never could get ahead.[40]

The hard truth was that Virginia had entered a long period of stagnation, both economic and political. Having been the most populous state at the nation's founding, it now ranked third behind New York and Pennsylvania. Ambitious Virginians moved west in search of new lands and opportunity. One of Madison's sisters was in Alabama. A nephew headed to Kentucky. Many of the Taylors, related to James's grandmother, also were in Kentucky. Dolley's cousin Edward Coles moved to Illinois.[41] In 1835, James Madison Cutts, nephew and namesake, wrote of the malaise that seemed to grip Virginia:

I am often disheartened—here having sacrificed years of my life. . . . I am not one iota advanced towards independence. . . . [Y]oung and old, it almost seems we cannot get a start. We are barely vegetating.[42]

As his financial situation declined, James also felt increasing concern about the path of the nation. Though long in retirement, he still worried over the future of the union he had done so much to form.

THE CONSTITUTIONAL SAGE
OF MONTPELIER

Madison always used time at Montpelier to study. As a young college graduate, while tutoring his brothers and sisters, he did much reading and thinking there. After finishing his term in the Confederation Congress in 1783, he used a winter at Montpelier to put himself through a course of law study. Montpelier was the scene for months of reading and analysis as he prepared for the Philadelphia Convention of 1787, and again when he drafted the Virginia Resolution of 1799. In retirement at Montpelier, he once more had time for study and thought, activities he performed better than most people. As one observer remarked, "Never have I seen so much mind in so little matter."[1]

Dolley's role in his studies was limited to helping organize his extensive papers, a project he thought would create an asset that could be sold for her support after his death. He badgered friends for copies of old letters to complete his records. Through this work, he aimed to shape the accounts that would be told of his time.[2]

His participation in events, he acknowledged, disqualified him from writing history. "The best history," he thought, "must be the fruit of contributions bequeathed by contemporary actors and witnesses, to successors who will make an unbiased use of them." Aging memories, he cautioned, "become no longer faithful depositories. Where oral tradition is the resort, all know the uncertainties and inaccuracies which beset it."[3]

Writers pestered him about events and people: how Kentucky split off from Virginia, or the difficulties of invading Canada and selecting army commanders during the War of 1812. Explaining cabinet appointments, a process that bedeviled his presidency, Madison stressed the many factors that come into play: "[the appointee's] political principles and connections, his personal temper and habits, his relations of feeling towards those with whom he is to be associated; and the quarter of the Union to which he belongs." Then the nominee also must win Senate confirmation. Madison added that the best candidates may decline the job: "You are probably very little aware of the number of refusals."[4]

He lauded Dr. Franklin and paid tribute to Washington's "modest dignity" and "greatness of character," adding a small man's appreciation for the general's "advantage of a stature and figure." Madison described Jefferson as a "walking library," with whom "the genius of philosophy ever walked hand in hand." Gouverneur Morris, he insisted, composed the final draft of the Constitution, and "a better choice could not have been made." He even praised Hamilton, his onetime partner, then long-time adversary.[5]

Madison took a proprietary attitude toward the Philadelphia Convention. Many knew that he retained notes of the deliberations, but he insisted that they not be published until the last delegate died. Madison kept a close eye on how many still lived. In 1827, he noted that only three were left, adding that "of the lamps still burning, none can be far from the socket."[6]

To one correspondent, Madison emphasized the steps leading to Philadelphia, especially the Annapolis Convention. He disputed another's interpretation of the Virginia Plan presented by Edmund Randolph. He disparaged "gross errors" in accounts by New York delegate Robert Yates, Luther Martin of Maryland, and Charles Pinckney of South Carolina.[7] In late 1835, when the eighty-four-year-old Madison was largely bedridden, his thoughts turned again to Philadelphia in 1787. In a single sentence of Madisonian dimensions (134 words), he paid a definitive tribute to the Philadelphia delegates, insisting there were never men "more pure in their motives, or more exclusively or anxiously devoted to the object committed to them."[8]

Madison's reflections ranged far beyond his own career. Commenting on an essay addressing the proof of God, he expressed religious doubt. In struggling with the idea of infinite time and space, he wrote, the human mind prefers "an invisible cause possessing infinite power, wisdom & goodness" to a "universe visibly destitute of those attributes." With a shrug, he allowed that belief "in a God all-powerful wise and good" is "essential to the moral order of the world and to the happiness of man." He did not, however, profess that belief in the letter.[9]

Madison puzzled over the diminutive size of Roman farms in classical writings. No family, he protested, could have survived on such a small "speck of earth." Cincinnatus, a wealthy man, supposedly farmed a mere five acres. Madison entertained a lively interest in the theories of economist Thomas Malthus, whose anxiety about overpopulation he shared. Madison criticized the idealistic socialism of Robert Owen and speculated on the nature of chemistry.[10]

Madison studied how language changes over time, a particular concern when writing constitutions. Can a constitution be preserved if its very medium—words—changes in meaning? Known for his command of Latin and Greek, Madison also examined hieroglyphics, Chinese grammar, and American Indian languages. He listed the influences that change language:

1. The taste for metaphorical terms, which gradually assume a simple and direct meaning. [That is, slang.]
2. Fashion as in dress which exchanges old terms and phrases for new. . . .
3. Imitation of peculiarities in Individuals. . . .
4. Euphony and abbreviation, which are constantly modifying words.
5. New objects and ideas which in the progress of knowledge call for new terms and phrases. . . .
6. The adoption from dead or foreign languages, of substitutes for words and expressions become immodest or offensive by vulgar use.

Because the meaning of a constitutional provision shifts with "the changeable meaning of the words composing it," then so must the "shape and attributes of the government" change. Writing in 1821, he thought the "language of our Constitution is already undergoing interpretations unknown to its founders." Madison often resisted those interpretations, such as Hamilton's expansion of the powers of Congress under the "necessary and proper" clause. Yet he also recognized that since words will change their meaning, so too will constitutions.[11]

In retirement, Madison wrote about constitutional disputes only in private letters until an issue flared that seemed to threaten the republic itself: the implications of the Virginia and Kentucky Resolutions that Madison and Jefferson had drafted so many years before.[12]

The issue arose in the sectional contest over protective tariffs adopted by Congress in the 1820s. Because southerners exported raw goods and imported manufactured goods, they wanted low tariffs. New

England and the middle Atlantic states, home to manufacturing, preferred high tariffs that excluded foreign goods. The South lost the battle when Congress in 1828 adopted what southerners dubbed the "Tariff of Abominations." Anger over that tariff helped sweep Andrew Jackson into the presidency that fall.[13]

Southern leaders nursed the constitutional argument that Congress had no power to impose a *protective* tariff, as opposed to one designed to raise revenue. Madison scoffed at their argument. He knew that the Philadelphia delegates had intended federal import taxes to support the government and that in most years the tariff raised more than 90 percent of the public revenue. Yet any tariff, no matter how low, would deter the import of some goods and thus would be at least somewhat protective.[14] Madison laid out these points in a public letter timed to appear in the *North American Review* after the 1828 election. Those who sought to limit the congressional power to impose tariffs, he warned, would "[destroy] all stability in social institutions, and all the advantages of known and certain rules in the intercourse of life."[15]

Friends applauded his essay but opponents dismissed him as a relic of bygone days. In fact, he was becoming an almost ghostly figure, speaking in first-person terms of events that had become mist-shrouded tales of yore. Madison was shocked by the "illiberal spirit" of his opponents. "So much effort," he complained to a friend, "is devoted to misunderstand." He was incredulous when opponents celebrated the views of his old nemesis Patrick Henry. By opposing ratification in 1788, Madison charged, Henry had preferred "every calamity involved in monarchy, aristocracy, oligarchy, and in military and fiscal oppression." By 1831, with some southerners still denying that Congress had the power to impose a protective tariff, Madison wrote privately that the basis for their position "will lie between an impenetrable stupidity and an incurable prejudice."[16]

Then the argument over the tariff took an ominous turn. South Carolina leaders were claiming that Jefferson's Kentucky Resolution and Madison's Virginia Resolution established that states could "nullify" the tariff. The theory of nullification, Madison feared, could destroy the union.

Though Congressman John C. Calhoun of South Carolina was a key Madison ally before and during the War of 1812, times had changed. In December 1828, then–Vice President Calhoun published *The South*

Carolina Exposition and Protest,[17] repeating the argument that the Constitution authorized only tariffs that would raise revenues, not protective tariffs.[18] Calhoun's new wrinkle was the claim that a special convention in a single state could declare a federal law "null and void." Because state conventions had ratified the Constitution in the first place, Calhoun reasoned, a new state convention could repudiate unconstitutional action by the federal government. The state would thus "interpose" its sovereignty to protect its citizens.

To support Calhoun's theory, nullificationists triumphantly pointed to the Virginia and Kentucky Resolutions of 1798. After all, Madison's Virginia Resolution said that states could "interpose" their views against unconstitutional federal actions. Though he had not taken Calhoun's last half-step of announcing a state power to nullify federal law, Madison's words were being used for purposes he abhorred.

As early as 1821, Madison had anticipated the nullification argument.[19] Madison later wrote to friends that if Calhoun was correct, then the Constitution did not allow the peaceful resolution of disputes between federal and state governments and provides "not a government, but merely a treaty between independent nations." The Virginia and Kentucky Resolutions, he protested, never contemplated that the states could "annul within themselves acts of the federal government." Only the United States Supreme Court could do that. To modify the Constitution, a state had to secure an amendment. Its other option, Madison conceded, was to secede from the union.[20]

Madison and Jefferson wrote the Virginia and Kentucky Resolutions because they thought Federalists in 1798 were using the threat of war with France to centralize power in the national government. Thirty years later, those resolutions were being used to undermine the Constitution. Madison and Jefferson had created intellectual weapons that now filled the Pandora's Box of secession. Nearing eighty, Madison applied his remaining strength to clamp down the lid to that box.

In early 1830, Madison composed a detailed refutation of nullification. The Virginia Resolution, Madison wrote, merely invited other states to protest the Alien and Sedition Acts. He stressed that Virginia legislators deleted from an early draft the statement (which had not come from Madison's pen) that the federal statutes were "utterly null and void and of no force or effect." With that passage specifically removed, how could the resolution possibly be thought to support nullification? In truth, Virginia had specifically rejected nullification. Madison emphasized the practical consequences of nullification theory:

that a single state could suspend federal law in that state, effectively dictating the meaning of the Constitution.[21]

Madison released his analysis in an essay in the *North American Review*. Much as he had in *The Federalist* and during the ratification fight, he called on his fellow citizens to embrace the Constitution as a series of difficult compromises. Possibly, he admitted, a majority of Americans would have rejected every individual provision of the Constitution, even though the entire package was unanimously adopted by the states: "Free constitutions will rarely if ever be formed without reciprocal concessions." Nullification would replace that delicately balanced document with the unilateral power of a single state to void a constitutional action it disliked.[22]

It was a frustrating business for Madison. The Virginia and Kentucky Resolutions had championed the states as a platform for challenging unconstitutional actions by the central government. Calhoun and his allies got that part right. But Madison knew that when he attacked the Alien and Sedition Acts three decades before, he always stopped short of any claim that the states could repudiate federal actions. The nullificationists were stretching his words, words he had chosen with care. They also were ignoring the difference in the risk to the republic posed by the oppressive actions of the Federalists in 1798 and the thoroughly unremarkable levying of tariffs in 1828. Madison was weary of having his arguments belittled because of "the weakening effect of age on the judgment." If a writer lives long enough, he griped to an editor in 1831, he "will find his arguments, whatever they be, answered with an 'I wonder how old he is?'"[23]

Madisonian logic would not resolve the nullification standoff, which smoldered for two more years. In late November 1832, a special South Carolina Convention declared the federal tariff null and void in that state as of February 1 of the following year. Then the state legislature approved a militia of twenty-five thousand men. In response, President Jackson declared the state's actions "subversive of the Constitution." If South Carolina spilled a single drop of blood, he thundered, "I will hang the first man of them I can get my hand on to the first tree I can find." In early 1833, Congress strengthened Jackson's power against the recalcitrant state. When no other state rallied to its cause, South Carolina repealed its attempted nullification.[24]

Madison did not again speak out on nullification. He was feeling the drag of time. His letters bristled with references to his "advanced years," his "octogenary age," and "feeble state." His physical limitations were maddening. "In explanation of my microscopic writing," he wrote apologetically to Monroe, "I must remark that the older I grow the more my stiffening fingers make smaller letters, as my feet take shorter steps." He added that both writing and walking had become "at the same time more fatiguing as well as more slow."[25]

Madison puzzled over the strength of public feeling over the tariff issue and the sectional antagonism it brought. After the crisis subsided, the old man at Montpelier continued to chew over the issue, finally drafting a lengthy memorandum rehashing his repudiation of nullification.[26]

Madison increasingly feared that a central flaw in the union would destroy it. In early 1833, he marveled to a friend that an issue as mundane as the tariff could lead states to contemplate secession, then shared an eerily prescient vision:

> [T]he prospect before us would be a rupture of the Union—a Southern Confederacy, mutual enmity with the Northern—the most dreadful animosities and border wars springing from the case of slaves—rival alliances abroad, standing armies at home . . . and Federal Governments with powers of a more consolidating and Monarchical tendency than the greatest jealousy has charged on the existing system.[27]

He would not live to see that vision realized, but he understood that the core of the tariff and nullification controversies was not federal fiscal policy. Rather, it was sectional animosity between North and South, an animosity that naturally focused on slavery.

In his final years, slavery haunted Madison. He had thought through many challenges to America's system of self-government, then worked with his partners to vanquish them. But when it came to slavery, he had done little beyond wringing his hands. It was the problem he could never solve.

26

---◆---

"A Sad Blot on Our Free Country"

Through most of their life together, James and Dolley owned more than a hundred slaves. At Montpelier, up to a dozen slaves cared for their personal needs: preparing their food, washing their clothes, keeping their home clean, disposing of their waste. Other slaves operated the smithy and the carpentry shop, built barrels and wheels, cut ice from ponds in winter, made shoes and operated mills. Some were hired out for construction work, while James and Dolley hired neighbors' slaves to meet short-term labor needs. A few of the Montpelier slaves' names have survived, but most have been lost.[1]

James and Dolley's closest friends were slaveowners. Jefferson at times owned twice as many slaves as the Madisons. Monroe, less wealthy, owned more than thirty slaves at one point. Visitors to Monticello observed the close resemblance between several of Jefferson's young house slaves and their owner; one was named James Madison Hemings, at Dolley's suggestion, one of several who were Jefferson's children by his slave, Sally Hemings. James and Dolley, frequent and intimate visitors to Monticello, must have noticed the resemblances. Madison and Jefferson spoke with each other of slave management. When Madison was looking for an overseer for Montpelier, Jefferson assessed one candidate as "harsh, severe, and tyrannical." Did Madison never comment to his friend on the resemblance between Jefferson and his young slaves? Did he accept his friend's paternity of the Hemings children as part of the customary pattern of southern slaveowning?[2]

Raised a slavemaster, Madison did the things that slavemasters did. As a young man, marooned in Philadelphia with a short purse, he considered covering his expenses by "selling a negro." When a slave owned by his father ran off, Madison bought an advertisement in a Richmond newspaper offering a reward for his return. When a mentor, Edmund Pendleton, asked for help in retrieving a runaway, Madison investigated Pennsylvania law on runaways, then asked a French diplomat to help recover the man from French troops. In instructions for his overseer and "laborers" (one of many euphemisms employed by slaveowners), Madison directed that the slaves be treated humanely, "consistent with their necessary subordination and work." A former Montpelier slave never saw Madison strike a slave and reported that Madison barred overseers from doing so. Yet beatings happened. In 1836, Payne Todd insisted that no slave had been flogged at Montpelier "for several years"; he admitted beating one in the past.[3]

Madison took seriously his duty to care for his slaves; he referred to them as part of his "family." He purchased "coarser" cloth for "my negro women." He regularly brought a physician to Montpelier to provide medical care. He mourned the deaths of slave members of his family, noting his "heavy loss" when fever killed a young cook who "was becoming moreover a competent gardener."[4]

Some slavemaster duties were more odious than others. After Madison's father died in early 1801, Madison convened a meeting of the heirs to parcel out his father's slaves while imposing the least disruption on slave families. Madison told Jefferson that the complex negotiation consumed an entire week. Day after day, the Madison relatives bargained with each other, valuing the age, health, and skills of each slave to ensure that each heir received his or her fair value in human property, while making an effort to preserve the family relationships that the slaves had formed. The naked power of slave ownership, as well as its awful consequences, was on full display.[5]

Through Madison's long life, his ambivalence about slavery passed through at least three stages. Until he was roughly forty, his profound discomfort with slavery could be seen both in his public career and his private statements. With middle age and marriage, holding ever more responsible government offices, Madison seemed to put aside those feelings; at least he largely avoided comment on slavery. After his retirement, as conflict over slavery increasingly erupted in America's political life, Madison could no longer avert his eyes from the injustice and violence of the slave system. Surrounded by slaves at Montpelier, where the legend of his grandfather's poisoning by a slave would never be spoken and could never be forgotten, Madison could not escape the specter of slavery and the risk that it would sever the American union.

As a young politician, Madison struggled with the contradiction between slavery and America's revolutionary ideals—his ideals. "Where slavery exists," he wrote at Montpelier while preparing for the Philadelphia Convention, "the republican theory becomes still more fallacious." As a young man, he flirted with the idea of moving to frontier lands in western New York, where he could "depend as little as possible on the labor of slaves."[6]

Madison had not absorbed the race prejudices of his time and place. He never denied that the African-Americans he owned were human beings like him. The slave Billey, who accompanied him to Philadelphia in the early 1780s, so absorbed the spirit of liberty that he sought his freedom. Madison wrote to his father that he would not "force Billey back to Virginia even if it could be done." Madison did not blame Billey "for coveting that liberty for which we have paid the price of so much blood, and have proclaimed so often to be the right, and worth the pursuit, of every human being." Yet he did not free Billey but sold him for not "near the worth of him" to a Philadelphian, who could hold him under that state's laws for only seven years. After Billey became a free man and a merchant's agent, James purchased goods for Montpelier through him. When Billey was lost at sea, Madison sent the news home to be relayed to Billey's parents, still slaves.[7]

Madison accepted emancipated blacks on equal footing. On his northern tour with Jefferson in the summer of 1791, he met a free Negro farmer who worked his land with white laborers. "He is intelligent," Madison recorded, "reads, writes, and understands accounts, and is dexterous in his affairs." When a free black man brought a message to Montpelier nine years later, James and Dolley invited the man to join the company for dinner and evening conversation. The visitor spent the night at Montpelier. After breakfast, he borrowed a horse to continue his journey.[8]

Dolley's views of slavery and race questions are more difficult to divine. She never complained about her father's decision to emancipate his slaves; neither did she express reservations about marrying a large slaveholder or running a household with slave labor. Her silence on the subject is all the more striking because slavery tormented her husband, and it did so increasingly as he aged. She and James certainly discussed those omnipresent questions. Her silence may have reflected a pragmatic acceptance of the world as she found it, or a resolve to say nothing to heighten James's uneasiness over being a slaveholder.

According to a former slave at Montpelier, the Madison slaves preferred to present their requests to James, not Dolley. He was more lenient, as even-tempered with slaves as he was with everyone else. If slaves misbehaved, one recalled, James "would send for them and admonish them privately, and never mortify them by doing it before others." A French cook employed at the Executive Mansion confirmed in 1814 that the slaves did not fear James. The household slaves, he reported, "wasted and cheated as much as they could." When the cook threatened to report them to the master, they replied that James "was a joke to them."[9]

Dolley's disposition could be stormier. Early in their retirement years, she became exasperated with Sukey, her best house servant, and banished her to work with the field hands. "Sukey has made so many depredations on everything in every part of the house," Dolley complained, "that I sent her to Black meadow last week." But, Dolley admitted, it was "terribly inconvenient to do without her, and I suppose I shall take her again . . . so I must let her steal from me."

Despite such episodes, Dolley maintained a personal connection with the slaves around her. To a nephew in Washington, she sent from Montpelier "the love of all here . . . even the black faces." In the fall of 1829, she and James took several slaves to Richmond for the state constitutional convention. Her letter to home included news sent by those slaves for their family members back at Montpelier.[10]

Though Dolley's letters never included a Quaker woman's remorse for owning other people, at least twice she conducted transactions that would bring freedom to an individual slave: on one occasion advancing funds for a slave to purchase his wife and child, who could then work off the purchase price with the Madisons, and on another occasion buying five years of service from a slave who would then be freed.[11]

James was the third American president—after Washington and Jefferson—to bring slaves to serve him while in office. Before the British burned the Executive Mansion, his slaves slept in the cellar. When they moved to the Octagon House, they slept in that cellar.[12]

For the house slaves at Montpelier, James built side-by-side duplex housing close to the main house. Unlike the much simpler cabins for the field hands, the slave duplexes had plank walls, glazed windows, wood floors, and brick chimneys. By providing visible and comfortable slave quarters, James aimed to make a good impression—even a misleading one—on visitors from the North and Europe, who often brought antislavery views with them.[13]

Three of Madison's friends would not let him forget the contradiction between his ideals and his immersion in the world of slavery. Each harangued him over his continuing acquiescence in the slave system.

An early political colleague, Francis Corbin, was also a Virginia slaveholder. Like Madison, Corbin dreamt of moving north to satisfy his "aversions to slavery," but he also never did. By 1819, Corbin was disgusted with slavery, which he thought economically ruinous and morally indefensible. "We must either abandon all the pure morality of republicanism," Corbin wrote to Madison, "or the gross and glaring immorality of slavery. They cannot co-exist many years longer." Two years later, Corbin's feelings were just as sharp: "Vice, especially the vice of slavery, is its own punishment, and punished we shall be most severely before we have done with it." He predicted that slavery would break the nation in two. Though Madison resisted Corbin's more dramatic assertions, he assured his old colleague that "[o]ur opinions agree as to the evil—moral, political and economical—of [slavery]."[14]

Lafayette urged Madison to oppose slavery. If only Madison could hear how slavery "lessens the credit of the American people and the progress of American principles," the Frenchman wrote, he would "feel redoubled anxiety that the difficulties . . . might be in time overcome." Madison agreed in principle, calling "Negro slavery . . . a sad blot on our free country," but he mustered a forest of practical objections to emancipation. Lafayette, he insisted, did not understand how difficult it was to find a solution.[15]

The most persistent antislavery voice in Madison's ear came from his onetime secretary, Edward Coles, Dolley's cousin. Coles was difficult to ignore because he was family, because he was devoted to James and Dolley—and because he freed his own slaves.

While working in the Executive Mansion, Coles recalled, he and the president "frequently talked unreservedly about the enslavement of Negroes." Coles would not hold his tongue when he and the president saw a coffle of slaves being led in chains to be auctioned nearby. It was fortunate, the young man taunted, that Madison was spared the mortification of having a foreign diplomat present to witness "such a revolting sight" in the nation's capital.[16]

Coles did not merely talk against slavery. He developed a plan to emancipate the dozen slaves he inherited from his father. In 1815, he purchased land in the Illinois Territory on the Mississippi River. By 1819, Coles was ready. He led his slaves to Illinois, telling them of their freedom as they drifted down the Ohio River. The moment, he recalled, was "electrical."

> In breathless silence they stood before me, unable to utter a word, but with countenances beaming with expression which no words could convey, and which no language can now describe. As they began to see the truth of what they had heard . . . there came on a kind of hysterical, giggling laugh. After a pause of intense and unutterable emotion, bathed in tears, and with tremulous voices, they gave vent to their gratitude.

Coles gave each family a plot of land in Illinois and employed some on his farm in the new territory.[17]

Madison called Coles's action "the true course," but doubted its ultimate success. Those freed would retain, he warned, "the habits of the slave," not "the instruction, the property or the employments of a freeman." Worse, Coles could not "chang[e] their color as well as their legal condition." As blacks in white society, "they seem destined to a privation of that moral rank and those social blessings which give to freedom more than half its value."[18]

Yet slavery did not merely suffuse and confuse James's private life. It also permeated his public career for forty years.

In his early years, Madison's discomfort over slavery was often on display. When America moved toward rebellion in 1774, young Madison immediately feared that "an insurrection among the slaves may and will be promoted." Six months later, he predicted that Virginia's slaves posed its greatest vulnerability, "and if we should be subdued, we shall fall like Achilles by the hand of one that knows the secret." Some four thousand slaves sought freedom with the British during the invasion of Virginia in 1780.[19]

When Virginia ran short on currency to pay its soldiers, some proposed to pay recruiting bounties in the form of slaves. Madison suggested an alternative: "Liberate and make soldiers at once of the blacks," which "would certainly be more consonant to the principles of liberty." Joseph Jones (Monroe's uncle) replied that Madison's idea would encourage the British to arm slaves, which would bring the South to "probably inevitable ruin." Jones wished for ultimate emancipation, but gradually, with the arrival of new laborers to take over the slaves' work, "or we shall suffer exceedingly."[20]

When Madison served as a delegate to Congress at the end of the war, the peace negotiations almost broke down over American demands for compensation for escaped slaves. Despite his reservations about slavery, Madison resented Britain's evasion of its commitment to pay for runaways. Madison also engaged in the thorny congressional debate over whether slaves should count in state population totals when allocating tax burdens among the states. That debate produced the "three-fifths" rule—counting slaves at three-fifths of their number—which would be incorporated in the new Constitution after an equally acrimonious debate.[21]

Serving in the Virginia General Assembly in Richmond in November 1785, Madison voted twice to retain the law allowing masters to emancipate their property. When petitions arrived calling for the gradual abolition of slavery, he objected to the "indignity" with which they were dismissed.[22]

In the summer of 1787, Madison watched with dismay as the Philadelphia Convention careened toward failure because of disagreements between northern and southern delegates. The principal division between the states, he noted, turned on "their having or not having slaves." Although he had identified the great fault line of the emerging republic, no delegate supported his structural proposals for balancing power between slave and nonslave regions. As a Georgian said later, slavery was too volatile an issue: "The moment we go to jostle on that ground, I fear we shall feel it tremble under our feet." The Philadelphia delegates strained to paper over that fault line. James agreed to their temporizing compromises, though he decried as "dishonorable" the twenty-year protection for slave imports. In two of his *Federalist* essays, and then at the Richmond ratifying convention in 1788, Madison defended the Constitution's compromises on slavery. "Great as the evil is," he said of the slave trade, "a dismemberment of the Union would be worse."[23]

Through those early years, most American leaders hoped for gradual emancipation. By 1804, every state above the Mason-Dixon Line had such a law, which pronounced the offspring of slaves to be free at some future time, usually at their twenty-first birthday. Under those laws, the eradication of slavery could take two generations. Many northern slaveowners responded to gradual emancipation laws by selling their slaves to southern masters.

In southern states, however, gradual emancipation held little appeal. Four southern states—Maryland, Virginia, and the Carolinas—held 80 percent of the 700,000 slaves counted in the 1790 census. If they confronted a gradual emancipation law, slaveowners in those states would find little market for their property in any other states, so they would have to swallow tremendous financial losses. Moreover, gradual emancipation could fundamentally transform their societies in disturbing ways. In many rural areas, freed slaves would become a majority. Gradual emancipation stopped at the Mason-Dixon Line.[24]

In the autumn of 1789, James turned to a new idea. The transportation of freed slaves to Africa, he wrote in a memorandum to himself, "might prove a great encouragement to manumission in the Southern [states]" and offer "the best hope yet presented of putting an end to the slavery in which not less than 600,000 unhappy negroes are now involved." Madison stressed the barrier of race prejudice, "the difference of color [which] must be considered permanent and insuperable," which made it impossible for freed slaves to prosper in the United States. To avoid the violence that white Americans would inflict on freed slaves, all freed people should be sent to a "proper external receptacle" outside the country.[25]

Having analyzed the question, Madison attempted to put it aside, but slavery could not be ignored. In the new Congress, the tariff debate devolved into an argument over slavery; southerners claimed they would pay more than their share of the tariffs because they relied on foreign imports, while northerners retorted that since slaveowners never bought imported goods for their slaves, the South would pay less than its proportionate share of the tax. Then Georgians demanded action against Spaniards and Indian tribes who enticed slaves to run away. Abolition petitions from Quakers triggered virulent debate in 1790. Madison voted with northerners during the episode, finding his fellow southerners "intemperate beyond all example." After that experience, Madison began to turn aside from public issues that involved slavery. Perhaps in response to increasing fears of slave uprisings, he displayed less public discomfort with slavery.[26]

In 1792, the slave rebellion in Saint-Domingue terrified southerners. "It is high time," Jefferson wrote of that rebellion, "we should foresee the bloody scenes which our children certainly, and possibly ourselves (South of the Potomac) [will] have to wade through." The Jay Treaty of 1795 proposed to drop claims for compensation for slave runaways during the Revolution. In early 1797, four emancipated slaves in North

Carolina asked Congress to protect them from reenslavement. Madison urged his colleagues to ignore the request because it involved only "the laws of a particular state."[27]

During his four years back in Montpelier after leaving Congress, Madison did not have to address slavery issues in public, not even the abortive Gabriel's Rebellion near Richmond in September 1800. But as Jefferson's Secretary of State, he dealt with slavery in many contexts, especially in the new Louisiana Territory. A congressional ban on slave imports infuriated Louisiana slaveowners and refugees from French Caribbean islands who wished to bring their human property to New Orleans. Free blacks in New Orleans began to organize themselves, raising fears of insurrection there, while Louisiana slaves fled to freedom in nearby Spanish lands.

The situation was inverted on the nation's northwestern border, where the Northwest Ordinance of 1787 banned slavery. Slaves from Canada ran to freedom in Michigan, bringing complaints from Canadian slaveholders. When British ships tied up in southern ports, runaway slaves crept aboard to seek freedom in British territories, while British sailors crept off to find freedom in America.[28]

An awkward situation developed in Washington City when a black man employed by the British Minister was arrested as a runaway. In response to the Minister's protest, Madison said that the slave could not legally form an employment contract, then stalled for time, pleading that the question was "not without difficulty or delicacy."[29]

In 1807, the Constitution's protection for slave imports expired, allowing Congress to ban them, though it failed to provide adequate enforcement tools. The Monroe-Pinkney treaty of 1807, though never ratified, included a pledge of cooperation between the United States and Britain in achieving the "complete abolition" of the international slave trade.

As president, Madison faced still more slave-related issues. Antislavery settlers in Indiana Territory opposed proslavery Governor William Henry Harrison. When Jefferson's embargo ended, smugglers shifted from carrying trade goods to delivering African slaves to Georgia and South Carolina. Madison was frustrated by how difficult it was to shut down the illegal slave trade. His annual message to Congress in December 1810 called for legislation to choke off the "traffic in enslaved Africans."[30]

As the prospect of war with Britain grew, so did southerners' anxiety. A friend of Dolley's referred to the slaves as the "home enemy." Vice

President Gerry's son feared that, in the event of a British attack, "there will be great danger of the blacks rising." A British commander urged slaves to flee their masters, triggering more fear among white Americans. A New Englander wrote to Madison of the "millions of slaves in the Southern states, who must be carefully watched." Executions of unruly or defiant slaves doubled from 1812 to 1813.[31]

Slaves on the frontiers ran off throughout the war, but the runaway problem became acute in the summers of 1813 and 1814, when British fleets rampaged through Chesapeake Bay. A Marylander herded his slaves to high ground every night, fearful of runaways or uprisings. A Virginian wrote candidly to the president at the end of 1813:

> The spirit of defection among the negroes has greatly increased . . . and becomes more and more manifest in every moment of our daily business. No doubt remains on our minds that concert and disaffection among the negroes is daily increasing, and that we are wholly at the mercy of the enemy.

The following year, Chesapeake runaways formed an effective unit of Britain's Colonial Marines. An American general described them as "vindictive and rapacious—with a most minute knowledge of every bye path." An American militia general attributed his men's flight from the Battle of Bladensburg to a rumor of slave revolt around Washington City: "[E]ach man more feared the enemy he had left behind, in the shape of a slave."[32]

After peace came, Madison and Monroe spent months pressing for the return of the roughly thirty-four hundred runaways, or for compensation for them. Madison acknowledged that Britain, which "professes to be the champion" of the slaves, could hardly be expected to agree to "a perfidious surrender of them to their masters." He and Monroe seized on reports that British commanders sold the runaways into slavery in the West Indies or forced them into lifetime enlistments in the British military. If either report were true, it would remove the "odium" of returning the runaways to American masters. When the reports proved untrue, Madison and Monroe gave up the effort. The British returned no runaways.[33]

In his final message to Congress in December 1816, Madison again called for legislation against the illegal slave trade. A Georgian noted two years later that "African and West India negroes are almost daily introduced into Georgia for sale or settlement."[34]

When Madison left Washington City in spring 1817, he could point to no action of his that reduced the nation's dependence on slavery or improved the condition of slaves.

In February 1819, Representative James Tallmadge of New York pushed slavery into the center of American political life. He proposed to amend a bill that allowed settlers in the Missouri Territory to form a government and seek statehood. Tallmadge's amendment would close that territory to additional slaves and would decree gradual emancipation for slaves already there. The legislation, with Tallmadge's amendment, passed the House but died in the Senate. A year later, proslavery congressmen forced the Missouri Compromise, which admitted Missouri as a slave state, Maine as a free state, and barred slavery from lands north of Missouri's southern border, except for Missouri itself.[35]

The Missouri fight revived Madison's nightmare that slavery would destroy the union. He could not turn away from the question any longer. Accustomed to solving problems with reason, to balancing competing interests, Madison soon was tangled in the incendiary mixture of emotion, self-interest, rage, and inverted morality that beset Americans when they addressed race and slavery.

In March 1819, Madison responded defensively to a Philadelphian's inquiry about the condition of slaves in Virginia. Their situation, he wrote, was "better, beyond comparison, than . . . before the Revolution . . . better fed, better clad, better lodged, and better treated in every respect."[36]

A few months later, another Philadelphian asked Madison's advice on a plan for "the eventual total extirpation of slavery from the United States." In his lengthy response, which he specified was not for public distribution, Madison called slavery "a national evil." He endorsed the efforts of the American Colonization Society to transport freed slaves to Africa's western coast. That colonization scheme eventually produced the nation of Liberia but involved only free blacks. The problem was far larger than the American Colonization Society could address.[37]

Emancipation, Madison began, had to meet three criteria. First, it must be gradual. Few disputed that proposition.

Second, it must be "equitable and satisfactory to the individuals concerned"—that is, to slaveowners and slaves alike. That would require compensation to masters for all the slaves in the United States. Madison did some back-of-the-envelope calculations. A million and one-half slaves, at an average price of $400, would cost $600 million. The federal budget that year was $22.6 million.

To purchase the slaves, Madison proposed that all revenues from public land sales be devoted to the effort. At two dollars an acre, he figured, that would require the sale of only 300 million acres, or no more than one-third of the existing public lands. The effort would have to be gradual; any attempt to sell so much land at once would destroy its price. Also, some slaves were "disabled or worn out" and should be left with their masters.

Madison's third standard, however, imposed the greatest barrier: that emancipation not disturb the "probably unalterable prejudices in the United States." If freed slaves were to live with whites, they would be denied equal political and civil rights and "must be always dissatisfied with their condition as a change only from one to another species of oppression." Consequently, freed slaves must be "permanently removed beyond the region occupied by or allotted to a white population." The freed people would have to be transported across the ocean to large tracts of African land.[38]

Madison greatly underestimated the costs and challenges of this course. If emancipation was gradual, the slave population would continue to grow. From 1790 to 1820, that population had doubled. So even more slaves would need to be purchased and transported and placed on African land. And the Constitution would have to be amended to create the government power to undertake the massive effort.[39]

Knowing he had not yet found a feasible way to end slavery, Madison kept gnawing on the problem. He tried out another approach in a letter addressing the constitutional power to emancipate slaves. The best policy, he suggested, might be to disperse the slaves around the country. That would improve their condition "by lessening the number belonging to individual masters and intermixing both with greater masses of free people." It also, he suggested, would increase the number of voluntary emancipations. Though Jefferson endorsed this approach to ending slavery, there was little basis for believing that dispersion of slaves would bring any of the positive results Madison foresaw.[40]

During the winter months of 1821, Madison's reflections on slavery led him to a new literary form. He penned an allegorical story titled "Jonathan Bull and Mary Bull," effectively acknowledging that the slavery issue might not yield to purely rational analysis. Through the more indirect approach of allegory, he sought a way to reach into the hearts where prejudice lay. Tellingly, the prejudice he hoped to dispel was that of northern whites against southern whites, not that of white against black.

In Madison's allegory, Jonathan Bull (the North) and Mary Bull (the South) are both descendants of John Bull (Britain). They marry and live happily on an expanding farm. A dispute arises over how to settle a new farm (presumably Missouri), whereupon Jonathan suddenly contrives a prejudice against Mary because her left arm has a black stain on it and is weaker than her right. The stain came from a dye that arrived as part of a "noxious cargo" from Africa. Jonathan taunts Mary for her "misfortune" and declares he can no longer "consort with one marked with such a deformity."

Mary responds with a passionate appeal that reads like a list of debater's points. First, she notes, Jonathan knew about Mary's deformity when they married. Moreover, he has a mild version of the deformity himself, in the form of "spots and specks scattered over your body as black as the skin on my arm." Most important, Mary is not responsible for "the origin of the sad mishap" and is "as anxious as you can be to get rid of it," but no surgeon can safely "[tear] off the skin or [cut] off the unfortunate limb." And in any event, Jonathan has profited greatly from their marriage with his boats and fisheries and "looms and other machineries."

In the end, Jonathan yields to Mary's plea. A hint of Madison's wit comes through in the final line, which declares that the dispute ends happily, "as the quarrels of lovers always, and of married folks sometimes do."

The story, which went unpublished until 1835 and then appeared anonymously, reveals a good deal about its author. Madison always described slavery as an evil, yet his allegory insisted the slaveowner was blameless, having suffered a "misfortune," a "mishap." Madison's sympathy extends exclusively to the slaveowner, not to northern harpies like Jonathan who criticize Mary's stain. The slaves are simply a stain, nothing like actual human beings. The only permanent solution is to remove the stain, but it cannot be done. So, the story concludes, Jonathan (the North) needs to stop whining and carry on. That was the best Madison could come up with. The technique of putting the apologia for slavery into the mouth of another recalls Madison's use of the same device many years earlier in *The Federalist* No. 54; there he summoned an imaginary southerner to defend the Constitution's slavery provisions. In both instances, Madison shied from defending slavery in his own voice.[41]

Through his retirement years, he continued to worry the slavery question. Its evil, he assured the social reformer Frances Wright, "is so deeply felt, and so universally acknowledged, that no merit could be greater than that of devising a satisfactory remedy for it." But he could find none. The problems seemed intractable. There were the "physical peculiarities of those held in bondage, which preclude their incorporation with the white population." To Lafayette, he repeated that "the great sine qua non therefore is some external asylum for the colored race." But widespread emancipation would leave the South without adequate labor, so new labor sources had to be found.[42]

Madison's public statements rarely challenged race prejudice, though he thought prejudice was the largest barrier to ending slavery. At the Richmond convention in December 1829, he came near to the issue. If the slaves "were of our own complexion, much of the difficulty would be removed," he said. "But the mere circumstance of complexion cannot deprive them of the character of men." Madison believed in that principle, but he never pressed the point. Such an exploration of unreasoning prejudice was foreign to his nature. Also, he may have judged correctly that challenging white prejudice could not succeed in 1829. Traveling the country in that year, the Frenchman Alexis de Tocqueville observed that "the prejudice of the race appears to be stronger in the states which have abolished slavery . . . and nowhere is it so intolerant as in those states where servitude has never been known." After the Richmond convention, Madison told Lafayette that any mention of emancipation at that gathering "would have been a spark to a mass of gunpowder."[43]

Madison, a charter member of the American Colonization Society, hung his membership certificate on his dining-room wall. In 1831, he still urged using revenues from public land sales to purchase slaves and ship them to Africa. By then, America had two million slaves.[44]

Shortly after his eighty-second birthday in 1833, after becoming the ceremonial president of the colonization society, Madison tinkered again with the return-to-Africa plan. The government, he suggested, could purchase female children born to slaves but leave them in bondage until they worked off their purchase price. The expenses of emancipation, he suggested, could be met by a combination of voluntary emancipations, gifts from "the philanthropic and the conscientious," state grants, and public land sales. Ships that brought immigrants to America could take the freed slaves to "adequate asylums" in Africa—or the West Indies, or the West. Someplace far away.

But there was yet another problem with his scheme: Most blacks had no wish to go to Africa. Free blacks had a "known repugnance" to the idea, Madison admitted, while "among the slaves there is an almost

universal preference of their present condition to freedom in a distant
and unknown land." That resistance, he suggested, would dwindle with
news of successful African settlements. Similarly, the replacement of
slave labor with free white labor would be "slow, [and] attended with
much inconvenience," but Madison clung to a core belief: Even a complex and improbable plan was "preferable to acquiescence in a perpetu-
ation of slavery," or to ending slavery "by convulsions more disastrous
in their character and consequences than slavery itself." In short, a bad
plan was better than no plan.[45]

Always, Madison's purpose was to preserve the union and domestic
peace. Though he and Dolley lived in pastoral quiet, they read about and
dreaded the social and political turbulence of the times, especially the
Nat Turner rebellion in 1831.

Turner was a black lay preacher in Southampton County, Virginia,
just west of Norfolk. In late August, inspired by Turner, slaves in the
county began to kill their owners. Before it was over, sixty whites and
more than one hundred slaves lay dead. The episode shook Virginia's
white leadership so profoundly that the Virginia General Assembly seriously debated a proposal to end slavery by shipping Virginia's slaves to
other southern states. The legislation, presented by Jefferson's grandson,
failed.[46]

The shadow of Turner's Rebellion reached Montpelier. "I hope the
bustle and alarm of *Insurrections* are over," Dolley wrote to a niece,
"though I hope all will be on their guard ever after this." She voiced the
anxiety that many whites felt, living in isolated places surrounded by
black slaves. "I am quiet, knowing little about it and that I cannot help
myself if I am in danger."[47]

The battle over American slavery was under way. An 1829 pamphlet
by a free black man, David Walker, called for slaves to rebel against
their masters. In 1831, William Lloyd Garrison founded *The Liberator*
in Boston, an abolitionist weekly that circulated nationally. In the next
year Garrison published *Thoughts on African Colonization*, dismissing
colonization as a fantasy and calling for abolition and racial equality. In
1833, the British Parliament voted to end slavery in the British Empire.
In the summer of 1835, the Tappan brothers of New York bankrolled
the mailing of abolitionist pamphlets throughout the South. Slaveowners responded against these challenges. A popular 1832 publication in
Virginia defended slavery as humane and necessary.[48]

At the same time, violence exploded in American cities and towns.
In 1835, 147 riots broke out, many of them caused by race conflict.

Thirty-five times, mobs swarmed abolitionists. On another eleven occasions, they responded to rumors of slave insurrection. Fifteen more riots were battles between blacks and whites. More than seventy people died in street fighting.[49]

Strife over slavery seemed to threaten the union, just as Madison had feared more than forty-five years before. In a letter to Madison in late spring of 1833, Senator Henry Clay despaired over "political malcontents" among southerners. They were transferring their rage from the tariff issue to slavery, and they had begun to "disseminate sentiments unfriendly to the union." In reply, Madison repeated his vexation over the passions that seized his fellow southerners:

> [W]hat madness in the South, to look for greater safety in disunion. It would be worse than jumping out of the frying pan into the fire. It would be jumping into the fire from a fear of the frying pan.[50]

In February 1835, the abolitionist Harriet Martineau visited Montpelier. Though Madison had been close to an invalid for months, he and Martineau and Dolley talked for hours in his study. Dolley reported that they enjoyed Martineau's "enlightened conversation and unassuming manners," which spurred the Madisons to begin reading their guest's multivolume biographies of political economists. During the visit, James spoke of many things, but he spoke most about slavery. That was where his faith in the American experiment in self-government faltered.

He confirmed to Martineau the criticisms of slavery. Indeed, he "talked more on the subject of slavery than on all other subjects together, returning to it morning, noon, and night." Slavery, he said, dehumanized the enslaved as creatures to be bred, with "every slave girl being expected to be mother by the time she is fifteen." Even when well treated, slaves suffered "degradation of their minds" which led to "their carelessness of each other in their nearest relations, and their cruelty to brutes." He complained that "the whole bible is against negro slavery, but that the clergy do not preach this; and the people do not see it."

Despite this unblinking view of the evils of slavery, James expressed a peculiar moral myopia when he said that slavery's worst impact was on white women who "cannot trust their slaves in the smallest particulars"—a complaint he presumably had heard many times from southern women. Madison added that plantations like Montpelier were "surrounded by vicious free blacks, who induce thievery among the

negroes, and keep the minds of the owners in a state of perpetual suspicion, fear, and anger." During their conversations, Martineau noted, two
or three slaves "lounged about the room," while other slaves continually
came to Dolley for the keys that unlocked the containers that held most
of the food and valuables of the house.

In the end, Martineau recorded, Madison's naturally sunny disposition cut through even these mournful observations. He dwelt "cheerfully, gaily, to the last, on his faith in the people's power of wise
self-government."[51]

27

FAREWELLS

As a young man, beset with recurring ailments, Madison anticipated an early death. Instead, he lived into his mideighties and
watched his closest friends and partners fall away. Growing ever
more frail and often ill, Madison survived longer than anyone expected.
When he reached eighty in 1831, he wrote that he had "outlived so
many of my contemporaries, I ought not to forget that I may be thought
to have outlived myself."[1]

As the years passed, Dolley became more indispensable to him and
James became a less equal partner. She endured illness as well as her
own aches and indignities—she turned sixty-three in 1831—yet remained vigorous. A visitor in the summer of 1832, who had not seen the
couple for more than fifteen years, marveled at her vitality. "It seemed to
me as though I had parted with her only yesterday," he wrote, "so little
had time been able to change her personal appearance—not a wrinkle,
no alteration in her complexion, no difference in her walk."[2]

Jefferson's death in 1826 was a great loss, though not an unexpected
one. In a letter that winter, Jefferson wrote sadly of his desperate financial situation, bemoaning the "abject depression" of Virginia's agriculture. He then bade farewell to his old friend: "To myself you have been
a pillar of support through life . . . be assured that I shall leave with you
my last affections." Madison replied immediately with a heartfelt, if
slightly stiff, tribute:

> You cannot look back to the long period of our private friendship
> and political harmony, with more affecting recollections than I
> do. If they are a source of pleasure to you, what ought they not
> be to me? We cannot be deprived of the happy consciousness of
> the pure devotion to the public good with which we discharged

the trusts committed to us. . . . I offer you the fullest return of affectionate assurances.[3]

Jefferson's death on July 4 seemed an almost divine event, occurring on the fiftieth anniversary of the Declaration of Independence, and on the same day that John Adams died.

Jefferson's farewell letter made a final request of his old friend: "[T]ake care of me when dead." Madison did. During the tariff uproar, he stoutly defended Jefferson's Kentucky Resolution, insisting that it provided no support for nullification. He continued that defense even after discovering that Jefferson had used the term "nullify" in his draft of the resolution. When controversy arose over the jockeying for votes in the House of Representatives in the presidential election of 1800, Madison studied court testimony to mount a skillful defense of Jefferson's conduct. To a young friend, he issued his enduring dictum that Jefferson's words should not always be taken at face value, ascribing to him "a habit . . . as in others of great genius, of expressing in strong and round terms impressions of the moment."[4]

Several years later, Monroe's physical decline alarmed Madison. His friend, seven years younger, had always been a robust figure. In early 1830, after returning home from the Richmond constitutional convention, Madison was "full of anxiety" over Monroe's health. Several months later he exhorted Monroe to attend a board meeting at the University of Virginia. "Your constitution, though like mine the worse for wear," he urged, "has remains of good stamina."[5]

Warm words could not arrest Monroe's troubles. His wife died in late September and Monroe, dead broke, moved in with his daughter and son-in-law in New York. "Our sympathies," Madison wrote, "have been fully with you during the afflictions which have befallen you." By spring of 1831, Monroe sent his friend an emotional farewell. "I deeply regret," he wrote, "that there is no prospect of our ever meeting again, since so long have we been connected, and in the most friendly intercourse, in public and private life, that a final separation is among the most distressing incidents that would occur."

James felt the same sorrow, and for once he said so directly. "The pain I feel," he wrote, "associated as it is with a recollection of the long, close, and uninterrupted friendship which united us, amounts to a pang which I cannot well express."[6]

Monroe's death on July 4, 1831—fifty-five years after the Declaration of Independence and five years after Jefferson and Adams—evoked more wonder. It seemed that all former presidents might be fated to die on the Fourth of July.

James's health took a sour turn in 1831. His rheumatism flared in the cold months, swelling his hands and leaving them mostly useless. He endured periodic fevers and influenza. In May, he apologized for being slow in responding to a letter, explaining that, "in addition to my very advanced age . . . I have had several relapses." The rheumatism returned the following winter. His "hands and fingers are still so swelled and sore as to be nearly useless," Dolley wrote, "but I lend him mine." At the end of that long winter, he reported to a friend, "I am still confined to my bed with my malady, my debility, and my age, in triple alliance against me."[7]

A year later, he corrected a correspondent who congratulated him on his health. "I am still laboring under the continued effects of a chronic disease which has confined me for many months to my House, and much of the time to my bed," James wrote, "and has reduced me to a very emaciated and feeble condition, with my hands & fingers so stiffened, that writing is laborious & painful." Always cold, he constantly wore gloves and a nightcap. Increasingly, he dictated letters to Dolley or her brother, John Payne.[8]

James's world shrank as his body failed. He spent his days in two rooms, the main bedroom shared with Dolley, and a small adjacent room, which contained a bed and opened to the dining room. James sometimes took his meals at a small table set up in the doorway of that room so he could converse with guests as they ate at the main table.[9]

In nightcap and flannel dressing gown, James received visitors seated in a rocking chair or lying on a couch, or even on his bed. The contrast between his appearance and his conversation could be unsettling. "His face was extremely emaciated," one visitor recalled, "and his eyes rested in their orbits with a quiet and almost dull inexpressiveness." Yet he "gave warm and welcome greeting in a voice, whose clearness, strength and readiness astonished me." After dinner, they talked for hours. "I made several movements to leave his bedside, saying I feared that he fatigued himself," the guest recalled, "but he would not hear of it, replying that his lungs were the strongest part of him that was left."

Despite his confinement, James's mind roamed the world. "Whilst reflecting in my sick bed . . . on the dangers hovering over our Constitution," he wrote to a friend, he had "a few ideas which, tho' not occurring for the first time, had become particularly impressive." His conversation ranged from African colonization to expeditions of exploration, from Virginia's constitution to tales of past exploits. He followed the issues of the day—President Jackson's battle against the Second Bank of the United States, nullification, and Supreme Court decisions. But he also talked of the novels of Daniel Defoe or the new railroads springing up in the northeast. He was not content to recycle old prejudices or opinions. He was, one guest observed, "very fully posted as to facts."[10]

James's decline involved little pain, which may have helped him retain his sunny demeanor. At age eighty-three, he wrote to one of Dolley's cousins, he should not expect his health to improve, adding: "I ought rather to consider myself as greatly favored by the degree in which an enjoyment of life is still granted me." Dolley described him as "very feeble," but she added that "his mind is cheerful."[11]

Much of that cheerfulness derived from Dolley's unceasing attentions. Physically and emotionally, James was entirely dependent on her. He referred to her when he wrote of his gratitude for "the preservation of another life, without which mine would cease to be an enjoyment."

As his nurse and devoted partner, Dolley made James her life. James, she wrote to her sister Anna, continued to receive "letters, and visitors as if he was made of iron—to his great disadvantage and mine." Dolley grieved when Anna died in the summer of 1832, but her attention to James did not slacken. In 1834, she wrote that she had "not left the enclosure around our house for the last eight months, on account of his continued indisposition." For two years, she had not left him for more than half an hour, "so deep is the interest and sympathy I feel for him!"[12]

The parade of visitors to Montpelier would have worn out much younger and heartier people. In the summer of 1832, the leading presidential candidates—incumbent Andrew Jackson and Senator Henry Clay—called at Montpelier, invoking Madison's implied blessing. A year later, Dolley wrote to a niece that "we have had more company this summer than I can describe." Even when James could no longer taste the wine, he insisted that it be passed around with a liberal hand. Dolley tried to keep up with fashion, urging her nieces in Washington to find her pretty fabric for a dress or a turban, "suitable for ladies 'of a certain age.'" Her letters could stray into a peevishness brought on by her isolation and her cares. "My days," she wrote in May 1835, "are devoted to nursing and comforting my patient, who walks only from the bed in which he breakfasts to one in the little chamber."[13]

As the days ticked by, steadily draining him of life, Madison's mind turned to his legacy: his legacy to Dolley and his family, and his legacy to the nation. Like so much of his life, it was all wrapped up with slavery.

James and Dolley's financial situation was untenable. They had to sell assets to pay their bills. Their principal assets were land, slaves, and James's papers. James had long intended that his papers be sold after his death. He had never sold slaves for revenue, which uprooted slave families and would implicate him more deeply in the hateful commerce. Also, if he sold slaves, he would have less labor for raising crops. So he sold land.[14]

His strategy was a desperate gamble against his own life span—that his life would run out before his land did. It was a losing gamble. With so much western land opening for settlement, Virginia land prices sank. Every acre that James sold meant that the next year would produce a smaller crop and less revenue, but the population at Montpelier, black and white, never shrank. James knew his strategy could not be sustained. "In order to avoid the sale of Negroes," he wrote in 1834, he had "sold land till the residue will not support them." James could not conceal the crisis from Dolley. Though she had little natural aptitude for thrift, she hunted for "cheap" secondhand carpets from auctions.[15]

Slavery was never far from James's mind. Despite his dismay over it, he had never freed a slave. In early 1832, his conscience took voice in a letter from Edward Coles, who had freed his own slaves more than a decade before. Coles spoke plainly: "[I]t would be a blot and stigma on your otherwise spotless escutcheon, not to restore to your slaves that liberty and those rights which you have been through life so zealous and able a champion." Coles pointed out that Jefferson's reputation suffered from his failure to free his slaves in his will, as Washington had. Ignoring stepson Payne, Coles argued that since James had no children, "the obligation is the stronger to do what duty, consistency and your own peculiar character imperiously require."[16]

General Washington had blundered, Coles wrote, in tying his slaves' emancipation to the death of his widow. That placed her life at risk, since slaves eager for freedom might hasten her demise. To protect Dolley, Coles argued that James's will should free slaves below a certain age after a set term of years, during which time they could earn enough to pay for their resettlement in Africa. Those not wishing to travel to Africa could be swapped for more liberty-craving slaves on neighboring plantations. Older slaves might continue as dependents upon James's heirs.

Based on earlier conversations, Coles addressed James's reservations, notably "the advanced age and helpless situation of many of your slaves, and their matrimonial connection with the slaves of your neighbors," as well as the need to remove them from the race prejudices in Virginia. All of these difficulties, Coles insisted, were "nothing compared to the example of your . . . perpetuating the bondage of so many unfortunate human beings." Freeing his slaves, Coles concluded, "will redound to your fame, and may be calculated to induce others to follow your example."

Two years later, in early 1834, economic reality overtook Coles's high-sounding words. James and Dolley were submerged in debt. They could sell no more land without starving the residents of Montpelier. James decided to sell sixteen slaves to William Taylor, a distant cousin, who took them to Louisiana. Taylor would, James told Coles, "do better by them than I can." James insisted that the slaves consented to the sale, an assertion that might or might not have been true; the slaves certainly could see that Montpelier was a failing enterprise and might have hoped for better conditions elsewhere. After the sale, James and Dolley still were mired in debt. Dolley wrote to a niece that James had considered leaving Montpelier and moving to the Washington, D.C., house occupied for years by her sister Anna's family. It was a "last resort."[17]

During the earlier visit of the abolitionist Harriet Martineau in the first half of 1835, she received a warm welcome from Madison. "His relish for conversation," Martineau wrote later, "could never have been keener." Nevertheless she found it "as painful as it was strange to listen to the cheerful old man" extol African colonization. His final outside visitor, in May 1836, reported that James deplored abolitionism, which he believed was driving southerners to take extreme positions.[18]

He was fading daily. Dolley wrote to her surviving sister that James was "unable to write, or even to exert his thoughts, without oppressive fatigue." In late June, he was offered "stimulants"—most likely liquor—to sustain him for a few more days, perhaps even to reach the sixtieth anniversary of independence on the Fourth of July, when he might become the fourth ex-president to die on that date. He declined the offer.[19]

Despite Dolley's steady attendance on him, she was not present for his death on June 28, 1836. It was a quiet morning, little different from many others. Valet Paul Jennings, the slave who shaved James every other morning, was in James's small room with him. For six months before, Jennings recalled, his master could not walk. During the days, James reclined on a couch, though "his mind was bright." On that morning, Dolley's servant Sukey brought James's breakfast. He could not swallow it. His niece Nelly Willis grew concerned and asked, "What is the matter, Uncle James?"

"Nothing more," he answered, "than a change of mind, my dear." His head drooped to his chest. Death took him, Jennings recalled, "as quietly as the snuff of a candle goes out." The change, of course, was not of James's mind. It was his body that finally gave out.[20]

He was buried on the grounds of Montpelier, while his neighbors and slaves watched. Tributes poured forth around the nation. Madison's death marked the end of America's birth. No one remained who had attended the Philadelphia Convention of 1787. He did not outlive himself, but he outlived everyone else.

James had long since prepared a statement for release upon his death. In a final expression of their partnership, it was written in Dolley's hand. His message addressed his lifelong horror that slavery—which both afflicted and cosseted his days, and which he had never challenged—would undermine the nation and destroy the work of his life.

His last words, he asked, should be received "as issuing from the tomb where truth alone can be respected, and the happiness of man alone consulted." After that melodramatic introduction, his advice was simple: "that the Union of the States be cherished and perpetuated." Any enemy to union, he urged, should "be regarded as a Pandora with her box opened" or as "the Serpent creeping with his deadly wills into Paradise."[21]

Only one former president was alive to mark his death. John Quincy Adams called on his countrymen to hear "the still small voice . . . that spoke the words of peace—of harmony—of union. And for that voice . . . fix your eyes upon the memory, and listen with your ears to the life of James Madison."[22]

Of the five principal partners of James's life, only Dolley survived him. She struggled with grief after his death. A week later, she confessed "to have no power over my confused and oppressed mind to speak fully of the enduring goodness of my beloved husband." She added that James "left me many pledges of his confidence and love. Especially do I value all his writings." A month after his death, she described herself as "in a troubled dream." For James, she wrote, "my affection was perfect, as was his character and conduct through life." She repeated James's request of her: "that I should be calm, and strive to live long after him—that I should proceed to fulfill the trust he reposed in me of many things."[23]

In fact, he left her much to do.

He left Montpelier to her, but only so long as she paid nine thousand dollars to various relatives and another six thousand dollars in bequests to educational institutions. If Dolley could not make the payments, the estate would be sold to raise the money. He also left her the Washington City house long occupied by the Cutts family, as well as the "negroes and people of color held by me." He left some land to his favored niece, Nelly Willis. The will said nothing about freeing slaves.[24]

In the months after James's death, Dolley attempted to sell his papers to a publisher. James had projected their value at a hundred thousand dollars, but Payne, acting as Dolley's agent, elicited no offers at all. In the spring of 1837, Congress bought the first three volumes (including his notes from the Philadelphia Convention) for thirty thousand dollars. That allowed Dolley to pay James's bequests and live comfortably for several years. Spending only summers at Montpelier, she otherwise resided in the Washington house, which sat a block from the White House on what had been named Lafayette Square. Once more, Dolley mixed in society, dining with President Martin Van Buren and Senator Henry Clay. No doors were closed to Mrs. Madison. Senator Daniel Webster called her "the only permanent power in Washington, all others are transient."[25]

Montpelier, run by overseers, could not support the life she chose to lead. A publishing contract for the balance of James's papers provided little help. By 1843, Dolley was negotiating to sell the estate and its slaves. Payne sold off furniture and objects James had collected. The following year, the estate passed out of the Madison family for the first time in more than a century. "No one," Dolley wrote to the purchaser, "can appreciate my feeling of grief and dismay."[26]

Dolley's final years in Washington City were not easy. Paul Jennings, who purchased his freedom with funds borrowed from Senator Webster, recalled Webster sending him with baskets of provisions for Dolley. The Massachusetts senator instructed Jennings that when he noticed "anything in the house that I thought she was in need of, to take it to her."[27]

Dolley died in 1849, at age eighty-one. Her funeral was the largest Washington had yet seen. Hundreds attended the service at St. John's Episcopal Church in Lafayette Square. President Zachary Taylor—the twelfth president Dolley knew personally—led the procession to Congressional Cemetery. Her body was moved to Montpelier in 1858 and buried next to James.[28]

A final indignity remained. Edward Coles was disappointed to learn that Dolley's will did not release the few remaining slaves she owned but instead left them to Payne Todd. Coles then encountered William Taylor, the Madison cousin who bought slaves from James in 1834. Taylor reported that his brother had prepared James's will, and that James and Dolley had an oral understanding that Dolley would release the Montpelier slaves upon her death. Coles confirmed that story with Henry Clay and with James's niece Nelly Willis, who witnessed James's will. Dolley had failed, Coles concluded, to implement James's wishes. Coles proclaimed that James not only intended to free his slaves but also "died under the impression he had done so."[29] Coles's conclusion was not entirely fair. A student of the law like James would certainly know that he had freed no slave. Rather, he pushed that task to his widow, though she was poorly suited to it and he had left her too few assets to see the job through.

For all of the years Madison spent analyzing and worrying about slavery, he never found a way out of its vicious grip—not for himself and not for the nation. No one else found that path either, and there was some honor in his continuing search for it. Instead, the nation was destined to stagger through what Madison feared most: a bloody civil war pitting North against South that left more than seven hundred thousand dead.

Though not mentioned in his final advice to his country, Madison's legacy to that nation was a rich one. With Alexander Hamilton, he did much of the hard intellectual work of creating the constitutional government, leading the fight to ratify the Constitution and writing *The Federalist*. With George Washington, he undertook the challenges of building the new government and creating the Bill of Rights. He and Thomas Jefferson, though professing to disdain political parties, created a model party that could translate public opinion into a governing mandate while facilitating peaceful changes in government. With James Monroe, he demonstrated that a republican nation could war with a powerful foe, acquit itself decently if not gloriously, and remain true to its ideals. And with Dolley, he created a republican style that matched the open and well-intentioned government over which he presided.

That glittering list of achievements reflects Madison's extraordinary gifts, and also the gifts of his partners. From Hamilton, Madison gained the vision, fire, and audacity to imagine an entirely new form of government and then win its approval. Madison's alliance with Washington drew on the incomparable stature and political weight of America's first citizen. Jefferson shared with Madison his idealism, his sure political instincts, and his intuitive sympathy for individual rights. The partnership with Monroe brought soldierly gravitas and ballast to a presidential administration that was not naturally warlike. And Dolley blessed his days with personal magnetism, warmth, and laughter.

That Madison's achievements were tied to his remarkable partnerships reflects his focus on making a success of the American experiment in self-government, whether it meant designing a new system of government, solving a specific problem, or respecting the people's rights. He was ever eager to make common cause with like-minded souls to reach those overarching goals, without regard for credit or blame. Madison's great good fortune was to find so many remarkable partners with whom he could join in the important work, and theirs was to be able to call upon Madison's profound yet affable brilliance. As he said of the writing of the Constitution, redeeming the promise of the American Revolution was the work of many hands and many heads. By approaching all with an open hand and a willing heart, Madison did as much as anyone to translate that promise into reality.

He was proud of how he and his partners had changed the world by creating a government that intended to provide liberty and freedom for its citizens. He knew that many had been left behind—beginning with America's slaves—and there was much more to be done, but he believed it would be done. "Despotism can only exist in darkness," he wrote to his old colleague Lafayette, "and there are too many lights now in the political firmament to permit it to remain anywhere."[30]

ACKNOWLEDGMENTS

I am grateful for the assistance I received from several people with deep knowledge and understanding of Madison's remarkable life. Because I set myself the task of reviewing all available correspondence to and from Dolley and James Madison, I was most fortunate that Keith Donohue of the National Historic Publications and Records Commission arranged for me to have early access to the online site that is now called "Founders Online." David Mattern and J.C.A. Stagg of the Madison Papers project at the University of Virginia granted me access to unedited transcriptions of correspondence as yet unpublished, while David responded patiently to a variety of inquiries that might charitably be described as partially informed. The professional and curatorial staff at Montpelier were unfailingly helpful. It was a blessing to have access to their minds and to Montpelier's grounds during a stay there. Doug Smith, Christian Cotz, Matthew Reeves, and especially Meg Kennedy provided invaluable insights.

Fellow practitioners of the dark arts of historical research and writing also provided important help along my way. Ralph Ketcham, whose Madison biography informs the work of all coming after him, was encouraging and instructive, and he made the supreme sacrifice of reading the entire manuscript, a chore discharged generously and without complaint by two other colleagues and friends, James McGrath Morris and Gregory E. May. I learned as well from Elizabeth Dowling Taylor and Fergus Bordewich, and from Richard Beeman, John Vile, and Mary Sarah Bilder. (The last three provided reassuring confirmation that they too have not figured out how the delegates to the Philadelphia Convention selected the members of committees, an ellipsis in the historical record that annoyed me when I was writing my first book, *The Summer of 1787*, and continues to annoy me. Doctoral candidates, please take note: Someone needs to solve that.) None of the foregoing can be blamed for those instances in which I have persisted in error. More's the pity.

This is my fourth book with Alice Mayhew, a gifted editor who cares so much about publishing good books and who still thinks of writers having careers, not one-night stands with the publishing house du jour. I benefit also from the guidance and friendship of my agent, Will Lippincott, who has been willing to journey with me into publishing thickets from which the fainter of heart might turn back.

I'm running out of ways to thank Nancy, who has graced my life for many days and nights, even after I said I thought I'd like to try writing books.

NOTES

Much of the research for this book involved reviewing the collected correspondence of James Madison and his contemporaries, a large portion of which has been assembled, edited, and published through multidecade efforts at major research universities. For Madison, this effort has been centered at the University of Virginia, currently under the direction of J.C.A. Stagg and David Mattern. While this book was under way, however, most of those published materials were placed online by the National Archives at its Founders Online website, www.founders.archives.gov. This is a magnificent step forward for those who wish to research the Founding era, and it was a huge convenience in the preparation of this book, particularly because I was granted early access to the site through the efforts of Keith Donohue. Because these materials are available online through the use of simple search tools, I have cited them only by reference to the collections of papers from which they come:

- *The Adams Papers (AP).*
- *The Papers of Alexander Hamilton (PAH).*
- *The Papers of Thomas Jefferson (PTJ).*
- *The Papers of James Madison (PJM).*
- *The Papers of George Washington (PGW).*
- *Annals of Congress (Annals)* (which is accessible through the Library of Congress home page, at www.memory.loc.gov).

Because the scholarly editing process of these papers has been so painstaking, there are still some ellipses in the published papers from these collections. For the Madison Papers, materials from the second volume of the Retirement Series, which cover the period from February 1, 1820, to February 26, 1823, are not yet online and thus must be reviewed in the bound volume. While I was conducting my research, the Madison Papers project had not yet published those materials for the period after February 26, 1823—as well as those in the periods from July 1, 1805, to February 28, 1809, and from July 1, 1814, to March 3, 1817—so those are not available at Founders Online. Through the kindness of Messrs. Stagg and Mattern, I was granted early access to the unedited and unannotated versions of those collections. I am extremely grateful for that accommodation. I occasionally cite the published volume of a series when I refer to an editorial note in the collections.

For other frequently cited sources, I have used the following abbreviations:

- Max Farrand, ed., *The Records of the Federal Convention of 1787,* New Haven: Yale University Press (1911), vols. 1–3 (Farrand).
- James H. Hutson, ed., *Supplement to Max Farrand's The Records of the Federal Convention,* New Haven: Yale University Press (1987) (Hutson).
- *Documentary Digital Edition of the Papers of Dolley Madison (DEPDM).*
- David B. Mattern and Holly C. Shulman, *The Selected Letters of Dolley Payne Madison,* Charlottesville: University of Virginia Press (2003) (*Selected Letters*).
- *Documentary History of the Ratification of the Constitution (DHRC).*
- Stanislaus Murray Hamilton, *Writings of James Monroe,* New York: G.P. Putnam's Sons (1898) (*WJM*).
- Correspondence of Richard Rush in Richard Rush Collection, Library of Congress (microfilm) (Richard Rush Collection).
- Catherine Allgor, ed., *The Queen of America: Mary Cutts's Life of Dolley Madison,* Charlottesville: University of Virginia Press (2012) *(Queen of America).*

Many fine works have been written on Madison, so I mention only a few. For a view of Madison's complete career, the best single-volume treatment is Ralph Ketcham's excellent *James Madison,* which I cite below only as "Ketcham." Irving Brant's seven-volume study of Madison, which truly was the work of a lifetime, still yields insights to the diligent reader, though Brant lacked access to some sources that have become available since he wrote. A thorough biography recently was published by Lynne Cheney, *James Madison: A Life Reconsidered.* Jack Rakove has written several powerful studies of Madison, particularly his political ideas, which I have consulted and cite within. Particular periods in Madison's life have been illuminated in Stuart Leibiger's *Founding Friendship* (1780s and 1790s) and Drew McCoy's *Last of the Fathers* (retirement). Madison's relationship with Jefferson, first highlighted in Adrienne Koch's *Jefferson and Madison*, has been further explored by the more recent *Madison and Jefferson*, by Andrew Burstein and Nancy Isenberg. In quoting from correspondence and other primary sources, I have sometimes modernized spelling and punctuation without altering the words actually used.

CHAPTER 1: THE END OF THE BEGINNING

1. Madison to Jefferson, April 22, 1783, May 6, 1783, in *PJM*; Jefferson to Madison, May 7, 1783, ibid.
2. Madison to Jefferson, August 11, 1783, in *PJM*; Jefferson to Madison, August 31, 1783, in ibid.; Irving Brant, *James Madison: The Nationalist 1780–1787*, Indianapolis: Bobbs-Merrill Co. (1948), pp. 285–86.
3. Madison's Notes, February 20, 1783, in *PJM*.
4. Ron Chernow, *Alexander Hamilton*, New York: Penguin Press (2004), pp. 176–77.
5. Ron Chernow, *Washington: A Life*, New York: Penguin Press (2010), pp. 433–34; "Memorandum on Conversation Regarding the Continental Army," February 20, 1783, in Jack N. Rakove, ed., *James Madison, Writings*, New York: Library of America (1999), pp. 16–17. Ironically, the author of one of the mutinous letters, a young officer named John Armstrong, later served as a most controversial Secretary of War in President Madison's administration.
6. Madison to Edmund Randolph, February 25, 1783, in *PJM*.
7. "Report on Address to the States," April 26, 1783, ibid.
8. "From George Washington to the States," in *PGW*, June 8, 1783.
9. "After-Dinner Anecdotes of James Madison: Excerpt from Jared Sparks' Journal for 1829–31," *Virginia Magazine of History and Biography*, 60:155, 164 (1952); Madison to Jefferson, September 20, 1783, in *PJM*.
10. Introduction, *PJM*, 7:xvii; Madison to his father, September 8, 1783, in *PJM*; Madison to Edmund Randolph, July 15, 1783, ibid.; Madison to John Francis Mercer, July 16, 1783, ibid.; Madison to Edmund Randolph, June 24, 1783, ibid.
11. Madison to Jefferson, August 11, 1783, ibid.
12. Jefferson to Madison, June 1, 1783, ibid.
13. James Maury to Madison, June 19, 1829, ibid.
14. Madison to James Madison Sr., June 5, 1783, May 27, 1783, ibid.
15. Madison to Jefferson, February 11, 1784, ibid.
16. Madison to William Cogswell, March 10, 1834, ibid.
17. Edward Coles to Hugh Blair Grigsby, December 23, 1854, cited in Stuart Leibiger, *Founding Friendship*, Charlottesville: University of Virginia Press (1999), p. 23. An interesting consideration of Madison's personality appears in T.V. Smith, "Saints: Secular and Sacerdotal—James Madison and Mahatma Gandhi," *Ethics*, 59:49 (1948).
18. Gordon Wood, *Empire of Liberty*, New York: Oxford University Press (2011), p. 699.
19. John Church Hamilton, *The History of the Republic of the United States of America as Traced in the Writings of Alexander Hamilton*, Philadelphia: J.B. Lippincott & Co. (1850), 7:686; Sarah N. Randolph, *The Domestic Life of Thomas Jefferson*, New York: Harper & Brothers (1871), p. 427; Editor's Note, in *PJM* 8:37.
20. I am grateful to Professor Ralph Ketcham for sharing with me an extraordinary family tree of the Madison clan, without which the statements in the text would have been impossible.

CHAPTER 2: IMPATIENT YOUNG MEN

1. This overview of Hamilton's youth is drawn in considerable degree from the first two chapters of Chernow, *Alexander Hamilton*.
2. Ann L. Miller, *The Short Life and Strange Death of Ambrose Madison*, Orange, VA: Orange County Historical Society (2001), p. 32.
3. Miller, *Short Life*, pp. 26–28; Douglas Chambers, *Murder at Montpelier*, Jackson: University Press of Mississippi (2005), pp. 5–9. The head of an executed slave was exhibited on a stake in Orange County as an object lesson to other slaves, while another was burned at the stake in 1748 for poisoning her master. Ibid., p. 10; Irving Brant, *James Madison: The Virginia Revolutionist, 1751–1780*, Indianapolis: Bobbs-Merrill Co. (1941), pp. 27–49; Ketcham, pp. 4–5.
4. Madison to William Bradford, November 9, 1772, January 24, 1772, in *PJM*; Brant, *Virginia Revolutionist*, 1:113.
5. Madison to William Bradford, April 1, 1774, in *PJM*.
6. Madison to William Bradford, November 26, 1774, ibid.
7. *DHRC*, 20:1104 (Hamilton to G. Morris, May 19, 1789).
8. John Adams to Benjamin Rush, November 11, 1806, in John A. Schultz and Douglass Adair, eds., *The Spur of Fame: Dialogues of John Adams and Benjamin Rush, 1805–1813*, San Marino, CA: Huntington Library, p. 68.
9. Richard B. Morris, *Witnesses at the Creation: Hamilton, Madison, Jay, and the Constitution*, New York: Holt, Rinehart and Winston (1985), p. 4; *DHRC*, 23:2360 (*Poughkeepsie Country Journal*, July 1, 1788).
10. Richard Labunski, *James Madison and the Struggle for the Bill of Rights*, New York: Oxford University Press (2006), p. 89; Martha Dangerfield Bland to Frances Bland Tucker, March 30, 1781, quoted in Ketcham, p. 107.
11. William Pierce notes, in Farrand, 3:94; Eliza House Trist to Jefferson, in *PTJ*, April 13, 1784.
12. Louis Guillaume Otto, in Farrand, 3:237.
13. Hamilton to James Duane, September 3, 1780, in *PAH*, 2:401.
14. "Resolution of the New York Legislature Calling for a Convention of the States to Revise and Amend the Articles of Confederation," July 20, 1782, in *PAH*, 1:110–13.
15. Articles of Confederation, Art. IX, §§ 5, 6; Art. XIII; Madison's Notes, November 25, 1782.
16. "Report on Property Recaptured on Land," December 23, 1782, in *PJM*; Madison's Notes, January 13, 1783, ibid.; Madison's Notes, January 21, 1783, ibid.
17. Notes on Debates, January 27, 1783, in *PJM*; Ed. Note, ibid.
18. E. James Ferguson's *The Power of the Purse: A History of American Public Finance, 1776–1790*, Chapel Hill: University of North Carolina Press (1961), provides an authoritative review of these experiences.
19. Articles of Confederation, Art. VIII; Notes on Debates, January 27, 1783, in *PJM* (James Wilson); Madison to Edmund Randolph, February 4, 1783, ibid., 6:193; Notes on Debates, January 14–15, 1783, and January 31, 1783, ibid. During a debate on soldiers' pay, Hamilton electrified his listeners by suggesting that federal officers should have coercive powers to collect funds from the states. The remark, Madison clucked in his notes, "was imprudent and injurious to the cause which it was meant to serve." Those opposing federal taxing powers claimed "that Mr. Hamilton had let out the secret" that broad coercive powers were intended for Congress. Hamilton, unrepentant, went on to denounce individual states for opposing a federal import tax. Notes on Debates, January 28, 1783, ibid. (note); Notes on Debates, February 18, 1783, ibid.; Notes on Debates, February 19, 1783, ibid. Even the more restrained Madison erupted against congressional impotence in late

January, urging a tortured argument that the Articles implied the power for Congress to impose a tax without consent of the states; the Articles empowered Congress to borrow money, he reasoned, so imposing a tax to repay such borrowing was within their "spirit." Notes on Debates, January 28, 1783, ibid.

20. Notes on Debates, April 1, 1783, ibid.; "Unsubmitted Resolution Calling for a Convention to Amend the Articles of Confederation," July 1783, in *PAH*.

21. Madison to Jefferson, April 22, 1783, in *PJM*.

22. "An Address to the States," ibid.; Joseph Jones to Madison, June 14, 1783, ibid.; Edmund Randolph to Madison, June 14, 1783, ibid.

23. Hamilton to Madison, July 6, 1783, ibid.; Madison to Hamilton, October 16, 1783, ibid.

24. Hamilton to John Jay, July 25, 1783, in *PAH*.

25. Chernow, *Alexander Hamilton*, pp. 184–90; Hamilton to Nathanael Greene, June 10, 1783, in *PAH*, 3:376.

26. Madison to Jefferson, December 10, 1783, in *PJM*, 7:401.

27. David O. Stewart, *The Summer of 1787: The Men Who Invented the Constitution*, New York: Simon & Schuster (2007), pp. 20–21; Edmund Randolph to Madison, August 6, 1782, in *PJM*; Madison to James Monroe, April 28, 1785, ibid.

28. John Francis Mercer to Madison, March 28, 1786, in *PJM*; Madison to Jefferson, July 3, 1784, ibid.; R.H. Lee to Madison, November 20, 1784, ibid.; Madison to James Madison, Sr., December 24, 1784, ibid.; "Bill Providing for Installment payments on British Debts," December 19, 1785, ibid.

29. Madison to Pendleton, January 22, 1782, in *PJM*; Madison, "Observations Relating to the Influence of Vermont, and the Territorial Claims on the Politics of Congress," May 1, 1782, ibid.; Madison to Washington, March 18, 1787, ibid.; Madison to Jefferson, January 22, 1786, ibid.; Madison, "Preface to Debates in the Convention of 1787," in Farrand, 3:542 (undated); Morris, *Witnesses at the Creation*, p. 124.

30. "Resolution Appointing Virginia Members of a Potomac River Commission," June 28, 1784, in *PJM*; Madison to R.H. Lee, December 11, 1784, ibid.; Washington to Madison, December 28, 1784, ibid.; "Resolutions Authorizing an Interstate Compact on Navigation and Jurisdiction of the Potomac," December 28, 1784, ibid.

31. Stewart, *Summer of 1787*, pp. 1–7; Mason to Madison, August 9, 1785, in *PJM*. Mason and his colleague conducted the talks without ever seeing their instructions from the legislature, including the requirement that three Virginia commissioners be present at all times.

32. "Act Ratifying the Chesapeake Compact with Maryland," December 24–26, 1785, ibid.

33. Jefferson to Madison, July 1, 1784, ibid., 8:90; John Francis Mercer to Madison, November 26, 1784, ibid.; R.H. Lee to Madison, November 26, 1784, ibid.

34. Madison to R.H. Lee, December 25, 1784, ibid.

35. Ed. Note, in *PJM*, 8:406; Madison to Washington, December 9, 1785, ibid.

36. Ibid. Twenty years later, Madison claimed credit for drafting the substituted legislation, though at the time he attributed it to John Tyler (grandfather of the tenth president). Madison to Jefferson, January 22, 1786, ibid.; Madison to Monroe, January 22, 1785, ibid.; Madison to Noah Webster, October 12, 1804, ibid.; Madison, "Preface to the Debates in the Convention of 1787," in Farrand, 3:543–44; "Resolution Authorizing a Commission to Examine Trade Regulations," in *PJM*, 8:471. The legislature also approved the agreement with Maryland on maritime issues. "Act Ratifying the Chesapeake Compact with Maryland," December 24–26, 1785, and Ed. Note, ibid., 8:457–61.

37. Madison to Monroe, January 22, 1785, in *PJM*.

38. Edmund Randolph to Madison, March 1, 1786, ibid.; Daniel Carroll to Madison, March 13, 1786, ibid. & n.1; Michael Meyerson, *Liberty's Blueprint: How Madison and*

Hamilton Wrote The Federalist, *Defined the Constitution, and Made Democracy Safe for the World,* New York: Basic Books (2008), p. 54; Madison to Jefferson, March 18, 1786, in *PJM*; Edmund Randolph to Madison, June 12, 1786, ibid.; Madison to Jefferson, August 10, 1786, ibid.; William Grayson to Madison, May 28, 1786, ibid. Others did not share Madison's pessimism. James Monroe, then a young Virginia delegate to Congress, reported that New Englanders intended to push the Annapolis Convention beyond commercial issues, while a leading Pennsylvania politician, James Wilson, had "great expectations" for the Annapolis meeting. A Massachusetts delegate to Congress stressed that giving Congress power to regulate commerce would "run deep into the authorities of the individual states" and even require a federal court system. Madison to Monroe, August 15, 1786, ibid.; Monroe to Madison, September 3, 1786, ibid.; Rufus King to Jonathan Jackson, September 3, 1786, cited in Ed. Note, *PJM*, 9:115.

39. Meyerson, *Liberty's Blueprint*, p. 51; John C. Hamilton, *The Life of Alexander Hamilton,* New York: D. Appleton & Co., 2:374–75 (1840); Egbert Benson, *Memoir Read Before the Historical Society of the State of New York, December 31, 1816,* New York: Henry C. Sleight, 2d ed., p. 98.

40. Madison to Jefferson, March 16, 1784, in *PJM*, 8:11; Jefferson to Madison, May 8, 1784, in *PJM*, 8:31; Jeff Broadwater, *James Madison: A Son of Virginia & a Founder of the Nation,* Chapel Hill: University of North Carolina Press (2012), p. 36.

41. Madison to Jefferson, March 18, 1786, in *PJM*. Ever particular, Madison asked his friend to acquire two additional volumes that were missing from multivolume sets shipped from France.

42. "Notes on Ancient and Modern Confederacies," ibid.; Madison to Jefferson, March 18, 1786, ibid.

43. Meyerson, *Liberty's Blueprint*, p. 54; Madison to Jefferson, August 12, 1786, in *PJM*, 9:95.

44. Hamilton to Elizabeth Hamilton, September 8, 1786, in *PAH*, 3:684.

45. Madison to Ambrose Madison, September 11, 1786, in *PJM*; Madison to Noah Webster, October 12, 1804, ibid.

46. Thomas Cushing, Francis Dana, and Samuel Breck to Hamilton and Egbert Benson, September 10, 1786, in *PAH*; Meyerson, *Liberty's Blueprint*, pp. 56–57.

47. Tench Coxe to Madison, September 9, 1789, in *PJM*.

48. Farrand, 3:545; Madison to Noah Webster, October 12, 1804, in *PJM*.

49. *DHRC*, 1:181–85. The Massachusetts men were shocked to encounter Hamilton and other delegates going home. Another New Yorker was boarding a ship for Annapolis when he also met Hamilton traveling north. When a North Carolina delegate arrived in Annapolis on September 15, he found that Mann's tavern no longer held any delegates at all.

50. Pauline Maier, *Ratification: The People Debate the Constitution, 1787–1788,* New York: Simon & Schuster (2010), p. 256; David Jameson to Madison, May 21, 1780, in *PJM*; Joseph Jones to Madison, October 17, 1780, ibid.; Louis B. Wright and Marion Tinling, eds., *Quebec to Carolina in 1785–1786, Being the Travel Diary of Robert Hunter Jr., a Young Merchant of London,* San Marino, CA: The Huntington Library (1943), p. 236; Johan David Schoepf, *Travels in the Confederation [1783–1784],* Philadelphia: William J. Campbell (1911), pp. 51–55.

51. Madison to Washington, November 1, 1786, in *PJM*; Madison to Monroe, October 30, 1786, ibid.

52. Madison to James Madison, Sr., November 1, 1786, ibid.; Madison to Washington, November 8, 1786, ibid.; Madison, "Preface," in Farrand, 3:547.

53. Madison to Noah Webster, October 12, 1804, in *PJM*.

54. Madison to Washington, November 8, 1786, ibid.; Meyerson, *Liberty's Blueprint*, p. 61;

Irving Brant, *James Madison, The Nationalist, 1780–1787,* Indianapolis: Bobbs-Merrill (1948), pp. 394–96.

55. Linda Grant DePauw, *The Eleventh Pillar: New York State and the Federal Constitution,* Ithaca, NY: Cornell University Press (1966), p. 49; Monroe to Madison, October 2, 1786, in *PJM*; Monroe to Madison, October 7, 1786, ibid.; Peter Onuf, "It Is Not a Union," *Wilson Quarterly,* 11:102 (1987).

56. Madison to Monroe, February 25, 1787, in *PJM*; Journals of Congress, 32:71–74 (February 21, 1787); Chernow, *Alexander Hamilton,* pp. 226–27; DePauw, *Eleventh Pillar,* pp. 49–50.

57. For a representative example of the attitude toward Rhode Island, see Edward Carrington's letter to Washington on June 9, 1787, in Farrand, 3:37: Rhode Island's "apostasy from every moral, as well as political, obligation, has placed her perfectly without the views of her confederates." Washington to David Stuart, July 1, 1787, in Farrand, 3:51.

CHAPTER 3: A POWERFUL EFFECT ON OUR DESTINY

1. Leonard L. Richards, *Shays's Rebellion,* Philadelphia: University of Pennsylvania Press (2002); Madison to Edmund Randolph, March 11, 1787, in *PJM*; Edmund Randolph to Madison, ibid.; Madison to Washington, March 18, 1787, ibid.; Madison to Jefferson, March 19, 1787, ibid.

2. Madison to Edmund Pendleton, February 24, 1787, ibid.; Monroe to Madison, September 3, 1787, ibid.; Timothy Bloodworth to Richard Caswell, September 4, 1786, in Walter Clark, ed., *State Records of North Carolina,* Goldsboro, NC: Nash Brothers (1900), 18:724; William Pierce to George Turner, May 19, 1787, in Hutson, pp. 9, 10; Madison to Edmund Randolph, February 25, 1787, in *PJM*.

3. "Vices," in *PJM*; Samuel Johnson, "Taxation Not Tyranny," in *The Works of Samuel Johnson,* Troy, NY: Pafraets & Co. (1903), 14:144.

4. Madison to Washington, April 16, 1787, in *PJM*; Madison to Edmund Randolph, April 8, 1787, ibid.; Madison to Jefferson, March 19, 1787, ibid.

5. Madison to Ambrose Madison, September 8, 1786, ibid.; Madison to James Madison, Sr., April 1, 1787, ibid.; Madison to James Madison, Sr., November 18, 1785, ibid.; Madison to James Madison, Sr., December 24, 1785, ibid.

6. Madison to James Madison, Sr., November 1, 1786, ibid. & n.1; Madison to Ambrose Madison, November 16, 1787, ibid.; Madison to Ambrose Madison, January 21, 1786, ibid.; Madison to James Madison, Sr., December 7, 1786, ibid.; Madison to James Madison, Sr., February 25, 1787, April 1, 1787, and May 27, 1787, ibid.

7. *Pennsylvania Herald,* May 16, 1787, p. 3.

8. William Shippen to Thomas Shippen, May 14, 1787, in Hutson, p. 1.

9. Madison to Edmund Randolph, April 8, 1787, in *PJM*; Madison to Noah Webster, October 12, 1804, ibid.

10. George Mason to George Mason, Jr., May 20, 1787, in Farrand, 3:23, 24.

11. Note by Madison, Farrand, 1:10; George Read to John Dickinson, May 21, 1787, in Farrand, 3:24–25; Mason to George Mason, Jr., May 20 and May 27, 1787, in Farrand, 3:23, 3:28; Jacob Broom to Thomas Collins, May 23, 1787, in Hutson, p. 16.

12. Hamilton to Robert Morris, August 13, 1782, in *PAH*; William Pierce, "Character Sketches of Delegates to the Federal Convention," in Farrand, 3:89–90; DePauw, *Eleventh Pillar,* pp. 52–58; Madison to Washington, March 18, 1787, in *PJM*.

13. Washington Diary, May 18, 1787, in Farrand, 3:21; *Pennsylvania Journal and Weekly Advertiser,* May 19, 1787, in Farrand, 3:22; "George Mason's Account of certain proceedings in Convention," September 30, 1792, in Farrand, 3:367.

14. Jared Ingersoll to Thomas Shippen, May 18, 1787, in Hutson, p. 6; Madison to James Madison, Sr., May 27, 1787, in *PJM*; George Read to John Dickinson, May 21, 1787,

in Farrand, 3:24; Washington to Arthur Lee, May 20, 1787, in Farrand, 3:22; William Grayson to Monroe, May 29, 1787, in Farrand, 3:30; John Dickinson to Polly Dickinson, May 29, 1787, in Hutson, p. 28.

15. Madison, "Preface," in Farrand, 3:550; Hugh Blair Grigsby, *The History of the Virginia Convention of 1788*, Richmond: Virginia Historical Society (1890), 1:95 n.107.

16. Farrand, 1:10 (Mason, May 28, 1787); Madison to Jefferson, June 6, 1787, in *PJM*.

17. Farrand, 1:18–23 (Randolph, May 29, 1787); Mason to George Mason, Jr., May 27, 1787, in Farrand, 3:28.

18. Farrand, 1:25 (McHenry notes, May 29, 1787), 1:24 (Yates notes, May 29, 1787); Robert Yates to Abraham Yates, June 1, 1787, in Hutson, p. 41; Abraham Lansing to Abraham Yates, August 26, 1787, in Hutson, p. 243.

19. James Parton, *The Life and Times of Aaron Burr*, Boston: Houghton Mifflin Co. (1892), 1:153n (quoting New York Attorney General Erastus Root).

20. Farrand, 3:94 (Pierce); Grigsby, *Virginia Convention of 1788*, 1:96; Fisher Ames Correspondence, quoted in Irving Brant, *James Madison: Father of the Constitution, 1787–1800*, Indianapolis: Bobbs-Merrill (1950), p. 249; Stewart, *Summer of 1787*, p. 158.

21. In an early debate over whether each state should have an equal legislative vote, Hamilton moved that representatives be allocated based on "the number of free inhabitants" in each state, a proposition that troubled both small states (who wanted each state to have an equal vote) and slave states (who wanted their slaves counted); Madison softened the proposition by substituting a vague proposal that the allocation not be "according to the present system." The delegates would be able to fill in the blanks as the convention proceeded. Farrand, 1:36 (May 30); Farrand, 1:121 (June 5).

22. Farrand, 1:110 (June 4) (Madison, in notes by Pierce); Farrand, 2:34–35 (July 17) (Madison); Farrand, 2:73–74 (July 21) (Madison); Farrand, 2:56 (July 19) (Madison).

23. Farrand, 1:72–73 (June 1), 1:145–57 (June 6).

24. Farrand, 1:60 (Madison, May 31, 1787).

25. Farrand, 1:48 (May 31) (Roger Sherman, Elbridge Gerry); ibid., 1:101 (June 4) (Mason). George Washington expressed amazement that New Englanders, who had been the most prodemocratic American leaders, swung toward more authoritarian models of government after the Shays uprising. He expected such sentiments more from southerners, in view of "the habitual distinctions which have always existed among the people" there. Washington to Madison, March 31, 1787, in *PJM*.

26. Farrand, 1:49–50 (May 31) (Madison); Farrand, 1:196 (June 11) (Hamilton).

27. Stewart, *Summer of 1787*, pp. 59–74.

28. Farrand, 1:258 (June 16) (Lansing); Farrand, 1:242–45 (June 15) (New Jersey Plan).

29. Farrand, 1:246 (June 15) (Hamilton).

30. Farrand, 1:288–93 (June 18) (Hamilton).

31. Farrand, 1:322 (June 19) (Wilson); Farrand, 1:337 (June 20) (Lansing); Farrand, 1:363 (June 21) (Johnson). A lone Delaware delegate, George Read, expressed his preference for Hamilton's outline of government during debate a week later; Farrand, 1:461 (June 29) (Read). After the convention, a Maryland delegate claimed that "more than 20 members of the convention were in favor of a kingly gov't," an assertion that was never actually documented beyond barroom blustering. Daniel Carroll to James Madison, May 28, 1788, in Farrand, 3:305–6.

32. N.P. Trist, "Memoranda," in Farrand, 3:533–34. Years later, Madison stressed that Hamilton's support for strong government grew from "views which he made no secret of." Ibid.

33. Farrand, 1:323 (June 20) (Hamilton); Farrand, 1:358 (June 21) (Hamilton); Farrand, 1:373 (June 22) (Hamilton).

34. Farrand, 1:314–22 (June 19) (Madison).
35. Farrand, 1:465 (June 29) (Madison); Farrand, 1:466–67 (June 29) (Hamilton).
36. Farrand, 1:447 (June 28) (Madison); Farrand, 1:476 (June 29) (Madison); Farrand, 1:486 (June 30) (Madison).
37. Farrand, 1:486 (June 30) (Madison).
38. Farrand, 1:136 (June 6) (Dickinson); Farrand, 1:526–27 (July 5) (Gerry); Farrand, 1:128 (July 5) (Madison).
39. Farrand, 1:536 (July 5) (Yates notes); Hamilton to Washington, July 3, 1787, in Farrand, 3:53–54.
40. Washington to Hamilton, July 10, 1787, in Farrand, 3:56–57.
41. Farrand, 1:562 (July 9) (Madison); Farrand, 2:9, 10 (July 14) (Madison).
42. The delegates likely were not much charmed by Madison's schoolmasterish tendency to correct the reasoning employed by other delegates. E.g., Farrand, 1:485 (correcting error by Oliver Ellsworth of Connecticut); Farrand, 1:584 (correcting error by Gouverneur Morris).
43. Stewart, *Summer of 1787*, pp. 101–25; Farrand, 1:20 (July 16).

CHAPTER 4: A SYSTEM TO LAST FOR AGES

1. In the second week of July, Madison was named to a second committee that worked out the initial apportionment of representatives among the states. Farrand, 1:562 (July 9).
2. Madison to James Madison, Sr., July 28, 1787, in *PJM*.
3. Gerry to Ann Gerry, August 9, 1787, in Hutson, p. 215; Gerry to Ann Gerry, August 15, 1787, in Hutson, p. 222.
4. Farrand, 2:318–19 (August 17) (Madison); Farrand, 2:431 (August 27) (Madison); Farrand, 2:203 (August 7) (Madison).
5. Farrand, 2:254 (August 10) (Madison); Farrand, 2:301 (August 15) (Madison); Farrand, 2:316 (August 17) (Madison); Farrand, 2:427 (August 27) (Madison); Farrand, 2:430 (August 27) (Madison); Farrand, 2:440–41 (August 28) (Madison); Farrand, 2:486 (September 3).
6. Farrand, 1:421 (June 26) (Madison); Farrand, 2:221 (August 8) (Madison). He made a similar argument on July 26. Farrand, 2:124 (July 26) (Madison).
7. Farrand, 2:268–72 (August 13).
8. Farrand, 2:366 (August 22). For a more extensive review of this dispute, see Stewart, *Summer of 1787*, pp. 191–206.
9. Farrand, 2:416, 417 (August 25) (Madison).
10. Farrand, 1:449 (August 29) (Madison).
11. Dickinson to George Logan, January 16, 1802, in Hutson, pp. 300–301. Wilson first proposed the elector system in early June. Farrand, 1:80 (June 2) (Wilson).
12. Washington to Henry Knox, August 19, 1787, in Farrand, 3:70; see Alexander Martin to Governor Caswell, August 20, 1787, in Farrand, 3:72; David Brearley to William Paterson, August 21, 1787, in Farrand, 3:73.
13. Farrand, 2:524 (September 6) (Hamilton). Earlier in the summer Hamilton said he did not "think favorably of republican government," but he would support the Constitution. Farrand, 1:424 (June 26) (Hamilton).
14. Farrand, 2:553–54 (September 8); Farrand, 1:558, 560 (September 10); Farrand, 585–86 (September 12).
15. Farrand, 2:587–88 (September 12).
16. Farrand, 2:645–46 (September 17) (Hamilton).
17. Madison to Jefferson, September 6, 1787, in *PJM*.

CHAPTER 5: CREATING *THE FEDERALIST*

1. Morris, *Witnesses at the Creation*, p. 225.
2. Madison to Washington, October 18, 1787, in *PJM*, 10:197; Meyerson, *Liberty's Blueprint*, pp. 78–79; Morris, *Witnesses at the Creation*, p. 22.
3. Washington to David Humphreys, October 10, 1787, in Farrand, 3:103.
4. Meyerson, *Liberty's Blueprint*, p. 82.
5. "Liste des Membres et Officiers du Congres," 1788, in Farrand, 3:232, 234; Joseph Barrell to Samuel Blachley Webb, May 4, 1788, in *DHRC*, 20:1086 ("The Pamphlet wrote by Mr. Jay is excellent"); Maier, *Ratification*, pp. 336–37; DePauw, *Eleventh Pillar*, p. 132.
6. Pierce, in Farrand, 3:89.
7. Chernow, *Alexander Hamilton*, p. 249; Jefferson to Madison, November 18, 1788, in *PJM*, 10:353; Meyerson, *Liberty's Blueprint*, p. 142.
8. Elizabeth Fleet, ed., "Madison's 'Detached Memoranda,'" *William and Mary Quarterly*, 3:534–68 (1946).
9. Meyerson, *Liberty's Blueprint*, pp. 82–86; Walter Stahr, *John Jay, Founding Father*, New York: Hambledon & Continuum (2006), pp. 248–49.
10. Madison to Randolph, November 18, 1787, in *PJM*, 10:252; Madison to Washington, November 18, 1787, *PJM*, 10:253.
11. DePauw, *Eleventh Pillar*, p. 85; Chernow, *Alexander Hamilton*, p. 261.
12. DePauw, *Eleventh Pillar*, pp. 110–11.
13. Fleet, "Madison's Detached Memoranda."
14. Henrietta Maria Colden to Frances Bland Tucker, December 28, 1787, in *DHRC*, 19:479; Edmund Randolph to Madison, January 3, 1788, in *PJM*, 10:350; Cyrus Griffin to Madison, March 24, 1788, in *PJM*, 10:4. A friend in Fredericksburg, Virginia, reported the same response to the Constitution, which was "at this moment the subject of general conversation in every part of the town, and will soon be in every quarter of the state." John Dawson to Madison, September 25, 1787, in *PJM*, 10:173.
15. Madison to Washington, October 18, 1787, in *PJM*, 10:196; Madison to Washington, February 8, 1787, in *PJM*, 10:481.
16. Tench Coxe to Madison, September 27, 1787, in *PJM*, 10:175; Randolph to Madison, September 30, 1787, in *PJM*, 10:181–82; Madison to Coxe, October 1, 1787, in *PJM*, 10:183; Washington to Madison, October 10, 1787, in *PJM*, 10:189; Madison to Washington, October 14, 1787, in *PJM*, 10:194; Henry Lee to Madison, December 20, 1787, in *PJM*, 10:339; Coxe to Madison, December 28, 1787, in *PJM*, 10:347; Rufus King to Madison, January 6, 1788, in *PJM*, 10:351; Rufus King to Madison, February 3, 1788, in *PJM*, 10:465 & n.3; Daniel Carroll to Madison, February 10, 1788, in *PJM*, 10:495. This list of Madison's correspondence about the ratification process is by no means exhaustive.
17. Ketcham, p. 232; Madison to Tench Coxe, January 3, 1788, in *PJM*, 10:349; Edwin G. Burrows & Mike Wallace, *Gotham: A History of New York City to 1898*, New York: Oxford University Press (1999), pp. 265–66; John C. Hamilton, *History of the Republic as Traced in the Writings of Alexander Hamilton and His Contemporaries*, New York: D. Appleton & Co. (1859), 4:29n; Stanley Elkins and Eric McKitrick, *The Age of Federalism*, New York: Oxford University Press (1993), p. 113.
18. Madison to Archibald Stuart, October 30, 1787, in *PJM*, 10:232.
19. Madison to Washington, November 18, 1787, in *PJM*, 10:252; Madison to Edmund Randolph, December 2, 1787, in *PJM*, 10:289; Joseph Jones to Madison, December 18, 1787, in *PJM*, 10:329; Rev. James Madison to Madison, February 9, 1789, in *PJM*, 10:487; Henry Knox to Washington, March 10, 1788, in *DHRC*, 20:852.
20. Maier, *Ratification*, p. 93; DePauw, *Eleventh Pillar*, p. 170.
21. While still in his twenties, Hamilton wrote in one letter, "Experience is a continued

comment on the worthlessness of the human race." Hamilton to Meade, August 27, 1782, in John Church Hamilton, *The Life of Alexander Hamilton*, New York: D. Appleton & Co. (1840), 1:241.

22. Madison dwells on this concern in *The Federalist* No. 48.

23. A reader wishing to delve more deeply into *The Federalist* has many choices for a learned guide to aid the effort. Michael Meyerson's *Liberty's Blueprint* tells the story of how the famous papers were written and reviews them at greater length than this volume can. Powerful scholarly treatments can be found in Jack N. Rakove's *Original Meanings: Politics and Ideas in the Making of the Constitution*, New York: Vintage Books (1996), and Garry Wills's *Explaining America: The Federalist*, Garden City, NY: Doubleday (1981). Older studies that reward careful reading include Robert Dahl, *A Preface to Democratic Theory* (1956), and Charles Beard's *An Economic Interpretation of the Constitution of the United States* (1913).

24. Hamilton to Madison, April 3, 1788, in *PJM*, 11:7; Meyerson, *Liberty's Blueprint*, pp. 91–99. In delivering the message, he wrote as though he and Madison had not written the Publius essays, aiming to conceal their authorship if his letter should go astray, as some postmasters perused letters they conveyed. "If our suspicions of the author be right," Hamilton wrote archly, "he must be too much engaged to make a rapid progress in what remains." He added that the New York courts were in session, thus explaining his inability to keep writing.

25. In the final essay, now published as No. 85, Hamilton admitted that Publius never reached the final two topics in his original outline: how the Constitution resembled state constitutions and how it would preserve republican government. But, he insisted, those points were covered in the geyser of earlier Publius essays.

26. Washington to Madison, February 5, 1788, in *PJM*, 10:468; George Nicholson to Madison, April 5, 1788, in *PJM*, 11:9; Hamilton to Madison, May 11, 1788, in *PJM*, 11:41; Hamilton to Madison, May 19, 1788, in *PJM*, 11:53; Archibald M'Lean to Stephen Van Rensselaer, April 10, 1788, in *DHRC*, 20:906; Leonard Gansevoort to Stephen Van Rensselaer, April 11, 1788, in *DHRC*, 20:913.

27. Comte de Moustier to Comte de Montmorin, June 25, 1788, in *DHRC*, 21:1227.

28. Madison to Jefferson, February 8, 1825, in *PJM*.

29. Hamilton to Madison, April 3, 1788, in *PJM*, 11:7; Hamilton to Madison, May 11, 1788, in *PJM*, 11:41; Hamilton to Madison, May 19, 1788, in *PJM*, 11:54; Madison to Hamilton, June 9, 1788, in *PJM*, 11:101; Hamilton to Madison, July 8, 1788, in *PJM*, 11:186. Meyerson points out this same pattern in his excellent work, pp. 102–3.

CHAPTER 6: RATIFICATION BATTLES

1. "From Alexander Hamilton to *The Daily Advertiser*," July 21, 1787, in *PAH*.

2. *DHRC*, 9:14–15 (*New York Daily Advertiser*, July 26, 1787); *DHRC*, 9:16–20 (*New York Journal*, September 6, 1787); *DHRC*, 9:24 (*New York Journal*, September 13, 1787); *DHRC*, 9:31 (*New York Journal*, September 20, 1787).

3. Edward Carrington to Madison, September 23, 1787, in *DHRC*, 9:34.

4. Rufus King to Madison, January 20, 1788, in *PJM*; Rufus King to Madison, January 27, 1788, ibid.; Madison to Washington, February 8, 1788, ibid. General Washington fretted that if the antis prevailed in Massachusetts it would "invigorate the opposition." Washington to Madison, February 5, 1788, ibid.

5. Rufus King to Madison, January 23, 1788, ibid.; Maier, *Ratification*, pp. 196–207. The Massachusetts amendments are discussed at *DHRC*, 20:751 (ed. note).

6. Madison to Jefferson, February 19, 1788, in *PJM*.

7. Madison to Ambrose Madison, November 8, 1788, ibid.; Archibald Stuart to Madison, December 2, 1787, ibid.; Joseph Jones to Madison, December 18, 1787, ibid.; Washington to Madison, February 5, 1788, ibid.

43. Madison to Hamilton, June 16, 1788, in *PJM*; Madison to Hamilton, June 22, 1788, ibid.; Madison to Hamilton, June 20, 1788, ibid., 11:157.

44. *DHRC,* 10:1179–81 (ed. note); *DHRC,* 10:1223, 1225 (June 12, 1788) (Madison); *DHRC,* 10:1220 (June 12, 1788) (Henry); Maier, *Ratification,* pp. 276–77.

45. *DHRC,* 10:1223 (June 12, 1788) (Madison); Lafayette to Washington, February 4, 1788, in *PGW.*

46. Madison to Hamilton, June 16, 1788, in *PJM.*

47. *DHRC,* 10:1476–79 (June 24, 1788) (Henry).

48. *DHRC,* 10:1488 (June 24, 1788) (Randolph); *DHRC,* 10:1498–99 (June 24, 1788) (Madison).

49. *DHRC,* 10:1506 (June 24, 1788) (Henry); *DHRC,* 10:1512 (Spencer Roane); *DHRC* 10:1511 (Archibald Stuart).

50. *DHRC,* 10:1538–41 (June 25, 1788) (vote on resolution); Madison to Hamilton, June 25, 1788, in *PJM,* 11:177.

51. *DHRC,* 10:1551–56 (June 27, 1788) (motion and amendments); Madison to Hamilton, June 27, 1788, in *PJM,* 11:181.

52. Maier, *Ratification,* pp. 345, 348; DePauw, *Eleventh Pillar,* pp. 187–88; *New York Daily Advertiser,* July 8, 1788, in *DHRC,* 22:2080; Hamilton to Madison, July 2, 1788, in *PJM.*

53. Jay to Washington, June 20, 1788, in *DHRC,* 23:2349; Hamilton to Madison, July 2, 1788, in *PJM*; Hamilton to Madison, June 25, 1788, ibid.

54. Melancton Smith to Robert Yates, Jr., January 28, 1788, in *DHRC,* 20:671; James M. Hughes to John Lamb, June 18, 1788, in *DHRC,* 21:1202; Samuel Blachley Webb to Joseph Barrell, July 1–2, 1788, in *DHRC,* 11:1243; Jay to Washington, February 3, 1788, in *DHRC,* 20:746; *DHRC,* 22:1751 (June 17, 1788) (Smith).

55. Abraham Yates, Jr., to George Clinton, July 1, 1788, in *DHRC,* 20:1245; *DHRC,* 22:1875–76 (June 24, 1788) (Philip Schuyler letter); *DHRC,* 22:1903 (June 26, 1788) (Lansing).

56. DeWitt Clinton to Charles Tillinghast, July 3, 1788, in *DHRC,* 22:2082; Cornelius C. Schoonmaker to Peter Van Gaasbeck, July 2, 1788, in *DHRC,* 22:2083.

57. Abraham Bancker to Evert Bancker, July 5, 1788, in *DHRC,* 22: 2086; *DHRC,* 22:2094 (*New York Daily Advertiser,* July 8, 1788); *DHRC,* 22:2084–85 (ed. note) (quoting letter from Philip Schuyler to Stephen Van Rensselaer, July 2, 1788).

58. Hamilton to Madison, June 8, 1788, in *PJM*; Jay to Washington, May 29, 1788, in *DHRC,* 10:119; Maier, *Ratification,* pp. 376–77; *Journal of Congress,* July 8, 1788, 34:304; Madison to Washington, July 21, 1788, in *PJM*; Madison to Jefferson, August 10, 1788, ibid.

59. *DHRC,* 22:2099 (July 5, 1788); *DHRC,* 2106, 2110–12 (July 7, 1788).

60. *DHRC,* 22:2113 (*New York Morning Advertiser,* July 16, 1788); DeWitt Clinton to Charles Tillinghast, July 12, 1788, in *DHRC,* 22:2150; *DHRC,* 22:2131, 22:2145–46 (July 11, 1788) (Governor Clinton).

61. *DHRC,* 22:1712 (June 20, 1788) (M. Smith).

62. Maier, *Ratification,* p. 347 (quoting James Kent); *New York Daily Advertiser,* July 8, 1788, in *DHRC,* 22:2079.

63. M. Smith to Nathan Dane, June 28, 1788, in *DHRC,* 22:2015.

64. Ibid.; *DHRC,* 22:2195–98 (July 17, 1788) (Hamilton); *New York Daily Advertiser,* July 21, 1788, in *DHRC,* 22:2198.

65. *DHRC,* 22:2211–15 (July 17, 1788) (M. Smith).

66. Abraham Bancker to Evert Bancker, July 18, 1788, in *DHRC,* 22:2226; *DHRC,* 22:2232 (DeWitt Clinton diary, July 18, 1788).

67. The procession was originally scheduled for July 3. Victor Marie DuPont to Pierre

Samuel DuPont de Nemours, July 1–4, 1788, in *DHRC*, 20:1241. The procession is described at length in *DHRC*, 21:1584–1659.

68. *DHRC*, 22:2277–83; *New York Independent Journal*, July 28, 1788, in *DHRC*, 22:2282; Maier, *Ratification*, p. 392.

69. *DHRC*, 23:2291 (July 24, 1788); *DHRC*, 23:2300 (July 25, 1788); *New York Independent Journal*, July 28, 1788, in *DHRC*, 23:2298.

70. *Poughkeepsie Country Journal*, July 28, 1788, in *DHRC*, 23:2324.

71. Samuel Blachley Webb to Catherine Hogeboom, June 27, 1788, in *DHRC*, 22:1977.

72. Clinton to John Lamb, June 28, 1788, in *DHRC*, 23:2357; *DHRC*, 22:1989 (June 28, 1788).

73. This is the conclusion of both Maier and DePauw in their respective studies of the New York convention.

74. Hamilton to Edward Carrington, May 26, 1792, in *PAH*.

75. Madison to James K. Paulding, April 1, 1831, in *PJM*; N.P. Trist, "Memoranda," September 27, 1834, in Farrand, 3:534.

76. Monroe to Jefferson, July 12, 1788, in *DHRC*, 10:1705.

CHAPTER 7: COURTING THE GENERAL

1. Stuart Leibiger, *Founding Friendship: George Washington, James Madison, and the Creation of the American Republic*, Charlottesville, VA: University Press of Virginia (1999), p. 31; Virginia Delegates to Governor Harrison, August 23, 1783, in *PJM*.

2. Samuel Shaw to Francis Shaw, January 7, 1777, in Josiah Quincy, ed., *The Journals of Major Samuel Shaw*, Boston: Wm. Crosby and H.P. Nichols (1847), pp. 29–30 ("Our army love our general very much, but yet they have one thing against him, which is the little care he takes of himself in any action. His personal bravery, and the desire he has of animating his troops by example, make him fearless of any danger."); Abigail Adams to Mary Cranch, July 12, 1789, January 5, 1790, in *AP*.

3. Chernow, *Washington*, pp. 19–21, 40–51; Kenneth R. Bowling, *Creating the Federal City, 1774–1800: Potomac Fever*, Washington, D.C.: American Institute of Architects Press (1988), p. 44.

4. Leibiger, *Founding Friendship*, p. 38.

5. E.g., Madison to Jones, October 17, 1780, in *PJM*; "Draft of letter to John Jay, Explaining His Instructions," October 17, 1780, ibid.; Madison to Jefferson, November 18, 1781, March 24, 1782, ibid.

6. Jefferson to Washington, March 15, 1784, in *PTJ*; Jefferson to Madison, February 20, 1784, in *PJM*; Jefferson to Madison, May 25, 1784, ibid.

7. Joel Achenbach, *The Grand Idea: George Washington's Potomac and the Race to the West*, New York: Simon & Schuster (2004).

8. Ketcham, pp. 169–70; Madison to R.H. Lee, December 11, 1784, in *PJM*; "Resolutions Authorizing an Interstate Compact on Navigation and Jurisdiction of the Potomac," December 28, 1784, ibid.; Washington to Madison, December 28, 1784, ibid.; Madison to Jefferson, January 9, 1785, ibid.

9. Madison to Jefferson, January 9, 1785, ibid.; Elkanah Watson, *Men and Times of the Revolution, or Memoirs of Elkanah Watson, including Journal of Travels in Europe and America, 1777–1842*, New York: Dana and Co. (1856), p. 246; Madison to Washington, January 1, 1785, in *PJM*; Madison to Washington, January 9, 1785, ibid.; Madison to Jefferson, April 27, 1785, ibid.; Mason to Madison, August 9, 1785, ibid.; Mason to Madison, December 7, 1785, ibid.; "Act Ratifying the Chesapeake Compact with Maryland," ibid., December 24–26, 1785.

10. Madison to Jefferson, August 12, 1786, ibid.; Madison to Jefferson, October 3, 1785,

ibid.; "Amendments to the Act Conveying Canal Shares to George Washington," November 16, 1785, ibid.; Washington to Madison, October 29, 1785, ibid.

11. Wright and Tinling, *Quebec to Carolina*, pp. 191–94; Watson, *Men and Times of the Revolution*, p. 244.

12. Washington to Madison, November 30, 1785, in *PJM*; Madison to Washington, November 11, 1785, ibid.; Madison to Washington, December 9, 1785, ibid.

13. In contrast, during the Revolutionary War, the more ego-driven Hamilton resented his subordination to Washington while longing for a battlefield command. Hamilton to Philip Schuyler, February 18, 1781, in *PAH*.

14. Ketcham, p. 149; Madison to Monroe, June 4, 1789, in *PJM*.

15. Madison to Monroe, July 11, 1786, ibid.; Monroe to Madison, July 15, 1786, ibid.; Madison to Jefferson, August 12, 1786, ibid.; Madison to Ambrose Madison, August 7, 1786, ibid.

16. Madison to Edmund Randolph, July 26, 1785, ibid.

17. Madison to Washington, November 1, 1786, ibid.; Madison to Washington, November 8, 1786, ibid.; Washington to Madison, November 17, 1786, ibid.; Washington to Madison, December 16, 1786, ibid.; Madison to Washington, December 7, 1786, ibid.

18. Madison to Washington, February 21, 1787, ibid.; Madison to Washington, March 18, 1787, ibid.; Washington to Madison, March 31, 1787, ibid.; Madison to Washington, April 16, 1787, ibid.

19. Leibiger, *Founding Friendship*, pp. 79–81.

20. Madison to Washington, September 30, 1787, in *PJM*; Madison to Washington, October 14, 1787, ibid.; Washington to Madison, October 10, 1787, ibid.; Madison to Washington, October 18, 1787, ibid.; Washington to Madison, October 22, 1787, ibid.; Madison to Washington, October 28, 1787, ibid.; Madison to Washington, January 14, 1787, ibid.; Madison to Washington, January 25, 1788, ibid.

21. Madison to Washington, November 20, 1787, ibid.; Madison to Washington, December 7, 1787, ibid.; Washington to Madison, December 7, 1787, ibid.; Madison to Washington, December 14, 1787, ibid.; Madison to Washington, December 20, 1787, ibid.; Madison to Washington, April 10, 1788, ibid.; Washington to Thomas Johnson, April 20, 1788, in *PGW*.

22. Washington to Madison, February 5, 1788, in *PJM*, 10:468; Madison to Washington, February 20, 1788, ibid.; Washington to Madison, March 2, 1788, ibid.

23. Madison to Washington, June 4, 1788, ibid.; Madison to Washington, June 13, 1788, ibid.; Madison to Washington, June 18, 1788, ibid.; Madison to Washington, June 23, 1788, ibid.; Washington to Madison, June 23, 1788, ibid.

24. Ketcham, p. 269; Washington Diary, July 5, 1788, in *PGW*.

25. Washington to Benjamin Lincoln, August 28, 1788, in *DHRC*, 23:2463; Washington to John Armstrong, April 25, 1788, in *PGW*; Madison to Washington, August 24, 1788, in *PJM*; Madison to Edmund Randolph, September 14, 1788, ibid. (within the first seven or eight years, "the great business of the union will be settled").

26. Madison to Washington, August 11, 1788, ibid.

Chapter 8: Starting from Scratch

1. William L. Smith to Edward Rutledge, August 9, 1789, in George C. Rogers, Jr., "Letters of William Loughton Smith to Edward Rutledge," *South Carolina Hist. Rev.*, 69:1, 14–15 (1968).

2. Carrington to Madison, October 22, 1788, in *PJM*; Randolph to Madison, October 23, 1788, ibid.

3. Madison to Randolph, November 2, 1788, ibid.; George Turberville to Madison, No-

vember 16, 1788, ibid.; Henry Lee to Madison, November 19, 1788, ibid.; Washington to Madison, November 17, 1788, ibid.

4. Edward Carrington to Madison, November 15, 1788, November 18, 1788, November 26, 1788, ibid.; Labunski, *Struggle for the Bill of Rights*, pp. 150–66.

5. Alexander White to Madison, December 4, 1788, ibid.; Burgess Ball to Madison, December 8, 1788, ibid.; Richard Bland Lee to Madison, December 12, 1788, ibid.; Andrew Shepherd to Madison, December 14, 1788, ibid.; Hardin Burley to Madison, December 16, 1788, ibid.; Madison to Henry Lee, November 30, 1788, ibid.; Madison to James Madison, Sr., December 18, 1788, ibid.

6. Washington to Henry Lee, December 23, 1788, *PGW*; Washington Diary, December 25, 1788, ibid.; Washington to David Stuart, December 2, 1788, ibid.; Washington to Thomas Newton, December 17, 1788, ibid.; Washington to Warner Lewis, December 19, 1788, ibid.

7. These totals were derived from Founders Online, www.founders.archives.gov, the project of the National Archives that has digitized the correspondence of many of the Founders, including Washington and Madison. Washington's other frequent correspondents—his former army colleagues Henry Knox and the Marquis de Lafayette and his business agent in Philadelphia, Clement Biddle—were not engaged in the sorts of political projects that drew Madison and Washington together.

8. Washington Diary, December 20, 22, 23, 24, 1788, in *PGW*; Washington to Gouverneur Morris, November 28, 1788, ibid.; Hamilton to Madison, November 23, 1788, in *PJM*, 11:367; Ingersoll, "Notes of a Visit to Montpelier," quoted in Labunski, *Struggle for the Bill of Rights*, p. 99. Madison's potential investment at Great Falls, where Henry Lee projected a new town of Matildaville, is described in a sequence of correspondence: Henry Lee to Madison, October 29, 1788, in *PJM*; Madison to Washington, November 5, 1788, ibid.; Washington to Madison, November 17, 1788, ibid.; Henry Lee to Washington, February 9, 1789, in *PGW*.

9. "Memorandum on a Discussion of the President's Retirement," May 5, 1792, in *PJM*.

10. Henry Randall, *Life of Thomas Jefferson*, New York: Derby & Jackson (1858), 3:255 n.2 (comments written by Madison on December 3, 1827, as recorded by Nicholas Trist).

11. Madison to George Eve, January 2, 1789, in *PJM*. Other surviving letters from Madison's campaign went to Thomas Mann Randolph (Jefferson's son-in-law), January 13, 1789, ibid., 11:415; George Thompson, January 29, 1789, ibid.; and one headed "To A Resident of Spotsylvania County," January 27, 1789, ibid.

12. Benjamin Johnson to Madison, January 19, 1789, ibid., 11:423; Labunski, *Struggle for the Bill of Rights*, p. 175. Labunski's book provides a careful analysis of the Madison-Monroe election campaign.

13. Washington to Madison, February 16, 1789, in *PJM*; Ketcham, p. 278; Leibiger, *Founding Friendship*, p. 104; Nathaniel E. Stein and Ralph Ketcham, "Two New Letters on Washington's Inaugural," *Manuscripts*, 11:54 (1959).

14. Labunski, *Struggle for the Bill of Rights*, pp. 182–83; Burrows and Wallace, *Gotham*, p. 300.

15. Labunski, *Struggle for the Bill of Rights*, p. 181; Burrows and Wallace, *Gotham*, p. 301.

16. Madison to Washington, March 5, 1789, March 8, 1789, March 19, 1789, March 26, 1789, in *PJM*; Madison to Edmund Randolph, March 1, 1789, ibid.

17. Ketcham, p. 278; Madison to James Madison, Sr., February 24, 1789, in *PJM*. A sample of the requests for federal appointments, all in *PJM*, might include William Lindsay to Madison, March 2, 1789 (naval position); Miles King to Madison, March 3, 1789 (naval position); Gustavus B. Wallace to Madison, March 4, 1789 (tax collector); Thomas Thompson to Madison, March 8, 1789 (consul to Portugal); Richard Morris to Madison,

March 10, 1789 (supply and arms depot manager); John Beckley to Madison (clerk of House of Representatives); Elias Langham to Madison, March 15 (commissary of military stores); Edward Stevens to Madison, March 16, 1789 (customs agent); Christian Feibiger to Madison, April 2, 1789 (naval officer); Tench Coxe to Madison, April 5, 1789 ("anything proper").

18. Madison to Edmund Randolph, March 1, 1789, in *PJM*; Madison to Jefferson, March 29, 1789, ibid.

19. *Annals,* 1:107 (April 8, 1789); 1:135 (April 14); 1:181 (April 20); 1:227–28 (April 28); 1:269 (May 4).

20. Henry Knox to Washington, May 13, 1789, in *PGW*; Board of Treasury to Washington, June 10, 1789, ibid.; Robert Cullen, "Early U.S. Postal Routes and the Communications Infrastructure," American Association of State Highway and Transportation Officials, at http://web.mit.edu/comm-forum/mit6/papers/Cullen.pdf; Brooke Jackson and Charles Johnson, "Government Employment in Oregon," Oregon Employment Department, www.qualityinfo.org/olmisj.

21. Burrows and Wallace, *Gotham,* p. 297; Edgar Maclay, ed., *Personal Journal of William Maclay,* New York: D. Appleton and Co. (1890), p. 9; Fisher Ames to George Richards Minot, May 3, 1789, in Seth Ames, ed., *Works of Fisher Ames,* Boston: Little, Brown & Co. (1854), 1:34.

22. Washington to Hamilton, October 3, 1788, in *PAH*; James Hart, *The American Presidency in Action, 1789,* New York: Macmillan Co. (1948), p. 8.

23. Burrows and Wallace, *Gotham,* p. 297; Diary of Tobias Lear, April 30, 1789, reprinted in *New York Times,* August 13, 1898.

24. Washington to Madison, May 5, 1789, in *PJM*.

25. Washington to Madison, March 30, 1789, ibid.; Washington to Adams, May 10, 1789, in *PGW*; Hamilton to Washington, May 5, 1789, in *PAH*; Robert Livingston to Washington, May 2, 1789, in *PGW*.

26. Washington to David Stuart, July 26, 1789, in *PGW*; Kenneth R. Bowling and Helen E. Veit, eds., *The Diary of William Maclay and Other Notes on Senate Debates,* Baltimore: Johns Hopkins University Press (1988), pp. 136–37, 251, 342; Chernow, *Washington,* p. 581; Washington Diary, January 12, 1790, January 8, 1790, in *PGW*; Edmund Randolph to Madison, July 23, 1789, in *PJM*; Washington to Madison, May 12, 1789, ibid. Washington often noted in his diary the attendance level at his levees.

27. Hart, *American Presidency,* pp. 34–39; Leibiger, *Founding Friendship,* pp. 118–19; Washington to David Stuart, July 26, 1789, in *PGW*; *Annals,* 1:257 (May 5, 1789), 1:333–34 (May 11, 1789) (Madison). A full discussion of this sequence appears in James H. Hutson, "John Adams' Title Campaign," *New England Quarterly,* 41:34 (1968). Jefferson had the last word, describing the episode as "the most superlatively ridiculous thing I have ever heard of." Jefferson to Madison, July 29, 1789, in *PJM,* 12:315.

28. Madison to Jefferson, June 30, 1789, in *PJM*; Madison to Samuel Johnston, June 21, 1789, ibid.

29. *Annals,* 1:385–88 (May 19, 1789).

30. *Annals,* 1:480 (June 16, 1789) (Madison); 1:514–19 (June 17, 1789) (Madison).

31. Madison to Randolph, May 31, 1789, in *PJM*.

32. Washington to Madison, May 11, 1789, ibid.; Washington to Madison, May 17, 1789, ibid.; Washington to Madison, June 12, 1789, ibid.; Washington to Madison, July 25, 1789, ibid.; Washington to Madison, August 5, 1789, ibid.; Washington to Madison, September 8, 1789, ibid.; Washington to Madison, September 23, 1789, ibid.

33. Madison to Randolph, June 24, 1789, ibid.; Washington to James Craik, September 8, 1789, in *PGW*; Chernow, *Washington,* pp. 586–87.

34. *Annals*, 1:189–90, 192–93 (April 21, 1789); 1:209–10 (April 25, 1789); 1:246 (May 4, 1789); Elkins and McKitrick, *Age of Federalism*, pp. 67–71; Leibiger, *Founding Friendship*, p. 120.

35. Burgess Ball to Washington, August 25, 1789, in *PGW*; Charles Carter and Burgess Ball to Washington, October 8, 1789, ibid.; Burgess Ball to Washington, December 26, 1789, ibid.; Chernow, *Washington*, pp. 524–26; Washington to Betty Lewis, September 13, 1789, in *PGW*.

36. Madison to Eliza House Trist, May 21, 1789, in *PJM*; Samuel Mitchill to Mrs. Mitchill, January 3, 1802, in "Dr. Mitchill's Letters from Washington City," *Harper's New Monthly Magazine*, 58:743 (1879); Madison to Jefferson, May 23, 1789, in *PJM*; Andrew Burstein and Nancy Isenberg, *Madison and Jefferson*, New York: Random House (2010), p. 682, n. 63; Journal of Comte de Moustier, July 28, 1788, in Merrill Jensen and Robert A. Becker, eds., *Documentary History of the First Federal Elections, 1788–1790*, Madison: University of Wisconsin Press (1976), p. 52; Mary Coxe to Tench Coxe, January 1789, ibid., p. 53. On at least two occasions, the wife of Henry Lee in Virginia sent regards to Mrs. Colden in letters from her husband to Madison, as did another Virginian, suggesting an understanding that Madison was regularly in Mrs. Colden's company. Henry Lee to Madison, June 10, 1789, in *PJM*; Henry Lee to Madison, March 4, 1790, ibid.; Richard Bland Lee to Madison, April 17, 1791, ibid.

CHAPTER 9: NOT ALTOGETHER USELESS

1. Madison to Jefferson, October 17, 1788, in *PJM*; *Federalist*, No. 48; Washington to Benjamin Lincoln, October 26, 1788; "Pacificus" [Noah Webster] to James Madison, August 14, 1789, in Helen E. Veit et al., eds., *Creating the Bill of Rights: The Documentary Record from the First Federal Congress*, Baltimore: The Johns Hopkins University Press (1991), p. 276; Labunski, *Struggle for the Bill of Rights*, pp. 199–200.

2. Kenneth R. Bowling, "'A Tub to the Whale': The Founding Fathers and the Adoption of the Federal Bill of Rights," *J. of the Early Republic*, 8:223, 228 (1988).

3. *DHRC*, 10:1331 (June 16, 1788) (Henry); Paul Finkelman, "James Madison and the Bill of Rights: A Reluctant Paternity," *Supreme Court Review*, 1990:301; Maier, *Ratification*, pp. 196–98, 307, 398; *DHRC*, 10:1551 (June 27, 1788) (George Wythe); Jefferson to Madison, December 20, 1787, in *PJM*; Jefferson to Madison, July 31, 1788, ibid.

4. Madison to Jefferson, August 10, 1788, ibid.; Madison to George Turberville, November 2, 1788, ibid.; Madison to Hamilton, June 27, 1788, ibid.; Washington to Jefferson, August 31, 1788, in *PGW*.

5. Madison to Jefferson, August 23, 1788, in *PJM*; "Virginia's Application for a Second Convention, May 5, 1789," and "New York's Application for a Second Convention," in Veit, *Creating the Bill of Rights*, pp. 235–38; Madison to George Turberville, November 2, 1789, in *PJM*.

6. Madison to Edmund Pendleton, October 20, 1788, ibid.; Madison to Washington, December 2, 1788, ibid.; Madison to Jefferson, December 8, 1788, ibid.; Madison to Thomas Mann Randolph, January 13, 1789, ibid.

7. Madison to George Eve, January 2, 1789, ibid.

8. "Address of the House of Representatives to the President, May 5, 1789," ibid.; Washington to Madison, May 31, 1789, ibid.

9. *Annals*, 1:441–48 (June 8, 1789); *Annals*, 1:445 (Sherman).

10. *Annals*, 1:453 (June 8, 1789) (Madison).

11. *Annals*, 1:449 (June 8, 1789) (Madison).

12. *Annals*, 1:450–53 (June 8, 1789) (Madison); Labunski, *Struggle for the Bill of Rights*, pp. 198–99.

13. *Annals*, 1:784 (August 17, 1789) (Madison).

14. *Annals*, 1:455 (June 8, 1789) (Madison).

15. William R. Davie to Madison, June 10, 1789, in *PJM*; Benjamin Hawkins to Madison, July 3, 1788, ibid.; Samuel Johnston to Madison, July 8, 1789, ibid.; George Turberville to Madison, June 16, 1788, ibid.; Edmund Randolph to Madison, June 30, 1788, ibid.; Madison to Tench Coxe, June 18, 1788, ibid.

16. Brant, *Father of the Constitution*, p. 249 (Ames letter); Theodore Sedgwick to Benjamin Lincoln, July 19, 1789, in Veit, *Creating the Bill of Rights*, pp. 263–64; Bowling, "'A Tub to the Whale,'" pp. 233, 236–37 (1988) (Pennsylvanians); George Clymer to Richard Peters, June 8, 1789, in Veit, *Creating the Bill of Rights*, p. 245; George Clymer to Tench Coxe, June 28, 1789, ibid., p. 255.

17. Labunski, *Struggle for the Bill of Rights*, pp. 216–17. Madison wanted the amendments folded directly into each provision of the Constitution that was being revised, not tacked on at the end (as they are now). He thought that revising the constitutional text would "preserve neatness and propriety" and ensure that the "system would remain uniform and entire." By the end of the debates, he conceded on this question of form. *Annals*, 1:735 (August 13, 1789) (Madison); Labunski, *Struggle for the Bill of Rights*, p. 219.

18. William L. Smith to Edward Rutledge, August 15, 1789, in Veit, *Creating the Bill of Rights*, p. 278; William Smith to Otho H. Williams, August 22, 1789, ibid., p. 285; *Annals*, 1:774 (August 15, 1789) (Aedanus Burke).

19. Madison to Richard Peters, August 19, 1789, in *PJM*; Madison to Edmund Randolph, August 21, 1789, ibid.; Madison to Pendleton, August 21, 1789, ibid.

20. In late August, President Washington conducted the first in-person consultation with the Senate over treaty making. Prompted by the constitutional provision that the Senate's role on treaties was to "advise and consent," the president visited the Senate chamber to seek senators' views on upcoming negotiations with the Creek and Cherokee tribes. Both sides found the procedure awkward in the extreme. When one senator proposed that his colleagues needed more time to consider the question, Washington burst out, "This defeats every purpose of my coming here." The experiment was never repeated. In the future, the Senate's "advice" would be offered privately by individual senators, and "consent" would be granted or withheld outside the presence of the president. Maclay, *Journal*, pp. 127–29.

21. Labunski, *Struggle for the Bill of Rights*, pp. 236–37; Madison to Edmund Pendleton, September 14, 1789, in *PJM*; Paine Wingate to John Langdon, September 17, 1789, in Veit, *Creating the Bill of Rights*, p. 297; Bowling, "'A Tub to the Whale,'" p. 245; William Grayson to Patrick Henry, September 29, 1789, in Henry, *Patrick Henry*, 3:406.

22. From the Rhode Island Legislature, Sept. 10–19, 1789, in *PGW*.

23. Three of the original states—Connecticut, Massachusetts, and Georgia—did not ratify the Bill of Rights until 1939. Two of the proposed amendments were not ratified in Madison's lifetime, but one took effect two centuries later. In 1992, the Twenty-seventh Amendment was adopted, barring changes in congressional compensation from taking effect until the next Congress takes office. The twelfth proposed amendment would have limited congressional districts to different population levels depending on the size of the House of Representatives; with the nation's growth, that proposed restriction became irrelevant.

24. Madison to Richard Peters, August 19, 1789, in *PJM*.

25. *Annals*, 1:455, 457 (June 8, 1789) (Madison).

CHAPTER 10: THE DEAL

1. Madison to Jefferson, October 8, 1789, in *PJM*; Madison to Jefferson, November 1, 1789, ibid.; Madison to Washington, January 4, 1789, ibid.

2. Washington to John Beale Bordley, August 17, 1788, in *PGW*; Washington Diary, October 20, 1789, October 28, 1789, October 30, 1789, November 4, 1789, ibid.

3. Maclay, *Journal*, p. 173 (January 14, 1790); Rogers, "Letters of William Loughton Smith," pp. 199–202; Woody Holton, *Unruly Americans and the Origins of the Constitution*, New York: Hill and Wang (2007), pp. 34–39; Ferguson, *Power of the Purse*, pp. 291–96. A South Carolina congressman complained that wealthy investors were "sending pilot-boats secretly from New York to Charleston, while the people there were asleep, as it were, and totally unacquainted with the councils or view of the administration, with information on the one side only." *Annals*, 1:1340 (February 19, 1790) (Burke).

4. Richard Sylla, "U.S. Securities Markets and the Banking System, 1790–1840," in *Review of the Federal Reserve Bank of St. Louis*, May/June 1998, p. 86. By comparison, today's United States government debt is roughly 100 percent of the national gross domestic product, though today's American economy is far more dynamic and the machinery of revenue collection is far more developed.

5. This discussion grows from a number of sources, principally Ferguson's *Power of the Purse*, which provides an extraordinarily thorough and incisive treatment of the financial realities of America in its birth pangs.

6. Madison, "Money," (1779–80), in *PJM*; Ketcham, pp. 85–87.

7. Ferguson, *Power of the Purse*, pp. 251–81.

8. Hamilton to Madison, October 12, 1789, in *PJM*; Madison to Hamilton, November 19, 1789, ibid.; Ferguson, *Power of the Purse*, pp. 289–90; Madison to Henry Lee, April 13, 1790, in *PJM*.

9. Madison to Jefferson, January 24, 1790, in *PJM*; Maclay, *Journal*, p. 174 (January 18, 1790); Gustavus B. Wallace to Madison, March 25, 1790, April 20, 1790, in *PJM*.

10. *Annals*, 1:1333–37 (February 11, 1790) (Madison). Shortly before the legislative debate began, Hamilton learned that Madison would propose this "discrimination" between original and current debt holders. When the Treasury Secretary pointed out to Madison that he had opposed such discrimination when they both served in Congress in 1783, Madison insisted that rampant speculation over the intervening seven years had "changed the state of the question." Hamilton to Edward Carrington, May 26, 1792, in *PAH*.

11. *Annals*, 1:1261 (February 15, 1790) (Sedgwick).

12. *Annals*, 1:1308–9 (February 18, 1790) (Madison).

13. *Annals*, 1:1344 (February 22, 1790); Madison to James Madison, Sr., February 27, 1790; Washington to David Stuart, March 28, 1790, in *PGW*; Stuart to Washington, June 2, 1790, ibid.

14. *Annals*, 1:1224–25 (February 11, 1790) (Fitzsimons), 1:1228 (February 11, 1790) (Jackson), 1:1240 (February 12, 1790) (Tucker), 1:1246 (February 12, 1790) (Madison).

15. *Annals*, 1:1505–6 (March 17, 1790) (Smith).

16. *Annals*, 1:1517–20 (March 22, 1790) (Boudinot), 1523–24 (March 23, 1790) (final report, as amended); Madison to Benjamin Rush, March 20, 1790, in *PJM*; Madison to Edmund Randolph, March 21, 1790, ibid.; Washington to David Stuart, June 15, 1790, in *PGW*.

17. "Memorandum on an African Colony for Freed Slaves," October 20, 1789, in *PJM*.

18. E.g., *Annals*, 1:1405 (February 25, 1790) (White).

19. Ferguson, *Power of the Purse*, pp. 209–11; William Davies to Madison, May 8, 1790, in *PJM*.

20. *Annals*, 1:1386–89 (February 24, 1790) (Madison); 1:1426 (February 26, 1790) (Madison); 1:1427–28, 1434, 1437 (March 1, 1790) (Madison); 1:1454 (March 2, 1790) (Madison); 1:1590–91 (April 22, 1790) (Madison).

21. *Annals*, 1:1578 (April 12, 1790) (Sedgwick); 1:1597 (April 26, 1790).

22. Elkins and McKitrick, *Age of Federalism*, p. 207. Americans were applying to state capitals that rationale of easy accessibility, moving them to central locations within states—from New York to Albany, from Philadelphia to Lancaster to Harrisburg, from Charleston to Columbia. Bowling, *Creating the Federal City*, pp. 3–11; *Annals*, 1:818 (August 27, 1789) (Scott).

23. *Annals*, 1:894–901 (September 4, 1789) (Madison); 1:890 (September 3, 1789) (Madison); Maclay, *Journal*, p. 143. At one point Madison suggested that Virginians might not have ratified the Constitution if they had anticipated the antisouthern biases revealed in the congressional debates.

24. Madison to Pendleton, September 14, 1789, in *PJM*; Madison to Henry Lee, October 4, 1789, ibid.

25. Bowling, *Creating the Federal City*, pp. 158–59; Madison to Henry Lee, October 4, 1789, in *PJM*.

26. Fitzsimons to Tench Coxe, September 6, 1790, in Tench Coxe Papers, Historical Society of Pennsylvania, quoted in Bowling, *Creating the Federal City*, p. 146; Maclay, *Journal*, p. 247; Fergus Bordewich, *Washington: The Making of the American Capital*, New York: Amistad (2008), pp. 27–28.

27. Maclay, *Journal*, p. 158; Wright and Tinling, *Quebec to Carolina*, pp. 187–89; Benjamin Rush to John Adams, 1789, in Lyman Butterfield, ed., *Letters of Benjamin Rush*, Princeton University Press (1951), 1:508.

28. Madison to Washington, November 20, 1789, in *PJM*; Bordewich, *Making of the American Capital*, p. 29.

29. Madison to Henry Lee, October 4, 1789, in *PJM*.

30. Maclay, *Journal*, p. 202.

31. Bowling, *Creating the Federal City*, pp. 175–76.

32. Madison to Henry Lee, April 13, 1790, in *PJM*; J.P.G. [Peter] Muhlenberg to Benj. Rush, June 17, 1790, in "A survey of Benjamin Rush Papers," *Pennsylvania Mag. of Hist. and Biography*, 70:78 (1946); Madison to Pendleton, June 22, 1790, in *PJM*; Madison to Edmund Randolph, May 19, 1790, ibid.; Madison to Governor of Virginia, May 25, 1790, ibid.; Smith to Edward Rutledge, June 14, 1790, in Rogers, "Letters of William L. Smith to Edward Rutledge," *S. Car. Hist. Rev.* 69:101, 118–19 (1968).

33. Maclay, *Journal*, pp. 284–86; Bowling, *Creating the Federal City*, pp. 180–81; Madison to Monroe, June 17, 1790, in *PJM*.

34. Washington to David Stuart, June 15, 1790, in *PGW*.

35. The only accounts of the meal come from Jefferson and were written some time later, yet the external facts largely confirm those accounts, except for Jefferson's portrayal of himself as almost entirely aloof from the political bargaining between Hamilton and Madison. Franklin B. Sawvel, ed., *The Complete Anas of Thomas Jefferson*, New York: Round Table Press (1903), pp. 32–34; Jefferson to Washington, September 9, 1792, in *PTJ*, 17:205.

36. *Annals*, 1:1719 (July 6, 1790) (Burke); *Annals*, 1:1723 (July 6, 1790) (Madison).

37. Ferguson, *Power of the Purse*, pp. 322–24.

38. William Loughton Smith to Edward Rutledge, July 25, 1790, in *S.C. Hist. Mag.* 69:125 (1965). The four were Richard Bland Lee and Alexander White of Virginia, and George Gale and Daniel Carroll of Maryland.

39. Maclay, *Journal*, pp. 231, 235, 268, 308, 328–29. Daniel Carroll of Maryland, fittingly enough, was appointed one of the three commissioners for the construction of the new District of Columbia, which was located largely on the site of his own farm. George Gale was appointed supervisor of distilled liquors for the district of Maryland.

40. Madison to James Monroe, July 25, 1790, in *PJM*.

41. Ketcham, p. 349; Washington to Madison, March 6, 1796, in *PJM*.

42. Madison to James Madison, Sr., August 14, 1790, ibid.

43. Ketcham, pp. 317–18.

44. "Instructions for the Montpelier Overseer and Laborers," November 1790, in *PJM*.

CHAPTER 11: FIRST, FRIENDSHIP

1. Dumas Malone, ed., *Autobiography of Thomas Jefferson*, New York: Capricorn Books (1959), p. 55; Madison to Margaret B. Smith, September 1830, in *PJM*; e.g., Madison to Jefferson, May 6, 1780, ibid.; Jefferson to Madison, November 18, 1781, ibid.; Madison to Jefferson, June 2, 1780, ibid.; Madison to Jefferson, January 9, 1781, ibid.

2. Sarah N. Randolph, *The Domestic Life of Thomas Jefferson*, New York: Harper & Brothers (1871), p. 63; Jefferson to Elizabeth Wayles Eppes, October 3, 1782, in *PTJ*; Edmund Randolph to Madison, September 20, 1782, in *PJM*.

3. Notes on Congress, November 12, 1782, in *PJM*, 5:268; Edmund Randolph to Madison, November 22, 1782, ibid.; Jefferson to Monroe, May 20, 1782, ibid. This episode during Jefferson's term as governor is the subject of Michael Kranish's *Flight from Monticello: Thomas Jefferson at War*, New York: Oxford University Press (2011).

4. Madison to James Madison, Sr., January 1, 1783, in *PJM*; Burstein and Isenberg, *Madison and Jefferson*, p. 95.

5. Isaac Jefferson, *Memoirs of a Monticello Slave*, Charlottesville: University of Virginia Press (1951), p. 25; Margaret Bayard Smith, *The First Forty Years of Washington Society*, New York: C. Scribner's Sons (1906), p. 8.

6. Jefferson to Ann Cary et al., March 2, 1802, in *PTJ*; Smith, *First Forty Years*, pp. 6–7; Randolph, *Domestic Life of Thomas Jefferson*, pp. 58–60. Dr. Benjamin Rush of Philadelphia offered a comparable tribute to Jefferson as polymath. "He possessed a genius of the first order," Rush wrote. "It was universal in its objects. He was not less distinguished for his political than his mathematical and philosophical knowledge," George W. Corner, ed., *The Autobiography of Benjamin Rush*, Princeton University Press (1948), p. 151. Madison, pasty-faced and reticent with new acquaintances, did not show to advantage while in Jefferson's company. As one contemporary recorded, Madison's stiff manners made a first impression of "sternness rather than . . . the mildness and suavity which I found afterwards." Irving Brant, *James Madison: Secretary of State 1800–1809*, Indianapolis: Bobbs-Merrill Co. (1953), p. 13.

7. "Report on Books for Congress," January 23, 1783, and editorial note, in *PJM*.

8. Jefferson to Madison, April 14, 1783, ibid.

9. Jefferson to Madison, May 7, 1783, ibid.; Madison to Jefferson, June 10, 1783, ibid.; Jefferson to Madison, August 31, 1783, ibid.

10. John Quincy Adams, *Jubilee of the Constitution: A Discourse*, New York: Samuel Colman (1839), p. 111.

11. Madison to Jefferson, December 10, 1783, February 17, 1784, April 25, 1784, in *PJM*; Jefferson to Madison, February 20, 1784, and March 16, 1784, ibid.; Madison to Jefferson, April 25, 1784, ibid.

12. Jefferson to Madison, November 11, 1784, April 27, 1785, ibid.

13. Madison to Jefferson, May 12, 1786, June 19, 1786, in *PJM*; Jefferson to John Sullivan, January 7, 1786, October 5, 1787, January 26, 1787, April 16, 1787, in *PTJ*; Jefferson to William Stephens Smith, September 28, 1787, ibid.; Jefferson to Archibald Cary, January 7, 1787, ibid.; Jefferson to Madison, May 18, 1792, in *PJM*.

14. Jefferson to Madison, May 25, 1784, ibid.; Madison to Jefferson, April 27, 1785, ibid.

15. Jefferson to Madison, February 8, 1786, May 3, 1788, ibid.

16. Madison to Jefferson, May 12, 1786, December 9, 1787, September 21, 1788, ibid. Ironi

cally, the pamphlet on the Mohegan language was prepared by an uncle of Aaron Burr, Jefferson's first vice president, who became Jefferson's political bête noire. Mary-Jo Kline, ed., *Political Correspondence and Public Papers of Aaron Burr,* Princeton University Press (1983), 1:lviii–lx.

17. Jefferson to Madison, May 8, 1784, in *PJM*; Madison to Jefferson, November 15, 1785, January 22, 1786, November 25, 1786, ibid.
18. Jefferson to Madison, May 15, 1787, ibid.; Madison to Jefferson, January 22, 1786, ibid.
19. Jefferson to Madison, October 28, 1785, ibid.
20. Madison to Jefferson, February 4, 1790, ibid. Madison, still living with his parents as he neared forty, was well positioned to appreciate the interdependence of generations.
21. Jefferson to Madison, June 29, 1797, ibid.
22. John Adams, *Autobiography of John Adams,* Cambridge, MA: Belknap Press (1962), 3:335; Madison to Nicholas Trist, May 29, 1832, in *PJM*; Joseph J. Ellis, *American Sphinx: The Character of Thomas Jefferson,* New York: Alfred A. Knopf (1997).
23. Jefferson to Madison, December 16, 1786, in *PJM*; Jefferson to Madison, January 30, 1787, ibid.
24. Jefferson to Madison, June 20, 1787, ibid. Jefferson would prove less enthusiastic about judicial review as pronounced by Chief Justice John Marshall in his 1803 ruling in *Marbury v. Madison.*
25. Madison to Jefferson, October 24, 1787, ibid.
26. Jefferson to Madison, December 20, 1787, ibid.; Jefferson to Madison, July 31, 1788, ibid.
27. Madison to Jefferson, October 17, 1788, ibid.
28. Jefferson to Madison, November 18, 1788, ibid.
29. Jefferson to Madison, February 20, 1784, ibid.
30. Madison to Jefferson, March 16, 1784, ibid.
31. Jefferson to Madison, December 4, 1787, ibid.
32. Madison to Jefferson, April 27, 1785, ibid.
33. Madison to Jefferson, January 22, 1786, ibid.; Ketcham, pp. 161–68; Malone, *Jefferson,* 1:261–63; David John Mays, *Edmund Pendleton: A Biography,* Cambridge: Harvard University Press (1952), 2:161. In *The Age of Federalism* (p. 198), Elkins and McKitrick enumerate an extensive list of reforms that Jefferson proposed yet was never able to turn into law.
34. Madison to Jefferson, October 8, 1789, and November 1, 1789, in *PJM*; John Dawson to Madison, December 17, 1789, ibid.; Jon Meacham, *Thomas Jefferson: The Art of Power,* New York: Random House (2012), p. 232.

CHAPTER 12: THE HAMILTON PROBLEM

1. Madison to Washington, January 4, 1790, in *PJM*; Jefferson to Madison, February 14, 1790, ibid.; Corner, *Autobiography of Benjamin Rush,* p. 181 (March 17, 1790); Jefferson to Madison, February 14, 1790, in *PJM*. Like Washington, Jefferson consulted Madison on proper procedures under the Constitution that Madison knew so well, beginning with the proper method for conveying to Congress any communications the president received from state governments. Jefferson to Madison, March 30, 1790, ibid.
2. Madison to Monroe, July 24, 1790, in *PJM*; Jefferson to George Gilmer, June 27, 1790, in *PTJ*.
3. Jefferson's *Anas,* in Paul Leicester Ford, ed., *The Works of Thomas Jefferson,* New York: G.P. Putnam's Sons (1904–05), 1:159–60; Jefferson to Benjamin Rush, January 16, 1811, in *PTJ*; Madison to Jefferson, January 24, 1790, in *PJM*. Jefferson's dislike for cities and their merchant classes was deeply etched. A few years earlier, he wrote: "The mobs of great cities add just so much to the support of pure government, as sores do to the strength of the human body." *Notes on the State of Virginia,* pp. 157–58.

4. *Annals*, 1:1894 (January 6, 1791) (Madison).
5. Chernow, *Alexander Hamilton*, pp. 347–48; "National Bank," December 13, 1790, in *PAH*; Elkins and McKitrick, *Age of Federalism*, pp. 226–27.
6. "Memorandum for Thomas Jefferson," January 31, 1791, in *PJM*; "Notes on the Bank of England," February 1, 1791, ibid.; "Notes on Banks," February 1, 1791, ibid.
7. *Annals*, 1:1944–52 (February 2, 1791) (Madison).
8. *Annals*, 1:1957 (February 3, 1791) (Fisher Ames); "Final Version of an Opinion on the Constitutionality of an Act to Establish a Bank," February 23, 1791, in *PAH*.
9. *Annals*, 1:1954–55 (February 3, 1791) (Fisher Ames); *Annals*, 1:1977 (February 4, 1791) (Elias Boudinot). For a discussion of the congressional debate, see Benjamin B. Klubes, "The First Federal Congress and the First National Bank: A Case Study in Constitutional Interpretation," *Journal of the Early Republic*, 10:19 (1990). Because only Hamilton knew that Madison was the author of *The Federalist* No. 44, he very likely brought the passage to the attention of the congressman who recited it.
10. Elkins and McKitrick, *Age of Federalism*, p. 232; *Annals*, 1:2012 (February 8, 1791).
11. Fleet, "Madison's Detached Memoranda," 3:542–43.
12. "Final Version of an Opinion on the Constitutionality of an Act to Establish a Bank," February 23, 1791, in *PAH*; Elkins and McKitrick, *Age of Federalism*, pp. 229–32; Jefferson to Madison, September 21, 1795, in *PJM*.
13. Memoranda of N P Trist, September 27, 1834, in Farrand, 3:534 (emphasis added).
14. Madison expressed his conviction that his positions did not change in an exchange in 1795 with Samuel Dexter, a New England congressman who found himself increasingly attracted to the Republican cause. Dexter proposed a conversation with Madison to understand "the motives for your present line of politics, when compared with your former measures." Agreeing to a dinner meeting "en famille," Madison assured Dexter that he wished "an opportunity of removing one at least of the impressions you are under, which may not do justice to the consistency between my present and former line of politics." Samuel Dexter, Jr., to Madison, February 3, 1795, in *PJM*; Madison to Dexter, February 5, 1795, ibid.
15. Madison to Jefferson, May 1, 1791, ibid.
16. Maclay, *Journal*, p. 68.
17. Jefferson to Benjamin Rush, January 16, 1811, in *PTJ*; "Notes of a Conversation with Alexander Hamilton," August 13, 1791, in *PTJ*; Jefferson to Madison, June 10, 1792, in *PJM*.
18. Maclay, *Journal*, pp. 23–25.
19. Madison to Edmund Pendleton, December 6, 1792, in *PJM*; Jefferson to Madison, June 9, 1793, ibid.; see Maclay, *Journal*, p. 351.
20. Jefferson to Madison, September 8, 1793, in *PTJ*; "Jefferson's Account of the Bargain on the Assumption and Residence Bills," ibid.
21. Thoughtful discussions of this question appear in an essay titled "Is There a 'James Madison Problem'?" in Gordon Wood, *Revolutionary Characters: What Made the Founders Different*, New York: Penguin Press (2006), pp. 143–72, and in Burstein and Isenberg, *Madison and Jefferson*, pp. 222–24. For an extended argument that Madison consistently adhered to Virginian agrarian views even during what has been understood as his nationalist phase, see Lance Banning, *The Sacred Fire of Liberty: James Madison and the Founding of the Federal Republic*, Ithaca: Cornell University Press (1995).
22. Jefferson to Madison, March 13, 1791, in *PJM*; Madison to Jefferson, March 13, 1791, ibid.
23. Madison to Ambrose Madison, April 11, 1791, in *PJM*; Ed. Note, "Lake Country Tour," in *PJM* (May 31, 1791); "Jefferson's Journal of the Tour," May 21–June 10, 1791, *in PTJ*;

Jefferson to Mary Jefferson, May 30, 1791, ibid.; Jefferson to Martha Jefferson Randolph, May 31, 1791, in *PTJ*; Ketcham, pp. 323–25. A careful study of the botanical elements of the tour appears in Andrea Wulf, *Founding Gardeners: The Revolutionary Generation, Nature, and the Shaping of the American Nation*, New York: Alfred A. Knopf (2011), pp. 87–97.

24. Madison to Margaret B. Smith, September 1830, in *PJM*; Wulf, *Founding Gardeners*, pp. 94–96.

25. Lewis Leary, *That Rascal Freneau: A Study in Literary Failure*, New Brunswick, NJ: Rutgers University Press (1941).

26. Jefferson to Philip Freneau, February 28, 1791, in *PTJ*; Jefferson to Thomas Mann Randolph, May 15, 1791, ibid.; Madison to Jefferson, May 1, 1791, in *PJM*; Jefferson to Madison, May 9, 1791, ibid.; Jefferson to Madison, July 21, 1791, ibid.

27. Jefferson to Madison, July 21, 1791, ibid.; Madison to Jefferson, July 24, 1791, ibid.; Philip Freneau to Madison, July 25, 1791, ibid.; Freneau to Jefferson, August 4, 1791, in *PTJ*; Leary, *That Rascal Freneau*, pp. 186–87. For months, Madison, Jefferson, and their friends hectored political allies to subscribe to Freneau's paper. E.g., Henry Lee to Madison, December 8, 1791, in *PJM*; Daniel Carroll to Madison, December 12, 1791, ibid.; Jefferson to Thomas Mann Randolph, November 20, 1791, in *PTJ*; Jefferson to Philip Freneau, March 13, 1791, ibid.

28. *National Gazette*, December 19, 1791 (emphasis added), in *PJM*; *National Gazette*, "Charters," January 18, 1792, ibid.

29. *National Gazette*, "Parties," January 23, 1792, ibid.; *National Gazette*, "Government of the United States," February 3, 1792, ibid.

30. *National Gazette*, "Republican Distribution of Citizens," March 3, 1792, ibid.; *National Gazette*, "Fashion," March 20, 1792, ibid.; *National Gazette*, "Property," March 27, 1792, ibid. Madison wrote in "Property" that freedom of conscience was "the most sacred of all property . . . more sacred than [a man's] castle." The assertion rings somewhat hollow to modern ears in an essay on property that never addresses the human property that prevailed in many parts of the nation, including at Madison's home.

31. *National Gazette*, March 31, 1792, ibid.

32. Noble E. Cunningham, Jr., *The Jeffersonian Republicans, The Formation of Party Organization, 1789–1801*, Chapel Hill: University of North Carolina Press (1957), p. 22 [hereafter *Jeffersonian Republicans I*"].

33. Benjamin Rush, *The Autobiography of Benjamin Rush: His Travels Through Life Together with His Commonplace Book for 1789–1813*, George W. Corner, ed. New York: Praeger (1947), pp. 202–3 (August 10–12, 1791); Jefferson to Edward Rutledge, August 29, 1791.

34. Rush, *Autobiography*, pp. 217–19; Madison to Henry Lee, April 15, 1792; Chernow, *Alexander Hamilton*, pp. 382–83.

35. Madison to Pendleton, April 9, 1792; Madison to Henry Lee, April 15, 1792.

36. Rush, *Autobiography*, p. 217; Cunningham, *Jeffersonian Republicans I*, p. 61; Jefferson, "Note on Stockholders in Congress," March 25, 1793, in *PTJ*; Leary, *That Rascal Freneau*, p. 225. That Madison's father also owned public debt seems never to have given Madison any second thoughts about characterizing such financial interests as inherently corrupting. Madison was supposed to redeem his father's debt certificates during this period, but on at least two occasions he mislaid the power of attorney required to complete the transactions. James Madison, Sr., to Madison, February 28, 1792, in *PJM*; Madison to James Madison, Sr., March 15, 1792, ibid.; Madison to James Madison, Sr., April 7, 1794, ibid.; Madison to James Madison, Sr., April 21, 1794, ibid.

37. Elkins and McKitrick, *Age of Federalism*, pp. 257–58, 262–63, 276–77.

38. Madison to Henry Lee, January 1, 1792, in *PJM*.

39. Madison actually supported the assistance to fishermen that Hamilton proposed. In an adroit maneuver, he persuaded Congress to rename Hamilton's bounties as "allowances," thereby preserving aid to fishermen but blocking Hamilton from extending bounties to other industries. *Annals* 2:388 (February 6, 1792) (Madison), 2:400–401 (February 9, 1792).

40. Jefferson, "Conversations with the President," February 28 and 29, 1792, in Sawvel, *Complete Anas*, pp. 50–55.

41. Elkins and McKitrick, *Age of Federalism*, pp. 275–79.

42. Elkins and McKitrick, *Age of Federalism*, p. 282; Jefferson to Washington, May 23, 1792, in *PTJ*.

43. Hamilton to Edward Carrington, May 26, 1792, in *PAH*.

44. Madison, "Memorandum on a Discussion of the President's Retirement," May 5, 9, 1792, in *PJM*; Madison to Washington, June 20, 1792, ibid.; Jefferson to Madison, October 1, 1792, ibid.

45. Denver Brunsman, "James Madison and the *National Gazette* Essays: The Birth of a Party Politician," in Stuart Leibiger, ed., *A Companion to James Madison and James Monroe*, Malden, MA: Wiley-Blackwell (2013), p. 154.

46. Cunningham, *Jeffersonian Republicans I*, pp. 36–38, 44–48; John Beckley to Madison, August 1, 1792, September 2, 1792, October 17, 1792, in *PJM*; John Dawson to Madison, November 27, 1792, ibid.; Ed. Note, "Madison in the Third Congress, 2 December 1793–3 March 1795," ibid.; Harry Ammon, "The Formation of the Republican Party in Virginia, 1789–1796," *Journal of Southern History*, 19:283, 298 (1953); Jefferson to Thomas Pinckney, December 3, 1792, in *PTJ*.

47. William L. Smith, "The Politicks and Views of a Certain Party Displayed" (1792); Brant, *Father of the Constitution*, p. 368 (quoting letter from Fisher Ames to Timothy Dwight, January 1793).

48. Madison, "Who Are the Best Keepers of the People's Liberties?" *National Gazette* (December 20, 1792), in *PJM*.

CHAPTER 13: BECOMING REPUBLICANS

1. Meacham, *Art of Power*, pp. 222–24.

2. For more on the complex course of the early years of the French Revolution, good sources are Georges Lefebvre, *The French Revolution from Its Origins to 1793*, New York: Columbia University Press (1962), and Simon Schama, *Citizens: A Chronicle of the French Revolution*, New York: Alfred A. Knopf (1989).

3. Elkins and McKitrick, *Age of Federalism*, pp. 309–10; George Turberville to Madison, January 28, 1793, in *PJM*; Madison to George Nicholas, March 15, 1793, ibid.; Madison to Minister of Interior of the French Republic, April 1793, ibid.

4. Hamilton to Edward Carrington, May 26, 1792, in *PAH*; Jefferson to William Short, January 3, 1793, in *PTJ*.

5. Elkins and McKitrick, *Age of Federalism*, pp. 70–71. In 1792, according to one writer, the French navy numbered 246 ships, including 86 ships of the line and 78 frigates. William James, *Naval History of Great Britain*, London: Harding, Lepard & Co. (1826), 1:45 and App. 4.

6. Jefferson to Madison, June 23, 1793, in *PJM*; Madison to Jefferson, June 19, 1793, ibid.

7. Jefferson to Madison, April 28, 1793, ibid.; Madison to Jefferson, May 8, 1793, ibid.; "[Jefferson's] Notes of Cabinet Meeting on Edmond Charles Genet," August 1, 1793, in Sawvel, *Complete Anas*, pp. 156–57; Jefferson to Madison, May 15, 1793, in *PJM*. Hamilton's perorations in cabinet sessions continued to grate on Jefferson. In August he complained that Hamilton delivered "three speeches of ¾ of an hour length each." Jefferson to Madison, August 11, 1793, ibid.

8. One historian has suggested that the Republicans pressed the foreign policy issue in American politics because they had few domestic policy ideas to offer as alternatives to Hamilton's financial system. Harry Ammon, "The Jeffersonian Republicans in Virginia: An Interpretation," *Virginia Magazine of History and Biography*, 71:153, 159 (1963). This conclusion is consistent with a report from Attorney General Edmund Randolph after a trip home that Virginians were dissatisfied with Hamilton personally but not with his policies. Jefferson to Madison, July 21, 1793, in *PJM*.

9. Harry Ammon, *The Genet Mission*, New York: W.W. Norton (1973), pp. vii, 52–55.

10. Ammon, *Genet Mission*, pp. 65–66, 69–70, 73, 80, 82–83; Jefferson to Madison, July 7, 1793, in *PJM*; Richard Beeman, *The Old Dominion and the New Nation*, Lexington: University Press of Kentucky (1972), p. 126.

11. Jefferson to Madison, June 9, 1793, ibid.

12. Jefferson to Madison, August 11, 1793, ibid.

13. Jefferson to Madison, July 7, 1793, in *PJM*.

14. "Helvidius" No. 4, September 14, 1793, ibid. Helvidius Priscus was a determined republican in Rome in the first century A.D., who opposed the increasing centralization of power under the emperors. Madison also had the private pleasure of relying on Hamilton's *Federalist* No. 75 for its warning against trusting the executive to make treaties on his own.

15. Madison to Jefferson, August 27, 1793, in *PJM*; Ketcham, pp. 344–45; Cunningham, *Jeffersonian Republicans I*, pp. 58–59; Madison to Archibald Stuart, September 1, 1793, in *PJM*.

16. Jefferson to Madison, September 1, 1793, ibid.; Madison to Archibald Stuart, September 1, 1793, ibid.

17. Jefferson to Madison, September 1, 1793, ibid.; J. H. Powell, *Bring Out Your Dead: The Great Plague of Yellow Fever in Philadelphia in 1793*, Philadelphia: University of Pennsylvania Press (1949), pp. 48, 114.

18. Jefferson to Madison, September 8, 1793, September 12, 1793, in *PJM*.

19. Powell, *Bring Out Your Dead*, pp. 216, 252.

20. For years, Madison would struggle to retrieve Kentucky lands that Ambrose had purchased for both of them without securing sound title. E.g., Madison to Hubbard Taylor, November 15, 1794, in *PJM*.

21. Washington to Madison, October 14, 1793, ibid.; Jefferson to Madison, November 17, 1793, ibid.; John Beckley to Madison, November 20, 1793, ibid.

22. Cunningham, *Jeffersonian Republicans I*, p. 69.

23. Ibid., p. 71; *Annals*, 3:157 (January 3, 1794) (Madison).

24. *Annals*, 3:213, 215 (January 14, 1794) (Madison).

25. Editor's Note, "Madison in the Third Congress, 2 December 1793–3 March 1795," in *PJM* (quoting William Lyman to Samuel Henshaw, January 17, 1794). After only six weeks back at Monticello, Jefferson shared with Madison a sobering insight that retirement had brought him. "I could not have supposed, when at Philadelphia," he wrote, "that so little of what was passing there could be known . . . here." The public's ignorance, he concluded, meant that "the people are not in a condition either to approve or disapprove of their government, nor consequently to influence it." Jefferson to Madison, February 15, 1794, in *PJM*. For men who aimed to represent the people, it was a depressing realization.

26. Madison to Jefferson, March 12, 1794, in *PJM*; Chernow, *Washington*, p. 715; Joshua Barney and others to Madison, March 13, 1794, in *PJM*; Madison to Jefferson, March 14, 1794, ibid.; Jefferson to Madison, April 3, 1794, ibid.

27. Madison to Jefferson, April 14, 1794, ibid.; Walter Stahr, *John Jay*, pp. 314–19; Samuel

Flagg Bemis, *Jay's Treaty: A Study in Commerce and Diplomacy*, New Haven: Yale University Press (1962), pp. 269–78.

28. Elkins and McKitrick, *Age of Federalism*, pp. 394–95; Madison to Jefferson, May 25, 1794, in *PJM*.

29. Eugene Perry Link, *Democratic-Republican Societies, 1790–1800*, New York: Columbia University Press (1942), passim.

30. Link, *Democratic-Republican Societies*, pp. 67, 143–44; Cunningham, *Jeffersonian Republicans I*, pp. 150–52.

31. Elkins and McKitrick, *Age of Federalism*, pp. 474–75; Jefferson to James Monroe, May 1795, in *PTJ*.

32. Madison to Monroe, December 4, 1794, in *PJM*.

33. Jefferson to Madison, December 28, 1794, ibid.

34. Jefferson to Madison, April 28, May 5, May 13, May 19, May 27, June 2, June 9, June 17, June 23, June 29, July 7, July 14, July 21, July 28, August 11, August 18, August 25, September 1, September 8, September 12, and September 15, 1793, in *PJM*; Madison to Jefferson, March 2, March 9, March 12, March 14, March 24, March 26, and March 31, 1794, ibid.; see Burstein and Isenberg, *Madison and Jefferson*, p. 284.

35. Jefferson to Madison, June 29, 1793 (crop rotation), in *PJM*; Madison to Jefferson, July 1, 1791 (Jamaica corn), ibid.; Madison to James Madison, Sr., June 15, 1791, ibid.; Jefferson to Madison, July 6, 1791 (African rice), ibid.; Madison to Jefferson, June 17, 1793, ibid.; Jefferson to Madison, May 5, 1793, and May 19, 1793 (threshing machine), ibid.; Madison to Jefferson, May 1, 1791 (table mechanism, with design drawing), ibid.; Jefferson to Madison, May 10, 1798 (locks and hinges), ibid.; Madison to Jefferson, May 20, 1798 (same), Madison to Jefferson, June 19, 1793, ibid.

36. Jefferson to Madison, April 27, 1795, ibid.

37. *Queen of America*, pp. 94–95; Catherine Allgor, *A Perfect Union: Dolley Madison and the Creation of the American Nation*, New York: Henry Holt and Co. (2006), pp. 25–29.

38. Catharine Coles to Dolley Payne Todd, June 1, 1794, in *PJM*.

39. Madison to Dolley Payne Todd, August 18, 1794, ibid.

40. Dolley Payne Todd to Eliza Collins Lee, September 16, 1794, in *Selected Letters*, p. 31.

41. Madison to Jefferson, October 5, 1794, in *PJM*.

CHAPTER 14: PARTY WARRIOR

1. Pierce Butler to Madison, June 26, 1795, in *PJM*; Madison to Monroe, December 20, 1795, ibid.

2. Hamilton to Washington, April 14, 1794, in *PGW*.

3. Bemis, *Jay Treaty*, pp. 372–73; Ketcham, pp. 356–57.

4. Madison to Robert R. Livingston, August 10, 1795, in *PJM*; Madison to Jefferson, August 6, 1795, ibid.; Madison to Henry Tazewell, September 25, 1795, ibid.; Elkins and McKitrick, *Age of Federalism*, pp. 420–21.

5. Chernow, *Alexander Hamilton*, pp. 494–96; Elkins and McKitrick, *Age of Federalism*, p. 432; Jefferson to Madison, September 21, 1795, in *PJM*.

6. Maclay, *Journal*, p. 205.

7. Curtis P. Nettles, *The Emergence of a National Economy, 1775–1815*, New York: Holt, Rinehart & Winston (1962), p. 222; Elkins and McKitrick, *Age of Federalism*, pp. 441, 842–43.

8. Madison to Jefferson, December 13, 1795, in *PJM*.

9. Madison to Jefferson, October 18, 1795, November 8, 1795, in *PJM*; Jefferson to Madison, November 21, 1795, ibid.; Ellis, *American Sphinx*, pp. 187–88.

10. Madison to Monroe, December 20, 1795, January 26, 1796, in *PJM*; Madison to Pendleton,

February 7, 1796, in *PJM*; William Branch Giles to Jefferson, December 9, 1795, and December 20, 1795, in *PTJ*.

11. *Annals*, 4:490–91, 493 (March 10, 1796) (Madison).

12. *Annals*, 4:760–62 (March 30, 1796); Cunningham, *Jeffersonian Republicans I*, p. 82.

13. *Annals*, 4:776–77 (Madison) (April 6, 1796). Rather than pin his argument on the supposed authoritativeness of the ratifying conventions, Madison could have insisted that the Convention's rejection of the provision requiring House approval of treaties simply avoided a redundancy in the Constitution: Since all legislative power was confided jointly to the House and the Senate, the House's ability to reject legislation implementing treaties was already established by Article I.

14. Ketcham, p. 362.

15. *Annals*, 4:969–76 (April 15, 1796) (Madison).

16. For example, Madison had voted on one occasion for the chief executive officer to be chosen for life—a vote that would deeply embarrass him (should it ever come to light) as the opponent of supposed monarchist forces in American politics. Farrand, 2:34n, 2:36n; Stewart, *Summer of 1787*, p. 308n.

17. See Burstein and Isenberg, *Madison and Jefferson*, p. 308; Brant, *Father of the Constitution*, 3:437.

18. Adams to Abigail Adams, April 28, 1796, in *AP*; Ketcham, p. 365; Madison to Jefferson, May 1, 1796, in *PJM*.

19. Madison to Jefferson, May 22, 1796, in *PJM*.

20. Madison to Monroe, May 14, 1796, ibid.

21. Jefferson to Madison, December 28, 1794 (emphasis added), ibid.

22. Madison to Jefferson, March 23, 1795, ibid.

23. Jefferson to Madison, April 27, 1795, ibid.

24. For a party manager like Madison, Jefferson's greatest negative was his occasional indulgence in a well-turned but ill-considered phrase. In 1791, arranging an American edition for Thomas Paine's controversial volume *The Rights of Man*, Jefferson dashed off a cover letter to the printer applauding Paine's challenge to "the political heresies that have sprung up among us." When the printer included those words as a book preface, a brief furor forced Jefferson to write a letter of explanation to President Washington, though the episode confirmed Jefferson's identity as a sturdy opponent of the Federalists. In 1797, a comparable brouhaha broke out with the release of a letter from Jefferson to Philip Mazzei referring to "apostates who have gone over to those heresies, men who were Samsons in the field and Solomons in the council, but who have had their heads shorn by the harlot England." The passage was widely understood to refer to President Washington, but that controversy blew over as well. Meacham, *Art of Power*, pp. 252, 309.

25. Madison to Monroe, February 26, 1796, in *PJM*.

26. Virginia had 822,000 people, both free and slave, of the 3.9 million in the entire nation. Its land area, which included the future West Virginia, represented 18.9 percent of the total for all of the states, or 109,465 square miles out of 549,813.

27. Jeffrey L. Pasley, "'A Journeyman, Either in Law or Politics': John Beckley and the Social Origins of Political Campaigning," *Journal of the Early Republic*, 16:531, 553 (1996); Noble E. Cunningham, "John Beckley: An Early American Party Manager," *William and Mary Quarterly*, 13:40 (1956); John Beckley to Madison, September 10, 1795, in *PJM*; Jefferson to Madison, September 21, 1795, in *PJM* (has received a box of pamphlets from Beckley); John Beckley to Madison, October 15, 1796, ibid. (30,000 pamphlets). Beckley epitomized the upward social mobility that America came to represent. After emigrating from England as an indentured servant at age twelve, Beckley attended the College of

William and Mary and rose to be mayor of Richmond. As an ally of Madison's in 1789, he became clerk of the new House of Representatives and roomed in the same New York boardinghouse with him.

28. Cunningham, *Jeffersonian Republicans I*, pp. 91–92; John Beckley to Madison, June 20, 1796, in *PJM*.

29. Cunningham, *Jeffersonian Republicans I*, pp. 92–108; John Beckley to Madison, October 15, 1796, in *PJM*.

30. Madison to Henry Tazewell, October 18, 1796, ibid.; Madison to Jefferson, December 10, 1796, ibid.; Jefferson to Madison, December 17, 1796, ibid.

31. Jefferson to Madison, January 8, 1797, ibid.

32. Jefferson to Adams, December 28, 1796 (unsent), in *PTJ*; Jefferson to Madison, January 1, 1797, in *PJM*; Madison to Jefferson, January 15, 1797, ibid.; Jefferson to Madison, January 30, 1797, ibid.

33. Monroe to Madison, February 27, 1796; Madison to Jefferson, January 15, 1797, ibid.; Jefferson to Madison, January 8, 1797, ibid.; Madison to James Madison, Sr., March 27, 1797, ibid.

34. Leibiger, *Founding Friendship*, p. 216; Washington to Madison, January 22, 1796, March 16, 1796, ibid.; Hamilton to Washington, January 25–31, 1797, ibid.; Hamilton to Timothy Pickering, March 22, 1797, ibid.; Hamilton to Oliver Wolcott, Jr., January 25–31, 1797, in *PAH*; Elkins and McKitrick, *Age of Federalism*, pp. 542–44.

35. Jefferson to Madison, March 6, 1796, in *PJM*; Madison to Jefferson, April 4, 1796, ibid.

36. Madison to James Madison, Sr., March 13, December 19, and December 25, 1796; February 5, February 13, March 12, March 19, and March 27, 1797, ibid.

37. Adams to Abigail Adams, January 14, 1797, in *AP*.

CHAPTER 15: NO TIME FOR QUALMS

1. Madison to William Bradford, April 28, 1773, in *PJM*.

2. Ketcham, pp. 368–70; Francis Taylor Diary, April 10, 1786, in Southern Historical Collection, University of North Carolina Library.

3. Wulf, *Founding Gardeners*, p. 195.

4. Madison to Jefferson, April 15, 1798, December 11, 1798; Madison to Monroe, December 17, 1797, January 30, 1799, July 20, 1799, in *PJM*.

5. Vernon G. Setser, *The Commercial Reciprocity Policy of the United States, 1774–1829*, Philadelphia: University of Pennsylvania Press (1937), p. 184; Ketcham, pp. 373–74; Madison to Jefferson, April 15, 1798, in *PJM* (bemoaning frost and heavy rains); Madison to Jefferson, May 20, 1798 (drought), ibid.; Madison to Jefferson, October 1, 1800 (Hessian fly devastating fields), ibid.

6. Ketcham, p. 371; Allgor, *Perfect Union*, passim.

7. Jefferson to Madison, November 26, 1799, February 5, 1799; January 16, 1799, in *PJM*.

8. "Political Reflections," February 23, 1799, ibid.

9. Madison to James Madison, Sr., March 12, 1797, ibid.; Jefferson to Madison, June 1, 1797, February 12, 1797, March 29, 1798, ibid.; Henry Tazewell to Madison, June 4, 1797, ibid.; Elkins and McKitrick, *Age of Federalism*, p. 510. Madison predicted that Jay's Treaty "will have annihilated the marine of a maritime country by a single stroke of his pen." Madison to Jefferson, March 4, 1798, in *PJM*.

10. Jefferson to Madison, June 8, June 15, 1797, ibid.; Henry Tazewell to Madison, June 11, 1797, ibid.

11. James Monroe, *A View of the Conduct of the Executive in the Foreign Affairs of the United States Connected with the Mission to the French Republic During the Years 1794, 5 & 6*, Philadelphia: Benjamin Franklin Bache (1797); Jefferson to Madison, February 15, 1798,

in *PJM*. Madison's comment on the contest between Representative Lyon (iron tongs) and Griswold (wooden cane) came very close to endorsing dueling, a surprising statement from a man not known for physical truculence. The worst feature of the incident, Madison wrote to Jefferson, was that it became the subject of House debate. "[I]f Griswold be a man of the sword, he should not have permitted the step to be taken; if not he does not deserve to be avenged by the House. No man ought to reproach another with cowardice, who is not ready to give proof of his own courage." February 18, 1798, ibid.

12. Madison to Jefferson, April 15, 1798, ibid.

13. Jefferson to Madison, March 21, 1798, April 19, 1798, May 10, 1798, ibid.; David McCullough, *John Adams,* New York: Simon & Schuster (2000), pp. 496–98, 501; Jefferson to John Taylor, June 4, 1798, in *PTJ*.

14. Elkins and McKitrick, *Age of Federalism*, pp. 595–96; McCullough, *John Adams*, p. 501; Adams proclamation, March 23, 1798, in *AP*.

15. Madison to Jefferson, May 13, 1798, in *PJM*.

16. *Annals*, 5:589–91 (June 26, 1798); Elkins and McKitrick, *Age of Federalism*, pp. 591–92.

17. James Fairfax McLaughlin, *Matthew Lyon, the Hampden of Congress,* New York: Wynkoop Hallenbeck Crawford Company (1900), pp. 343–44, 374–75; Jefferson to Madison, November 3, 1798, in *PJM*.

18. E.g., Circular letter from John Dawson, July 19, 1798 (arguing that Sedition Act violates First Amendment), in *PJM*; Jefferson to Madison, June 7, 1798, ibid.

19. Cunningham, *Jeffersonian Republicans I*, p. 126; Koch, *Jefferson and Madison*, pp. 185–87.

20. Adrienne Koch and Harry Ammon, "The Virginia and Kentucky Resolutions: An Episode in Jefferson's and Madison's Defense of Civil Liberties," *William and Mary Quarterly*, 5:145, 156 (1948).

21. When Jefferson reviewed Madison's draft resolution, he objected that it should include language that the Alien and Sedition Acts were "no law, but utterly void, and of no force or effect." That bold language was included in the draft presented to the Virginia legislature but then was deleted by the legislature. Madison had not included such language in his draft and surely did not wish to see it in the final version. Ed. Note, "Virginia Resolutions: December 21, 1798," in *PJM*; Jefferson to Wilson Cary Nicholas, November 29, 1798, in *PTJ*.

22. Elkins and McKitrick, *Age of Federalism*, p. 720; Beeman, *Old Dominion*, pp. 204, 209.

23. Jefferson to Madison, August 23, 1799, in *PJM*.

24. Jefferson to Wilson Cary Nicholas, September 5, 1799, in *PTJ*.

25. Beeman, *Old Dominion*, p. 210.

26. John Taylor of Caroline to Madison, March 4, 1799, in *PJM*; Edmund Pendleton to Madison, May 12, 1799, ibid.; Ketcham, pp. 397–98.

27. In the "Report of 1800," Madison again flogged his dubious theory that the actions of the state ratifying conventions should guide construction of the Constitution. He stressed that several states had requested an amendment protecting free speech, which he called "the most satisfactory and authentic proof" that the First Amendment was authoritative. Of course, the most satisfactory and authentic proof of the power of the First Amendment was that it had been ratified as part of the Bill of Rights. That it was proposed in several state ratifying conventions in 1788 gave it no additional force whatever.

28. Garrett Ward Sheldon, "James Madison, the Virginia Resolutions, and the Philosophy of Modern Democracy," in Leibiger, *Companion to James Madison*, p. 174.

29. Madison to Jefferson, January 9, 1800, in *PJM*. One scholar fairly attributes the more sober tone of the "Report of 1800" to the pending presidential election, as well as the negative response by other states to the Virginia and Kentucky Resolutions. Kevin Gutzman, "A 'Troublesome Legacy': James Madison and 'The Principles of '98,'" *J. Early*

Rep., 15:569, 583 (1995). An equally strong factor was Madison's characteristic caution in qualifying his positions and avoiding extreme statements.

30. *Ableman v. Booth*, 62 U.S. 506 (1859); *Cooper v. Aaron*, 358 U.S. 1 (1958).

31. Notably, Admiral Horatio Nelson's fleet had demolished a French fleet at the Battle of the Nile in August 1798.

32. McCullough, *John Adams*, pp. 523–25; Jefferson to Madison, January 30, 1799, in *PJM*.

33. *Richmond Examiner*, December 20, 1799; Madison to Jefferson, February 18, 1798, in *PJM*.

34. James Callender, *The Prospect Before Us*, Richmond: M. Jones, S. Pleasants, Jun., and J. Lyon (1800), pp. 30–31; Cunningham, *Jeffersonian Republicans I*, p. 219.

35. Meacham, *Art of Power*, p. 322; Jefferson to Madison, August 29, 1800, in *PJM*; Fawn M. Brodie, *Thomas Jefferson: An Intimate History*, New York: W.W. Norton & Co. (1974), p. 325; William P. Cutler and Julia Cutler, eds., *Life, Journals, and Correspondence of Rev. Manasseh Cutler*, Cincinnati: Robert Clarke & Co. (1888), 2:56.

36. *Philadelphia Aurora*, January 23, 1799.

37. Cunningham, *Jeffersonian Republicans I*, p. 139; Charles Pinckney to Madison, May 16, 1799, in *PJM*; Madison to Jefferson, November 22, 1799, ibid. For example, Charles Pinckney of South Carolina sent letters to Madison and Monroe in the care of Joseph Alston, a fellow South Carolina Republican and the prospective son-in-law of Aaron Burr. Madison to Jefferson, October 21, 1800, ibid.; Madison to Monroe, October 21, 1800, ibid.

38. Charles Pinckney to Madison, May 16, 1799, September 30, 1799, ibid.; John Dawson to Madison, November 28, 1799, ibid.; Stevens Mason to Madison, January 16, 1800, ibid.; Madison to Monroe, October 21, 1800, ibid.

39. Beeman, *Old Dominion*, pp. 216, 221–22; Cunningham, *Jeffersonian Republicans I*, pp. 155, 159–60, 195, 197–98; Brodie, *Intimate History*, p. 324.

40. John Dawson to Madison, November 28, 1799, in *PJM*; Jefferson to Madison, March 8, 1799, ibid.; John Dawson to Madison, May 4, 1800, ibid.

41. Charles Peale Polk to Madison, June 20, 1800, ibid.; Dawson to Madison, July 28, 1800, August 17, 1800, ibid.

42. Jefferson to Monroe, February 16, 1800, in *PJM*; Cunningham, *Jeffersonian Republicans I*, p. 146; Madison to Jefferson, March 15, 1800, in *PJM*; Elkins and McKitrick, *Age of Federalism*, p. 730.

43. Stevens Mason to Madison, April 23, 1800, in *PJM*; Madison to Jefferson, May 23, 1800, ibid.; John C. Miller, *Crisis in Freedom: The Alien and Sedition Acts*, Boston: Little, Brown & Co. (1951), pp. 203–5, 223.

44. Madison to Jefferson, November 1–3, 1800, quoted in Ed. Note, "Introductory Note: Letter from Alexander Hamilton, Concerning the Public Conduct and Character of John Adams, Esq., President of the United States," October 24, 1800, in *PAH*. Madison later wrote to Jefferson that Hamilton's pamphlet "has perhaps more deeply wounded the author than the object it was discharged at." Madison to Jefferson, January 10, 1801, in *PJM*.

45. Cunningham, *Jeffersonian Republicans I*, pp. 236–37.

46. Monroe to Madison, November 6, 1800, in *PJM*; Madison to Monroe, November 10, 1800, ibid.; Madison to Jefferson, January 10, 1801, ibid.; Madison, "Autobiography," December 1830, ibid.

47. Edward J. Larson, *A Magnificent Catastrophe: The Tumultuous Election of 1800, America's First Presidential Campaign*, New York: Free Press (2007), pp. 244–54, 259–70; David O. Stewart, *American Emperor: Aaron Burr's Challenge to Jefferson's America*, New York: Simon & Schuster (2009), pp. 18–24; Madison to Jefferson, January 10, 1801, in *PJM*.

48. Madison to Jefferson, January 10, 1801, February 28, 1801, ibid.
49. Monroe to Madison, September 29, 1800, in *PJM*; Douglas R. Egerton, *Gabriel's Rebellion: The Virginia Slave Conspiracies of 1800 and 1802,* Chapel Hill: University of North Carolina Press (1993); Monroe to Madison, September 9, 1800, in *PJM*; ; Link, *Democratic-Republican Societies,* pp. 184–85. Months after the uprising, one of Madison's cousins explained he would not be moving to a farm because "the late insurrection has rendered [my wife] very averse to the increase of the number of our slaves, which the settlement of a farm would make necessary." Reverend James Madison to Madison, December 28, 1800, in *PJM*.

CHAPTER 16: FRIENDS AND RIVALS AND FRIENDS

1. Joseph Jones to Madison, September 19, 1780, in *PJM*; Joseph Jones to Madison, November 10, 1780, ibid.; Madison to Edmund Randolph, February 4, 1783, ibid.; Joseph Jones to Madison, August 30, 1783, ibid.; Joseph Jones to Madison, June 8, 1783, ibid.
2. Harry Ammon, *James Monroe: The Quest for National Identity,* Charlottesville: University of Virginia Press (1971), pp. 8–28.
3. Ammon, *James Monroe,* p. 46 (quoting Sarah Vaughan to Catherine Livingston, October 10, 1784).
4. Jefferson to Madison, May 8, 1784, in *PJM*; Madison to Monroe, November 27, 1784, August 7, 1785, ibid.
5. Ammon, *James Monroe,* pp. 258 (Lord Henry Holland), 369 (William Wirt). John C. Calhoun of South Carolina, who knew Monroe much later in his career, offered a very similar description (ibid., p. 369): "I have known many much more rapid in reaching a conclusion, but few with a certainty so unerring."
6. In 1867, Monroe's grandson published a short and unfinished book that Monroe wrote during his retirement, which purported to compare the United States government with different republics of antiquity. Samuel Gouverneur, ed., James Monroe, *The People the Sovereigns,* Philadelphia: J.B. Lippincott & Co. (1867).
7. See *DHRC*, 9:845–76 (May 25, 1788) (reproducing entire text); Andrew Burstein, "Jefferson's Madison versus Jefferson's Monroe," *Presidential Studies Quarterly* (Spring 1998), p. 397.
8. Jefferson to Madison, January 30, 1787, in *PJM*.
9. Quoted in Noble Cunningham, *The Presidency of James Monroe,* Lawrence: University Press of Kansas (1996), p. 16 (Morgan Lewis).
10. Madison to Monroe, November 14, 1784, in *PJM*; Madison to Monroe, July 28, 1785, ibid.; Monroe to Madison, August 14, 1785, ibid.; Madison to Jefferson, October 3, 1785, ibid.; Ammon, *James Monroe,* p. 53.
11. Monroe to Madison, September 3, 1786, in *PJM*; Madison to Monroe, October 5, 1786, ibid.
12. Monroe to Madison, February 9, 1786, ibid.; Madison to Monroe, March 14, 1786, ibid.; Madison to Monroe, March 19, 1786, ibid.; Madison to Monroe, April 9, 1786, ibid.; Madison to Monroe, July 11, 1786, ibid.; Monroe to Madison, July 15, 1786, ibid. Separately, each man also bought Kentucky lands; Monroe claimed them through a land bounty earned for his military service, while Madison invested with his father and brother Ambrose. Madison to Jefferson, August 12, 1786, ibid.; Ammon, *James Monroe,* pp. 38–39; Ketcham, pp. 145–46. Monroe's domestic arrangements are addressed in Monroe to Madison, February 11, 1786, in *PJM*; March 19, 1786, ibid.; Madison to Monroe, February 6, 1787, ibid.; Madison to Monroe, February 25, 1787, ibid.
13. Monroe to Madison, February 6, 1787, ibid.; Madison to Monroe, February 25, 1787, ibid.

14. Madison to Monroe, March 14, 1786, ibid.; Monroe to Madison, September 3, 1786, ibid.; Burstein, "Jefferson's Madison," pp. 395–96.
15. Monroe to Jefferson, July 27, 1787, in *PJM*.
16. Monroe to Madison, October 13, 1787, ibid.; Monroe to Jefferson, April 10, 1788, ibid.; Madison to Jefferson, April 22, 1788, ibid.; Ammon, *James Monroe*, p. 68.
17. *DHRC*, 9:850, 853–54, 869, 874–75 (May 25, 1788) (Monroe's largely unpublished commentary on the Constitution); ibid., 9:1108–11 (June 10, 1788) (Monroe).
18. Monroe to Madison, November 22, 1788, in *PJM*; Edward Carrington to Madison, November 15 and November 26, 1788, ibid.; Henry Lee to Madison, December 8, 1788, ibid.; Joseph Jones to Madison, December 14, 1788, ibid.
19. The fullest description and analysis of the Madison-Monroe race in 1788 appears in Labunski, *Struggle for the Bill of Rights*, pp. 147–77. The account in this chapter draws on that work.
20. Monroe to Jefferson, February 15, 1789, in *PTJ*.
21. Madison to George Eve, January 2, 1789, in *PJM*; Madison to Thomas Mann Randolph, January 13, 1789, ibid.; Madison to a Resident of Spotsylvania County, January 27, 1789, ibid.; Madison to George Thompson, January 29, 1789, ibid.
22. Memorandum of N.P. Trist, December 3, 1827, in *PJM*; Gaillard Hunt, *The Life of James Madison*, New York: Doubleday, Page & Co. (1902), p. 165.
23. Edward Stevens to Madison, January 31, 1790, in *PJM*. Labunski presents a county-by-county analysis of the voting results. *Struggle for the Bill of Rights*, p. 175.
24. Madison to Jefferson, March 29, 1789, in *PJM*; Monroe to Jefferson, February 15, 1789, in *PTJ*.
25. Monroe to Madison, April 26, 1789, in *PJM*, Madison to Monroe, May 13, 1789, ibid.
26. Ammon, *James Monroe*, pp. 78–79; Jefferson to William Short, December 14, 1789, in *PTJ*. Monroe's property became the site of the University of Virginia in Charlottesville.
27. Madison to Jefferson, June 12, 1792, in *PJM*; Monroe to Madison, June 27, 1792, ibid.; Monroe to Madison, September 18, 1792, ibid.; Madison to Jefferson, August 27, 1793, ibid.; Madison to Jefferson, September 2, 1793, ibid.; Madison to Archibald Stuart, September 1, 1793, ibid.; Madison to Monroe, September 15, 1793, ibid.; Madison to Monroe, October 29, 1793, ibid.; Jefferson to Madison, November 17, 1793, ibid.
28. Ketcham, p. 353; Ammon, *James Monroe*, p. 113; Milton Lomask, *Aaron Burr: The Years from Princeton to Vice President, 1756–1805*, New York: Farrar Straus Giroux (1979), pp. 44–45; Stewart, *American Emperor*, pp. 295–96. Madison recommended Aaron Burr for the post, but Washington's mistrust of the New Yorker reached back to Continental Army days so he passed over Burr. Washington offered the post to another New Yorker, Robert Livingston, who also declined.
29. Monroe to Madison, May 26, 1794, in *PJM*; Monroe to Jefferson, May 27, 1794, in *PTJ*; Madison to James Madison, Sr., June 6, 1794, in *PJM*; Catharine Coles to Dolley Payne Todd, June 1, 1794, ibid.; Burstein and Isenberg, *Madison and Jefferson*, p. 293.
30. Monroe to Madison, November 30, 1794, in *PJM*; Madison to Monroe, March 26, 1795, ibid.; Madison to Monroe, March 27, 1795, ibid.
31. Monroe to Madison, October 23, 1795, in *PJM*; Monroe to Madison, January 20, 1796, ibid.; Madison to Monroe, January 25, 1796, ibid.; Monroe to Madison, June 7, 1796, ibid.
32. Monroe to Madison, September 2, 1794, ibid.; "Address to the National Convention," in *WJM*, 2:14 (August 14, 1794); Monroe to Secretary of State, ibid., 2:16 (August 15, 1794); Monroe to Madison, November 30, 1794, in *PJM*.
33. Monroe to Madison, September 2, 1794, ibid.
34. Monroe to Madison, February 18, 1795, ibid.; Monroe to Madison, December 18, 1795, ibid.; Madison to Monroe, March 11, 1795, ibid.

35. Monroe to Madison, November 30, 1794, ibid.; Monroe to Madison, September 8, 1795, ibid.; Monroe to Madison, October 23, 1795, ibid.

36. Madison to Monroe, April 7, 1796, ibid.; Monroe to Madison, September 20, 1796, ibid.; Monroe to Madison, September 20, 1796, ibid.; Madison to Monroe, September 29, 1796, ibid.; Ammon, *James Monroe,* pp. 139–40.

37. Monroe to Madison, December 10, 1797, ibid.; Madison to Monroe, February 5, 1798, ibid.; Monroe to Madison, February 6, 1798, ibid.; Monroe to Madison, July 13, 1799, ibid.

38. Madison to Jefferson, January 21, 1798, ibid.; Monroe to Madison, June 8, 1798, ibid.; Madison to Monroe, June 9, 1798, ibid.

39. Monroe to Madison, November 17, 1798, ibid.; Editorial Note, "Election of James Monroe" (December 6, 1799), ibid.

40. Monroe to Madison, May 15, 1800, ibid.; Monroe to Madison, September 9, 1800, ibid.; Monroe to Madison, October 8, 1800, ibid.; Egerton, *Gabriel's Rebellion*; Ammon, *James Monroe,* pp. 186–88.

41. Monroe to Madison, September 29, 1800, ibid.

42. Monroe to Madison, November 5, 1800, ibid.; Madison to Monroe, November 10, 1800, ibid.; Monroe to Madison, December 16, 1800, ibid.; Stewart, *American Emperor,* pp. 19–25.

CHAPTER 17: DISTANT DIPLOMACY

1. Wood, *Empire of Liberty,* pp. 302, 318–19, 479.

2. Ketcham, pp. 410–11; Mary Hackett, "James Madison's Secretary of State Years, 1801–1809: Successes and Failures in Foreign Relations," in Leibiger, *Companion to James Madison,* p. 177; Smelser, *Democratic Republic,* p. 52.

3. Smelser, *Democratic Republic,* pp. 22, 37; Madison to Jefferson, May 11, 15, 1808, in *PJM*; Ketcham, p. 409.

4. Madison to Wilson Cary Nicholas, July 10, 1801, in *PJM*; Madison to Jefferson, September 11, 1801, ibid.

5. Edward Thornton to Madison, March 17, 1802, ibid.

6. Madison to William Pinkney, October 21, 1807, ibid.

7. Augustus John Foster, *Jeffersonian America: Notes on the United States of America, Collected in the Years 1805–6–7 and 11–12,* San Marino, CA: Huntington Library (1954), p. 155. Madison's aggressive diplomacy raises the far less significant—but still intriguing—question whether his chess-playing style was equally pugnacious.

8. Monroe and Charles Pinckney to Madison, May 25, 1805, in *PJM*; George Erving to Madison, June 22, 1807, ibid.

9. Jon Kukla, *A Wilderness So Immense: The Louisiana Purchase and the Destiny of America,* New York: Anchor (2004), pp. 261–66. Monroe received official credentials to negotiate with both France and Spain, because France was in the process of acquiring Spain's Louisiana province under an earlier agreement. Whichever nation controlled New Orleans, Monroe would be authorized to make a deal with it.

10. Monroe to Madison, February 25, 1803, in *PJM*; Monroe to Madison, March 7, 1803, in *PJM*; Madison to Samuel Coleman, March 13, 1803, ibid.

11. Madison to Monroe and Robert Livingston, March 2, 1803, ibid.

12. Madison to Monroe and Livingston, July 29, 1803, ibid.

13. Monroe to Madison, May 14, 1803, ibid.; Livingston to Madison, July 30, 1803, ibid.; Monroe to Madison, August 11, 1803, ibid.; Monroe to Madison, August 23, 1803, ibid.; Monroe to Madison, September 6, 1803, ibid.; Livingston to Madison, September 17, 1803, ibid.; Monroe to Madison, June 28, 1804, ibid. Jefferson took Monroe's part

in the quarrel. After reviewing letters between Livingston and American commissioners negotiating a financial settlement over seized ships, the president decreed: "A more disgusting correspondence between men of sense . . . I have never read." Of Livingston, he added that "he has quarreled with every public agent with whom he had anything to do." Jefferson to Madison, August 18, 1804, ibid.

14. Livingston to Madison, May 20, 1803, ibid.; Monroe to Madison, May 23, 1803, ibid.; Livingston and Monroe to Madison, June 7, 1803, ibid.; Monroe to Madison, August 15, 1803, ibid.

15. Madison to Monroe, July 29, 1803, ibid. West Florida became part of the United States in 1810, following a brief rebellion and attendant political maneuvering. William C. Davis, *The Rogue Republic: How Would-Be Patriots Waged the Shortest Revolution in American History*, New York: Houghton Mifflin, Harcourt (2011).

16. Setser, *Commercial Reciprocity*, p. 161; Smelser, *Democratic Republic*, p. 144; James Stephen, *War in Disguise; or The Frauds of the Neutral Flags*, pp. 108–9, New York: Hopkins & Seymour (1806).

17. Bradford Perkins, *Prologue to War: England and the United States 1805–1812*, Berkeley: University of California Press (1961), pp. 73–74.

18. Ibid., p. 85.

19. Smelser, *Democratic Republic*, p. 141; Stephen, *War in Disguise*, pp. 117–18.

20. Madison to Monroe, May 15, 1806, in *PJM*; DeWitt Clinton to Madison, April 26, 1804, ibid.; Madison to DeWitt Clinton, June 25, 1804, ibid.; DeWitt Clinton to Madison, June 25, 1804, ibid.

21. Anthony Steel, "Anthony Merry and the Anglo-American Dispute about Impressment," *Cambridge Historical Journal*, 9:331, 338–39 (1949).

22. Perkins, *Prologue to War*, p. 91; Smelser, *Democratic Republic*, pp. 143, 206. John Quincy Adams denounced impressment as "an authorized system of kidnapping on the ocean." Dumas Malone, *Jefferson the President: Second Term, 1805–1809*, Charlottesville: University of Virginia Press (2d ed., 2005), p. 401.

23. Madison to Rufus King, July 24, 1801, in *PJM*; Madison to Monroe, January 5, 1804, ibid.

24. Monroe to Madison, September 20, 1803, ibid.; Monroe to Madison, October 21, 1803, ibid.; Madison to Monroe, December 26, 1803, ibid.

25. Perkins, *Prologue to War*, p. 8.

26. Ammon, *James Monroe*, p. 235; Monroe to Madison, May 26, 1805, in *PJM*.

27. Monroe and Charles Pinckney to Madison, March 1, 1805, ibid.; Charles Pinckney to Madison, March 3–17, 1805, ibid. ("I own I wish we had some more naval force; while my residence in Europe has given me the means of seeing the dreadful and atrocious consequences of anything like standing armies and increased my hostility to them, it has at the same time convinced me if we continue a commercial nation we must have some moderate increase of our [navy]."); Armstrong to Madison, October 3, 1805, ibid. After several years in Napoleonic France, United States Minister Robert Livingston sounded the same note: "I cannot again too strongly recommend putting ourselves in a posture of defense and having at least six ships of the line [battleships]. . . . [A] few ships would render us respectable abroad and safe at home." Robert Livingston to Madison, November 21, 1804, ibid.

28. Madison to Anthony Merry, July 7, 1804, ibid.; DeWitt Clinton to Madison, July 30, 1804, ibid.; Pichon to Madison, June 28, 1804, ibid.; Pichon to Madison, August 27, 1804, ibid.; Perkins, *Prologue to War*, p. 75; Ammon, *James Monroe*, p. 250. Two of the passengers trapped in New York with the French ships were Jerome Bonaparte, brother of the emperor, and his American then-wife, Elizabeth Patterson of Baltimore.

29. Monroe to Madison, August 10, 1804, in *PJM*.
30. Monroe and Charles Pinckney to Madison, March 1, 1805, ibid.; Monroe to Madison, May 16, 1805, ibid.
31. Monroe to Madison, March 5, 1807, ibid.; Monroe to Madison, May 3, 1805, ibid.; Monroe to Madison, May 26, 1805, ibid.; Monroe to Madison, June 30, 1805, ibid.; Monroe to Madison, July 14, 1804, ibid.; Monroe to Madison, May 26, 1805, ibid.; Monroe to Madison, February 2, 1806, ibid.; Monroe to Madison, December 14, 1804, ibid.
32. Madison to Monroe, April 23, 1806, ibid.; Madison to Monroe, May 18, 1806, ibid. In the fall of 1805, while Dolley was receiving treatment in Philadelphia for an abscess on her leg, Madison composed a lengthy study of the legal doctrines that underlay British intrusions on the mercantile rights of neutral nations. In a long, dense pamphlet, he concluded that the British legal theories were contrary to British law. Although Madison's pamphlet was far too learned to influence public opinion—one senator found it "often obscure and sometimes unintelligible . . . I have never read a book that fatigued me more"—the exercise of preparing it may well have had the effect of further cementing his hostility to British claims. E.S. Brown, ed., *William Plumer's Memorandum of Proceedings in the United States Senate 1803–1807*, New York: Macmillan (1923), pp. 387–89, 444.
33. Monroe and Pinkney to Madison, November 11, 1806, in *PJM*; Monroe and Pinkney to Madison, December 27, 1806, ibid.; Monroe and Pinckney to Madison, January 3, 1807, ibid.

CHAPTER 18: THE RUPTURE

1. Madison to Monroe and William Pinkney, February 3, 1807, in *PJM*.
2. Brant, *Secretary of State* (quoting from David Erskine, British Minister), p. 375; Perkins, *Prologue to War*, p. 135; Jefferson to Madison, April 21, 1807, in *PJM*.
3. Jacob Crowninshield to Madison, April 7, 1807, ibid.; Madison to Samuel Smith, March 25, 1807, ibid.; Samuel Smith to Madison, March 14, 1807, April 3, 1807, April 18, 1807, ibid.; Tench Coxe to Madison, April 1, 1807, ibid.
4. Madison to Monroe, March 20, 1807, ibid.; Madison to Monroe and William Pinkney, March 18, 1807, ibid.
5. Monroe to Jefferson, January 11, 1807, ibid.; Ketcham, pp. 450–52; Ammon, *James Monroe*, pp. 266–67.
6. Monroe and William Pinkney to Madison, April 22, 1807, in *PJM*.
7. Gallatin to Madison, April 13, 1807, in *PJM*; Donald R. Hickey, *The War of 1812: A Forgotten Conflict*, Urbana: University of Illinois Press (2012), p. 11; Jefferson to Madison, April 21, 1807, in *PJM*; Madison to Jefferson, May 4, 1807, ibid.
8. Madison to Monroe and William Pinkney, May 20, 1807, ibid.
9. Brant, *Secretary of State*, pp. 376–77; Ammon, *James Monroe*, p. 267.
10. Madison to Monroe, May 25, 1807, in *PJM*.
11. Monroe and Pinkney to Madison, April 22, 1807, and July 23, 1807, ibid.; Ammon, *James Monroe*, p. 269; Perkins, *Prologue to War*, pp. 137–38. The draft letter dated June 1, 1807, from Monroe to Jefferson, never sent, is published at *WJM*, 5:5.
12. In the words of a British historian, the British viewed the American warship as "a sort of fly-paper for deserters." Anthony Steel, "More Light on the *Chesapeake*," *Mariners' Mirror*, 39:265 (1953).
13. Ian Toll, *Six Frigates: The Epic History of the Founding of the U.S. Navy*, New York: W.W. Norton (2007), pp. 294–308; Mary Hackett, "James Madison's Secretary of State Years: 1801–1809," in Leibiger, *Companion to James Madison*, p. 186; Thomas Matthews to Madison, June 23, 1807, in *PJM*.

14. Madison to Jefferson, June 19, 1807, ibid.; Madison to James Bowdoin, July 15, 1807, ibid.

15. James Jay to Madison, July 4, 1807, ibid.; John Dawson to Madison, June 28, 1807, ibid.; Elbridge Gerry to Madison, July 5, 1807, ibid.; Jefferson to Lafayette, July 14, 1807, Library of Congress website, Thomas Jefferson Papers, http://memory.loc.gov /ammem/collections/jefferson_papers/; William Wirt to Carr, July 19, 1807, in John P. Kennedy, *Memoirs of the Life of William Wirt*, Philadelphia: J.B. Lippincott & Co. (1860), 1:197–99; Winfield Scott, *Memoirs of Lieutenant-General Scott*, New York: Sheldon & Co. (1864), 1:18–21; John G. Jackson to Madison, July 5, 1807, in *PJM*; Perkins, *Prologue to War*, pp. 144–48.

16. Monroe to Madison, October 10, 1807, in *PJM*; Monroe and Pinkney to Madison, October 10, 1807, ibid.; Pinkney to Madison, October 10, 1807, ibid.; Monroe and Pinkney to Madison, October 22, 1807, ibid.

17. Gerry to Madison, February 19, 1806, ibid.; Armstrong to Madison, September 24, 1807, ibid.; Perkins, *Prologue to War*, pp. 150, 163.

18. *National Intelligencer*, December 25, 1807.

19. Ketcham, pp. 461–62; Perkins, *Prologue to War*, pp. 162–63.

20. James Duncan Phillips, "Jefferson's 'Wicked Tyrannical Embargo,'" *New England Quarterly*, 18:466 (1945); James Jay to Madison, May 11, 1808; Charles Sellers, *The Market Revolution: Jacksonian America, 1815–1846*, New York: Oxford University Press (1991), p. 225.

21. James Sullivan to Madison, April 30, 1808, in *PJM*; Madison to Jefferson, August 10, 1808, ibid.; Smelser, *Democratic Republic*, pp. 167–69. Madison proposed sending federal gunboats to police the northern coastal trade.

22. John Willard to Madison, August 14, 1808, in *PJM*; Ray W. Irwin, "Governor Tompkins and the Embargo, 1807–1809," *New York History*, 22:311, 316–17 (1941); Douglas Lamar Jones, "'The Caprice of Juries': The Enforcement of the Jeffersonian Embargo in Massachusetts," *Am. J. Legal Hist.*, 24:307 (1980); Perkins, *Prologue to War*, p. 179; Alan Taylor, *The Civil War of 1812: American Citizens, British Subjects, Irish Rebels, and Indian Allies*, New York: Vintage (2011), p. 119; Perkins, *Prologue to War*, pp. 157, 162.

23. William Pinkney to Madison, August 2, 1808, in *PJM*; Ketcham, p. 462; Smelser, *Democratic Republic*, p. 162; Louis Martin Sears, "British Industry and the American Embargo," *Q.J. Econ.*, 34:88 (1919); William Pinkney to Madison, September 7, 1808, in *PJM*; John Armstrong to Madison, August 30, 1808, ibid. For economic analyses of the impact of the embargo, see Jeffrey A. Frankel, "The 1807–1809 Embargo Against Great Britain," *J. Econ. Hist.* 42:291 (1982); Sears, "British Industry and the American Embargo," supra. Gallatin, the Treasury Secretary whose revenue officers enforced the embargo, presciently predicted the policy's failure (Gallatin to Jefferson, December 18, 1807, in *PTJ*):

> [I]n every point of view, privations, sufferings, revenue, effect on the enemy, politics at home, etc., I prefer war to a permanent embargo. . . . [I]t is not without much hesitation that a statesman should hazard to regulate the concerns of individuals as if he could do it better than themselves. . . . As to the hope that it may . . . induce England to treat us better, I think it entirely groundless.

24. Madison to Monroe, May 17, 1806, in *PJM*; J.C.A. Stagg, "James Madison and the 'Malcontents': The Political Origins of the War of 1812," *William and Mary Q.*, 33:557, 565 (1976).

25. John Beckley to Monroe, July 13, 1806, in Noble Cunningham, *Jeffersonian Republicans in Power*, Chapel Hill: University of North Carolina Press (1963), p. 232 (hereafter *Jeffersonian Republicans II*).

26. Brown, *Plumer's Memorandum*, pp. 464–65; C. Peter Magrath, *Yazoo: Law and Politics in the New Republic, Case of* Fletcher v. Peck, Providence: Brown University Press (1966).

27. John S. Pancake, "The 'Invisibles': A Chapter in the Opposition to President Madison," *J. Southern Hist.*, 21:17 (1955) (quoting from *National Intelligencer,* March 8, 1808); Perkins, *Prologue to War,* p. 49.

28. John Randolph to James Monroe, September 6, 1806, in *WJM,* 4:486 n.1; Monroe to Randolph, November 12, 1806, ibid., 4:486; Monroe to Randolph, June 16, 1806, ibid., 4:460; Ammon, *James Monroe,* pp. 255–56. Some Republicans had approached Monroe about running for president in 1804, near the end of Jefferson's first term, but Monroe rejected their suggestions. Harry Ammon, "James Monroe and the Election of 1808 in VA," *WMQ,* 20:33, 37 (Jan. 1963).

29. Gov. William Cabell to Wilson Nicholas, January 9, 1808, in Cunningham, *Jeffersonian Republicans II,* p. 110; Irving Brant, "Election of 1808," in Arthur Schlesinger, Jr., ed., *History of American Presidential Elections, 1789–1968,* New York: McGraw-Hill (1971), 1:191 (quoting Representative Barent Gardenier of New York).

30. Cunningham, *Jeffersonian Republicans II,* pp. 108–14; Ammon, *James Monroe,* pp. 271–73.

31. Monroe to Dr. Walter Jones, January 24, 1808, in *WJM,* 5:22; Jefferson to Monroe, February 18, 1808, in *PTJ*; Monroe to Jefferson, February 27, 1808, in *PTJ.*

32. Madison to Monroe, January 5, 1808, in *PJM*; Monroe to Madison, January 19, 1808, ibid.

33. Monroe to Madison, February 3, 1808, ibid.; Madison to Monroe, February 6, 1808, ibid.

34. Monroe to Madison, February 28, 1808, ibid.; Monroe to Madison, March 5, 1808, ibid.; *Colvin's Weekly Register,* February 2, 1808 (noting that Monroe's partisans were attacking Madison for rejecting the treaty).

35. Madison to Monroe, March 21, 1808, in *PJM*; Monroe to Madison, March 26, 1808, ibid.; Monroe to Madison, March 28, 1808, ibid.; Madison to Monroe, March 30, 1808, ibid.; Monroe to Madison, April 5, 1808, ibid.; Madison to Monroe, April 18, 1808, ibid.

36. Morgan Lewis to Madison, January 9, 1808, ibid.; Henry Lee to Madison, February 10, 1808, ibid.; John Main to Madison, March 7, 1808, ibid.; Ketcham, p. 468; Cunningham, *Jeffersonian Republicans II,* pp. 118–21.

37. Monroe to [unidentified], July 13, 1808, in *WJM,* 5:53; Monroe to L.W. Tazewell, October 30, 1808, ibid., 5:66; Monroe to William Wirt, December 30, 1808, ibid., 5:84; Monroe to Sir Francis Baring, October 15, 1809, *Bull. NYPL* (1905), 5:380; Ammon, *James Monroe,* pp. 274–76; J.C.A. Stagg, "Madison, Monroe, and the War of 1812," in Leibiger, *Companion to James Madison,* p. 423. Monroe's letter to William Wirt reflects his unabashed expression of his feelings, so atypical for the era. "Your letter of this day," he wrote, "has equally surprised and hurt me."

38. Irving Brant elegantly summarized Madison's electoral victory ("Election of 1808," in Schlesinger, *American Presidential Elections,* 1:221):

    > Madison was fortunate in his competitors. Monroe, who started strongly, faded like a ghost. . . . Clinton had nothing to offer but personal ambition, the ground-out eulogies of a political machine, and the slanderous pen of the . . . press. Pinckney was the sacrificial offering of a disorganized party—a figurehead out of the dead political past—as unassailable and as potent as a tombstone.

39. Monroe to Jefferson, January 28, 1809, in *PTJ*; Harry Ammon, "James Monroe and the Election of 1808 in Virginia," *William & Mary Q.,* 20:33 (1963); Norman K. Risjord, *J. Southern Hist.,* 33:486 (1967). The Virginia popular vote reflects the very narrow franchise in that state. Though there were nearly a million people living in the state, almost 40 percent were enslaved. Assuming that women (also ineligible to vote) made up half of the white population of about 600,000, that left approximately 300,000 free males, perhaps two-thirds of whom were of voting age. Yet only 17,000 votes were cast.

40. Gallatin to William B. Giles, November 24, 1808, in E. James Ferguson, *Selected Writings of Albert Gallatin,* Indianapolis: Bobbs-Merrill Company, Inc. (1967), p. 301; Jefferson to Madison, March 11, 1808, in *PJM*. Jefferson's early withdrawal from the business of government was noted in his own letter in November 1808: "I think it fair to leave to those who are to act on them, the decisions they prefer, being to be myself but a spectator." Jefferson to Levi Lincoln, November 13, 1808, in *PTJ*; Gallatin to Madison, September 9, 1808, in *PJM*.

41. Madison to William Pinkney, February 11, 1809, in *PJM*.

42. Perkins, *Prologue to War,* pp. 226–33.

43. Jefferson to DuPont de Nemours, March 2, 1809, in *PTJ*.

Chapter 19: Reclaiming a Friend

1. Margaret Bayard Smith to Susan Bayard Smith, February 26, 1809, and March 1809, in Smith, *First Forty Years,* pp. 54–64; Allgor, *A Perfect Union,* p. 141; Charles Francis Adams, ed., *Memoirs of John Quincy Adams,* Philadelphia: J.B. Lippincott & Co. (1874), 1:544; Washington Irving to Henry Brevoort, September 22, 1810, quoted in Brian Jay Jones, *Washington Irving: An American Original,* New York: Arcade Publishing (2008), p. 107; Brant, *The President,* pp. 11–15 (1956).

2. "The New President," *The Ordeal,* 1:162 (March 18, 1809); Madison to William Pinkney, March 17, 1809, in *PJM*; Jefferson to Madison, March 17, 1809, ibid.; Elbridge Gerry to Madison, March 26, 1809, ibid.

3. William Branch Giles to Madison, February 27, 1809, ibid.; Wilson Cary Nicholas to Madison, March 3, 1809, ibid.; Ketcham, pp. 481–82.

4. Gallatin to Joseph H. Nicholson, December 29, 1808, in Henry Adams, *The Life of Albert Gallatin,* Philadelphia: J.B. Lippincott & Co. (1880), p. 384.

5. Monroe to Richard Brent, February 25, 1810; Monroe to Sir Francis Baring, *Bull. NYPL* (1905), 5:380.

6. Ketcham, p. 477.

7. Perkins, *Prologue to War,* pp. 233–34; Brant, *The President,* 5:48–49.

8. Ketcham, pp. 492–93; Perkins, *Prologue to War,* pp. 210–12; Madison to Gallatin, July 30, 1809, in *PJM*.

9. Robert Smith to Madison, April 15, 1809, in *PJM*; Perkins, *Prologue to War,* pp. 211–13; Ketcham, pp. 493–94.

10. Madison to Jefferson, April 24, 1809, in *PJM*; Jefferson to Madison, April 27, 1809, ibid.

11. Madison to Jefferson, June 20, 1809, ibid.; Gallatin to Madison, July 24, 1809, July 26, 1809, ibid.; Robert Smith to Madison, July 24, 1809, ibid.

12. Gallatin to John Montgomery, July 27, 1809, quoted in Perkins, *Prologue to War,* p. 219; Madison to Gallatin, July 28, 1809, in *PJM*; Richard Forrest to Madison, July 25, 1809, in *PJM* ("The attack on the *Chesapeake* did not produce half so violent a sensation" among Americans); John G. Jackson to Madison, July 28, 1809, ibid. ("British perfidy has kindled a flame throughout the country").

13. Presidential Proclamation, August 9, 1809, ibid.; Madison to Dolley Madison, August 7, 1809, ibid.; Perkins, *Prologue to War,* p. 219.

14. In his Message to Congress on November 29, 1809, Madison tried to distinguish the British repudiation of Erskine's agreement from his own repudiation of Monroe-Pinkney by claiming that Erskine had not departed from his instructions. That contention, however, does not bear scrutiny. Indeed, Madison might have avoided the political injury from the Agreement if he or Secretary Smith had asked to see Erskine's diplomatic instructions, a request that was not out of bounds in that era. Nevertheless, the Americans were entitled to rely on Erskine to represent his government's views accurately.

15. Caesar Rodney to Madison, September 6, 1809, in *PJM*; Robert Smith to Francis Jackson, October 19, 1809, November 1, 1809, November 8, 1809, ibid.; Madison to William Pinkney, December 4, 1809, ibid.; William Pinkney to Madison, March 23, 1810, November 24, 1810, ibid.; Smelser, *Democratic Republic,* p. 195.

16. David Bailie Warren to Madison, October 18, 1809, in *PJM*; Madison to William Pinkney, May 23, 1810, ibid.; J.C.A. Stagg, "James Madison and the 'Malcontents': The Political Origins of the War of 1812," *William and Mary Q.,* 33:557, 564 (1976).

17. Annual Message to Congress, November 29, 1809, in *PJM*.

18. Henry Adams, *History of the United States of America during the First Administration of James Madison, 1809–1813,* New York: Library of America (1986), pp. 221, 248; Madison to Jefferson, December 11, 1809, in *PJM*; Ketcham, pp. 498–99; Brant, *The President,* 5:113–15. The months-long argument that led to Representative John G. Jackson's duel is described in Stephen W. Brown, *Voice of the New West: John G. Jackson, His Life and Times,* Macon, GA: Mercer University Press (1985), pp. 85–91. Isaac Coles paid a twenty-dollar fine for the whipping incident. Allgor, *Perfect Union,* p. 258.

19. *Annals,* 11:754–55 (December 19, 1809) (Representative Macon); Madison to William Pinkney, January 20, 1810, in *PJM*; Henry Adams, *History,* pp. 130–31; Perkins, *Prologue to War,* p. 239.

20. Perkins, *Prologue to War,* pp. 241–42; Taggart to Rev. John Taylor, April 27, 1810, in George H. Hayne, ed., "Letters of Samuel Taggart, Representative in Congress, 1803–1814," American Antiquarian Society, *Proceedings,* 33:347; Madison to Jefferson, April 23, 1810, in *PJM*.

21. Madison to William Pinkney, May 23, 1810, ibid.; Madison to Jefferson, May 25, 1810, ibid.; James Hamilton to Francis Jackson, May 21, 1810, quoted in Perkins, *Prologue to War,* p. 243.

22. Perkins, *Prologue to War,* pp. 246–49; Jefferson to Madison, October 15, 1810, in *PJM*; Madison to Jefferson, October 19, 1810, ibid.

23. Madison to William Pinkney, January 20, 1810, in *PJM*; Madison to John Armstrong, October 29, 1810, ibid.; Madison to William Pinkney, October 30, 1810, ibid.; Presidential Proclamation restoring non-intercourse with Great Britain, November 2, 1810, ibid. The American Minister to France, John Armstrong, had advised Madison numerous times on the violent and unreliable nature of Napoleonic rule. E.g., John Armstrong to Madison, January 2, 1809, and June 6, 1809, ibid. On the choice between fighting Britain or France, Madison's advisers leaned toward challenging Britain. As Attorney General Caesar Rodney wrote to Madison on January 16, 1810, ibid.:

> England is our old and inveterate enemy. She has done us more injury. The impressment of our seamen alone is worse than all we have sustained from France. She is vulnerable by land & water. Her provinces we can conquer and the remnant of her commerce will become a prey to our privateers.

> Armstrong, Minister to France, raised the practical issue of how a war might be conducted against France on the other side of the Atlantic: "The Territory of this mighty Power is absolutely invulnerable; and there is no mode in which we could make her feel either physical or moral Coercion. We might as well declare War against the Inhabitants of the Moon." Armstrong to Madison, December 10, 1809, ibid.

24. Robert Smith to Louis-Marie Turreau, December 18, 1810, in *PJM*; Ketcham, pp. 505–6; Perkins, *Prologue to War,* p. 252; Annual Message to Congress, December 5, 1810, in *PJM*.

25. Ketcham, p. 505.

26. Perkins, *Prologue to War*, pp. 50–51; Smelser, *Democratic Republic*, p. 230. Elbridge Gerry, a prominent Massachusetts Republican, urged as early as 1806 that military spending be increased, though he preferred building up the navy rather than the army. E.g., Elbridge Gerry to Madison, February 19, 1806, and February 26, 1806, in *PJM*.

27. Albert Gallatin to Samuel Smith, June 29, 1809, in Adams, *Writings of Gallatin*, 1:454; Frank A. Cassell, *Merchant Congressman in the Young Republic: Samuel Smith of Maryland, 1752–1839*, Madison: University of Wisconsin Press (1971), pp. 134, 163–65.

28. Stagg, "James Madison and the 'Malcontents'": 5:562. In the 1790s, Samuel Smith, a merchant who usually sided with commercial interests, had opposed Madison's efforts in Congress to enact trade retaliation against Britain. Cassell, *Merchant Congressman*, pp. 49–54.

29. Drew R. McCoy, *The Last of the Fathers: James Madison and the Republican Legacy*, New York: Cambridge University Press (1989), pp. 80–81.

30. Cassell, *Merchant Congressman*, pp. 165–71.

31. Gallatin to Madison, March 7, 1811, in *PJM*. For an example of Smith's diplomatic correspondence first prepared by Madison, see Madison's draft of Robert Smith to John Armstrong, July 5, 1810, ibid.

32. Madison documented this exchange at some length: "Memorandum on Robert Smith," April 11, 1811, in *PJM*. Smith issued his own version of events, a pamphlet with the modest title "Robert Smith's Address to the People of the United States." One Virginian deftly summarized Smith's rhetorical shortcomings when he wrote that the pamphlet presented "a rare instance of a man's giving a finishing stroke to his own character, in his eagerness to ruin his enemy." Attorney General Caesar Rodney also captured the public response to Smith's effort: "O that mine enemy had written a book!" Ketcham, p. 490, quoting Henry St. George Tucker to James Garnett, July 1811; Caesar Rodney to Madison, August 24, 1811, in *PJM*.

33. Jefferson to Madison, March 30, 1809, ibid.

34. Jefferson to Madison, November 27, 1809, and November 30, 1809, ibid. When Jefferson sounded him out about a military post, Monroe answered that "he would sooner be shot than take a command under [General-in-Chief James] Wilkinson." As Wilkinson had been a secret agent of the Spanish king and a participant in Aaron Burr's extraordinary plan for the private conquest of Spanish Mexico and Florida—and was arguably an incompetent buffoon—Monroe's judgment on that point seems impeccable. Stewart, *American Emperor*, pp. 60–62, passim.

35. Ammon, *James Monroe*, pp. 282–83.

36. Ibid.; Jefferson to Madison, May 25, 1810, in *PJM*; Madison to Monroe, July 16, 1810, ibid.; Monroe to Madison, July 25, 1810, ibid.

37. Ammon, *James Monroe*, p. 286; Madison to Monroe, March 20, 1811, in *PJM*.

38. Monroe to Madison, March 23, 1811, ibid.; Madison to Monroe, March 26, 1811, ibid.; Monroe to Jefferson, April 3, 1811, in *PTJ*. The core of Madison's reply to Monroe was the following:

> [W]ith the mutual knowledge of our respective views of the foreign as well as domestic interests of our Country, I see no serious obstacle on either side, to an association of our labors in promoting them. In the general policy of avoiding war, by a strict and fair neutrality towards the Belligerents, and of settling amicably, our differences with both; or with either, as leading to a settlement with the other; or that failing, as putting us on better ground against him, there is and has been an entire concurrence among the most enlightened who have shared in the public Councils since the year 1800. A like concurrence has prevailed in the opinion, that whilst on one hand, it is of great importance to the interests of the U. S. that peace should be

preserved, and commerce obtained with the Continent of Europe, there are on the other hand, powerful reasons in favor of an adjustment with the great Maritime power, who, tho' liable to suffer much from our enmity, is capable also of doing us much harm or good, according to her disposition towards us. In favor of a cordial accommodation with G. Britain, there has certainly never ceased to be a prevailing disposition in the Executive Councils, since I became connected with them. In the terms of accommodation, with that as with other powers, differences of opinion must be looked for, even among those most agreed in the same general views. These differences however lie fairly within the compass of free consultation and mutual concession, as subordinate to the necessary Unity belonging to the Executive Dept.

39. Monroe to Dr. Charles Everett, April 23, 1811, in *WJM*, 5:185.
40. Ammon, *James Monroe*, pp. 282–86; J.H. Powell, *Richard Rush, Republican Diplomat 1780–1859*, Philadelphia: University of Pennsylvania Press (1942), p. 38; Jefferson to Monroe, May 5, 1811, in *PTJ*.
41. Abbot Smith, "Mr. Madison's War: An Unsuccessful Experiment in the Conduct of National Policy," *Pol. Sci. Q.*, 57:229, 240 (1942) (arguing that Madison was resolved upon war before taking the oath of office in 1809); Paul Jennings, "A Colored Man's Reminiscences of James Madison," in Elizabeth Dowling Taylor, *A Slave in the White House: Paul Jennings and the Madisons*, New York: Palgrave Macmillan (2012), p. 230; Annual Message to Congress, November 5, 1811, in *PJM*.

CHAPTER 20: THE REPUBLICAN WAY OF WAR

1. Smelser, *Democratic Republic*, pp. 219–24; Monroe to Lord Auckland, Fall 1811, in *WJM*, 5:191–93; Wood, *Empire of Liberty*, p. 659 (quoting John Taylor). In a similar vein were the views of Monroe's successor as governor of Virginia and John Quincy Adams. James Barbour to Madison, January 29, 1812, in *PJM*; John Quincy Adams to Abigail Adams, August 10, 1812, in Worthington Chauncey Ford, ed., *Writings of John Quincy Adams*, New York: The Macmillan Co. (1914), 4:388.
2. Ketcham, p. 516; J.C.A. Stagg, "James Madison and the 'Malcontents,'" pp. 383–84; Hickey, *The War of 1812*, p. 30; Dolley Madison to Anna Cutts, December 22, 1811, in *Selected Letters*, p. 153; Jefferson to Madison, February 19, 1812, in *PJM*; Henry Clay to Caesar Rodney, August 17, 1811, in James F. Hopkins, *Papers of Henry Clay*, Lexington: University of Kentucky Press (1959), 1:574; Madison to Jefferson, March 6, 1812, February 7, 1812, and April 3, 1812, in *PJM*; Dearborn to Madison, April 6, 1812, ibid. Many Americans had an exaggerated sense of how easy it would be to conquer Canada. One correspondent assured Madison it could be achieved "without the loss of a drop of blood!" Samuel DuPont de Nemours to Madison, January 20, 1812, ibid.
3. Message to Congress, March 9, 1812, in *PJM*; Ketcham, p. 518. The Henry episode was best captured in Samuel Eliot Morison, *By Land and By Sea*, New York: Alfred A. Knopf (1953), pp. 266–83, on which this passage draws.
4. Stagg, *Mr. Madison's War*, pp. 93–98.
5. Message to Congress, April 1, 1812, in *PJM*; Madison to Jefferson, May 25, 1812, in ibid.; Message to Congress, June 1, 1812, ibid.
6. Richard Rush to Benjamin Rush, June 20, 1812, in Richard Rush Collection.
7. Christopher Ellery to Madison, June 24, 1812, in *PJM*; Samuel Thurber to Madison, July 27, 1812, ibid.; Henry Dearborn to Madison, June 26, 1812, and July 3, 1812, ibid.; Ketcham, p. 537; Madison to Richard Cutts, August 8, 1812, ibid.
8. Paul A. Gilje, "The Baltimore Riots of 1812 and the Breakdown of the Anglo-American Mob Tradition," *J. Social History* 13:547 (1980); Benjamin Wittes and Ritika Singh, "James Madison, Presidential Power, and Civil Liberties in the War of 1812," in Pietro

S. Nivola and Peter J. Kastor, eds., *What So Proudly We Hailed: Essays on the Contemporary Meaning of the War of 1812*, Washington, DC: Brookings Institution Press (2012), p. 109.

9. Monroe to Col. John Taylor, June 13, 1812, in *WJM*, 5:205.

10. Wood, *Empire of Liberty*, p. 674; Edward K. Eckert, "William Jones: Mr. Madison's Secretary of the Navy," *Pa. Mag. Hist. & Biog.*, 96:167, 168 (1972); Taylor, *Civil War of 1812*, p. 128.

11. Memorandum of George Bancroft, March 1836, enclosed in Bancroft to Henry Adams, April 11, 1878, in Henry Adams, *Life of Albert Gallatin*, pp. 460–61, n.1.

12. Madison to Gallatin, August 8, 1812, ibid.; Stagg, *Mr. Madison's War*, pp. 118–19.

13. Powell, *Richard Rush*, p. 42; Scott, *Memoirs*, 1:35–36; David Jones to Madison, August 28, 1812, in *PJM*; Richard Rush to Charles J. Ingersoll, September 9, 1812, September 18, 1812, in Richard Rush Collection.

14. Madison to Jefferson, August 17, 1812, in *PJM*; Samuel Spring to Madison, August 26, 1812, ibid.; William Keteltas to Madison, September 12, 1812, ibid.; Hickey, *War of 1812*, p. 86.

15. J.C.A. Stagg, "James Monroe, James Madison, and the War of 1812: A Difficult Interlude," in Leibiger, ed., *Companion to James Madison*, p. 426; Monroe to Madison, September 2, 1812, September 7, 1812, September 8, 1812, September 9, 1812, September 10, 1812, and September 12, 1812, in *PJM*; Madison to Monroe, September 5, 1812, and September 6, 1812, ibid.; Madison to William Eustis, September 6, 1812, and September 8, 1812, ibid.; Richard Rush to Charles J. Ingersoll, September 19, 1812, in Richard Rush Collection; Smelser, *Democratic Republic*, p. 248.

16. C. Edward Skeen, *John Armstrong, Jr., 1758–1843: A Biography*, Syracuse University Press (1981), p. 127; Toll, *Six Frigates*, pp. 337–83; Message to Congress, November 4, 1812, in *PJM*; Message to Congress, December 11, 1812, ibid.; Message to Congress, February 22, 1813, ibid.

17. Madison to Jefferson, October 14, 1812, ibid.; Madison to the South Carolina Legislature, October 10, 1812, ibid.

18. Norman K. Risjord, "Election of 1812," in Schlesinger, *American Presidential Elections*, 1:255–56; Evan Cornog, *The Birth of Empire: DeWitt Clinton and the American Experience, 1769–1828*, New York: Oxford University Press (1998), pp. 96–101. John Quincy Adams deplored DeWitt Clinton's campaign because of its hypocritical demand for both peace and a more aggressive war policy, depending upon Clinton's audience. Ketcham, p. 545.

19. Gerry is often remembered as the author of a Massachusetts redistricting that spawned the term "gerrymander," because one electoral district had a distorted shape that an artist portrayed as a salamander.

20. Message to Congress, November 4, 1812, in *PJM*.

21. Stagg, *Mr. Madison's War*, pp. 277–78; Hickey, *War of 1812*, p. 105; Ammon, *James Monroe*, pp. 314–15; Monroe to Jefferson, June 7, 1813, in *PTJ*. In addition, some senators opposed a Monroe appointment as further evidence of Virginia's unwarranted domination of the national government.

22. Taylor, *Civil War of 1812*, p. 140; J.C.A. Stagg, "James Madison and the Coercion of Great Britain: Canada, the West Indies, and the War of 1812," *William and Mary Q.*, 38:3, 4–6 (1981).

23. Madison to Gallatin, August 26, 1812, in *PJM*; Madison to Dearborn, February 6, 1813, ibid. Even former president John Adams, in retirement in Massachusetts, wrote to Madison to make this point, as did other self-appointed advisers. John Adams to Madison, May 14, 1813, ibid.; Jonathan Dayton to Madison, September 17, 1812, ibid.; Marinus Willett to Madison, January 26, 1813, ibid.

24. Ammon, *James Monroe*, pp. 316–17; Stagg, *Mr. Madison's War*, p. 280; Richard Rush to Charles J. Ingersoll, December 28, 1812, in Richard Rush Collection.

25. Jefferson to Madison, April 24, 1811, note 4, in *PJM*; Skeen, *Armstrong*, pp. 100, 123; Armstrong to Madison, March 25, 1809, in *PJM*. Gallatin, who supported the appointment, admitted that the New Yorker might not generate an "entire unity of feeling, that disinterested zeal, that personal attachment which are so useful in producing hearty cooperation." Gallatin to Madison, January 7, 1813, ibid.

26. Monroe to Madison, February 25, 1813, note 1, in *PJM* (reproducing draft letter to Madison); Mackubin Thomas Owens, "James Monroe as Secretary of State and Secretary of War, 1809–1817: Toward Republican Strategic Sobriety," in Leibiger, ed., *Companion to James Madison*, pp. 414–15; Stagg, ibid., pp. 427–28; Brook Poston, "James Monroe and James Madison: Republican Partners," ibid., p. 516.

27. For a number of years, Wilkinson had been a secret agent of the Spanish king while also serving as general-in-chief of the American army. He quartered his troops in Louisiana Territory in such an unhealthful location that he lost half of them to disease and desertion. Stewart, *American Emperor*, pp. 61–66; Hickey, *War of 1812*, pp. 141–42. Jefferson to Theodorus Bailey, February 6, 1813, in *PJM*. John Adams shared the general frustration with the nation's generals, some of whom—like Wilkinson—he had appointed to high position. "We want generals," he wrote in September 1813, "who know how to form an army, and such, as yet we have not." John Adams to Richard Rush, September 6, 1813, in Richard Rush Collection.

28. Smelser, *Democratic Republic*, p. 294; Skeen, *Armstrong*, p. 186; Taylor, *Civil War of 1812*, pp. 325–26; Hickey, *War of 1812*, pp. 167, 230. In late 1814, construction began on Fulton's proposed steam-powered warship, but it was not completed until after the war ended. Jefferson to Madison, July 13, 1813, in *PJM*; Robert Fulton to Madison, July 25, 1813, December 24, 1813, September 8, 1814, and November 5, 1814, ibid.; Benjamin Crowninshield to Madison, April 18, 1815, ibid.

29. Taylor, *Civil War of 1812*, pp. 245–46; Harrison to Armstrong, September 15, 1813, in *PJM*; Hubbard Taylor to Madison, November 5, 1813, ibid.; Annual Message to Congress, December 7, 1813, ibid.

30. Monroe to Madison, April 13, 1813, ibid.; Armstrong to Madison, July 16, 1813, ibid.; Monroe to Madison, July 18, 1813, ibid.; Madison to Monroe, July 19, 1813, ibid.; Ketcham, pp. 562–63.

31. Dolley Madison to Edward Coles, July 2, 1813, and Dolley Madison to Hannah Gallatin, July 29, 1813, in *Selected Letters*, pp. 177, 179; Monroe to Jefferson, June 18, 1813, in *PJM*. Republicans were so concerned about Madison's illness that Vice President Gerry, who was sixty-nine, made a point of never yielding his presiding chair in the U.S. Senate, thereby preventing the Senate from designating one of its members the president pro tem. Under legislation in effect at the time, the Senate president pro tem would have succeeded to office if both the presidency and vice presidency were vacant. With the Senate position vacant, the presidency would have fallen to House Speaker Clay, a Madison ally. Hickey, *War of 1812*, p. 122.

32. "Autobiography," December 1830, in *PJM*.

33. Minnie Clare Yarborough, ed., *The Reminiscences of William C. Preston*, Chapel Hill: University of North Carolina Press (1933), p. 7; Powell, *Richard Rush*, p. 38; Dolley Madison to Hannah Gallatin, July 28, 1813, in *Selected Letters*, p. 189.

34. Adams, *Memoirs of John Quincy Adams*, at 6:5; Monroe to Madison, December 27, 1813, in *PJM*.

35. Richard Rush to John Adams, August 1813, in Richard Rush Collection; Madison to Gallatin, August 2, 1813, ibid.; Stagg, *Mr. Madison's War*, p. 299 and n.110; Henry Adams, *History of the United States*, pp. 660–61; Joseph Anderson to Madison, July 12, 1813, in *PJM*; Ketcham, pp. 560–64.

36. Richard Rush to Charles J. Ingersoll, October 28, 1813, in Richard Rush Collection; "Francis Jeffrey's Account of a Conversation with Madison," November 18, 1813, and n.1, in *PJM* (quoting Jeffrey's Journal for November 15, 1813).

37. Madison, "Annual Message to Congress," December 7, 1813, ibid.

38. Hickey, *War of 1812*, pp. 152–53; Jefferson to Madison, February 16, 1814, ibid.

39. Stagg, *Mr. Madison's War*, pp. 375–76; John Haff to [New York congressmen?], January 28, 1814, in *PJM*; William Jones to Madison, March 9, 1814, ibid.; Jones to Madison, March 17, 1814, ibid.; Madison to Congress, March 31, 1814, ibid.; Hickey, *War of 1812*, pp. 169, 172–74. With the decline of French power in Europe in early 1814, most European ports opened to British trade, making the American embargo ineffective. Only four months after the embargo took effect, Madison reversed himself and asked for its repeal, which Congress was delighted to enact. Ibid., pp. 174–75.

40. Barry J. Lohnes, "A New Look at the Invasion of Eastern Maine," *Maine Hist. Soc. Q.* (Summer 1975), p. 15; Stagg, *Mr. Madison's War*, p. 410; Taylor, *Civil War of 1812*, pp. 253–58.

41. Madison to Congress, January 6, 1814, in *PJM*; Gallatin to William H. Crawford, April 21, 1814, in Ferguson, *Selected Writings of Albert Gallatin*, p. 334.

42. Stagg, *Mr. Madison's War*, p. 381.

43. Madison to Armstrong, May 20, 1814, in *PJM*; Madison to Jones, May 20, 1814, ibid.; Daniel Rasmussen, *American Uprising: The Untold Story of America's Largest Slave Revolt*, New York: Harper (2011) passim; Philip Stuart to Madison, July 29, 1814, ibid.; Steve Vogel, *Through the Perilous Fight: Six Weeks that Saved the Nation*, New York: Random House (2013), pp. 35–37; Alexander Dallas to Richard Rush, July 2, 1814, in Richard Rush Collection.

44. Jones to Madison, May 25, 1814, in *PJM*; Madison to Armstrong, June 3, 1814, ibid.; Madison to Jones, June 3, 1814, ibid.; "Cabinet Meeting Memorandum," June 7, 1814, ibid.; Stagg, *Mr. Madison's War*, pp. 394–95; "Memorandum of Cabinet Meeting," June 23–24, 1814, in *PJM*.

45. "Memorandum of Cabinet Meeting," June 27, 1814, ibid.

46. Madison to Armstrong, June 15, 1814, ibid.; Armstrong to Madison, May 14, 1814, ibid.; William Henry Harrison to Madison, May 11, 1814, ibid.; Armstrong to Madison, June 29, 1814, ibid.; Madison, Memorandum, July 6, 1814, ibid.

47. Madison to Armstrong, May 20, 1814, ibid.; Madison to Armstrong, July 2, 1814, ibid.; Madison to Armstrong, July 18, 1814, ibid.; Ketcham, pp. 574–75; Vogel, *Through the Perilous Fight*, p. 54; Stagg, *Mr. Madison's War*, pp. 408–10; "Memorandum on Defense of the City of Washington," July 1, 1814, in *PJM*; Monroe to Richard Rush, August 9, 1814, in Richard Rush Collection; Dolley Madison to Hannah Gallatin, July 30, 1814, in *Selected Letters*, p. 189; Madison to Nelly Conway Madison, August 8, 1814, in *PJM*. The letter of August 8 is one of only three surviving letters from Madison to his mother.

48. Madison to Armstrong, August 13, 1814, ibid. A week before, Madison had sent a testy direction to Armstrong to issue no commissions for army officers without the president's prior approval. Madison to Armstrong, August 4, 1814, ibid.

49. Vogel, *Through the Perilous Fight*, pp. 68–69, 78; Ammon, *James Monroe*, pp. 330–31; Madison to Monroe, August 21, 1814 (5 a.m.), in *PJM*; Madison to Monroe, August 21, 1814 (8 a.m.), ibid.; Monroe to Madison, August 21, 1814 (twice), ibid.; Monroe to Madison, August 22, 1814 (twice), ibid.

50. Madison to Monroe, August 22, 1814, ibid.; Powell, *Richard Rush*, p. 61; Madison to Dolley Madison, August 23, 1814, in *PJM*.

51. "Memorandum of Conversation with John Armstrong," August 24, 1814, ibid.; Vogel, *Through the Perilous Fight*, pp. 130–31.

52. Smith, *First Forty Years*, p. 103; Powell, *Richard Rush*, pp. 63–64.

53. Smith, *First Forty Years*, pp. 101, 104, 107; Vogel, *Through the Perilous Fight*, pp. 158–59, 182–83, 202–03; Jennings, *Reminiscences*, in Taylor, *Slave in the White House*, pp. 232–34.

54. William Thornton to Madison, August 30, 1814, in *PJM*; Allgor, *More Perfect Union*, p. 315.

CHAPTER 21: NEAR TO A MIRACLE

1. Richard Rush to John Adams, September 5, 1814, in Richard Rush Collection.

2. Hickey, *War of 1812*, p. 207 (quoting William Wirt to Elizabeth Wirt, October 24, 1814); Richard Rush to Charles Jared Ingersoll, in Richard Rush Collection, September 8, 1814; William Thornton to Madison, August 30, 1814; Allgor, *More Perfect Union*, p. 319; "J.M.'s Notes Respecting the Burning City in 1814," in *WJM*, 5:373–75; Vogel, *Through the Perilous Fight*, pp. 249–50.

3. "Memorandum of Conversation with John Armstrong," August 29, 1814, in *PJM*.

4. Presidential Proclamation, September 1, 1814, ibid.

5. Message to Congress, September 20, 1814, ibid.

6. Wood, *Empire of Liberty*, p. 688; Stagg, in Leibiger, *Companion to James Madison*, p. 432; Jones to Madison, October 10, 1814, in *PJM*; Ketcham, pp. 588–89; Hickey, *War of 1812*, pp. 232–33. The song "James Madison, My Jo" is preserved and performed by David Hildebrand, an expert in early American music, on his CD album *Music of the War of 1812*.

7. Rufus King to Jeremiah Mason, September 2, 1814, in Charles R. King, ed., *The Life and Correspondence of Rufus King*, New York: G.P. Putnam's Sons (1898), 5:414.

8. Edward Coles to Hugh Blair Grigsby, December 23, 1854, cited in McCoy, *Last of the Fathers*, p. 21.

9. Gallatin to Monroe, June 13, 1814, in Ferguson, *Selected Writings of Gallatin*, p. 341.

10. Madison to Congress, October 13, 1814, in *PJM*; Madison to Jefferson, October 10, 1814, ibid.; Madison to Congress, October 10, 1814, ibid.; Hickey, *War of 1812*, p. 293.

11. Hickey, *War of 1812*, pp. 199–203; James Banner, Jr., *To the Hartford Convention: The Federalists and the Origins of Party Politics in Massachusetts*, New York: Alfred A. Knopf (1970), pp. 315–30; Hickey, *War of 1812*, pp. 278–79; Ketcham, pp. 592 (quoting letter from William Wirt to Mrs. Wirt, October 14, 1814), 597; William Eustis to Richard Rush, December 10, 1814, in Richard Rush Collection; Taylor, *Civil War of 1812*, pp. 415, 492; Reginald Horsman, "Nantucket's Peace Treaty with England in 1814," *New England Q.*, 54:180 (1981); Stagg, *Mr. Madison's War*, pp. 477–78.

12. Madison to Wilson Cary Nicholas, November 26, 1814, in *PJM*.

13. Ammon, *James Monroe*, pp. 342–43; Gallatin to Monroe, June 13, 1814, in Ferguson, *Selected Writings of Gallatin*, p. 344; Richard Rush to John Adams, October 23, 1814, in Richard Rush Collection.

14. Dolley attributed her husband's illness to the Octagon House itself: "Mr. M has not been well since we came to this house and our servants are constantly sick owing to the damp cellar in which they are confined." Dolley Madison to Hannah Gallatin, December 26 and 29, 1814, quoted in Ketcham, p. 594.

15. Banner, *To the Hartford Convention*, pp. 341–43; Stagg, *Mr. Madison's War*, pp. 477–83. The commander of the army regiments near Hartford found reasons for daily meetings with Hartford's mayor and made a point of parading recruiting parties through the city to the beat of martial drums. His efforts may have had a strong influence on the convention delegates.

16. Monroe to Madison, February 3, 1815, ibid.; Robert V. Remini, *The Battle of New Orleans: Andrew Jackson and America's First Military Victory*, New York: Viking (1999), pp. 168, 192; Madison to Andrew Jackson, February 5, 1815, in *PJM*; A.J. Langguth, *Union 1812: The Americans Who Fought the Second War of Independence*, New York: Simon &

Schuster (2007), pp. 343–71; Ketcham, p. 596; Monroe to Jackson, February 5, 1815, in Harold Moser, ed., *Papers of Andrew Jackson,* Knoxville: University of Tennessee Press (1991), 3:271. Three days after receiving news of the victory, Madison issued a pardon for the pirates of Barataria who fought with Jackson and "have manifested a sincere penitence [and] have abandoned the prosecution of the worst cause, for the support of the best." Presidential Proclamation, February 6, 1815, in *PJM.*

17. Hugh Howard, *Mr. and Mrs. Madison's War: America's First Couple and the Second War of Independence,* New York: Bloomsbury Press (2012), pp. 286–87; Robert Rutland, *The Presidency of James Madison,* Lawrence: University Press of Kansas (1990), pp. 186–87; Jonathan Roberts, "Memoirs of a Senator from Pennsylvania: Jonathan Roberts, 1771–1854," *Pennsylvania Magazine of History and Biography,* 62:373, 377–78 (1938).

18. Madison to Congress, February 18, 1815, in *PJM.*

19. Presidential Proclamation, March 4, 1815, ibid.

20. Dudley Mills, "The Duke of Wellington and the Peace Negotiations at Ghent," *Canadian Hist. Review,* 2:22, 27 (1921); Smelser, *Democratic Republic,* pp. 308–9.

21. Henry Clay to Caesar A. Rodney, December 29, 1812, in James F. Hopkins and Mary W.M. Hargreaves, eds., *Papers of Henry Clay,* Lexington: University of Kentucky Press (1959), 1:750; Smelser, *Democratic Republic,* p. 324.

22. John Adams to Richard Rush, October 8, 1813, in Richard Rush Collection.

23. Edward Coles to William Cabell Rives, January 21, 1856, in *William & Mary Q.,* 7:164 (1927). Some of Madison's contemporaries greatly valued his insistence on respecting constitutional rights in wartime. On the day Madison left office, Washington's mayor wrote to Madison: "Power and national glory, Sir, have often before, been acquired by the sword; but rarely without the sacrifice of civil or political liberty. It is here, preeminently, that the righteous triumph of the one, under the smiles of Heaven, secures the other." James Blake to Madison, March 4, 1817, in *PJM.*

24. "Veto Message," January 13, 1815, ibid. Sadly, William Jones's considerable talents did not extend to banking. After three years as president, he was forced out of the position in a scandal. Edward K. Eckert, "William Jones: Mr. Madison's Secretary of the Navy," *Pa. Mag. Hist. & Biog.,* 96:167 (1972). Jefferson parted company with Madison on the proposal for a second Bank of the United States. The former president worked through his son-in-law, Representative John Wayles Eppes, to try to defeat the new version of the bank. Daniel Walker Howe, *What Hath God Wrought: The Transformation of America, 1815–1848,* New York: Oxford University Press (2007), p. 68.

25. Madison to Congress, February 18, 1815, in *PJM.*

26. Curtis P. Nettels, *The Emergence of a National Economy,* New York: Holt, Rinehart and Winston (1962), p. 396, C. Edward Skeen, *1816: America Rising,* Lexington: University Press of Kentucky (2003), p. 18.

27. "Message to Congress," December 5, 1815, in *PJM;* Veto Message, March 3, 1817, ibid.

28. Jackson to Monroe, January 6, 1817, in Moser, *Papers of Andrew Jackson,* 4:82.

29. Ketcham, p. 586. On Madison's civil liberties record, see Wittes and Singh, "James Madison, Presidential Power, and Civil Liberties in the War of 1812"; Smelser, *Democratic Republic,* p. 319; Aaron N. Coleman, "James Madison's Domestic Policies, 1809–1817: Jeffersonian Factionalism and the Beginnings of American Nationalism," in Leibiger, *Companion to James Madison,* p. 204; David J. Siemers, "President James Madison and Foreign Affairs, 1809–1817: Years of Principle and Peril," ibid., p. 218.

30. Dolley Madison to Edward Coles, March 16, 1816, in *Selected Letters,* p. 207; Adams to Jefferson, February 2, 1817, in *PTJ.*

31. Madison to Jeremy Bentham, May 8, 1816, in *PJM.*

32. Monroe to Madison, June 3, 1815, ibid.; Jefferson to Madison, June 15, 1815, ibid.; Monroe to Madison, June 16, 1815, ibid.; Monroe to Madison, July 22, 1815, August 2, 1815, ibid.; Monroe to Madison, August 24, 1815, September 11, 1815, September 19, 1815, ibid.

33. Lynn W. Turner, "Elections of 1816 and 1820," in Schlesinger, *American Presidential Elections*, 1:299–311; Skeen, *1816: America Rising*, p. 230. John Adams, harboring presidential ambitions for his talented son John Quincy, complained that his son could not seek the presidency "till all Virginians shall be extinct." Turner, "Elections of 1816 and 1820," 1:304.

34. Ammon, *James Monroe*, pp. 367–68; Gallatin to Madison, July 17, 1817, in *PJM*.

35. Wulf, *Founding Gardeners*, p. 193.

36. Ralph L. Ketcham, ed., "An Unpublished Sketch of James Madison by James K. Paulding," *Va. Mag. Hist. & Biog.*, 67:432 (1959); Ketcham, pp. 610–12. After seeing Madison at a social event in January 1817, his former brother-in-law John G. Jackson reported that the retiring president "looks to the close of his great career with delight unaccompanied by a single regret." Brown, *Voice of the New West*, p. 183.

CHAPTER 22: ALL THINGS TO ALL MEN

1. *Queen of America*, p. 90; Will of Dolley Payne Todd, May 13, 1794, in *Selected Letters*, pp. 26–27. Dolley's sometimes erratic spelling in her letters has led some to question her educational attainments or intellectual gifts. This seems unfounded, particularly as spelling was a free-form exercise in her era. The volume and substance of Dolley's correspondence, combined with her skillful performance on the nation's most prominent political and social stage, reveals a woman of intelligence and understanding with a lively interest in her world.

2. *Selected Letters*, pp. 10–12.

3. Anthony Morris to Anna Payne, June 26, 1837, *Records of the Columbia Historical Society*, 44–45 (1942–43), 217–20.

4. Allgor, *Perfect Union*, pp. 17–25; *Selected Letters*, p. 15.

5. William W. Wilkins to Dolley Madison, August 22, 1794, in *Selected Letters*, pp. 29–30; Catharine Coles to Dolley Madison, June 1, 1794, ibid., pp. 27–28; Dolley Madison to Anna Cutts, August 19, 1805, ibid., pp. 63–64.

6. Dolley Madison to Elizabeth Collins Lee, [October 1794–1797], in *DEPDM*; Smith, *First Forty Years*, p. 237; M.T., "Days of My Youth," *Lippincott's Magazine*, 20:712 (1877).

7. Smith, *First Forty Years*, p. 64; Madison to Buckner Thruston, March 1, 1833, in *PJM*.

8. Dolley Madison to Elizabeth Collins Lee, September 16, 1794, in *Selected Letters*, p. 31; Madison to Dolley Madison, October 31, 1805, in *PJM*; Dolley Madison to Phoebe P. Morris, August 16, 1812, in *Selected Letters*, pp. 170–71; Dolley Madison to Madison, November 2, 1805, in *PJM*; Madison to Dolley Madison, November 19–20, 1805, ibid.; Dolley Madison to Anna Cutts, May 25, 1804, in *Selected Letters*, pp. 56–57.

9. Dolley Madison to Anna Payne Cutts, May 18, 1804, June 1819–1821, in *DEPDM*. A prominent appellate judge has called Todd the "most insignificant justice" ever to serve on the Supreme Court, partly because Todd authored only eleven opinions in nearly two decades of judicial service, barely one every two years. Frank H. Easterbrook, "The Most Insignificant Justice," *Univ. of Chicago Law Review*, 50:481, 496 (1983).

10. Abraham Joseph Hasbrouck to Severyn Bruyn, January 29, 1814, in *DEPDM*; Smith, *First Forty Years*, p. 235. The suspicion of a miscarriage arises from a statement by Jefferson that James was "not yet a father" after eleven years of marriage. The statement offers scant ground for the speculation. Jefferson to Benjamin Hawkins, March 14, 1801, in *PTJ*; Allgor, *Perfect Union*, p. 54.

11. Dolley Madison to Eliza Collins Lee, January 6, 1803, in *Selected Letters*, pp. 51–52; Dolley Madison to Anna Cutts, June 3, 1808, ibid., p. 86; Dolley Madison to Hannah Gallatin, March 5, 1815, ibid., pp. 198–99; Dolley Madison to Ruth Barlow, April 19, 1812, ibid., pp. 163–64; Dolley Madison to Anna Cutts, August 28, 1808, ibid., pp. 87–88.

12. Dolley Madison to Anna Cutts, July 29, 1805, ibid., p. 62; Dolley Madison to Edward Coles, July 2, 1813, ibid., p. 177; Dolley Madison to Hannah Gallatin, July 29, 1813, ibid., p. 179.

13. Ketcham, pp. 387–88; Taylor, *Slave in the White House*, pp. 13–14, 20–24.

14. *Selected Letters*, p. 41; Jefferson to Dolley Madison, May 27, 1801, in *PTJ*; Smith, *First Forty Years*, p. 28.

15. *Queen of America*, p. 110; Allgor, *Perfect Union*, pp. 72–73.

16. Eliza Collins Lee to Dolley Madison, March 2, 1809, in *Selected Letters*, pp. 107–8; William Winston Seaton, *A Biographical Sketch*, Boston: James R. Osgood & Co. (1871), p. 113; Allgor, *Perfect Union*, pp. 72, 74–75, 183, 232; Jeremiah Mason to Mary Means Mason, December 12, 1813, in *DFPDM*. Dolley could be very particular about the snuff she used. She relied on friends and relatives to send her high-quality snuff. Dolley Madison to John G. Jackson, October 23, 1809, in *Selected Letters*, p. 130; Dolley Madison to Payne Todd, May 24, 1821, ibid., pp. 244–45; Dolley Madison to Anna Cutts, April 23, 1827, ibid., pp. 268–70.

17. Dolley Madison to Anna Cutts, April 26, 1804, May 8, 1804, ibid., pp. 52–55.

18. Madison to Jefferson, July 22, 1805, in *PJM*.

19. Dolley Madison to Anna Cutts, July 29, 1805, in *Selected Letters*, p. 62; Madison to Jefferson, October 5, 1805, in *PJM*; E.S. Brown, ed., *William Plumer's Memorandum of Proceedings in the United States Senate 1803–1807*, New York: Macmillan (1923), pp. 387–89, 444 (January 22 and March 6, 1806).

20. Madison to Jefferson, October 5, 1805, in *PJM*; Dolley Madison to Madison, October 23, 1805, October 25, 1805, October 26, 1805, October 28, 1805, ibid.

21. Dolley Madison to Madison, November 23, 1805, ibid.

22. Madison to Dolley Madison, November 6, 1805, November 21, 1805, ibid.

23. Madison to Dolley Madison, November 6, 1805, November 11–18, 1805, November 15, 1805, ibid.; Lucy Washington Todd to Dolley Madison, April 18, 1812, in *Selected Letters*, pp. 161–62.

24. Dolley Madison to Madison, November 1, 1805, in *PJM*; Madison to Dolley Madison, November 6, 1805, ibid.; Dolley Madison to Madison, November 12, 1805, ibid.

25. Dolley Madison to Anna Cutts, August 19, 1805, in *Selected Letters*, pp. 63–64, n.1; Annette Gordon-Reed, *Thomas Jefferson and Sally Hemings: An American Controversy*, Charlottesville: University Press of Virginia (1997), p. 247; Annette Gordon-Reed, *The Hemingses of Monticello*, New York: W.W. Norton & Co. (2008), p. 589. The years brought more namesakes. Dolley's sister Lucy gave birth to James Madison Todd, while her brother John named a son James Madison Payne. James's sister Frances also bore a namesake, James Madison Hite, though she might have chosen that name to honor her father, James Madison, Sr. Dolley Madison to Mary E.P. Allen, February 25, 1834, in *Selected Letters*, pp. 303–4; Dolley Madison to Anna Cutts, June 6, 1829, in *Selected Letters*, pp. 278–80; Madison to James M. Hite, April 23, 1825, in *PJM*. Anna named a daughter for Dolley.

The Hemings family story about Dolley's supposed failure to redeem her promise of a gift to Sally Hemings contrasts sharply with the recollection of another Monticello slave of James's generosity to slaves. According to Peter Fossett, the older house slaves at Monticello looked forward to Madison's visits because "he never left without leaving each of them a substantial reminder of his visit." Taylor, *Slave in the White House*, p. 75, quoting "Once the Slave of Thomas Jefferson," *New York World*, January 30, 1898.

26. Dolley Madison to Anna Cutts, June 3, 1808, in *Selected Letters*, p. 86; *Queen of America*, p. 107; Dolley Madison to Eliza Collins Lee, February 26, 1808, in *Selected Letters*, pp. 84–85.

27. Dolley Madison to Anna Cutts, May 25, 1804, August 28, 1808, in *Selected Letters*, pp. 56–57, 87–88; Madison to Dolley Madison, August 7, 1809, in *PJM*.

28. John Randolph to James Monroe, September 6, 1806, in *WJM*, 4:486 n.1; Allgor, *Perfect Union*, p. 132; *Selected Letters*, p. 160, n.2.

29. Samuel Latham Mitchill to Catherine A. Mitchill, November 23, 1807, in "Dr. Mitchill's Letters from Washington," *Harper's New Monthly Magazine*, 58:752 (1879); Allgor, *Perfect Union*, p. 137.

CHAPTER 23: THE LADY PRESIDENTESS

1. Samuel Mitchill to Catherine Mitchill, January 25, 1808, in Allen Culling Clark, *Life and Letters of Dolly Madison*, Washington, D.C.: W.F. Roberts Co. (1914), p. 93; *Selected Letters*, pp. 92–94; Smith, *First Forty Years*, p. 62; Seaton, *Biographical Sketch*, p. 113; Allgor, *Perfect Union*, pp. 139–40, 144; Catherine Allgor, *Parlor Politics: In Which the Ladies of Washington Help Build a City and a Government*, Charlottesville: University Press of Virginia (2000), pp. 91, 94.

2. Benjamin Latrobe to Dolley Madison, March 22, 1809, March 29, 1809, April 21, 1809, September 8, 1809, in *Selected Letters*, pp. 111–14, 115–17; Dolley Madison to Benjamin Latrobe, September 12, 1809, ibid., pp. 127–28; Mary Latrobe to Dolley Madison, April 12, 1809, pp. 114–15; Allgor, *Perfect Union*, p. 159; Allgor, *Parlor Politics*, pp. 60–61. Client and decorator occasionally clashed, but Latrobe worked hard to smooth over points of contention.

3. Allgor, *Perfect Union*, pp. 188–89; Allgor, *Parlor Politics*, pp. 63–64, 76–77; George Waterston, *A Wanderer in Washington*, Washington: Washington Press (1827), p. 62.

4. Catherine Mitchill to Samuel Latham Mitchill, January 2, 1811, quoted in Allgor, *Perfect Union*, p. 172; Waterston, *Wanderer in Washington*, pp. 61–62.

5. Benjamin Henry Latrobe to George Harrison, June 30, 1809, quoted in Talbot Hamlin, *Benjamin Henry Latrobe*, New York: Oxford University Press (1955), p. 311; *Selected Letters*, pp. 95, 101; Allgor, *Perfect Union*, p. 174.

6. *Queen of America*, p. 110; Allgor, *Perfect Union*, pp. 183–86; Dolley Madison to Phoebe P. Morris, August 16, 1812, in *Selected Letters*, pp. 171–72.

7. Ketcham, p. 479; Smith, *First Forty Years*, p. 81.

8. Dolley Madison to Elizabeth Patterson Bonaparte, November 24, 1813, in *DEPDM*; Dolley Madison to Phoebe Morris, October 6, 1811, ibid.; Dolley Madison to Ruth Barlow, November 15, 1811, April 19, 1812, in *Selected Letters*, pp. 150–51, 163–64.

9. Allgor, *Parlor Politics*, p. 79; Richard Rush to Charles J. Ingersoll, December 3, 1812, in Richard Rush Collection.

10. Allgor, *Parlor Politics*, p. 84; Dolley Madison to James Taylor, November 10, 1810, in *Selected Letters*, p. 133; Dolley Madison to John G. Jackson, April 10, 1811, ibid., pp. 137–38; Dolley Madison to Edward Coles, June 15, 1811, ibid., p. 144; Dolley Madison to Anna Cutts, July 15, 1811, March 20, 1812, ibid., pp. 147–49, 157; Dolley Madison to Phoebe P. Morris, January 14, 1813, ibid., pp. 173–74.

11. Martha Jefferson Randolph to Dolley Madison, January 15, 1808, ibid., pp. 83–84; Thomas B. Johnson to Dolley Madison, March 11, 1809, ibid., pp. 109–10; Dolley Madison to Phoebe Morris, July 12, 1812, in *DEPDM*; Allgor, *Perfect Union*, pp. 209–24; Allgor, *Parlor Politics*, p. 81; *Selected Letters*, p. 100; Dolley Madison to Edward Coles, July 1, 1816, ibid., pp. 210–11.

12. Dolley Madison to Unknown Correspondent, June 3, 1810, in *DEPDM*.

13. Dolley Madison to Hannah Gallatin, August 1814, in *Selected Letters*, pp. 191–92.

14. *Queen of America*, p. 112; *Selected Letters*, p. 102.

15. Ketcham, p. 496; Allgor, *Parlor Politics*, p. 90; *Queen of America*, p. 112; Seaton, *Biographical Sketch*, p. 85.

16. Dolley Madison to Edward Coles, May 13, 1813, in *Selected Letters*, pp. 176–77; Dolley Madison to Anna Cutts, December 22, 1811, ibid., pp. 153–54; Dolley Madison to Ruth Barlow, April 19, 1812, ibid., pp. 163–64; Dolley Madison to Edward Coles, August 31, 1812, ibid., p. 172; Allgor, *Parlor Politics*, p. 95; Dolley Madison to John Payne Todd, August 6, 1814, in *Selected Letters*, p. 190.

17. Allgor, *Perfect Union*, p. 311; Jennings, "A Colored Man's Reminiscences," in Taylor, *Slave in the White House*, p. 231; Dolley Madison to Lucy Payne Washington Todd, August 23, 1814, in *Selected Letters*, pp. 193–94; Anna Cutts to Dolley Madison, August 23, 1814, ibid., p. 194.

18. Jennings, "Reminiscences," p. 233; Madison to Dolley Madison, August 27, 1814, in *PJM*.

19. Allgor, *Perfect Union*, pp. 319, 328–29; Smith, *First Forty Years*, p. 110; Taylor, *Slave in the White House*, p. 53; Dolley Madison to Hannah Gallatin, January 14, 1815, in *Selected Letters*, p. 197; Allgor, *Parlor Politics*, p. 98. Octagon House still stands at 18th Street and New York Avenue, Northwest.

20. Dolley Madison to Hannah Gallatin, March 5, 1815, ibid., pp. 198–99. The Madisons did not linger at Octagon House, where the dampness seemed to make both James and the servants ill. In October 1815, they moved to a townhouse at the corner of Pennsylvania Avenue and 19th Street, where Vice President Gerry had lived at the time of his death the previous year. They remained there through the end of James's second term as president. Dolley Madison to Hannah Gallatin, December 26, 1814, in *DEPDM*; Taylor, *Slave in the White House*, p. 35.

21. Dolley Madison to Edward Coles, March 6, 1816, in *Selected Letters*, p. 206.

22. Madison to William Eustis, March 31, 1817, in *PJM*; Jefferson to Madison, April 15, 1817, ibid.

23. Dolley Madison to Hannah Gallatin, March 19, 1815, in *Selected Letters*, pp. 199–200; Smith, *First Forty Years*, p. 141; Eliza Collins Lee to Dolley Madison, March 30, 1819, in *Selected Letters*, pp. 234–35.

CHAPTER 24: ADAM AND EVE AT MONTPELIER

1. Ketcham, p. 613; John H.B. Latrobe to Charles Carroll Harper, August, 4, 1832, in *PJM*; Smith, *First Forty Years*, p. 233; *Queen of America*, p. 158. For an extended view of the Madisons in retirement, there is Ralph Ketcham, *The Madisons at Montpelier: Reflections on the Founding Couple*, Charlottesville: University of Virginia Press (2011).

2. Madison to Richard Cutts, July 13, 1817, October 12, 1817, in *PJM*; Madison to Monroe, May 21, 1818, ibid.; Madison to Charles Caldwell, September 20, 1826, ibid.; Madison to Benjamin Henry Latrobe, July 24, 1818, ibid.

3. *Queen of America*, pp. 157–58; George Ticknor, *Life, Letters and Journals of George Ticknor*, Boston: Houghton Mifflin Co. (1909), p. 347.

4. Smith, *First Forty Years*, p. 235.

5. *Queen of America*, p. 174.

6. Ketcham, p. 621; *Queen of America*, pp. 158–59; Madison to Richard Peters, February 22, 1819 (commenting on Peters's proposed "pattern farm"), in *PJM*; Madison to Asher Robbins, August 8, 1818, ibid.; Abbe Serra to Madison, February 12, 1819, ibid. (sharing seeds of Missouri oranges and an unusual form of chestnut); Jefferson to Madison, February 16, 1820, ibid. (seakale seeds); James Ronaldson to Madison, August 4, 1828, ibid. (including seeds for New Zealand hemp).

7. Thomas Mann Randolph to Madison, October 14, 1817, ibid.; May 12, 1818, "Address to the Agricultural Society of Albemarle," ibid.

8. Madison recognized that he had lost the argument over the superiority of oxen to horses as draft animals, largely—he thought—because oxen fared poorly on roads and were slow in pulling carts. Madison to John Nicholas, January 4, 1819, ibid.

9. "Autobiography of George Tucker," *Bermuda Hist. Q.,* 18:141 (1961); Ticknor, *George Ticknor,* p. 347.

10. Dolley Madison to John G. Jackson, November 27, 1824, in *Selected Letters,* pp. 256–57.

11. Smith, *First Forty Years,* p. 234; Dolley Madison to Dolley Cutts, December 1831, in *DEPDM*; Dolley Madison to Sarah Coles Stevenson, December 31, 1834, ibid.; Dolley Madison to Sarah Coles Stevenson, February 1820, in *Selected Letters,* pp. 238–39.

12. Dolley Madison to Lucy Winston, March 10, 1823, ibid., p. 248; Dolley Madison to Elizabeth Coles, April 8, 1831, ibid., pp. 291–92; Monroe to Madison, November 24, 1817, April 28, 1818, in *PJM*; Madison to Monroe, November 29, 1817, November 28, 1818, ibid.; William Crawford to Madison, October 12, 1817, ibid.; Madison to William Crawford, October 24, 1817, ibid.; Madison to Richard Rush, July 24, 1818, May 10, 1819, ibid.

   Monroe's consultations with Madison closely resembled those Madison conducted with Jefferson during his presidency. In both situations, the former president was circumspect about offering advice and the incumbent president generally followed his own best judgment. For example, in the 1823 crisis over threatened French meddling with the emerging republics of South America, Madison endorsed a British proposal to make a joint statement that the French should abandon any such intentions. Monroe and his Secretary of State, John Quincy Adams, decided that the United States should not act with the British but should make that statement unilaterally, giving birth to the Monroe Doctrine. Madison to Monroe, October 20, 1823, ibid.

13. Dolley Madison to Anna Cutts, April 23, 1827, in *Selected Letters,* pp. 268–70; Dolley Madison to Margaret Bayard Smith, January 17, 1835, ibid., p. 308.

14. Dolley Madison to Payne Todd, April 12, 1823, ibid., pp. 249–50; Dolley Madison to Dolley Cutts, March 10, 1830, ibid., pp. 284–85; Dolley Madison to Dolley Cutts, December 1831, in *DEPDM*; Joseph Milligan to Dolley Madison, December 13, 1809, ibid.; Dolley Madison to Eliza Collins Lee, April 21, 1819, in *Selected Letters,* p. 236; Dolley Madison to Anna Cutts, May 18, 1825, ibid., pp. 261–62; Dolley Madison to Mary Cutts, May 1831, in *DEPDM*; Dolley Madison to Anna Cutts, May 15, 1832, in *Selected Letters,* p. 295; *Queen of America,* p. 159. Of one novel by James Fenimore Cooper (which scholars have concluded was probably *The Wept of Wish-ton-Wish*), Dolley complained that it was "too full of horrors." *Selected Letters,* p. 285, n.2.

15. Dolley Madison to Anna Cutts, April 3, 1818, July 23, 1818, ibid., pp. 228–29, 231–32; Dolley Madison to Anna Cutts, June–July 1819, in *DEPDM*.

16. Eliza Collins Lee to Dolley Madison, March 30, 1819, in *Selected Letters,* pp. 234–35. A similarly sunny view of the Madisons in retirement was published in the *National Intelligencer* in the following year. "Montpelier, the Seat of Mr. Madison," *National Intelligencer,* August 9, 1820.

17. Ketcham, pp. 646–58; "The Faculty Committee for General Purposes to the Visitors to the University of Virginia to James Madison," September 9, 1826, in *PJM* (appointing Madison rector of the university); Madison to Littleton Tazewell, May 17, 1834, ibid. (resigning as rector).

18. Madison to Dolley Madison, July 30, 1818, December 8, 1825, December 14, 1826, July 11, 1827, ibid.; Dolley Madison to Madison, December 7, 1826, ibid.

19. Madison to Jefferson, September 7, 1784, ibid.; Madison to Jefferson, October 17, 1784,

ibid.; Madison to Lafayette, August 21, 1824, ibid.; Madison to Jefferson, September 10, 1824, ibid. Months after offering to Jefferson his unvarnished view of Lafayette, Madison softened it. Upon reflection, he wrote to Jefferson, "Though his foibles did not disappear all the favorable traits presented themselves in a stronger light." Madison to Jefferson, August 20, 1785, ibid.

20. Fred Somkin, *Unquiet Eagle: Memory and Desire in the Idea of American Freedom, 1815–1860*, Ithaca: Cornell University Press (1967), pp. 131–74.

21. Madison to Dolley Madison, November 5, 1824, ibid.

22. Dolley Madison to John G. Jackson, November 27, 1824, in *Selected Letters*, pp. 256–57; Madison to Frances Wright, September 1, 1825, in *DEPDM*; *Queen of America*, p. 156; Ketcham, p. 627; Taylor, *Slave in the White House*, pp. 100–104. Chapter 26 of this book explores Madison's tortured view of slavery-related issues.

23. A. Lavasseur, *Lafayette in America in 1824 and 1825*, Philadelphia: Carey and Lea (1829), 2:245–46.

24. Monroe to Madison, September 10, 1829, October 4, 1829, in *PJM*; Madison to Monroe, September 15, 1829, ibid.

25. "Notes for the Virginia Constitutional Convention," October 1, 1829, ibid.; William G. Shade, *Democratizing the Old Dominion: Virginia and the Second Party System 1824–1861*, Charlottesville: University Press of Virginia (1995), pp. 66, 69–70; Ketcham, pp. 636–43; "Notes on Suffrage," December 1829, in *PJM*.

26. Ketcham, p. 637; Dickson C. Bruce, Jr., *The Virginia Convention of 1829–30 and the Conservative Tradition in the South*, San Marino, CA: The Huntington Library (1982), pp. 32–33; Taylor, *Slave in the White House*, p. 110; Hugh Blair Grigsby, *The Virginia Convention of 1829–30*, Richmond: McFarlane & Fergusson (1854), pp. 5–9.

27. Madison to Nicholas Trist, October 31, 1829, in *PJM*; Madison to Marquis de Lafayette, February 1, 1830, ibid.

28. "Speech in the Virginia Convention," December 2, 1829, ibid.; Grigsby, *Virginia Convention*, pp. 8–9; Taylor, *Slave in the White House*, p. 115.

29. McCoy, *Last of the Fathers*, pp. 242–44; Dolley Madison to John Payne, December 4, 1829, in *Selected Letters*, pp. 280–81; Madison, "Autobiography," December 1830, in *PJM*; Bruce, *Virginia Convention*, pp. 61, 90; Susan Dunn, *Dominion of Memories: Jefferson, Madison, and the Decline of Virginia*, New York: Basic Books (2007), pp. 156, 162–64; Madison to Marquis de Lafayette, February 1, 1830, in *PJM*.

30. Dolley Madison to John Payne, December 4, 1829, in *Selected Letters*, pp. 280–81.

31. Dolley Madison to Anna Cutts, December 28, 1829, ibid., pp. 282–83; Dolley Madison to Anna Cutts, January 25, 1830, ibid., pp. 283–84; Dolley Madison to Dolley Cutts, March 10, 1830, ibid., pp. 284–85. The scandal in the Jackson administration centered on Peggy Eaton, a lively widow who married Secretary of War John Eaton after the death of her first husband, possibly by suicide; some had suspected John and Peggy of having an affair before the death of Peggy's husband, and many thought she remarried too soon after his death. In pre-Victorian Washington, the wives of Jackson's other cabinet members snubbed Peggy. President Jackson, who long harbored resentment over slurs on his late wife's character, sided with the Eatons and fired his entire cabinet. Aside from its natural appeal as a story of the intersection of sex and power, the Eaton affair might have had particular resonance for Dolley, who had been criticized for remarrying too quickly after her first husband's death. For an excellent treatment of the affair, see Jon Meachem, *American Lion: Andrew Jackson in the White House*, New York: Random House (2008).

32. Albert Gallatin to Madison, September 4, 1815, June 4, 1816, in *PJM*.

33. Dolley Madison to Anna Cutts, June 1820, in *Selected Letters*, p. 243; Charles S. Fowler to Madison, June 25, 1825, in *PJM*; Richard Bache to Madison, December 1825, ibid.;

Levett Harris to Madison, October 31, 1826, ibid.; Madison to Payne Todd, November 13, 1825, ibid.

34. Madison to Payne Todd, April 26, 1826, ibid.; Madison to Edward Coles, February 23, 1827, ibid.

35. Dolley Madison to Anna Cutts, June 6, 1829, in *Selected Letters*, pp. 278–80.

36. Ibid., p. 220, quoting John C. Payne to James Madison Cutts, September 1, 1849.

37. Promissory note from Richard Cutts to James Madison for $7,500, April 4, 1817, in *PJM*; Madison to Richard Cutts, July 23, 1817, September 1, 1817, ibid.; William Thornton to Madison, September 2, 1823, ibid.; Madison to Nicholas Van Zandt, October 31, 1826, ibid.; "Memorandum on the Cutts House," September 1, 1828, ibid.; Dolley Madison to John G. Jackson, November 27, 1824, in *Selected Letters*, pp. 256–57. An overview of the Cutts-Madison financial dealings appears in volume 2 of the Retirement Series of the *Papers of James Madison*, at pp. 19–22. James's deep connection with Cutts became even more embarrassing when President Monroe advised him that Cutts was performing poorly in his War Department job and that Secretary of State John C. Calhoun wished to dismiss him. Monroe to Madison, December 23, 1820, in *PJM*. James did his best to defend his brother-in-law's position, and Cutts remained on the public payroll until Andrew Jackson became president in 1829. Madison to Monroe, December 28, 1820, in *PJM*. After Jackson fired Cutts, Dolley encouraged him to seek better opportunities in his native Maine. Dolley Madison to Richard Cutts, 1819–1822 (marked "Secret"), in *DEPDM*; Dolley Madison to John G. Jackson, November 29, 1822, in *Selected Letters*, p. 247; Dolley Madison to John Payne Todd, April 27, 1828, ibid., pp. 274–75; Dolley Madison to Anna Cutts, December 1822, June 6, 1829, in *DEPDM*.

38. Madison to George Graham, October 30, 1823, in *PJM*; Madison to Richard Cutts, March 27, 1824, September 13, 1824, ibid.; Madison to Bernard Peyton, June 7, 1827, ibid.; Madison to Edward Coles, June 28, 1831, ibid.

39. Monroe to Madison, June 15, 1826, January 22, 1827, September 23, 1827, March 28, 1828, ibid.

40. Madison to William Tapscott, July 29, 1826, ibid.; Madison to Hubbard Taylor, July 29, 1826, ibid.; Madison to W.S. Nicholls, December 22, 1826, ibid.; Ketcham, pp. 623–24; Madison to Nicholas Trist, January 26, 1828, ibid.; Indenture with Coleby Cowherd, March 9, 1830, ibid.; Indenture with John Lee and John Willis, June 5, 1832, ibid.

41. Ketcham, p. 623; Dolley Madison to Richard D. Cutts, October 23, 1835, in *Selected Letters*, p. 314; Dolley Madison to Lucy Payne Washington Todd, October 23, 1835, ibid., pp. 314–15; Dunn, *Dominion of Memories*, pp. 23–24, 118–19; Wulf, *Founding Gardeners*, p. 204.

42. James Madison Cutts to Dolley Madison, September 4, 1835, in *Selected Letters*, pp. 312–14.

CHAPTER 25: THE CONSTITUTIONAL SAGE OF MONTPELIER

1. McCoy, *Last of the Fathers*, p. xiii.

2. Ketcham, pp. 663–64; Andrew Stevenson to Madison, January 8, 1821, in *PJM*.

3. Madison to Joseph Gales, Jr., August 26, 1821, in *PJM*; Madison to Edward Everett, February 18, 1823, ibid.; Madison to James Paulding, April 1, 1831, ibid.

4. Madison to William King, May 20, 1819, ibid.; Madison to Henry Lee, February 16, 1827, ibid.

5. "Detached Memoranda," January 31, 1820, ibid.; Madison to Samuel H. Smith, November 4, 1826, ibid.; Madison to Jared Sparks, April 8, 1831, ibid.; Madison to James Paulding, April 1, 1831, ibid. In 1822, Madison sent to a leading editor a lengthy description of the controversy over the abortive Jay-Gardoqui negotiation over access

to the Mississippi River in 1786. In correcting Hamilton's account of the Federalist essays—Hamilton had claimed authorship of several that Madison wrote—Madison insisted that Hamilton's error was involuntary, adding that Hamilton "was incapable of any that was not so." Madison to Hezekiah Niles, January 8, 1822, ibid.

6. Madison to Thomas Ritchie, September 15, 1821, ibid.; Madison to John G. Jackson, December 28, 1821, ibid.; Madison to Samuel Harrison Smith, February 2, 1827, ibid.

7. Madison to John Tyler, March 1, 1833, ibid.; Madison to Joseph Gales, Jr., August 26, 1821, ibid.; Madison to Thomas Wharton, August 1, 1827, ibid.; Madison to James Robertson, Jr., March 27, 1831, ibid.; "Notes on Charles Pinckney Plan for Constitution," April 16, 1831, ibid.; Madison to Jared Sparks, November 25, 1831, ibid. When the official *Journal of the Philadelphia Convention* was published in 1820, James promptly wrote to Secretary of State Adams to correct errors in it. Madison to John Quincy Adams, June 13, 1820, ibid.

8. "Origin of the Constitutional Convention," December 1835, ibid.

9. Madison to Frederick Beasley, November 29, 1825, ibid. James also expressed doubts about Christian doctrines in a conversation with the Quaker Isaac Briggs, though Briggs claimed that his responses to James's doubts satisfied the former president "on every point." "Isaac Briggs' Account of Meeting with Madison," November 1, 1820, ibid. It seems more likely that Madison, out of courtesy, resolved to express no more doubts to Friend Briggs.

10. Madison to Richard Rush, April 21, 1821, ibid.; Madison to Nicholas Biddle, February 23, 1822, ibid.; Madison to Thomas Cooper, December 26, 1826, ibid.; Madison to Edward Everett, November 26, 1823, ibid.; Harriet Martineau, *Retrospect of Western Travel*, London: Saunders and Otley (1838), p. 9; Madison to Nicholas P. Trist, April 1827, in *PJM*; George W. Featherstonhaugh to Madison, December 7, 1820, ibid.; Madison to George W. Featherstonhaugh, March 6, 1821, ibid.

11. "Notes on Languages," post-December 31, 1819, ibid.; "Causes of Innovation in Language," December 1823, ibid.; Madison to Henry Lee, June 25, 1824, ibid.; Madison to Spencer Roane, September 2, 1819, May 6, 1821, June 29, 1821, ibid.; Madison to Jefferson, June 27, 1823, ibid.; Madison to Edward Everett, November 14, 1831, ibid.

12. Madison to Monroe, December 28, 1820, ibid.; "Power of the President to Appoint Ministers and Consuls During a Recess of the Senate," post–May 6, 1822, ibid.; Madison to Monroe, December 20, 1822, ibid.

13. Howe, *What Hath God Wrought*, pp. 270–75; Robert Remini, *Martin Van Buren and the Making of the Democratic Party*, New York: Columbia University Press (1959), pp. 170–85.

14. Robert L. Einhorn, *American Taxation, American Slavery*, Chicago: University of Chicago Press (2006), p. 117; Madison to Joseph C. Cabell, March 18, 1827.

15. Madison to Joseph C. Cabell, September 18, 1828, October 30, 1828, in *PJM*; Joseph C. Cabell to Madison, December 28, 1828, ibid.; McCoy, *Last of the Fathers*, pp. 124–26.

16. Richard Rush to Madison, January 10, 1828, in *PJM*; Madison to Joseph C. Cabell, February 2, 1829, February 13, 1829, ibid.; Madison to Joseph C. Cabell, March 19, 1829, ibid.; Madison to Nicholas Trist, September 23, 1831, May 15, 1832, ibid.

17. Clyde Wilson and Edwin Hemphill, eds., *The Papers of John C. Calhoun*, Columbia: University of South Carolina Press (1977), 10:442–534.

18. Calhoun's basic argument required an inventive interpretation of the tax clause in Article I, Section 8, of the Constitution, which gives Congress the power "to lay and collect taxes, duties, imposts, and excises, to pay the debts and provide for the common defense and general welfare of the United States." Calhoun insisted that the taxing power was restricted to those levies *necessary* "to pay debts" and all the rest. This construction of

the constitutional term, though possible, was contrary to the practice of Congress and the nation for the first forty years under the Constitution, and also is less plausible than an alternative construction: that the generic purposes described in the final phrases in Clause 8 (to pay the debts and prepare for the common defense and general welfare) simply directed that the taxing power be used for public purposes and not for private ones. Protective tariffs, of course, serve a public purpose of fostering domestic industries. Garrett Epps, *American Epic: Reading the U.S. Constitution,* New York: Oxford University Press (2013), p. 25. Calhoun also had to believe that Congress and the courts somehow could distinguish between tariffs that raise revenue and those that are protective, even though virtually all tariffs do both.

19. In a letter to a state-rights advocate, Madison insisted that the states' ratification of the Constitution involved "a surrender of certain portions of their respective authorities," including the ability to override federal law. Any other conclusion, he wrote, would mean that "the Constitution of the U. States might become different in every state." Madison to Spencer Roane, June 29, 1821, in *PJM*. Roane was a nephew of Patrick Henry.

20. Madison to Joseph Cabell, September 7, 1829, ibid.; Madison to Nicholas Trist, December 17, 1828, February 15, 1830, ibid. Trist was the grandson of Mrs. House, Madison's landlady in Philadelphia forty-five years before.

21. Nicholas Trist to Madison, February 6, 1830, ibid.; Robert Young Hayne, April 3 or 4, 1830, ibid.

22. Madison to Edward Everett, August 28, 1830, ibid. (published in *North American Review*).

23. Joseph C. Cabell to Madison, October 28, 1830, ibid.; Edward Coles to Madison, November 4, 1830, ibid.; Madison to Nicholas Trist, December 1, 1831, ibid.; "Notes on Nullification and the Nature of Union," December 1831, ibid.; Madison to Charles Eaton Hayne, August 27, 1832, ibid.

24. Richard Ellis, *The Union at Risk: Jacksonian Democracy, States' Rights, and the Nullification Crisis,* New York: Oxford University Press (1987), pp. 165–77; Merrill Peterson, *Olive Branch and Sword: The Compromise of 1833,* Baton Rouge: Louisiana State University Press (1982). The reconvened South Carolina Convention thumbed its nose at the federal government by purporting to nullify the legislation giving President Jackson powers to deal with the crisis, but the gesture was an empty one. With the state accepting the federal tariff policy, Jackson did not need the crisis powers.

25. Madison to Robert Walsh, February 15, 1831, in *PJM*; Madison to Frederick Beasley, March 22, 1831, ibid.; Madison to David Hosack, May 28, 1829, ibid.; Madison to Nicholas Trist, July 4, 1829, ibid.; Madison to Monroe, April 21, 1831, ibid.

26. Dunn, *Dominion of Memories,* p. 188; "On Nullification," December 1834, in *PJM*; Madison to Andrew Stevenson, February 10, 1833, ibid.; Madison to "A Friend of Union and State Rights," January 1, 1833, ibid.

27. Madison to Andrew Stevenson, February 10, 1833, ibid. Madison's fear of a permanent rupture between North and South, based on differences surrounding slavery, dated from at least the Philadelphia Convention. He referred to it in several letters throughout his retirement years. Madison to Richard Bland Lee, August 5, 1819, ibid.; Madison to Robert Walsh, Jr., November 28, 1819, ibid.; Madison to Nicholas Trist, May 29, 1832, ibid.; Madison to Henry Clay, April 2, 1833, ibid.

CHAPTER 26: "A SAD BLOT ON OUR FREE COUNTRY"

1. Taylor, *Slave in the White House,* p. 51. We know about Sawney, who accompanied James to Princeton in the early 1770s and became a foreman at Montpelier, though still a slave. Another slave foreman was Moses, who ran the blacksmith shop. Sukey was Dolley's

maid for decades, and Paul Jennings was a young house servant who became James's valet for the last decades of his life. Billey Gardner went to Philadelphia with James in the 1780s and was sold to a Philadelphian, later winning his freedom. Other house slaves included Nany, Benjamin Stewart, and Ralph Taylor and his wife, Catherine. Ailsey Payne was a cook. Anthony was a runaway from Montpelier in 1786. Taylor, *Slave in the White House*, pp. 26–28, 51, 122. The plantation account books for Montpelier have not been found, so the business of managing its slaves is nowhere near as well documented as it is for Jefferson's Monticello or Washington's Mount Vernon. One writer has estimated that John Payne, Dolley's father, operated a plantation with eighty slaves. Virginia Moore, *The Madisons: A Biography*, New York: McGraw-Hill (1979), p. 3.

2. Jefferson to Madison, August 16, 1810, ibid.

3. Madison to James Madison, Sr., March 30, 1782, November 1, 1786, ibid.; Madison to Edmund Pendleton, August 6, 1782, August 19, 1782, September 3, 1782, ibid.; "Instructions for the Montpelier Overseer and Laborers," November 1790, ibid.; Taylor, *Slave in the White House*, p. 97.

4. "Account with Charles Taylor," August 27, 1818, November 4, 1819, ibid.; "Account with Robley Dunglison," August 27, 1825, ibid.; Madison to James Madison, Sr., May 4, 1794, October 5, 1794, ibid.; Madison to Monroe, November 19, 1820, ibid.

5. David B. Mattern, "James Madison and Montpelier: The Rhythms of Rural Life," in Leibiger, *Companion to James Madison*, pp. 293–94; "Agreement," July 27, 1801, in *PJM* (Madison pays Benjamin Grayson Orr $250 to hire "Plato the slave" for five years); a creditor of Orr's attempted to take Plato from Madison to settle a claim against Orr, Benjamin Grayson Orr to Madison, June 25, 1802, Madison to Orr, June 28, 1801, ibid.; Francis H. Rozer to Madison, October 26, 1802, ibid.; William Madison to Madison, September 22, 1801, December 25, 1802, ibid.; Madison to Jefferson, October 3, 1801, ibid.

6. "Vices of the Political System of the United States," April 1787, ibid.; Madison to Edmund Randolph, July 26, 1785, ibid. Randolph shared Madison's ambivalence over owning slaves. "I should emancipate my slaves," Randolph wrote to Madison in 1789, "and thus end my days without undergoing any anxiety about the injustice of holding them." Edmund Randolph to Madison, May 19, 1789, ibid.

7. Madison to James Madison, Sr., September 8, 1783, September 6, 1788, December 27, 1795, ibid.; Madison to Jefferson, June 17, 1793, ibid. Billey Gardner's story is told in Taylor, *Slave in the White House*, pp. 26–28.

8. "Notes on Lake Country Tour," May 31–June 7, 1791, in *PJM* (entry for June 1, 1791); Edmund Berkeley, Jr., "Christopher McPherson: Prophet Without Honor," *Virginia Magazine of History and Biography*, 77:180, 184 (1969).

9. Gaillard Hunt, *Life of James Madison*, New York: Doubleday, Page & Co. (1902), pp. 380–81; Henry J. Doyhar to Madison, May 19, 1814, in *PJM*.

10. Dolley Madison to Anna Cutts, July 23, 1818, ibid.; Dolley Madison to Richard D. Cutts, 1827–1829, in *Selected Letters*, pp. 272–73; Dolley Madison to John C. Payne, December 4, 1829, ibid., pp. 280–81.

11. Francis Scott Key to Dolley Madison, June 30, 1810, in *DEPDM*; Dolley Madison to Elizabeth Parke Custis Law, October 17, 1804, in *Selected Letters*, p. 60.

12. Taylor, *Slave in the White House*, pp. 68, 92.

13. Ibid., p. 69; Wulf, *Founding Gardeners*, pp. 197–201; Mattern, "James Madison and Montpelier," p. 297.

14. Francis Corbin to Madison, October 21, 1788, in *PJM* ("We Virginians are too much accustomed to solitude and slavery—too much puffed up with our own foolish pride and vanity"), January 15, 1797, October 10, 1819, March 3, 1821, ibid.; Madison to Francis Corbin, November 26, 1820, ibid.

15. Madison to Jefferson, October 17, 1784, ibid.; Lafayette to Madison, April 22, 1805, August 28, 1826, ibid.

16. Kurt E. Leichtle and Bruce G. Carveth, *Crusade against Slavery: Edward Coles, Pioneer of Freedom*, Carbondale: Southern Illinois University Press (2011), p. 42; Ralph L. Ketcham, "The Dictates of Conscience: Edward Coles and Slavery," *Virginia Quarterly Review*, 36:52 (1960); "Governor Coles' Autobiography," *Journal of the Illinois State Historical Society*, 3:59 (1910). During the Madison administration, holding cells were maintained at six locations in Washington City for slaves who were coming up for auction or awaiting transportation to new masters. James Oliver Horton, "The Genesis of Washington's African American Community, in Francine Curro Cary, ed., *Urban Odyssey: A Multicultural History of Washington, D.C.*, Washington: Smithsonian Institution Press (1996), p. 26. In December 1808, another visitor to Washington City was stunned by a similar scene of slaves being led to market in "a country that boasts of being a land of liberty and an asylum for the oppressed." Noble E. Cunningham, Jr., ed., "The Diary of Frances Few, 1808–1809," *J. Southern Hist.*, 29:353 (1963).

   Edward Coles had worked for Jefferson before he worked for Madison. In 1814, Jefferson declined Coles's plea that he support emancipation, saying he had "overlived" his power to challenge slavery: "This enterprise is for the young, for those who can follow it up and bear it through to its consummation. It shall have all my prayers, and these are the only weapons of an old man." Jefferson to Edward Coles, August 25, 1814, in *PTJ*.

17. Leichtle and Carveth, *Crusade against Slavery*, pp. 58–70.

18. Madison to Edward Coles, September 3, 1819, in *PJM*.

19. Madison to William Bradford, November 26, 1774, June 19, 1775, ibid.; David Jameson to Madison, November 18, 1780, ibid.; George Mason to Virginia Delegates, April 3, 1781, ibid.; Edmund Pendleton to Madison, May 7, 1781, ibid.; David Jameson to Madison, August 10, 1781, ibid.

20. Madison to Joseph Jones, November 28, 1780, ibid.; Joseph Jones to Madison, December 8, 1780, ibid.

21. "Motion on Slaves taken by the British," September 10, 1782, ibid.; Alan Taylor, *The Internal Enemy: Slavery and War in Virginia, 1772–1832*, New York: W.W. Norton & Co. (2013), p. 28; Madison to Jefferson, May 13, 1783, in *PJM*; "Notes on March 28, 1783," Confederation Congress, ibid.; Thomas Walker to Virginia Delegates, May 3, 1783, ibid.

22. Madison to Washington, November 11, 1785, ibid.; Madison to Jefferson, January 22, 1786, ibid.

23. Farrand, 2:408 (August 25, 1787); *Annals*, 2:1242 (February 12, 1790) (Abraham Baldwin); *Federalist* Nos. 42, 54; *DHRC*, 9:1338–39 (June 17, 1788) (Madison).

24. Farrand, 3:161 (James Wilson in Pennsylvania ratifying convention, December 3, 1787); Alexis de Tocqueville, *Democracy in America*, New York: George Adlard (1839), 1:364–65.

25. "Memorandum on an African Colony for Freed Slaves," October 20, 1789, in *PJM*; Burstein and Isenberg, *Madison and Jefferson*, p. 200.

26. Einhorn, *American Taxation, American Slavery*, p. 151; Washington to Pierce Butler, August 10, 1789, in *PGW*; Anthony Wayne to Madison, June 15, 1789, in *PJM*; Madison to Benjamin Rush, March 20, 1790, ibid.; Diary of George Washington, March 16, 1790, in *PGW*; Madison to Robert Pleasants, October 30, 1791, in *PJM*.

27. Beeman, *Old Dominion*, pp. 95–96; Link, *Democratic-Republican Societies*, p. 184; Taylor, *Internal Enemy*, p. 94; Jefferson to Monroe, July 14, 1793, in *PTJ*; Elkins and McKitrick, *Age of Federalism*, pp. 143, 155, 197. The British and Americans quarreled for more than a decade over compensation for the runaway slaves. E.g., Gouverneur Morris to Washington, April 7, 1790, May 1, 1790, in *PGW*.

28. Monroe to Madison, September 9, 1800, October 8, 1800, in *PJM*; Egerton, *Gabriel's*

Rebellion; Ammon, *James Monroe*, pp. 186–89; Jefferson to Madison, November 22, 1801, in *PJM*; Daniel Brent to Madison, September 7, 1802, ibid.; William C.C. Claiborne to Madison, March 1, 1804, May 8, 1804, September 21, 1804, October 25, 1804, January 1, 1808, November 6, 1808, ibid.; William Hull to Madison, July 31, 1806, ibid. Britain had established a gradual emancipation policy for Upper Canada, but the runaways would not have benefited from that policy. Taylor, *Civil War of 1812*, pp. 45, 51. Madison received regular reports on the thriving slave trade in Havana, which supplied buyers in South Carolina and Georgia. Vincent Gray to Madison, October 29, 1802, November 10, 1802, in *PJM*.

29. Thomas Newton to Madison, August 3, 1807, ibid.; Madison to Thomas Newton, August 15, 1807, ibid.; Anthony Merry to Madison, May 4, 1804, ibid.; Levi Lincoln to Madison, May 9, 1804, ibid.; Madison to Anthony Merry, May 19, 1804, ibid. The inverted morality that Americans sometimes applied to slavery issues can be seen in a Virginian's plea to President Madison to waive the legal bar on slave imports in favor of French refugees from Saint-Domingue who arrived in Norfolk with their slaves: "The great laws of humanity and hospitality [to slaveowners] seemed to us superior to the rigid policy which forbids any slave to be brought into the United States; which policy could not embrace a subject so extraordinary and distressing." John Tyler to Madison, June 1, 1809, ibid. Madison declined to waive the ban on importing slaves in this instance, but Congress enacted legislation waiving penalties for such imports if the refugees had been forcibly expelled from their homelands.

30. "From Inhabitants of Michigan Territory," October 15, 1809, ibid.; "From Citizens of Clark County, Indiana," November 1, 1809, ibid.; Jonathan Jennings to Madison, February 13, 1811, ibid.; Paul Hamilton to Madison, October 29, 1810, ibid.; Madison to Benjamin Rush, November 6, 1810, ibid.

31. Smith, *First Forty Years*, p. 91; Claude G. Bowers, ed., *The Diary of Elbridge Gerry, Jr.*, New York: Brentano's (1927), pp. 198–99; William Tatham to Madison, March 16, 1812, in *PJM*; Stephen Belknap to Monroe, March 24, 1813, in *PJM*; William C.C. Claiborne to Madison, September 22, 1814, ibid.; Samuel Spring to Madison, August 26, 1812, ibid.; Wittes and Singh, "James Madison, Presidential Power, and Civil Liberties in the War of 1812," p. 112. After the war, James recalled that friends had told him that Elbridge Gerry, Jr., was "such a dolt" that he was not fit for a low government job, but James concluded that "some peculiarities in his manner led to an exaggeration of his deficiencies, and that he acquits himself well enough in the subordinate place he now holds." Madison to Jefferson, January 15, 1823, ibid.

32. Philip Stuart to Madison, July 29, 1814, ibid.; Walter Jones to Madison, November 8, 1813, ibid.; Taylor, *Internal Enemy*, pp. 283–86, 301.

33. Taylor, *Civil War of 1812*, p. 328; Ammon, *James Monroe*, p. 348; Madison to Monroe, April 5, 1815, in *PJM*; Madison to Monroe, March 26, 1815, ibid.; Monroe to Madison, February 28, 1815, ibid.; Madison to Monroe, July 26, 1816, ibid.; Taylor, *Internal Enemy*, pp. 430–32.

34. Madison to United States Congress, December 10, 1816, in *PJM*; Steven Deyle, *Carry Me Back: The Domestic Slave Trade in American Life*, New York: Oxford University Press (2005), p. 20.

35. Howe, *What Hath God Wrought*, pp. 147–60; Robert Pierce Forbes, *The Missouri Compromise and Its Aftermath*, Chapel Hill: University of North Carolina Press (2007).

36. Robert Walsh, Jr., to Madison, February 15, 1819, in *PJM*; Madison to Robert Walsh, Jr., March 2, 1819, ibid.

37. Robert J. Evans to Madison, June 3, 1819, ibid.; "From a Western Virginian" to Madison, March 13, 1806, ibid.; Aaron H. Palmer to Madison, April 20, 1809, ibid. (enclosing

minutes of the twelfth American convention for promoting the abolition of slavery); Benjamin Rush and others to Madison, February 12, 1813, ibid. (memorial from the Pennsylvania Society for promoting the abolition of slavery); S. Potter to Madison, February 7, 1813, ibid.; James B. Johnson to Madison, January 17, 1818, ibid.

38. Madison to Robert J. Evans, June 15, 1819, ibid.
39. Madison did not calculate the cost and time required to ship 1.5 million human beings (or more) across the Atlantic Ocean. Admittedly, international slave traders achieved a comparable feat in the other direction, carrying 1.9 million African slaves to the Americas between 1811 and 1870. OECD, *The World Economy*, 2006, p. 37. Five years later, Jefferson attempted a similar calculation of the expense of shipping all the slaves to Africa, with similarly unrealistic results. Jefferson to Jared Sparks, February 4, 1824, in *PTJ*. Neither man considered the cost of acquiring land in Africa for them.
40. Madison to Robert Walsh, Jr., November 28, 1819, in *PJM*; Madison to Lafayette, November 25, 1820, October 7, 1821, ibid.
41. Ed. Note, "Madison and the Allegory of Jonathan and Mary Bull" (1822), ibid.
42. Madison to Jedidiah Morse, March 14, 1823, ibid.; Madison to Frances Wright, September 1, 1825, ibid.; Madison to Lafayette, November 1826, ibid.; "Private Notes of Conversations with Mr. Madison," November 27–30, 1827, ibid.
43. Madison to Lafayette, February 1, 1830, ibid.; de Tocqueville, *Democracy in America*, 1:355. De Tocqueville concluded that freed slaves face "the prejudice of the master, the prejudice of the race, and the prejudice of color" and judged it nearly impossible that whites would abandon their prejudices. Ibid., 1:354 and n.
44. Taylor, *Slave in the White House*, p. 78; Madison to Ralph Randolph Gurley, February 19, 1832, December 29, 1831, in *PJM*; Amos J. Beyan, *The American Colonization Society and the Creation of the Liberian State: A Historical Perspective, 1822–1900*, Lanham: University Press of America (1991).
45. Madison to Thomas R. Dew, February 23, 1833, in *PJM*.
46. Leichtle and Carveth, *Crusade against Slavery*, pp. 152–55; McCoy, *Last of the Fathers*, pp. 297–98.
47. Dolley Madison to Mary E.E. Cutts, September 16, 1831, in *Selected Letters*, p. 293.
48. Peter P. Hinks, ed., *David Walker's Appeal to the Colored Citizens of the World*, University Park: Pennsylvania State University Press (2000); Eric Foner, *The Fiery Trial: Abraham Lincoln and Slavery*, New York: W.W. Norton & Co. (2010), pp. 15, 19; James B. Stewart, *Holy Warriors: The Abolitionists and American Slavery*, New York: Hill and Wang (1997); Jefferson Morley, *Snowstorm in August: Washington City, Francis Scott Key, and the Forgotten Race Riot of 1835*, New York: Nan A. Talese (2012), pp. 109, 116; Dunn, *Dominion of Memories*, p. 57. The British emancipation measure included a seven-year transitional period of "apprenticeship" for the freed slaves, which was cut short after only five years; the legislation appropriated £20 million to pay slaveowners.
49. David Grimsted, *American Mobbing, 1828–1861: Toward Civil War*, New York: Oxford University Press (1998), pp. 4, 12–14.
50. Henry Clay to Madison, May 28, 1833, in *PJM*; Madison to Henry Clay, June 1833, ibid.
51. Harriet Martineau, *Retrospect of Western Travel*, London: Saunders and Otley (1838), pp. 1–8, 13, 17; Dolley Madison to Mary Cutts, March 10, 1835, in *Selected Letters*, pp. 310–11; Dolley Madison to Ann Maury, March 31, 1835, in *DEPDM*. Martineau's description of the scene at Montpelier resembles the observations of another Englishwoman, Frances Trollope (mother of the novelist Anthony Trollope) when she traveled through the South at the same time. Trollope commented that in households with slaves, "all articles which can be taken and consumed are constantly locked up," which created a great focus on the mistress's keys, while slaveowners had a "habitual indifference to the

presence of their slaves. They talk of them, of their condition, of their faculties, exactly as if they were incapable of hearing." Frances Trollope, *Domestic Manners of the Americans*, London: Whittaker, Treacher & Co. (1832), 2:55–56.

James's negative view of free blacks was widely held. Henry Clay told the first meeting of the American Colonization Society that free blacks were "the most vicious" class of society, which was "the inevitable result of their moral and evil degradation. Contaminated themselves, they extended their vices all around them, to the slaves, to the whites." Beyan, *American Colonization Society*, p. 3. De Tocqueville offered a strikingly similar assessment of the status of free blacks, though he was more sympathetic to their plight. The Frenchman wrote that if a slave became free, "independence is often felt by him to be a heavier burden than slavery. . . . A thousand new desires beset him, and he is destitute of the knowledge and energy necessary to resist them: . . . [H]e sinks to such a depth of wretchedness that while servitude brutalizes, liberty destroys him." De Tocqueville, *Democracy in America*, 1:331.

CHAPTER 27: FAREWELLS

1. Madison to Jared Sparks, June 1, 1831, in *PJM*.
2. John Latrobe to Charles Carroll Harper, August 4, 1832, ibid.
3. Jefferson to Madison, February 17, 1826, ibid.; Madison to Jefferson, February 24, 1826, ibid.
4. Madison to Joseph C. Cabell, December 5, 1828, ibid.; Madison to Nicholas Trist, December 17, 1828, ibid.; Madison to William C. Rives, January 23, 1829, ibid.; Madison to Edward Everett, September 10, 1830, ibid.; Madison to Robert Walsh, January 25, 1831, ibid.; Madison to Nicholas Trist, May 15, 1832, ibid.
5. Madison to Monroe, January 21, 1830, ibid.; Madison to Monroe, May 18, 1830, ibid.
6. Monroe to Madison, December 7, 1830, ibid.; Madison to Monroe, December 15, 1830, ibid.; Edward Coles to Madison, January 16, 1831, ibid.; Monroe to Madison, April 11, 1831, ibid.; Madison to Monroe, April 21, 1831, ibid.
7. Madison to Alden Bradford, May 2, 1831, ibid.; Dolley Madison to Anna Cutts, December 1831, in *DEPDM*; Madison to Nicholas Trist, May 29, 1832, in *PJM*.
8. Madison to William B. Sprague, February 16, 1833, ibid.; Madison to Edward Coles, May 10, 1836, ibid.
9. Dolley Madison to Francis P. Lear, March 1832, in *Selected Letters*, p. 294; Taylor, *Slave in the White House*, pp. 119–20; Mattern, "James Madison and Montpelier," pp. 302–3.
10. John Latrobe to Charles Carroll Harper, August 4, 1832, in *PJM*; Madison to Nicholas Trist, May 29, 1832, ibid.
11. Madison to Sally Coles Stevenson, January 25, 1834, ibid.; Dolley Madison to Dolley Cutts, January 6, 1834, in *DEPDM*; Dolley Madison to Margaret Bayard Smith, August 31, 1834, in *Selected Letters*, p. 305.
12. Madison to Sally Coles Stevenson, January 25, 1834, in *PJM*; Dolley Madison to Frances P. Lear, March 1832, in *Selected Letters*, p. 294; Dolley Madison to Anna Cutts, May 15, 1832, ibid., p. 295; Dolley Madison to Richard Cutts, August 6, 1832, ibid., p. 297; Dolley Madison to Mary E.P. Allen, February 25, 1834, ibid., pp. 303–4.
13. Ketcham, p. 659; Dolley Madison to Anna Cutts, August 2, 1832, in *Selected Letters*, pp. 296–97; Mattern, "James Madison and Montpelier," pp. 302–3; Dolley Madison to Mary Cutts, August 1, 1833, in *Selected Letters*, pp. 299–300; Dolley Madison to Mary Cutts, November 4, 1833, ibid., p. 301; Dolley Madison to Mary Cutts, October 1834, in *DEPDM*; Dolley Madison to Dolley Cutts, May 11, 1835, in *Selected Letters*, pp. 311–12.
14. Madison to Edward Coles, February 23, 1827, in *PJM*.
15. Madison to Edward Coles, October 3, 1834, in *PJM*; Dolley Madison to Richard Cutts, August 11, 1833, in *Selected Letters*, pp. 300–301.

16. Edward Coles to Madison, January 8, 1832, in *PJM*.
17. Madison to Edward Coles, October 3, 1834, ibid.; McCoy, *Last of the Fathers*, pp. 155–59; Dolley Madison to Dolley Cutts, October 1834, in *DEPDM*. James's confidence in Taylor's probity may have been undermined when Taylor deducted $800 from the sale price because the "negro woman Betty" became ill in Louisiana. James protested the deduction, pointing out that there was no reason to believe she was ill at the time of Taylor's purchase. Madison to William Taylor, April 1835, in *PJM*.
18. Harriet Martineau, "The Brewing of the American Storm," *Macmillan's Magazine*, 6:97, 99 (1862); Ketcham, p. 669; William M. Meigs, Jr., *The Life of Charles Jared Ingersoll*, Philadelphia: J.B. Lippincott Co. (1897), pp. 244–45.
19. Dolley Madison to Lucy Todd, May 1836, in *DEPDM*; Ketcham, p. 669.
20. Paul Jennings, "Reminiscences," p. 236; John Payne Todd to Unknown Correspondent, June 28, 1836, in *PJM*.
21. "Advice to my Country," December 1830, ibid.
22. Ketcham, p. 669.
23. Dolley Madison to Richard Cutts, July 5, 1836, in *Selected Letters*, p. 328; Dolley Madison to Eliza Lee, July 26, 1836, ibid., pp. 329–30.
24. Will of James Madison, April 19, 1835, in *PJM*.
25. Allgor, *Parlor Politics*, p. 83.
26. Dolley Madison to Henry Moncure, August 12, 1844, in *Selected Letters*, p. 374.
27. Jennings, "Reminiscences," p. 234.
28. Elizabeth Collins Lee to Zaccheus Collins Lee, 1849, in *Selected Letters*, pp. 390–91; ibid., pp. 317–26.
29. McCoy, *Last of the Fathers*, pp. 320–21.
30. Madison to Marquis de Lafayette, November 25, 1820, in *PJM*.

INDEX

ABOUT THE AUTHOR

DAVID O. STEWART is the award-winning author of several acclaimed histories, including *The Summer of 1787: The Men Who Invented the Constitution* as well as *Impeached: The Trial of President Andrew Johnson and the Fight for Lincoln's Legacy* and *American Emperor: Aaron Burr's Challenge to Jefferson's America*. Stewart's most recent book, his first novel, is *The Lincoln Deception*. He also is the president of the *Washington Independent Review of Books*. Visit David at www.davidostewart.com.

Get email updates on

DAVID O. STEWART,

exclusive offers,

and other great book recommendations

from Simon & Schuster.

Visit **newsletters.simonandschuster.com**

or

scan below to sign up:

Chapman

MONTPE

the Seat of the late